Inner Secrets of the Path

INNER SECRETS
OF
THE PATH

Sayyid Haydar Amuli

With an introduction and explanatory notes by
Muhammad Khajavi

Translated from the original Arabic by
Assadullah ad-Dhaakir Yate

ELEMENT BOOKS
in association with
ZAHRA PUBLICATIONS

First published in 1989 by
Element Books Limited
Longmead, Shaftesbury, Dorset

Printed and bound in Great Britain
by Billings, Hylton Road, Worcester

Cover design by Max Fairbrother

Cover photo: Peter Sanders

British Library Cataloguing in Publication Data

Amuli, Sayyid Haydar
Inner secrets of the path
1. Sufi doctrine
I. Title
297′ .2

I S B N 1 - 85230 - 061 - 2

Contents

Introduction and Biographical
Background

Introduction and Biographical Background

In the name of Allah, the Beneficent, the Merciful.

Praise belongs to Allah, the Lord of the worlds who in His essential divine substance is before time and ever-existent, who in His own necessary independence is the beginning and the end and whose eternity does not admit of end.

Praise belongs to Him who by His essence is Him. The Beloved is He who is Allah, the Soul Being, the Beloved is Him. He is the Independent, the Eternal, who begets no one. The One, who was not begotten, without opponent or rival. He is the Possessor of Splendour, the One, the Eternal. His Oneness is not, however, of the kind to be counted. He is without likeness, existent before creation and time. There has been, nor is nothing similar to Him.

He is untouched by time and place. The chapter of The Unity (in the Qur'an) is an indication of this. He is Existence from before time and without need. He is the Real and the Creator of the different essences. He is without annihilation, subsistent of Himself. He exists by His essence, the Source of Outpouring of all essences.

May blessings and peace without end be on Muhammad, the first radiant manifestation of the Essence, the first of the messengers of Allah, whose reality is the radiant point of manifestation of the essence of the Lord of the Worlds, who is himself also the seal of His prophets, and on his caliph and successor, the greatest of caliphs, the most excellent of guardians and the seal of spiritual authority from the Maker of the heavens and the earth, the Commander of the Faithful and the just divider of people between the Fire and the Garden, the *'yamin of Allah'* — one of Allah's people of the right — as mentioned in the Qur'an.[1]

May peace and blessings be also on the family and progeny of Muhammad, the purest of the pure who are the joy and gladness of the worlds, and in particular on the last of these, the

---

[1] 'Ali is the *yamin* (right hand) of Allah, guarded by the army of Truth. The phrase *ashab al-yamin* (the Companions of the Right Hand) indicates none other than the people of 'Ali.

lord of the age and time itself, the caliph of the Merciful, the
leader of men and jinn — may God grant him great favours.
By the family of Muhammad was the correct path made known.
It was in their houses that the Book was revealed. They are the
proofs of Allah for mankind. In them and their forefathers there
is no doubt. In particular Abu Hasan 'Ali is revered for his high
station of knowledge. He is the tremendous news, the ark of
Noah, the door of Allah and the final word in eloquence.

> He is the first wave from the ocean of Allah's beauty
> and love.
> He is of the depths of the sea of nobility, from the Majestic.
> He is the witness and the witnessed and, by your life,
> endowed with great eloquence,
> He is the guide of the path leading to the fortunate abode.
> From God through him issues the intellect in its entirety.
> He is the king of the gathering of those messengers,
> The completion of the prophets by the divine overflowing
> from before endless time,
> The source of light for all the friends of Allah.
> There is one sole sun which possesses radiance,
> Although from him many lights of dawn appeared on the
> horizon.
> It was that same face of the moon whose light broke
> though,
> But it was by him that the twelve came to rejoice in their
> blessing.
> The state of Muhammad issues from the outpourings of
> the essence,
> And the family of Muhammad are the nobility of creation.
> The family of the Prophet are the lords of the two worlds.
> The family of the Prophet are the keys to the doors of the
> gardens.
> The family of the Prophet are the light of His beauty from
> before time.
> The family of the Prophet are a source of gnosis which
> never dries up.
> May the peace and blessings of Allah be upon them
> Until the moment the trumpet is sounded on the day of
> rising.

*   *   *   *

The divine decrees come into being in a world other than our own and they are governed by an order and time which is particular to them — such that whenever the will of Allah impinges on this world, then the decree passes from the Tablet of knowledge in the *malakut* (the invisible world of spirit and angel) to the pages of material forms in the world of men. Since different manifestations of the divine decrees become visible in this world, we have taken to calling them 'events which happen by chance' or 'occurrences.' It is because we interpret what happens in relation to ourselves that we react with surprise when the decree of Allah causes something to come into being, or not to come into being, and we become happy or unhappy accordingly.

The work before the reader came about in the following manner. One day some years ago one of my friends said that he had purchased a modest library wherein were several handwritten volumes. He asked me to take a look and to choose any book that I found interesting. However much I tried to refuse his offer — saying that, although handwriten, they remained for me a mere adornment and a financial investment for the book collectors, adding that after the death of their owner these papers would be sold again in the market for a ludicrous price — there was nothing I could do but peruse the books for the sake of our friendship and to avoid offending him. Of all the books — most of them of great value by reason of their illuminated pages, calligraphy and age — one in particular, which in contrast contained very bad calligraphy and not even the name of the author, attracted my attention. Despite its worn exterior, I purchased it at an extravagant price. This book was in fact 'The Mysteries of the Revealed Law, the Stations of the Way and the Light of the Truth' *(Asrar al-Shari'ah)* which the decree of God was now placing before my path.

By the style of the text I realised that it was the work of the lord of gnostics and divines Sayyid Haydar Amuli, an Iranian gnostic of great standing of the eighth century AH. His writing is eloquent and he fulfils the demand for spiritual knowledge among those persons whose mother tongue is Persian. Despite the poor calligraphy, it was nevertheless exceedingly correct and had been copied from the actual work of the author himself, may

Allah protect his secret; moreover, there were marginal notes elucidating most places in the book written in 950 AH. Despite research in different libraries of Iran and Turkey I could find no trace of another copy which would permit a cross-check of my copy. The copy possessed by the University of Tehran was only a selection containing no more than five or six pages of the book; the copy I found in the Islamic Consultative Assembly (previously the National Assembly) was half missing and full of defects. I thus made a photocopy of my copy and made up for the defects of the Assembly's copy. It was again the workings of the divine decree which caused me to then find a copy in the library of Ayatullah Mar'ashi of Qum.[1]

Although the copy from the library of Mar'ashi was good, having been written during the time of the Qacharis, it was not as correct as the copy I myself possessed. For this reason I made a further copy of my text and substituted it for the other which had been registered under the number of 388. I then completed correcting that work, spending many years in the process. It so happened that one day I went to meet some friends at the Iranian Academy of Philosophy; the head of the academy was talking about the lack of correct texts and the plethora of unedited annoted works. It was at this point that the manifestation of another divine decree caused the bringing to a head of those previous incidents of destiny which I had all but forgotten.[2] Thus I disclosed that a rare text, of which no more than two copies existed in the world, lay in my hands ready for printing. Mention

---

[1] It was with much charm and kindness that the employees of this fine library put a photocopy of the work at my disposition. The director of the library also supplied me with a copy of *Al-Muhit al-A'zam* (The Mighty Ocean), which had been handwritten by the author himself; this is the only copy which exists in Iran — the only other extant copy is in the library of Najaf — and I shall subsequently refer to it. When my eyes fell on the amber-like calligraphy of this *sayyid*, written as it were in the ink of the Cathay musk deer, they brightened with joy, and on a thorough reading I was apprised of his knowledge of the chains of transmission, of his way of the patched garment and granting of permission to his students.

---

[2] The reason for my forgetfulness was that I was totally absorbed in correcting the books of commentary of *Sadr al-Muta'lihin* The Core of the Divine Gnostics — which number fourteen detailed volumes — and *Kitab Mafatih al-Ghaib* (Book of Keys to the Unseen). The latter is the last introduction to the commentary of this great commentator and the key to understanding the deeper meanings of the Qur'an.

of this was greeted with great pleasure, and after attending to the technical matters of publication, the work was then actually printed.

As for the biography and historical importance of this divine prodigy, the men with whom he studied and the date of his death, in .the majority of cases such details are recorded inaccurately; biographers have plagiarised details from others and in their ignorance some have added material to inaccurate material of a previous date. In investigating these matters great care must be taken to look closely at what actually happened and to weigh the matters up with precision in order to discriminate the chaff from the grain and jumbled invention from reality. Most of the books containing such material are sources of erroneous data not only with regard to the life of this man but also with regard to his works.

One such book is *Al-Kashkul fi ma jara li ali'l-rasul* (Album of Events concerning the Family of the Prophet) which is attributed to Sayyid Amuli but in fact is the work of Haydar ibn 'Ali, a contemporary of Fakhr al-Muhaqqiqin, the teacher of Sayyid Amuli. He is mentioned with regard to the strife which broke out between the Sunnis and the Shiahs in 735 in Baghdad[1] when in fact at that time Sayyid Amuli was only sixteen years old and had never been in Iraq. The source of this and many other pieces of false information is the book *Majalis al-Mu'minin* (The Gatherings of the Believers).

As for the various (dubious) biographies there is that of Sayyid Haydar Tuni. It is significant that it is included in *Rawdat al-Jinnah* (The Meadow of Paradise) as an appendix to the biography of Sayyid Amuli wherein many miraculous feats are ascribed to him. It is for this resaon that we have not made any commentary on these matters. The stations, inner states and spiritual journeying are described in his own words, they being truer and clearer than any one else's, so that any contradictory statements may be avoided. We have thus avoided the usual method employed — which is to record anything which one has heard or read without

---

1 This strife — mostly occurring in the Karkh area of Baghdad inhabited by the Shiahs — was caused by political motives, according to historical testimonies (in particular that of al-Kamil Ibn Athir).

checking its veracity and without assuming any responsibility for the facts presented. Such writings only serve to obscure the true spiritual path of this friend of Allah and give a completely distorted picture of the story of his life; as a result his way of illumination has become hidden for subsequent generations and access to the right path, the path of light indicated by him, has been obstructed for the seeker, concealed from the sight of mankind.

Until now, no complete biographical commentary on this great gnostic, which is free from extraneous and erroneous material and which contains material written by himself, has been written in Persian. Little, moreover, has been written in Arabic: the introduction which precedes his book *Jami' al-Asrar* (A Compendium of Secrets) is lengthy and tiring, and that which accompanies his work *Nass al-Nusus* (The Text of Texts) is concise but uninformative and does nothing to elucidate those matters about which we are ignorant. It was for this reason that I decided to take the task upon myself. It was with the help of God that I set about composing this biography, using material from within his own works and avoiding any commentary or marginal notes.

Sayyid Amuli was born in 819 AH. His birth heralded the tremendous influence of his life. He illumined the world of darkness and tribulation, and embellished this world, this planting-ground for the next. He says himself at the end of the introduction to *Nass al-Nusus* (The Text of Texts), which is a commentary on the *Fusus al-Hikam* (The Bezels of Wisdom) of Shaykh Muhyi al-Din ibn 'Arabi: 'I completed this commentary in 782 AH at the age of sixty three.'

A brief genealogy and biography of his life appears in the first volume of his commentary entitled *Al-Muhit al-A'zam* (The Mighty Ocean) M.S. 301, Mar'ashi Library, Qum. The following is a translation of this: I am Rukn al-Din Haydar, the son of Sayyid Taj al-Din 'Ali Padashah, the son of Sayyid Rukn al-Din Haydar, the son of Sayyid Taj al-Din 'Ali Padashah, the son of Sayyid Muhammad Amir, the son of 'Ali Padashah, the son of Abu Ja'far Muhammad, the son of Zayd, the son of Abu Ja'far Muhammad, the son of Ibrahim, the son of Muhammad, the son of Husayn Kusaj, the son of Ibrahim, the son of Sana'illah,

the son of Muhammad Harun, the son of Hamzah, the son of
'Ubayd ullah al-'Araj, the son of Husayn Asghar, the son of
Imam 'Ali ibn al-Husayn Zayn al-'Abidin, the son of Husayn
the Shahid — the martyr, the son of the Commander of the
Faithful 'Ali ibn Abi Talib, may the peace of Allah be upon
them all.'.

In the introduction of *Jami' al-Asrar* (The Compendium of
Secrets) he further states: 'Know that from the earliest vigour
of my youth, namely from my childhood to the age of thirty or
thereabouts, I was engaged in studying the religion of my own
forefathers, the *ma'sumin* — the infallible ones. With regard to
the outer aspect of the *shari'ah*, I undertook a study of the Imamiyah sect and their juridical school *(madhhab)* — which is
daily practised amongst the Shiahs; and with regard to the inner,
namely the study of the truth and reality *(haqiqah)*, I devoted
my attention to the Sufis and the masters of the science of the
unity of Allah *(tawhid)*. The two aspects came together and a
joining of the outer *shari'ah* and the inner *haqiqah* was effected
such that I reached the station of constancy and firmness. This
I say not through any sense of pride, but rather as an expression
of the endless bounty of Allah. Indeed I swear by Allah that if
the seven heavens were made of paper and the trees of the earth
were pens, if the seas of the world were ink and the spirits,
mankind and the angels were scribes, then they would be unable
to write even a jot of what I had witnessed of the divine gnoses
and realities referred to in the authentic or divinely inspired
hadith, "I have prepared for the chosen of My slaves something
no eye has seen, no ear has heard and no heart has perceived"
and in the Qur'an, "So no soul knows what is hidden for them
of that which will refresh their eyes; a reward for what they did"
(32:17). The least of these truths was such that after seeing reality
from both sides and the true and false aspects of each side, after
perceiving in what manner the one was true and the other false,
I was able to understand how every one of these matters was
connected to a point of reality and *tawhid* — just as the line
which is drawn from circumference of a cycle is connected to
the central point. I was also able to understand the meaning of
Allah's words, "There is no living creature but He holds it by

its forelock; surely my Lord is on the right path" (11:56) and "Allah's is the East and the West, therefore, whither you turn, thither is Allah's purpose" (2:115); and the secret contained in the words of the Prophet, "The ways leading to the Real are as many as the persons in creation". The saying of the Commander of the Faithful, "Knowledge was no more than one point — and it was the ignorant who added to it" also became clear to me. I became as the incipient form before materialisation, the form which is capable of taking on any other form, the form which accepts and understands any belief structure or desire, such that all was swallowed up in my boundless existence. This is as the sublime station of the Prophet when he stood before Allah saying, "O Allah, show me the realities of the beings of creation just as they are"; this is highest of the stations of *tawhid* and the sublimest of positions in the world of unveilings. "That is Allah's grace; He grants it to whom He pleases, and Allah is the Lord of mighty grace" (62:4).

'From the poetry of Shaykh Muhyi al-Din ibn 'Arabi:

> Before this I used to deny my friend, for my heart could not accept his religion.
> Now my heart has adopted every shape of belief;
> It has become a pasture for the fine-eyed gazelles and a place of worship for the monk in his monastery.
> It is the temple of idols and also the Ka'bah above which they make the rounds.
> It is the tablets of the Torah and also the book of the Qur'an.
> I have drawn close to the religion of love and passion such that
> From wherever their caravans leave I set off too — for passion has become my way of life and faith.

'After my affirmation of the truth of Sufism, certain persons were troubled by some of its more abstruse and esoteric aspects with regard to the Real — such people imagined that I was availing myself of invalid and other spurious means. May they realise that this was not the case and that in reality I was only drawing upon the religion of my own forefathers — the infallible Imams. Because of their extreme ignorance, the majority of Sufis

think that the Imams were devoid of the excellencies and superior
insights of Sufism. Moreover many Shiahs also believe that the
knowledge of their Imams is restricted to that same knowledge
which is in common use amongst themselves. In fact there is not
a single form of knowledge but that the Imams are the source
of that knowledge; there is not a secret or hidden wisdom but
that they are the mine from which it may be extracted; they are
the teachers of the *shari'ah* and the leaders of the *tariqah* and the
poles of the *haqiqah;* they are the caliphs and the vicegerents of
Allah in the heavens and the earth; they are the manifestation
of the power and majesty of Allah in His *mulk* — the earth and
heavens — and in His *malakut* — the realm of the spirits and
angels. I swear by God that if they did not exist, then the heavens
would not be standing, the earth would not be outspread and
the creatures would not be living in them. This is the meaning
of Allah's words to His Prophet, "If you were not, then I would
not have created the cosmos"; here what is meant is the abode
of the different creatures. According to the scholars of the divine
sciences, the whole world is maintained in existence by reason
of the reality of the Perfect Man and the planets are kept in orbit
by his very breaths. Muhyi al-Din ibn 'Arabi says in his book
Nuskhat al-Haqq (Copy of the Truth): "Allah established the Perfect Man as the teacher of the angels and has caused the planets
to turn by his life and breath — and this by reason of his nobility,
sublimity and elevated station.' By the consensus of the nation
of Muslims, there are none greater than those great persons —
neither from an intellectual standpoint, nor from conclusions
drawn from the body of the traditions, nor from the station of
unveilings.

'It was the Prophet's own successor ('Ali) who proclaimed
with pride: "I am the sign and indication of Allah, the All-Powerful and the Conqueror; I am the reality of the secret truths; I
am the leader and guide of the heavens; I sit with the angels
who make praise and with Gabriel and I am the friend of Mika'il;
I am the guide of the planets; I am the tree of Sandalwood of
the planets; I am the guardian of the thunder and the dazzling
lightning; I am the face of Allah, the flank of Allah, the hand of
Allah; I am the first and the last, the manifest and the hidden." '

Sayyid Amuli also says in his own commentary: 'After understanding religion and its associated sciences and after mastering the different degrees of knowledge with regard both to the intellect and the related body of *ahadith* (traditions of the Prophet) — this study being undertaken partly in the town of Amul, birthplace and childhood home of myself and my forefathers, partly in Khurasan and Astarabad, and partly in Isfahan — I continued to strive until I arrived at the core and inner meaning of these matters.'

These studies lasted for approximately twenty years until for the second time I returned from Isfahan to Amul. Here I took up employment in the service of the just and temperate Padshah Fakhr al-Dawlah, the son of Shah Kay-Khisraw — may Allah grant them both a fair place in the Garden. Fakhr al-Dawlah treated me with particular respect and honour and placed me with those of his entourage who were intimate with him. After a while he made me one of his most trusted confidants and thereupon one of his special deputies and chamberlains; he accorded me this special treatment as he himself was descended from Anusharvan, Yazdagird and Perviz, one of his close relatives being a Padshah by the name of Ardishir, son of Hasan, the son of Taj al-Dawlah whom Tahir al-Din Faryabi Sha'ir, Siraj al-Din Qamari and other poets and reciters of *qasidahs* (odes) would honour and praise in their writings.

'After some time, the just padshah, the champion of his time, the living padshah of padshahs, the brave unflinching warior Fakhr al-Dawlah made a request to me. Thus it was that just as Jalal al-Dawlah Iskandar and the majestic Sultan Gustaham and Tus Malik came to be employed in the service of Fakhr al-Dawlah's brother, I also came to take up duties in his service. It was not long before — by the blessing of his company — I acquired such great position and wealth that it is impossible to imagine. In this way I came to live a life of luxury, prosperity and honour amongst the people, my friends and my fellow townsfolk.

'I passed some time in this state until a desire for the truth, a desire both instinctive and natural, began to flare up within me and Allah made me aware of the evil and corruption growing in me as a result of my ignorance and forgetfulness of Him. It became clear to me that I was following a way of perversity far from the straight path; it became manifest to me that I was treading the path of misguidance, close to the precipice of sin and crime. It was at this moment that I prayed to the Lord from deep within myself: I implored him to free me from these actions of mine — all my passion and desire was to leave this world and its pleasures. I found within myself that I was ready to turn in the direction of the Real and to set out on the path of *tawhid* (divine unity).

'It was for this reason that I no longer wished to keep the company of those padshahs nor to continue living in my own locality and place of birth, despite my love of that place; nor too could I continue to sit with my friends and brothers. It seemed the best thing to do was to abandon them completely and to move away to a place where I could carry out those duties necessary for a life devoted to the Real and where the form of my existence would be of the highest order. Thus it was that I freed myself forthwith from the rulers, as well as from the wealth of my sons and of my mother and brothers[1] and I put on a patch-ed garment — not worth more than a dirham — that had been thrown into an alley at the back of the house. It was in this that I set out via Ray, Qazvin and Isfahan with the intention of making the pilgrimage and visiting the sacred House of Allah and with the intention of visiting my forefather, the Messenger of Allah and the infallible Imams. In this way I arrived in Qazvin where I had previously spent a long period of my youth amidst wealth and honour.

'It was because a contract of brotherhood had been made with the young men of that town (and by this I mean with the group of Sufis) that a contract was also made between myself and the perfect shaykh, the one of arrival, Nur al-Din Tihrani — Tihran being a village on the way to Isfahan in the region of Dardasht

---

[1] Thus acting in accordance with the *ayah:* 'Say: If your fathers and your sons and your brethren and your mates and your kinsfolk and property which you have ac-quired, and the slackness of trade which you fear and dwellings which you like, are dearer to you than Allah and His Apostle and striving in His way, then wait till Allah brings about His command; and Allah does not guide the transgressing people' (9:24).

and which is pronounced with the open 't' sound by the people in contrast to the Arabic 't' with which it was originally spelt.

'Shaykh Nur al-Din Tihrani was a gnostic of Allah and an ascetic. All the people, both the common and the elite, accepted him and became his disciples. I spent a month, or rather, a little less than a month, in his company — until he gave me the real patched garment of the Sufis to wear,[1] and I came to master the *dhikr* (remembrance of Allah) of the elite rather than that of the common people; by sitting with him, I was able — by an alchemic transmission — to profit greatly, despite the extreme brevity of my stay. After this I went on from Isfahan to two other places, namely Aydhaj and Maliamir, where in company with another man of perfection and spiritual gnosis, I spent some time while waiting for the caravan to form which was bound for Baghdad. The caravan never materialised, however, and this, and the onset of a severe sickness, caused me to return to Isfahan. After a time, I did finally reach Baghdad and from there I had the honour of visiting the sacred site of the martyrdom of the Commander of the Faithful, the graves of Husayn, Musa and Jawad together with the Imams of Samarra. I spent a whole year in these places before setting out in the direction of the Ka'bah with the intention of performing the pilgrimage. I was alone and destitute when I set out.

'Having visited the tombs of the Messenger and the four Imams in Madinah, I returned to Iraq and in the holy city of Najaf —

---

[1] With regard to the patched robe, he himself says in *Al-Muhit al-A'zam* (The Mighty Ocean): 'This garment which is well-known amongst the common and elite of the *muwahhidin* — those who affirm the unity of Allah — is an indication of the secret of *wilayah* — friendship with Allah — and the secret wisdom of *tawhid* which came from Allah by means of Gabriel to Adam and then to his son Seth: this *wilayah* was transmitted as an inner reality by means of this lineage. Thereafter, it was transferred to Noah through a chain of prophets and saints *(awliya')* until it reached the Mahdi, may Allah speed his appearance on earth. With the Mahdi this transmission came to an end and it is for this reason that he is the seal of the *awliya'*. Thus the patched garment is not an indication, as the ignorant maintain, of something made of wool or cotton or the like — all are aware that the outer garment itself is not an indication of the taking on of the qualities of human perfection — rather it is connected to the right-guidance of the prophets, saints and the great amongst the shaykhs and men of perfection. As an explanation of the taking on of the inner meaning of the way of these great men — through an embodiment of their character and qualities and obedience to their way of life — the patched garment is a term both noble and subtle; thus it is that God says: 'Say: If you love Allah then follow me, Allah will love you, (3:31).'

may Allah bless those who visit it — I took up residence and busied myself with spiritual exercises, periods of isolation *(Khalwah)*, worship, and the seeking of *'ilm al-laduni* (knowledge bestowed by Allah on His slave through no effort of his own). There was no one in the region who had 'knowledge of this kind of activity and of these states. I associated, however, with a gnostic and man of perfection of this locality who, although living in obscurity, was in fact the leader of the saints of Allah; he was known amongst the people as 'Abd al-Rahman ibn Ahmad Muqaddasi and although enjoying the meagerest of means was among the finest and most excellent of the men of knowledge. I took to studying *Manazil al-Sa'irin* (The Stages of the Gnostic Travellers) together with its commentary, thereafter *Fusus al-Hikam* (The Bezels of Wisdom), together with its commentary and other books of the same nature. It was during this period of study that most of the realities contained in the books on Sufism (including both the simple and more detailed treatises) were revealed to me with clarity — and this by the blessing of that holy place, this holy person and the Imams. Thus it was that I came to write many commentaries, made many notes on this subject and then wrote several other books. Twenty years have elapsed since that date and the books which I have written now number between twenty and twenty-four; these I catalogued with an index, the last of the books being a commentary on the Quran.'

Up to this point Sayyid Amuli records in detail the spiritual journey upwards to his Lord by a process of divine attraction. As for the journey through the self and the death of desire, he continues the description of his own states in the introduction of his commentary of the *Fusus al-Hikam* entitled *Nass al-Nusus* (The Text of Texts) (with regards to the second aspect of the *wilayah* of Shaykh Muhyi al-Din ibn 'Arabi): 'I remained for a period in Isfahan occupied with the states of the spiritual path. It was then that, intending to go to Baghdad in order to visit the places of martyrdom of the Imams, the saints and the shaykhs of that region, and whilst planning to go to the house of Allah to perform the *hajj* and to remain forever close to this house, I suddenly saw one night in a dream that I was standing in the middle of a bazaar. I perceived that my body was as if dead, wrapped in a white shroud and fallen flat on the ground. While trying to discover the cause of this, I was at the same time in a state of great surprise: how was it that I was both standing and lying flat on the ground? It was in this state that I awoke. This in fact was the beginning of the death of desire and the start of my spiritual path — the same death alluded to by the Prophet when he says, "Die before you die" and the same as that described by the sage who said, "Die by your own will so that you may live the true and natural life".[1] God says: "Is he who was dead then We raised him to life and made for him a light by which he walks among the people, like him whose likeness is that of one of utter darkness whence he cannot come forth?" (6:122) I thanked God for His blessings; it is He who is the cause of eternal life and constant prosperity: "Most surely this is the mighty achievement. For the like of this then let the workers work). (37:60–61)

'Likewise I saw again on another occasion that I was sitting in the shop of some friends. On my back there was copper receptacle ornamented with gold, just like those of the water carriers who would tour the bazaars pouring water for the people to drink. This receptacle had a strange mouth, just like that of the large jars which they make out of fired clay. I was giving water to those present from this receptacle while at the same time I was searching for myself. I was also sitting at the same time as I was standing. Moreover, just as I was giving water to the people to drink, I would take a drink myself. Because of this strange picture, I would repeatedly burst out laughing at myself and I felt great amazement at this state until I finally woke up. This dream was instrumental in bringing me many tremendous insights.

'On another occasion, in Isfahan, I saw myself seated holding a severed head in my hand; at the same time my own head had

---

[1] That is according to the divine pattern or *sunnah* which holds sway over nature; this means that those whose desire has not died are, according to the natural pattern of life, themselves dead. This pattern of nature is an order of interconnected harmony based on wisdom and the whole cycle of beneficence is as a spark from the inner divine order.

been severed, although I had no knowledge of this. I was busy turning and playing with the head and at any moment would be seized by laughter at this strange picture, until I finally woke up. This dream was the means by which I arrived at many of the most precious spiritual truths; indeed a wealth of the finest insights were revealed to me as they flowed out from the generosity of the divine unseen. In a similar dream to this, I heard that my father gave no more nor less than a thousand dinars to the person who could interpret such dreams, and this sum was also paid without delay by some of the padshahs by the law of the exoteric. As for the inner world of meaning, a thousand things of note and worth, purer than the finest gold and clearer than the most translucent jewels promised to man in the Garden, were received from the real Padshah, namely Allah may He be exalted: "That is Allah's grace; He grants it to whom He pleases, and Allah is the Lord of mighty grace." (62:4); "And none are made to receive it but those who are patient, and none are made to receive it but those who have a mighty good fortune" (41:35). Such events often occur to myself and our spiritual friends, but despite being far-removed from the state of man, they are not extraordinary for God: "And this is not difficult for Allah" ' (14:20).

At the end of *Muqaddimah Fusus* (An Introduction to the Bezels), which is about the meaning for him of the unveilings and secrets of the *Fusus al-Hikam,* he describes the holy city of Najaf as being the cause of openings from the unseen occurring in his heart — just as one night Makkah became the cause of openings for Shaykh Muhyi al-Din and thereafter Madinah inspired the Madinan disclosures. He then goes on to explain the course of his own spiritual journey both in relation to himself and to the cosmos: 'Know that since God has commanded me to leave everything which is other than Him and to concentrate the heart completely on Him, there arose in my heart such a feeling of divine inspiration that I decided to take the noblest and sublimest locality on earth as my place of residence and worship of Him. Thus it was that I set out for Makkah — may Allah increase it in every way. It would be impossible to contain in a whole set of books the trials and hardships, the misfortune and toil which

I underwent on the journey from Isfahan to that place. Despite all this, however, the words of Allah were always on my tongue: "And whoever goes forth from his house flying to Allah and His Apostle, and then death overtakes him, his reward is indeed with Allah and Allah is Forgiving, Merciful" (4:100), and also the lines of that gnostic and lover of the Truth who says:

> I have left all men for the sake of Your satisfaction.
> I have abandoned as orphans my own sons for the sake of Your witnessing.
> Even if You cut me to pieces, my heart would still long for no one but You.

This was my state when I arrived in Makkah and completed the obligatory pilgrimage together with all the necessary and supererogatory rites. It was at this point — in 751 AH — that I conceived the desire and intention to stay forever in the proximity of that illustrious house. It was not long, however, that there arose within me the desire to live in the illuminated city of Madinah and it was for this reason that I set out for this city, where I visited the tomb of the Messenger of Allah and conceived the intention of staying within the confines of his splendid grave. At that moment, however, many obstacles were placed in my path, the greatest of these being a physical sickness, which made it necessary for me to return to Iraq and take up residence in the familiar surroundings of Najaf.

'Thus I returned without further trouble to this spiritual city and busied myself with religious exercises, pious seclusion and acts of worship — of an intensity and severity never before achieved. By this means, throughout all this period, meanings, gnoses, realities and truths flowed into my heart from the direction of Allah, the Lord of the unseen. It would be impossible to reckon these things for they are divine utterances and as such cannot be contained within clearly defined limits.[1] God, however, commanded me to reveal some of these gnoses to the elite of His slaves and so I set about writing a book about divine unity *(tawhid)*

---

1 This is an allusion to the *ayah:* 'And if you count Allah's favours, you will not be able to number them'. (14:34)

and an explanation of its secrets. Within a short time, I completed it and named it *Jami' al Asrar wa Manba' al-Anwar* (Compendium of Secrets and Source of Lights). I then wrote two more books called *Risalat al-Wujud fi ma'rifat il-Ma'bud* (Treatise on Existences on the Knowledge of the Worshipped One) and *Risalat al-Ma'ad fi ruju' al-'Ibad* (Treatise of Eschatology; on the Return to the Godhead). After these I composed some forty other books and essays in both Persian and Arabic. It was then that Allah commanded me to undertake a commentary of the Qur'an and so, after completion of the above-mentioned essays, I composed a work of seven thick volumes under the title of *Al-muhit al-A'zam wa'l-Tawd al-Asham fi Ta'wil Kitabillahi 'l-'Aziz al-Muhkam* (The Mighty Ocean and Lofty Mountain: esoteric exegesis on the clear and precious Book of Allah). With the help of the Lord it was completed in the best and most perfect manner and in the finest and most eloquent language such that no one surpassed me in this matter, neither in the way it was arranged nor in the way it was edited.

'Allah then commanded me to undertake a commentary on the *Fusus al-Hikam* which is a work directly inspired by His Messenger — it was the latter who gave it to Shaykh Muhyi al-Din in a dream saying: "Communicate it to those slaves who are worthy of it and who are ready to receive it". Thus I began this work, some thirty years after first taking up residence in Najaf, in 781 AH and completed it in 782 AH, a period of one year or less; my age at that time was sixty three years.'

The rest of what happened to him is described in different places of his own commentary; it is thus that he says: 'After this activity I began service with the great shaykh of perfection, the sultan of the scholars, the Honour of the Truth and the Religion, Abu Mutahhir Hilli. In his company I studied many of the books which contain both the foundation and ramifications of the sciences of the Family of the Prophet. The Shaykh bestowed on me a licence in which he addresses me as "Zayn al-'Abidin the Second" — having witnessed something in my behaviour which caused him to believe that my station was only second to that of infallibility. He also issued many other licences for me — both of a general and explicit nature — in all the sciences, one of which I shall now give:

> The most excellent Sayyid, the great Imam, the worthiest
> of the scholars of the world and the most knowledgeable
> of the noble amongst men, the guide to those on the
> spiritual path, the saviour of the souls of the gnostics, the
> renewer of the faith and the giver of life to the way of his
> forefathers, the one who combines the sciences of tradition
> with those of reason, and those of the foundations of juris-
> prudence with its branches, the possessor of a purified
> soul and the courtesy of a prophet, the pride of the family
> of the Propohet, which is the object of the special attention
> of the Lord of the Worlds, the pillar of the nation, of the
> truth and of the religion, Haydar ibn Sayyid al-Sa'id Taj
> al-Din 'Ali... (including the rest of his genealogy to the
> Commander of the Faithful) has read and studied with
> me in the most scrupulous manner the following books:
> the Qur'anic commentary, *Jawami' al-Jami'* by the great
> shaykh and protector of the faith, shaykh Tabrisi, *Shari'ah
> al-Islam* by the great jurist Shaykh Najm al-Din Muhaqqaq
> Hilli, *Manahij al-Yaqin* concerning the science of theology
> *(kalam)* by my father, may Allah have mercy on him,
> *Tahdhib al-Ahkam* (An Education of the Laws) by Shaykh
> Tayfah Tusi, *Nahj al-Balaghah* by the Commander of the
> Faithful and *Sharh Nahj al-Balaghah* by the sage Ibn
> Maytham. Thus do I give permission for him to transmit
> all of these books, just as I give permission for him to
> transmit all of his own works and writings concerning the
> sciences based both on the traditions and reason. I also
> hand over to him all the above-mentioned books which
> he may use with his own direct chain of transmission from
> them — in particular the books of my father which he
> has acquired through me. Moreover, he has permission
> to transmit the books of Shaykh Mufid (there being thus
> two paths of transmission from himself to Shaykh Mufid)
> together with the books of Shaykh Tusi, Sayyid Murtada
> and all the *ahadith* transmitted from the family of the
> Prophet (the "Four Books"), all with a complete chain of
> transmission.'

This detailed licence *(ijazah)* was given in Ramadan, 761 AH
in Hillah; the Arabic text is in my possession, but for reasons of

brevity I have omitted to mention the full chain of transmission, making do with a translation and resume of the whole.

After recording this *ijazah* he says: 'This kind of licence given to me with regard to the sciences based on the *ahadith* (traditions) and on reason is well-known only amongst the Arabs.' In Rajab 753 AH he was given a licence to teach *Manazil al-Sa'irin* and *Fusus al-Hikam,* together with their commentaries, by 'Abd al-Rahman ibn Ahmad al-Muqaddasi; this licence is written in much the same manner as that of Fakhr al-Muhaqqiqin and in it we read: 'I have benefited from him more than he (Sayyid Amuli) has benefited from me.'

He then mentions a method of *dhikr* (remembrance of Allah) from Muhammad ibn Abi Bakr Simnani. It is possible that he was instructed by this man himself because he was one his contemporaries. Sayyid Amuli goes on to say: 'Some of the *fuqara'* — the bereft in Allah — have explained their own way of *dhikr*', and the following is quoted: 'This poor fakir Muhammad ibn Abi Bakr Simnani — may God bestow on him the same as those who receive eternal life after the annihilation of this world — was instructed in the way (of *dhikr*) by Shaykh Salih al-Din Abi'l-Khayr Shams al-Din Muhammad ibn 'Ali ibn Muhammad Isfahani and the latter learnt the *dhikr la ilaha illa'llah* on the 'Id al-Fitr 703 AH in the *khanqah's* assembly (Sufi spiritual retreat) of Samisati in the Bayt al-Ahzan quarter near the Friday mosque in Damascus from Shaykh Salih Muhammad ibn Abi Bakr Isfarayni Zayn al-'Ibad, the Flag Bearer of the ascetics, the Honour of the virtuous, the one of constant *dhikr* in the morning and the evening. He in turn learnt it from Shaykh Sayf al-Din Abu'l-Mu'ali ibn Mutahhir ibn Sa'id Badarzay and he from the Shaykh and Pole of the Age, Abu'l-Janab Najm al-Din Ahmad ibn Muhammad ibn 'Abdullah Khiyuqi, the same Shaykh Najm al-Din al-Kubra, one of the poles of the "golden" chains of transmission (indeed any "golden" chain of transmission connected to him is known as a "major golden chain"); the latter in turn received it from Shaykh Isma'il Qasri and he from Shaykh Muhammad ibn Mankil who got it from Shaykh Daud ibn Muhammad known as the Servant of the Poor. The latter received it from 'Abbas ibn Idris who got it from Abu'l-Qasim ibn Ramadam who in turn got it from Abu Ya'qub Tabrisi, from Abu 'Abdullah ibn 'Uthman, from Abu Ya'qub Nahrjuri, from Abu Ya'qub Susi, from 'Abd al-Wahid ibn Zayd, from Kamil ibn Ziyad Nakh'i (may God be content with them all), from the Commander of the Faithful, from the Messenger of Allah, from Gabriel the Guardian of Revelation, from the Lord of Power may He be exalted.'[1]

Sayyid Amuli describes the method of instruction of the *dhikr*: 'Transmission of the *dhikr* takes on a distinct form and order amongst the people of this science'; a concise description is contained in the detailed *ijazah* of the above-mentioned fakir, namely Muhammad ibn Abi Bakr Simnani; in it we see an affirmation of the transmission of the following *hadith* by the Sufi shaykhs: 'One day 'Ali came in to see the Messenger of Allah saying: "Instruct me in the way which leads quickest to Allah and which is the most acceptable to Him and the way which is easiest for His slaves." He replied: "O 'Ali, may you be blessed in that which has come to you by way of prophethood." 'Ali then asked: "And what is that, O Messenger of Allah?" He replied: *"Dhikr* of Allah." He then said: "If the excellence of *dhikr* is so great, then all the people would make *dhikr* of Allah." He replied: "Abandon such thoughts — the Day of Resurrection will not take place so long as there is someone on the earth saying 'Allah Allah.' He then said: "O 'Ali, be silent. I will say this *dhikr* to you three times and you should listen; when I am silent, you should then say it so that I may hear it from you." Thus it was in this way that the Messenger of Allah instructed 'Ali in the way of *dhikr,* who then transmitted it to Hasan al-Basri, to Habib al-'Ajami — to Da'ud al-Ta'i, to Ma'ruf al-Karkhi, to Siri al-Saqti, to Junayd al-Baghdadi, to Mimshad Daynuri, to Ahmad Aswad Daynuri, to Muhammad ibn 'Abdillah Bakari Suhrawardi, known as 'Awami, to Qadi Wajih al-Din 'Umar ibn Muhammad Bakari, to Abu'l-Najib 'Abd al-Qahir

---

[1] A biography of each of these great shaykhs requires detailed investigation; there does in fact exist ample biographical material, but since it would be difficult to include in this introduction these golden chains of *wilayah* will be investigated according to the strict methodology of this science (of determining the veracity of the men and chains of transmission) if a suitable opportunity arises, God willing.

Suhrawardi, to Shihab al-Din 'Umar ibn Muhammad Suhrawardi Bakari, to Mu'in al-Din, one of the companions of the Shaykh of the Shaykhs of the land of Rum (the west or Byzantine), to Ahmad ibn Mas'ud in the town of Konya, one of the shaykhs of my father and forefathers, who then transmitted it to myself, the fakir, Muhammad ibn Abi Bakr Simnani on the 10 Jumada al-Ula in 731 AH.'

As for the taking on of the patched robe, this has been transmitted from the Commander of the Faithful in various chains of transmission. He goes on to say: 'The *kharqah* — the patched garment — both among the common and the elite is an expression of the secret of *wilayah* (intimacy with Allah) and the hidden wisdom of *tawhid*. This *wilayah* and wisdom was bestowed by Allah on Adam' (as we have explained earlier); he continues: 'As for an investigation into the relationship of the *kharqah* to the Commander of the Faithful and his infallible progeny — both in the outer realm of the manifest and in the inner realm of meaning — then it is as follows: 'as for what is manifest, I am Rukn al-Din Haydar, the son of Sayyid Taj al-Din...' and the ancestry here given is the same as that stated earlier. As for the realm of meaning, the account of his own childhood, spiritual development and his donning of the outer *kharqah* has already been mentioned; he himself says: 'Most of the chains of transmission of the *kharqah* come through Junayd al-Baghdadi, as he was the leader of a community, the Shaykh of a spiritual order and lived soon after the time of the infallible Imams.'[1]

He then relates the chain of transmission of the patched robe of the perfected shaykh Sa'd al-Din Hamawi and thereafter the chain of the gnostic and *muhaqqiq* (he who has arrived at the station of inner truth) Shihab al-Din Suhrawardi according to the licence that he had given to some of his own disciples — a chain which stretches back in three different paths of transmission to the Commander of the Faithful.

---

[1] The form of my *ijazah* to wear the outward *kharqah* — which I received from Shaykh Nur al-Din Isfahani — was in accordance with the way he himself had received it and under the same conditions imposed by the shaykhs of this realm; indeed all the shaykhs without exception took it on in this way — right up to the perfect shaykh, Junayd al-Baghdadi, who himself received it from his maternal uncle Sirri al-Saqti, who received it from Ma'ruf al-Karkhi and in turn from 'Ali bin Musa.

He quotes this licence given by Shaykh Shihab al-Din to his disciples saying: 'Know that the way of the Sufis has two aspects: the aspect of company and that of the patched robe. As for the aspect of company, I trace my relationship to my shaykh, Shaykh al-Islam Muhammad ibn Hamawi who himself held company with Khiḍr. As for the aspect of my *kharqah,* know that Muhammad ibn Hamawi took it on from his grandfather Imam Muhammad ibn Hamawi... from Ibn 'Ali Farmadi, from the pole of the age Abu'l-Qasim Gargani, from Ma'ruf al-Karkhi, from 'Ali ibn Musa al-Rida and the latter took it on from the Seal of the Prophets (Muhammad).

Shaykh Shihab al-Din Suhrawardi, known as Abu Hafs says: "My paternal uncle Shaykh al-Islam Abu'l-Najib Dia' al-Din 'Abd al-Qahir 'Abdullah ibn Muhammad Suhrawardi invested me with the patched robe and he himself was invested with it by his paternal uncle Wajih al-Din Muhammad known as 'Amawiyya... and he, by two great shaykhs, the first Akhi Faraj al-Din... whose chain of transmission reaches to 'Ali ibn Musa al-Rida and the second by his father Muhammad ibn 'Amawiyya from Shaykh Aswad Daynuri... whose chain also reaches to 'Ali ibn Musa al-Rida.'[1]

In the same book *Al-Muhit al-A'zam*, he relates how, besides the chain of transmission of the patched robe of Muhammad ibn Abi Bakr Simnani, he also took on another *kharqah* from the hand of Shaykh Nur al-Din Tihrani: 'I (Muhammad ibn Abi Bakr), the shaykh of the shaykhs of Abu'l-Hasan ibn 'Umar ibn Abi l-Hasan, have been invested with the *kharqah* from 'Imad al-Din 'Umar ibn Abi'l-Hasan 'Ali ibn Muhammad Hamawi and he held company with his grandfather Imam Muhammad ibn Hamawi (this being an indication that Sayyid Amuli also took on the *kharqah* from the hand of Muhammad ibn Abi Bakr Simnani).'

In conclusion he says: 'My arriving at the Truth and my unveilings were not dependent on the above; my arrival was first and foremost because of God rather than on account of my own

---

[1] The three dots indicate that some of the links in the chains are omitted to avoid repetition. They are delineated in Sufi books; it is possible that they will vary somewhat in who they include or omit.

spiritual progress. I was a *majdhub* — a person intoxicated by divine attraction — amongst spiritual travellers: I was of the beloved of Him rather than of those who love Him and the former have precedence over the latter — just like the prophets, the saints and their followers in the correct path for Allah says: "Those who have been recorded with good deeds from Ourselves they are far removed from the bad"; I had achieved the desired goal through the care and grace of God, not through any action on my part nor through any knowledge I possessed."[1]

Up to this point we have described the life of this great gnostic Sayyid Haydar Husayni Amuli, the pole of the gnostic cosmos and the moon in the heaven of glory and sublimity up to the year 782 AH, using his own words of truth and drawing from different places from a variety of his works.

Many of the works of this great gnostic resemble the name of the fabulous Simurgh; nothing remains of them but their titles. From 782 AH onwards we have no information about the life of this sage. We know nothing about when and where he died — except that he wrote a book entitled *Risalah fi'l-'Ulum il-'Aliyya'* (A Treatise concerning the Sublime Sciences) in 787 AH, and as Sahib Dhari'ah has noted: 'In it is mentioned that it was written after the book *Muntakhab al-Ta'wil* (An Anthology of Hermeneutics),' but other than this we have no other information or indication of any date.

As for the body of gnostic writings he has left us, it is better that I describe them by quoting from his own illuminating words which are the truest and most appropriate record of the matter; indeed his work is as a burning torch in the darkness of history and a shining lamp in the darkened hearts of the ignorant.

---

[1] My opinion was and still is that when the state of profound divine attraction overcomes a person — just as it overcame Ibrahim Adham and Shaykh 'Ala' al-Dawlah Simnani and many others like Uways al-Qarani, then the Real transports them to His court where He himself undertakes to bestow perfection and courtesy on them - this has been witnessed to be true in the case of many of the *majdhubs*, who are amongst the great saints of God: people such as Shaykh Abu l-Hasan al-Kharaqani who drew perfection from the spirituality of Bayazid Bastami; indeed Sayyid Amuli also received perfection directly from the spirituality of the infallible Imams, from the poles of previous ages and from the poles and saints of his time, and in the course of his spiritual path he crossed the station of the *majdhub* — and Allah knows best the truth of such matters.

In the introduction of *Nass al-Nusus* (The Text of Texts) he himself says, after the opening section entitled 'The historical circumstances related to the writing of the books':

1. Realise, O seeker of knowledge, that God painted the eye of the heart with the light of guidance and success after I finished writing *Majma' al-Asrar wa Manba' al-Anwar* (Collection of Secrets and the Source of Lights); [1] this work contains an explanation of *tawhid* (the unity of Allah) and the hidden truths, which are connected to *tawhid* (general definitions, classifications, states of doubt and ambiguity, subtleties and points of wisdom, secrets and indications), and a description of how *tawhid* may be defined in terms of divine *tawhid* or existential *tawhid*. It also shows how the science of *tawhid* may be divided in another way, namely into the *tawhid* of essence, of attribute and of action, or to express this otherwise, the *tawhid* of knowledge, of experience and of absolute truth; thereafter follows a clarification of these matters with respect to prophethood, to the message of prophecy and to *wilayah;* in conclusion there is an investigation into the *shari'ah, tariqah* and *haqiqah* together with an investigation into submission, faith and certainty accompanied by appropriate examples.

2. I then undertook *Risalat al-Wujud fi Ma'rifat al-Ma'bud* (Treatise on Existence; on the Knowledge of the Deity) concerning the nature of existence — with respect to absolute, accidental and necessary existence and also with respect to the oneness of existence, the manifest existence and the plurality of existence. In this work I have proved that He, that is "Existence", is the necessarily existent by His essence and that He necessarily cannot be conceived as non-existent; I have also shown that that which is in the outward is not other than Him for "He is the First and the Last and the Ascendant (over all) and the Knower of hidden things, and He is Cognizant of all things" (57:3).

3. After this I completed *Risalat al-Ma'ad fi Ruju'i'l-'Ibad* (Treatise of Eschatology, on the Return to the Godhead) together with a study of those matters pertaining to the Last Day and the rising from the grave, according to its three aspects: the minor day of rising, the intermediate day and the major day —

---

[1] This book was printed in 1347 (Persian solar calendar) by the Iran and France Institute.

and a proof of these according to the twelve risings of the outward and inward within the balanced framework of the cosmos as a whole and within that of the human self.

4. I then finished *Al-Usul wa 'l-Arkan fi tahdhibi 'l-Ashab wa 'l-Ikhwan* (Principles and Pillars, concerning the Reform of the Companions and Brothers). This work describes the five principles of belief, and each belief is examined with regard to the three classifications of *shari'ah, tariqah* and *haqiqah,* and the five pillars of the religion (prayer, fasting, almstax, pilgrimage and *jihad*).

5. I then completed *Risalat al-'Ilm* (Treatise of Knowledge) which deals with the three groups of men, namely the Sufis, the sages, and the scholastic theologians *(mutakallimun);* in it I describe the different spheres of knowledge of the three groups, including the principles, major subject matters and finer points associated with each.

6. There then followed the *Risalat al-'Aql wa 'l-Nafs* (Treatise on the Intellect and the Soul) which contains an examination of the difference between the intellect and the soul — with regard to both the particular and the general — together with an investigation into other related matters.

7. ...thereafter *Al-Amanat al-ilahiyah fi ta'yin al-khilafat al-rabaniyyah* (Divine Trusteeship in Man, determining the Divine Caliphate) which is concerned with the *ayah:* "Surely We offered the trust to the heavens and the earth..." (33:72) and offers an explanation of why the mention of the injustice and ignorance of man is as a form of praise of the highest order on behalf of Allah — in contrast to those shortsighted persons who think that this *ayah* refers to the disgrace and ignominy of man.[1]

8. ...*Al-Hujub wa Khulasatu 'l-Kutub* (The Veils and Quintessence of Books), containing a study of the *ayah:* "Then thrust him into a chain the length of which is seventy cubits" (69:32), an explanation of the saying of the Prophet, "There are seventy thousand veils of light and darkness before God...", and a comparison of these two statements. Such a comparison presents considerable difficulties, especially with regard to the whole sum and its parts,

---

[1] This work is wrongly entitled *Risalat al-Amanah* (Treatise of Divine Trusteeship) in some copies.

with regard to the parallel drawn between the Qur'an and the Prophetic traditions and with regard to the phrases "a thousand years," "five thousand years" and "three hundred thousand years"; such metaphors are similar to the statement of one of the great shaykhs: "I am two years younger than my Lord", and that of another: "Between myself and my Lord there is no difference except that I come first in the state of slavery."

9.   ...*Risalat al-Faqr wa Tahqiq al-Fakhr* (Treatise on Poverty and the Fulfilment of Glory) containing a comparison of the three *ahadith* related from the Prophet concerning *faqr* — poverty: "Poverty is my honour and by it I gain distinction over the rest of the prophets and messengers" and "Poverty means blackness of face in the two worlds" and "Poverty brings one almost to a state of unbelief *(kufr)*." [1]

10.   ...*Risalat al-Asma'i-Ilahi wa Ta'yin al-Mazahiruha min al-Ashkhas al-Insaniyah* (Treatise on the Divine Names and Identification of their Epiphanies among Human Beings) which deals with the prophets from Adam to Muhammad — may peace be upon them.

---

[1] Sayyid Qutub al-Din Nayrizi, one of the great gnostics and torch bearers during a time of declining Sufism and darkness, says in his book *Fasl al-Kitab* (The Decisive Book, on the subject of the gnostics who believe in the unity of existence). 'Sayyid Haydar bin 'Ali al-Husayni al-Amuli of the country of Tabaristan and Mazandaran possesses boundless excellence and is of the station of unveiling and witnessing; from among his beautiful works there are those entitled *Jami' al-Asrar* (Compendium of Secrets), *Muhit al-A'zam wa 'l-Bahr al-Khadam* (The Mighty Ocean and the Great Sea).' These works which are in my possession are amongst tne most precious of books. The commentator of *Fasl al-Kitab* who it appears had seen the *Risalat al-Faqr* (Treatise on Poverty), relates: 'I have written this book after seeing some of the ignorant believing that there is a contradiction in terms between the way of *faqr* (the state of the fakir on the path to Allah) and the way of the Shi'ah. In it I have demonstrated that any Shi'ah who is not of the people of poverty and spiritual journeying is not of the Shi'ah and every fakir who is not a Shi'ah is not a true fakir nor a *salik* (spiritual traveller), since these two matters are of their nature connected — the way of poverty being the way of the infallible Imams: to profess Shi'ism means that one follows them in their actions and their worship. Thus anyone who is neither a *faqir* nor a *salik* is in reality beyond the pale of Shi'ism, even though he may call himself a Shi'ah. I have composed the following lines about the people of the outward:

Such people are unaware of both the outward and the inner,
and so they go astray by their ignorance and lack of guidance;
They are immersed in worship of other than Him, while to tell the truth,
There is in reality no actor save Allah.'

11. ...*Risalat al-Nafs fi Ma'rifat al-Rabb* (Treatise of the Soul; on the Knowledge of God) which contains the saying of the Prophet: "Whoever knows himself knows his Lord" and which is composed in the light of the words of Allah: "And He is with you wherever you are (57:3) and "And in your own souls (too); will you not then see?" (51:21).

12. ...*Asrar al-Shari'ati wa Anwar al-Haqiqah* (Mysteries of the Law and Lights of the Truth) containing a description of each by the people of each group — just as Allah says: "For every one of you did We appoint a law and a way" (5:48) and just as the Prophet has said: "The law *(shari'ah)* is my speech, the spiritual way *(tairqah)* my work and the truth *(tariqah)* my inner state.[1]

13. ...*Risalat al-Jadawal* (Treatise of the Diagrams) also entitled *Madarij al-Salikin fi Maratib al-'Arifin* (Degrees of the pilgrims, concerning the Ranks of the Gnostics) describing the hundred basic stations of the journeying and the thousand subordinate grades, drawn from a cycle of one hundred divisions each containing ten grades.

14. ...*Naqd al-Nuqud fi Ma'rifat al-Wujud* (Final Examination of the Knowledge of Existence) which is a selection from our *Risalat al-Wujud.*[2]

15. ...*Muntaqa al-Ma'ad fi Murtada il-'Ibad* (A Quintessential Eschatology of the Chosen One amongst the Slaves) which is a selection from our work *Al-Ma'ad.*

16. ...*Risalat al-Tanbih fi l-Tanzih* (Treatise of Advice in the *via negationis*) which, as is clear (by its title), is about Allah — may He be exalted.

---

[1] This book is referred to sometimes as *Asrar al-Shari'ati wa Anwar al-Haqiqah* and sometimes as *Anwar al-Haqiqah wa Asrar al-Shari'ah* in the book *Jami'al Asrar;* according to the text in my possession it is *Anwar al-Haqiqah wa Atwar al-Tariqah wa Asrar al-Shari'ah;* according to the index of the university it is *Asrar al-Shari'ati wa Anwar al-Haqiqah;* in the library of Ma'rashi in Qum it is *Anwar al-Haqiqah wa Asrar al-Shari'ah.*

[2] This book together with *Jami' al-Asrar* was printed by the Iran and France Institute in 1347 AH (solar dating).

17. ...*Amthalat al-Tawhid wa Abniyat al-Tajrid* (Examples of Divine Unity and the Principles of Divestment) after the manner of the book *Lama'at 'Iraqi.* [1]

18. ...*Risalatu Kanz al-Kanuz wa Kashf al-Rumuz* (Treatise of the Treasure of Treasures and the Unveiling Symbols).

19. ...*Nihayat al-Tawhid fi 'Bidayat al-Tajrid* (The Conclusion of Divine Unity in the Beginning of Divestiment) which is a selection from *Jami' al-Asrar* and *Manba' al-Anwar.*

20. ...*Ta'yin al-Aqtab wa 'l-Awtad* (Identification of the Poles and Supports) containing mention of nineteen persons (seven great prophets and twelve Imams) — no more nor less (neither three hundred nor forty nor seven nor three nor one) since the number is nineteen with regard to the station of realisation; I have also composed a further forty or so writings in a similar vein, in both Arabic and Persian.

21. ...after completion of the above mentioned works — during a long period extending over thirty years — I wrote a commentary on the Qur'an entitled *Al-Muhit al-A'zam wal-Tawd al-Ashamm fi Ta'wil Kitab illahi 'l-'Aziz al-Muhkam* (The Mighty, Ocean and Lofty Mountain; esoteric exegesis of the clear and precious Book of Allah), comprising seven large volumes; I composed it in the manner of the great shaykh Najm al-Din Razi, known as "Dayah", who wrote a further six volumes of his book after completing the volume called *Bahr al-Haqa'iq wa Manba' al-Daqa'iq* (The Sea of Truths and Source of Subtleties). Our commentary is also written in accordance with the *hadith* of the Prophet which says "The Qur'an has an outer and an inner aspect: as for the inner there is always another aspect within this - extending to seven inner aspects"; all of the great and well-known figures of spiritual realisation and all those intimate with these matters affirm that this work has no equal, in particular with respect to Qur'anic knowledge. Moreover, this work is not a product of any effort of any effort on my part, but rather it is the result of the outpourings from the unseen — from the

---

[1] These two books, namely *Risalat al-Tanbih* and *Amthalat al-Tawhid* in addition to *Jami' al-Haqa'iq* were written in Persian and the another indicates this at the end of *Jami' al-Asrar.*

Beneficent Himself.[1]

22. After completion of all these writings a group of persons of perspicacity together with a number of eminent men of Allah were exceedingly desirous that I write for them a commentary on the *Fusus al-Hikam*... and this work is the same *Nass al-Nusus fi Sharh al-Fusus* (The Text of Texts Elucidating the Bezels) mentioned at the beginning of the introduction.'

These are books and essays *(Risa'il)* written by Sayyid Amuli up to 782 AH and which have been described by his own hand in the introduction to the *Nass al-Nusus* — the commentary on the *Fusus al-Hikam* of Shaykh Muhyi al-Din Ibn 'Arabi.

He has made no reference to any other essays, but other works written in his graceful hand have been recorded by the bibliographers:

23. *Risalat al-Ta'wilat* (Treatise of Spiritual Hermeneutics), a work of Qur'anic commentary which is a selection from the book *Al-Bahr al-Khadm* (The Great Sea) and which is also known as *Muntakhab al-Ta'wil* (Extract of Hermeneutics).

24. *Masa'il al-Amuliat* (Amuli Questions), a copy of which, consisting of approximately six pages and written in the hand of the author, exists in the Central University Library of Tehran (under the file no. 1022); in it he says: 'These treatises are concerned with questions of jurisprudence and take the form of questions, posed by myself (on various occasions), and the corresponding answers in the form of legal opinions *(fatwas)* by the great Shaykh, the sultan of the scholars of the earth, the honour of the Arab and non-Arab alike, the example and model of realisation for the whole or creation, the object of special favour by the Lord of the Worlds, the Imam and eminent scholar, Fakhr al-Haqq wa 'l-Millat wa 'l-Din, the son of 'Allamah Hilli; the first of these interviews took place at the end of the month of Rajab in 759 AH in the town of Hillah; I, the questioner, am the slave and fakir Haydar ibn 'Ali ibn Haydar al-'Alawi al-Husayni al-Amuli.' The questions are twelve in number and cover a variety of subjects in the realm of theology and jurisprudence. They, together

---

[1] In another volume of this book (No. 301 in the library of Mar'ashi in Qum) he says: 'I completed this at the end of the month of Shawwal 777 AH in Najaf.'

with the accompanying treatises, are all in Arabic and all are
written in the hand of Sayyid Amuli; the replies in the form of
fatwas are in the hand of Fakhr al-Muhaqqiqin Hilli; the date
of the writing of the *Masa'il* is 761 and the other *risalahs* 762 AH.[1]

1. *Masa'il Amuliat* consisting of twelve questions put to Fakhr al-Muhaqqiqin by
Sayyid Amuli: (1) concerning the necessity of divine gnosis and concerning the attributes which may or may not be associated with Him; (2) concerning the *mukallaf*
(the one on whom some duty is incumbent) who does not have the capacity to carry
out that duty, who by his ignorance is in a state of extreme weakness and by his
foolishness is in great need of sustenance; (3) concerning the duty of the *mukallaf*
and how a portion of it may be more difficult than the rest; (4) concerning the trader
who does not pay the *khums* tax on his wealth; (5) and (6) concerning the 'Alawi
Sadat (those who are descended from the Prophet by the lineage of 'Ali) and the
way in which *khums* is given to them; (7) and (8) concerning the *khums* of those who
are not descended from the Prophet and who are either employees or workers; (9)
concerning the love of the *mukallaf* for the Prophet and the Imams and concerning
what kind of love it should be — whether it should be the same as that associated
with mankind — a love caused by inclination, natural passion or some other kind
of love; (10) concerning the request for blessings on the Prophet and whether or not
it is obligatory or recommended and whether it is obligatory in the prayer and at
other times just recommended; it also concerns the question as to whether it is an
absolute obligation and deals with the difference between the asking of blessings on
Muhammad and his Family and the asking of blessings merely on His family; it
discusses too the difference between *ahl* and *al*, both linguistically and in terms of
their application; (11) concerning the saying of *amin* after the *al-Hamd surah* (something
which is done by the Sunnis), whether or not the saying of it invalidates the prayer
and whether or not this word is part of the Qur'an or not; (12) this particular page
is torn and patched up and the *fatwa* of Fakhr al-Muhaqqiqin is missing.
Within this collection — apart from the *Masa'il Amuliat* there are also twelve other
treatises, all written in the hand of Sayyid Amuli:
2. *Masa'il Madaniyat* (Madinan Questions) by 'Allamah Hilli; written on the back
of this manuscript is the *ijazah* of Fakhr al-Muhaqqiqin and in the work itself he
corrects several points of the *risalah* of his own father.
3. *Risalatu fi Hajj al-Mutamatti' bihi wa Wajibatuhu* (The Treatise of the Hajj al-
Tamattu' and its obligations) by Fakhr al-Muhaqqiqin.
4. *Risalatu Mi'raj al-Salamah wa Minhaj al-Karamah* (The Treatise of the Ascent to
Safety and the Miraculous Way) by 'Ali ibn Sulayman al-Bahrani.
5. *Kitab Suyun al-Hikmah* (The Book of the Springs of Wisdom) by Fakhr.
6. *Risalatu l-Hudud* (The Treatise on the Legal Parameters and Punishments) by
Ibn Sina.
7. *Masa'il Mutafarriqah* (Miscellaneous Questions).
8. *Risalat al-Tawhid* (The Treatise on Divine Unity).
9. *Istalahat Hukama* (The Terminology of the Wise).
10. *Risalah Khwajah Nasir al-Din Tusi.*
11. *Risalat al-'Ilm* (The Treatise on Knowledge).
12. Questions put by Shaykh Sadr al-Din Qunyawi to Khwajah Nasir al-Din Tusi.
13. *Risalat al-Qada' wa l-Qadr* (The Treatise of the Decree and Predestination) by
Hasan Basri.

---

[1] These *risalahs* are written in the hand of Sayyid Amuli, a hand more fair and
beautiful than a ravishing face; the *fatwas* of Fakhr al-Muhaqqiqin, the teacher of
Sayyid Amuli, are to be found in the margins and between the different sections of
the work; the following is a list of these thirteen *risalahs:*

25. *Risalatu fi'l-'Ulum al-'Aliyah* (Treatise on the Sublime Sciences), related by the author of *Al-Dhari'ah* and composed and written in 787 AH.[1]

As for the other treatise which have been attributed to him in such bibliographies as *'Iyan al-Shi'ah, Idah al-Maknun* (The Unveiling of the Hidden), *Majalis al-Mu'minin* (The Gatherings of the Believers), *Mu'ajam al-Mu'alifin* (The Encyclopaedia of Authors), *Fuwa'id al-Ridawayah* (The Benefits of al-Rida), *Hadiyat al-'Arifin* (The Guidance of the Gnostics), *Rawdat al-Jinnah* (The Meadow of Paradise), *Al-Dhari'atu* (The Dhari'ah), *Rayhan al-Adab* (The Scent of Courtesy), and others it should be said that it cannot be ascertained for certain whether they are actually his works or not; indeed there is more evidence to indicate the contrary; the following is a list of such works:

26. *Rafi'at al-Khilaf 'an Wajh Sukut Amir al-Mu'minin 'an al-Ikhtilaf* (Justification for the First Imam's attitude to the three first Caliphs).*

27. *Risalat al-Mu'tamid min al-Manqul fi-ma Awha ila al-Rasul* (Treatise of the Trustworthy Narrations concerning the Revelations to the Messenger).

---

[1] I saw this work — written in the hand of the author — included with the book *Muhit al-A'zam* in the library of Najaf (there is another copy of the same volume in the library of Mar'ashi in Qum). In it the author says: 'I wrote this brief treatise concerning the sciences of the three groups (the Sufis, the philosophers and the theologians) at the behest of certain respected persons. It consists of an introduction and ten subjects of investigation: the introduction deals with the three types of knowledge, the first an explanation of the knowledge of the people of Allah, the second concerning the way in which revelation and inspiration are transmitted, and the third concerning the nature of unveiling together with the different orders of divine names — the names of action, the names of the attributes and the names of the essence.' This *risalah* is the same *Risalat al-'Ilm* which has already been mentioned above (no. 5) or rather it is a shortened version of it; the year 787 AH, however, does seem rather late; Sayyid Amuli would describe each year of his life in the course of his writings but from 782 AH, the year in which he completed the commentary on the Fusus to 787 AH, there is an inexplicable gap of five years of which we know nothing; with regard to the date of writing of the commentary (in the library of Mar'ashi — written in the graceful hand of the author) the year 777 AH is recorded, and it is possible that this treatise, which is part of another volume of commentary, has been wrongly dated by the writer or has been misread — that is that the middle number has been inverted: and Allah knows better the truth of all matters.

---

* Henry Gorbin attributes this work to Haydar Amuli and states that it was written at the request of his teacher Fakhr al-Muhaqqiqin. See *La Philosophic shi'ite* (Tehran and Paris, 1969), p. 41

28. *Risalat al-Zad al-Musafirin* (The Treatise of the Travellers' Provision).

29. *Lubb al-Istilahat al-Sufiyah* (Kernel of Sufi Terms) — which is a selection of the *Istilahat* of Kamal al-Din 'Abd al-Razzaq al-Kashani.

30. *Kitab al-Kashkul fi-ma jara li'l Ali'l-Rasul* (Album of Events concerning the Family of the Prophet) which has already been mentioned.

If these works had actually been written by him, then he would have mentioned them in the introduction to *Nass al-Nusus* — in particular *al-Kashkul* which dates from 735 AH. *Nass al-Nusus* was composed in 782 AH; if we examine the rest of the books from this perspective, then it is clear, just as it is clear at first glance to those who are familiar with the style of Sayyid Amuli, which of the works are actually his and which are merely attributed to him: 'Whenever we scrutinise a particular art, it seems that art belongs to a particular person.'

In conclusion we should not forget that *Asrar al-Shari'ah* is twice mentioned by Sayyid Amuli in *Jami' al-Asrar;* as we have seen from above list many of the works of Sayyid Amuli are either shortened versions of his own books or — to use the language of the logicians — they are either complete abridgements or abridgements with regard to one aspect only; thus the content of one of his books may closely resemble that of another, or the structure of one may reflect that another. Thus, for example, the important work *Ta'wilat Qur'an al-Karim* (The Hermeneutics of the Noble Qur'an), which I read in the Mar'ashi library in Qum, usually treats the *ayat* according to the same three levels, namely *shari'ah, tariqah* and *haqiqah,* and the text of *Asrar al-Shari'ah* is almost always perceptible throughout the whole of the commentary. Similarly, the book *Jami' al-Asrar* revolves around the three levels of *tawhid* — essence, attribute and action — together with *tawhid* of knowledge, experience and truth, a study of prophethood, prophecy and *wilayah,* a study of *shari'ah, tariqah,* and *haqiqah,* and the subjects of submission *(islam),* faith *(iman)* and certainty *(iqan).* The *Risalat al-Ma'ad,* which is about the resurrection of God's slaves, contains amongst other matters the three-tiered aspect of the day of rising — the minor, intermediate and the major — which has already been dealt with in a more comprehensive manner in *Asrar al-Shari'ah*. Similarly, the book *Usul wa'l-Arkan* (Principles and Pillars) is an abridgement of this same book and the abridged text of *Risalat al-Hujub* (The Treatise of the Veils) is to be found in the chapter concerning the Day of Resurrection, just as the subjects of prophecy and the Final Day are dealt with in *Risalat al-Asma'* (Treatise of the Names) in an abridged and different form. *Risalat al-Tanbih* (Treatise of Advice) explains the three levels of divine unity, and *Risalat al-Wujud* (Treatise of Existence) — in particular in the introduction — deals with many of the questions of *tawhid*, albeit in a different manner.

Thus this precious work contains the subject matter for seven or eight of his main books of research into the divine truths; it contains the finest selection of Sayyid Amuli's ideas, both with regard to the Islamic system of belief and to the acts of worship — drawn from the Possessors of Divine Inspiration, the pillars of divine unity, the store-houses of boundless knowledge, namely the infallible Imams — drawn by way of unveilings and witnessing after long years of divine attraction, spiritual exercises and acts of worship and then set down in this book at the command of Allah as if without any effort on his part.

Shari'ah, *tariqah* and *haqiqah* are different names indicating one truth — namely the pattern of behaviour of Muhammad. Each, however, has its own specific realm of meaning: just as the almond consists of a shell, an outer skin and the kernel, so the shell is as the *shari'ah*, the outer skin the *tariqah* and the kernel the *haqiqah* — the inner core; the almond as a whole embraces all three.

In the *Majallah* (Place of Manifestation) of Ibn Abi Jamhur and *Bahr al-Ma'arif* (Sea of Gnosis) by Mulla 'Abd al-Samad Hamdani prayer is treated as consisting of three different levels: *khidmah* (service), *qurbah* (a drawing closer through humility) and *wuslah* (union); *khidmah* is thus on a level with *shari'ah* and the physical actions of the prayer, *qurbah* on a level with *tariqah* and the concentration of the heart during prayer, and *wuslah* on a level with *haqiqah* and the core meaning of prayer; all three are also contained in the word prayer. Sayyid Amuli also says in *Jami' al-Asrar*: '*Shari'ah* is on a par with the divine message, *tariqah* with the prophecy and *haqiqah* with *wilayah* (intimacy with Allah); all accept these truths: anyone who rejects them or who rejects just one of them is an unbeliever.'

Therefore, do not deny something simply because you cannot understand it. It is by purifying the heart of the impediments and troubles caused by this world, and by deep reflection on the words of these great people that the outward meaning of what they are saying will become comprehensible to you; this is because their speech comes from the world of witnessing and vision and not from the realm of mere knowledge and explanation; however much one tries to express this state in the language of knowledge and explanation, it is never more than secret compounded upon secret; God himself says: 'And they do not assign to Allah the attributes due to Him' (6:91). Imam Ahmad Ghazali has said: 'Anyone who has no portion of *tawhid*, then I fear for him that the outcome of his affair will be a bad one — that is his final seal and judgement on death will be as one of the unfortunate'; the minimum portion is that he accept and submit to the people of realisation — who are the saints or friends of Allah. Our Imams have also said: 'To deny is to cover up the truth: those who speak of the essence, the attributes and the actions of God are speaking only in order to increase our awareness and to encourage us'; in fact nobody really understands the *wali* (the intimate friend of Allah) and the attributes of the *wali* but the *wali* himself: the unripe cannot encompass the ripe so it is better to be brief and say: Peace! The denial of those who deny is merely a physical response to what they hear: their very efforts not to understand such matters are all-powerful and all contentment and submission have been extinguished in them. Since this group live on the level of the senses, they are incapable of understanding anything but tangible things; they are incapable of going beyond this level.

> Since the worm is hidden in the apple, it knows nothing
> but that as its world and heaven.

If they were to step out of the prison of the senses into the world of the heart, they would perceive that:

The heavens are contained in the *wali* whose divine intimacy causes the ordering of this world's heaven.

Most of mankind are in the station of those who are anxious
for their sustenance, who are greedy and miserly, and who are
caught up in all the material aspects of the world. Imam Baqir
has said:

Most men are beasts and four-footed animals.... .
Open the eye of your heart that you may see the soul and
the unseen.
If you enter the realms of divine passion, you will see all
horizons as a garden.
Rise above all the people of this world by your intent and
look around the heavens.
The heart wants that which you see and that which your
heart wants you shall see.
The heart will see its sun in every splitting of the atom.
If you give everything you have with passion, then call
me an unbeliever if you ever suffer loss in your desiring.
If the soul burns up with the fire of passion, then you will
see passion as the elixir of the soul.
Travel beyond the confines of this life and see the vastness
of His kingdom beyond space.
Let your ear listen to what it has not heard and your eye
see what it has not seen, until it leads you to where you
see the One of the world and all the worlds.
Express your passion for the One from your heart and
soul until you see Reality with the eye of certainty:
There is only One and nothing but Him, He is Alone and
there is no god but Him.[1]

---

[1] This set of verses ending (in the original) with the refrain 'you see' is an indication
of divine passion and the witnessing of the Truth — which is the basis of divine
gnoses. Such witnessing entails a divine attraction towards oneness by means of the
attributes of *tawhid*, then an entering into the different levels of unveiling — in which
the heart becomes aware of every molecule — and then a passing into the levels of
fana' (annihilation) whereby the spiritual traveller gives up everything he possesses
to his desire for the divine existence. In doing so, all excess or lack of material wealth
ceases to exist since his own illusory existence has disappeared into oneness with
God. Thereafter there is the *baqa'* — in which one abides in Allah; in this state
passion is transformed by alchemy into the elixir of existence and one moves beyond
the limits of the world of the senses and the four dimensions.

It is for this reason that the teaching shaykhs always warn their students and disciples against denying the people of Allah saying: The expressions of these people are obscure; it is hard to understand them when they talk about their thoughts and intentions because such matters are far removed from the minds of ordinary people. Shaykh Mahmud Shabistari comments in the following way: 'The saints of this path, both before (Muhammad) and after (him) have given indications of their inner experiences. When they became aware of the parameters of the self, they described both the one who acquires knowledge and the source of this knowledge. Since each man's speech is a reflection of his station, the common people find it difficult to understand this variety of experience.'

Shaykh Sa'd al-Din Hamawi said to some of his own disciples: 'Do not be duped by the variety of terms, and do not be negligent of their inner meanings, for on the day when the people are raised from their graves and when that which was hidden in their breasts becomes known, when the great plain of the Last Day encloses all of mankind, out of every thousand persons who are raised up, nine hundred and ninety nine of them will be killed by the sword of those expressions or by the arrow of those indications — blood will be split on the necks of those very people who were careless with regard to the meanings, who pursued the way of rejection and denial and abandoned the edifice of knowledge.'

Allah will forgive the person who desired that his actions be just and who, with the help of his intellect, avoided any dispute because he realised that he had no knowledge in these matters; this is the way of the spiritually advanced *(salihun)* and the sincere of His slaves. He says: 'Those who listen to the word, then follow the best of it; those are they whom Allah has guided, and those it is who are the men of understanding' (39:18)... .*

It remains to me to thank those at the Cultural Studies and Research Institute of the Islamic Iranian Academy of Philosophy and all those who, whatever the circumstances have a passion

---

* The editor's commentary on the text has been omitted since it largely comprises a selection of passages translated into Persian for the benefit of the Persian reader with a poor knowledge of Arabic.

for Islamic texts and who have a profound love for the truths of gnosis — all those who by the music of spirituality awakened my lifeless heart and broken spirit after an extended period away from any research of this nature. I have completed this introduction with the desire that it be of particular interest to the honoured scholars and researchers of this institute; I have added to it a list of contents which shows in detail the principles on which each section is based, principles which are as it were the links in the golden chain of this divine religion and which reflect the progression from *shari'ah,* through *tariqah* to *haqiqah.* I hope that I have managed to portray the beauty, radiance and splendour of these gnostic truths and subtleties which issue from behind the subtle veils of that garden of profundities, that abode of magnificence and elegance (which is the heart). I desire as reward for my efforts nothing but increase in God's grace and generosity, nothing but illumination by the lights of the Muhammadi realm and nothing but spiritual assistance on the path from Sayyid Haydar 'Alawi. It is thus that I present this brief work as a service to Allah who is reward can only be received in the next world.

This introduction was completed in the evening of the first of Muharram 1403 after the *hijrah,* lunar dating (26 Mehr 1361 AH, solar dating); I ask Allah that He bless all those who undertook that *hijrah.*

Sing the song of goodness in this echoing dome of the world.
For it shall return your song generously after death.

Muhammad Khajavi (26/7/1362 AH solar dating)

Postscript

The burial place of Sayyid Amuli is to be found in the town of Amul, at the lower end of the bazaar in a quarter known as Buqayye Mir Haydar ('Say Tan'); the building contained therein dates from the Seljuk period and the dome resembles that of Baba Rukn al-Din Shirazi, the renowned gnostic who died in 769 AD in Isfahan. On two small doors on either side of the building is written in Arabic: 'Construction of this revered burial ground was undertaken on the instructions of the Pole of the men of spiritual realisation and the Proof of the spiritual travellers, Sayyid 'Izz al-Din ibn Sayyid Baha' al-Din Amuli.' Again I express the hope that God willing, in the future, the illuminated visage of Sayyid Amuli will reveal itself more clearly to us from the dark mirror of history.

I
Ground Work

1

Introduction and the First Aspect:

a study of Theology and the Science of Gnosis

May Allah give me success in completion of this book, by the blessing of Muhammad, his pure family and progeny. Praise belongs to Allah, Who has illuminated the hearts of His slaves by the knowledge of the truth, tasting and witnessing, Who has cooled their eyes with the antimony of His divine grace and love from eternity, Who has brought them to the highest stations of witnessing in the world of pre-existent form and spiritual unveiling, and Who has enabled them to establish proof based on the intellect and clear evidence based on the traditions by way of the higher levels of the purified soul and the illuminated intellect.

May Allah bless the one who guides to such stations by means of the lights of inner vision and who indicates the path leading to these divine gnoses; may He bless the one who has made clear the meaning of the *shari'ah*, that is the merciful code of behaviour incumbent upon every Muslim. May He bless too his progeny, companions and family — the continuation of the lineage of the Prophet; it is in accordance with man's enmity or love of them that the different levels of the Garden and the Fire are apportioned in the hereafter.

Only the slaves of abundant excellence and of penetrating knowledge will be able to arrive at the Divine Presence and to fulfil the exigencies of the subtle divine states; such slaves alone will be able to come close to the Reality of Oneness and will be able to extinguish their own essence in the stations of unity after traversing the names and attributes of the Real by means of the station of oneness and arriving at knowledge of the higher and lower manifestations, together with the manifestations within the self and in the cosmos as a whole. Only these slaves will achieve the level of angelic attributes by their understanding of the most imperceptible of signs along the spiritual path, by their struggle and perseverance in the search for meanings, by their purification and refinement of behaviour and their capacity to free the self from the veil of animal urges. Only these slaves will be able to break the chains of bodily desires and the fetters of material bondage.

None will comprehend the nature of travel on this path but those experienced and knowledgeable in the science of true divinity and the stations of unveiling — that is the stations of the *awliya'* (the saints or intimate friends of Allah), the prophets and the greatest amongst the men of wisdom.

The spiritual gnoses and the rules of behaviour embodied in the *shari'ah* have come down to us from the Divine Presence by means of the Muhammadi reality; together they convey the blessings of the prophetic example and the stations of elevation. It was this important fact which spurred me to write a book expounding the way of perfection, which is the way of those able to unite what is separate by their gnosis and by applying the *shari'ah*. Moreover, I have composed this book with the view to comparing the way of the sincere Sufis and the way of the Imamiyah sect in the light of the divine insights and in accordance with each of the three levels of unity, namely the *shari'ah,* the *tariqah* and *haqiqah* of the Prophet, Mustafa ('the chosen one'). These three levels embrace the totality of the stations of the Muhammadi way, that is, both the inner and the outer stations. They embrace too all the degrees of perfection belonging to the prophets and the saints — who are the caliphs of Allah and the viceregents of divine Lordship.

In writing this book I have followed the path of the *shari'ah,* the path of specific duties and service made incumbent by Allah on His slaves. I have travelled lightly along this path with the minimum of hindrance and impediment, so much so it may be construed as an omission or negligence on my part. I have travelled thus along the spiritual path on seeing that this age and this country are devoid of men of excellence; I did not take upon myself this great task except after perceiving the absence of men of perfection and the absence of spiritual 'poles' (a group of spiritual guardians, appointed by God and specific in number) and after seeing the door to spiritual travel closed.

If we accept that knowledge is bestowed by Allah on certain of His slaves, then it is not surprising that He may store up this knowledge for certain of the later generations of gnostics. Thus it may be that understanding of that which was difficult for many of the earlier generations becomes easier for later generations. I feel there is no saying more apt than that of the one who said 'So much has been left by earlier generations to their successors. May Allah grant us refuge from envy which closes the door of justice and bars the way to attainment of man's finer qualities.' There are no more fitting words than those of Abu l-'Ala al-Mu'arra on the same topic:

> By your father's life, the man of nobility is never attributed
> with generosity
> As long as the Generous Himself exists in the world;
> But if the land becomes barren and the crops wither,
> Then one pastures on the dry stubble.

We should note too the famous words of the Commander of the Faithful ('Ali), words which have been related in an unbroken chain of transmission: 'Even if one does not attain everything, one does not abandon everything,' and 'Do not abandon what is easy because of what is difficult.'

Thus I composed this book and named it 'The Light of the Truth, the Stations of the Way and the Mysteries of the Revealed Law'. In doing so I sought from the Good, the Generous, that He grant us success by it and that He grant me success in its composition — success in delineating the spiritual path of right guidance — and that He enable us to avoid any mistakes in the exposition of the various topics under discussion; surely He is the Most Generous of those Who bestow goodness.

Before embarking on this study however I should present an introduction encompassing the numerous benefits awaiting the reader of this book; it is necessary that I provide the key with which to unlock the treasures contained therein for those desirous of such knowledge. Know therefore that this introduction includes an explanation of *shari'ah*, *tariqah* and *haqiqah*, together with a clarification of their various degrees according to the intellect, the body of traditions and the states of unveiling. Most of the elite and the common of this time think that *shari'ah* is at variance with *tariqah* and *tariqah* is at variance with *haqiqah*; they imagine that there are real differences between these various

levels and they attribute certain things to each of them which
are inappropriate, in particular to the group which affirms the
Oneness of Allah, namely the group known as the Sufis. The
reason for this is their lack of knowledge of the various spiritual
states of each of the three groups and their deficient understanding of their beliefs and principles. Thus I desired to make clear
these different states to those who had misconceptions about
them; I desired to reveal to them these spiritual states in a way
that would enable them to gain true knowledge of each of the
groups, in particular the people of Allah. I wanted to bring them
to a realisation that *shari'ah, tariqah* and *haqiqah* are synonyms
for one truth, albeit in different terms. By this means I desired
that they abandon their conflicts with the people of Allah, including the elite amongst them, and they leave off disputing with
the masters of the science of divine unity. I desired that, as a
result, they would rid their hearts and souls of the darkness of
ill-conduct and corruption and depart from the realm of doubt
and misgiving. Thus my clarification would be a purgative
medicine for their petrified minds and their coarse natures: it
would cause them to get rid of noxious waste material and cor-
rupting humours, with the result that they would acquire a capacity to listen to words which they had previously been unable to
digest, and they would be able to accept the beliefs (of the above-
mentioned groups) whenever anyone gave expression to them.

The words of the scholars, for example, confirm the prophetic
code of behaviour and the divine rules imposed on man. Indeed
each of the three levels, namely prophethood, delivery of the
message *(risalah)* and saintship or divine authority *(wilayah)* is a
pre-requisite of the other levels and all are interconnected. Thus,
shari'ah is the pre-requisite of *risalah, tariqah* is the pre-requisite
of prophethood and *haqiqah* is the pre-requisite of *wilayah*. This
is because *risalah* is the term for the transmission of that which
was revealed to the Prophet giving his period of prophecy; it is the
Prophet's instruction of the people in jurisprudence, politics,
social behaviour and divine wisdom — and this is precisely the
nature of the *shari'ah* as a whole. Prophethood is also the expression of that which manifests during the state of *wilayah,* that is
it is the perception of gnoses which arises from the Essence of

the Truth, through His names, attributes, actions and laws. It is an expression of the state of those who take on His attributes and His code of behaviour — and this is precisely the nature of *haqiqah* itself. The totality of this wisdom is dependent upon one person, namely the messenger, or upon one reality and that is the *shari'ah*. This concurs with our earlier statement that the prophetic code of behaviour and the divine body of laws imposed on man is one truth which encompasses all three levels and that the different names are synonyms for this one truth.

There are many examples of this in other spheres of investigation: the names *'aql* (intellect), *qalam* (pen) and *nur* (light) all indicate one reality, namely the reality of the Cosmic Man — as in the authoritative traditions which say, 'The first thing created by Allah was the *'aql* and 'The first thing created by Allah was the Pen' and 'The first thing created by Allah was My light.' Likewise, Allah's use of the words *fu'ad, qalb* and *sadr* all refer to one reality, namely the reality of the lesser man: 'The *fu'ad* or heart was not untrue in making him see what he saw' and 'The Faithful Spirit has descended with it, upon your heart *(qalb)*' and 'Have We not expanded for you your breast *(sadr)* and taken off from you your burden'. Thus there is no dispute between the prophets and the messengers with regard to the basic question of truth and reality, namely the question of the religion of Islam and its pillars or foundations. Allah says: 'He has made plain to you of the religion what He enjoined upon Noah and that which We have revealed to you, and that which We enjoined upon Abraham and Moses and Jesus, that you keep to obedience and be not divided therein' and 'The same did Abraham enjoin on his sons and (so did) Jacob. O my sons! Surely Allah has chosen for you (this) faith, therefore die not unless you are Muslims' and His words on the tongue of His Prophet: 'And (know) that this is My path, the right one, therefore follow it, and follow not (other) ways, for they will lead you away from His way; thus He has enjoined you with that you may guard against (evil)' and finally His words: 'That is the right religion, but most people know it not.' With these words Allah is indicating the right way — the way of Muhammad — whereby man must establish the three pillars of the *shari'ah*, *tariqah* and *haqiqah* and fulfil the demands of each, according to the different levels. The fact that 'most do not know' is because of their ignorance and blindness.

If one understands that there has never been any dispute amongst the prophets and messengers with regard to the foundations and pillars of Islam, then one should realise too that if differences do occur in the details and branches of the law, then these differences are of quality or quantity and do not indicate any difference in the essence or reality. Thus the reality of the *shari'ah* has been the same in all ages and locations; indeed it is untouched by contention and difference. What variations in law and rule there are arise because of the diversity of situation and time or because of the difference of degree in people's spiritual rank and understanding. Thus Allah has said: 'We make no difference between any of His apostles.' On further investigation we realise too that this divergence results from the complexity of the creational order and harmony and as such could not be imagined otherwise. Thus it has been said that there is no more perfect a creation in the realm of the possible than the creation of this world, since if there were a creation more intricate in workmanship and He were storing it up, then that would imply meanness on His part and a deficiency in His generosity; it would also imply incapacity and a negation of His power. Moreover, if existence were not organised and arranged to this degree of sophistication, then it would not be possible for any of His slaves (that is all of creation) to attain their own individual reality in accordance with their own individual capacity: it is clear that it would be impossible to channel all the varying capacities into one single path and at one simple level. Allah Himself says: 'For every one of you did We appoint a law and a way.' Thus these differences are in accordance with the nature of existence and a state of affairs other than this would not be possible.

The expressions and indications of the Sufis to describe these degrees and levels are difficult to understand; indeed their profundity of meaning is not intended to be comprehended by all. Thus the teaching shaykhs strove always to advise and guide their disciples in such matters, saying for example, 'Do not be duped by the diversity of the terms; surely when those in their graves are raised up and what is in their breasts becomes known, when mankind comes before Allah on the Day of Resurrection, then of every thousand so raised up, nine hundred and ninety nine will be killed by the gnostic terms or be slaughtered by the swords of gnostic signs: they will be covered in blood and wounds through their neglect of the meanings and their abandonment of the principles of this matter.'

If this point is understood, then the reader should also realise that the ultimate intention of this study is to explain that all these names refer to one reality, albeit using different terms; thus there is no fundamental difference between them. Moreover, we must have recourse to the three aspects of *shari'ah, tariqah* and *haqiqah* in order to demonstrate this fact in more detail. We must explain, first, that these three names are, in fact, aspects of one reality; secondly, that the people of *haqiqah* are greater than the people of *tariqah* and the people of *tariqah* are greater than the people of *shari'ah,* and that between them there exists no essential divergence; and thirdly, that an explanation of the *shari'ah* must be based on the intellect and the intellect on the *shari'ah.* This third section will also contain a study of other related matters.

With regard to the first aspect — to its definition and its reality as a unified whole — then know that the *shari'ah* is the name of the God-given path which lies before man in his life in this world; it encompasses both the principles and the branches of the religion; it encompasses both the duties and prescriptions which admit of a certain degree of choice for man in their method or time of undertaking and also the obligatory duties; it also encompasses all those actions which are most excellent in the eyes of God. As for the *tariqah,* it is the way of maximum prudence, the path of the best and surest action: thus any path which leads man to the best and surest in speech or action, in the attributes he acquires or the states he experiences, is called *tariqah.* As for *haqiqah,* it is affirmation of the existence of Being, either through unveiling and vision of its substance, or experiencing spiritual states, or affirming the Oneness of God. It has also been said that the meaning of *shari'ah* is that you worship Him, of *tariqah* that you attain His presence, and of *haqiqah* that you witness Him. Furthermore, it has been said that *shari'ah* means that you are maintained in existence by His command, *tariqah* that you carry out His command and *haqiqah* that you exist by and in Him. This meaning is supported by the words of the Prophet who said: 'The *shari'ah* is my words, *tariqah* my actions, *haqiqah* my states, gnosis is my capital, intellect the basis of my religion, love my foundation, passion my mount, fear my companion, knowledge my weapon, forbearance my friend, trust my cloak, contentment my treasure, truthfulness my residence, certainty my refuge, poverty my glory — and by it I attain to an honour above the rest of the prophets and messengers.' Likewise the words of the Prophet (on the occasion when he asked Harith 'How are you this morning?' and the latter answered: 'I have become a true believer'): 'For every truth there is a reality, so what is the reality of your belief?' He replied: 'I saw the people of the Garden visiting each other and the people of the Fire howling at each other; I saw plainly the throne of my Lord.' He then said: 'You have spoken correctly, so persevere.' Thus his true faith in the unseen was his *shari'ah*, his unveiling and consciousness of the Garden, the Fire and the throne was his *haqiqah* and his doing-without in this world and the actions undertaken by him such that he merited this degree were his *tariqah*. Moreover all three levels are encompassed by the prescribed laws of Islam and are in no way outside of it: we have seen earlier how the Islamic code includes all of them.

It has also been said that the Islamic code is like the almond nut, which consists of the oil, the kernel and the shell: the almond as a whole is the *shari'ah*, the kernel is the *tariqah* and the oil the *haqiqah*. A similar meaning has also been applied to prayer: 'Surely prayer is service, a coming closer and an arrival;' the service corresponds to the *shari'ah*, the coming closer to the *tariqah*, and the arrival to the *haqiqah*. Moreover, the word prayer includes all three of these. Allah Himself has referred to these three degrees by the phrases: *'ilm al-yaqin* (the knowledge of certainty), *'ayn al-yaqin* (the vision or experience of certainty) and *haqq al-yaqin* (the truth of reality of certainty) — an explanation of these terms will follow later in this work.

On investigation we realise that *shari'ah* expresses man's affirmation of the words of the Prophet in the heart and man's acting in accordance with the laws of Islam; we realise that *tariqah* is the fulfilment and realisation of these laws together with the prophetic pattern of behaviour and the putting into practice of this way (or *tariqah*) by the taking on of the appropriate attributes; we realise too that *haqiqah* is the witnessing through unveiling of the states and stations of the prophets — for as Allah has said: 'Certainly you have in the Apostle of Allah an excellent exemplar.' Attainment of this degree of *haqiqah* is only possible by taking upon oneself the attributes and behaviour pattern of the Prophet and by perception of prophetic knowledge through unveiling; indeed one only attains to this model of behaviour through establishing the duties of the Islamic code. This meaning is also indicated in the words of the Sultan of the Saints and Spiritual Inheritors, the Commander of the Faithful: 'I am going to attribute what has never been attributed to Islam by anyone before: Islam is submission and submission is affirmation and affirmation is certainty and certainty is constancy and constancy is performance and performance is righteous action. Thus whoever wishes to model himself on his Prophet as is fitting, then he should take on all these qualities and not reject any of those who themselves have taken on these qualities in their behaviour because... .'[1]

By its nature the essential cannot be separated from the essence. Allah's words 'And they shall continue to differ, except those on whom your Lord has mercy; and for this did He create them' confirm, this insomuch as differences in the outward arise from differences in the inner realm of meaning and differences in the meaning arise from differences in the realm of truth and substance. Truth and substance, however, are not established in time by the Creator; thus what is meant by 'He created them' is not that they are coerced in their distinct creational form, but rather that they are bestowed existence in accordance with their original substance and reality. This bestowal is not an in-time

---

[1] The text of the copy in my possession as well those copies in the Mar'ashi and Consultative Assembly Libraries were all interrupted here; in the book *Jami' al-Asrar*, however, the text reads: (after 'because') 'the source of all, even if there are differences in the code of rules, according to circumstance and condition, is the one reality, namely the Prophetic *Shari'ah* and the Divine Rule imposed on man.' In all three copies there is an empty space of half a line. And Allah knows best.

initiation of something on the part of the Creator, for in reality they are non-existent and in annihilation, and that which is non-existent and in annihilation is not a creation of the Creator, rather it is inherent and inseparable from His knowledge.

A dispute of vast dimensions exists concerning this subject, namely the nature of the beginnings of things and whether or not they are created by the Creator. This question is of utmost importance with regard to the science of *tawhid* (unity); indeed a proper investigation of the truth of divine unity is not feasible without an understanding of these beginnings. Since the scholars involved in this argument continue to infer and deduce other matters related to this question, and they continue to accuse each other of misinterpretation and deception, we decided to set out in this book the basic conclusions arrived at in this matter by the people of Allah and their elite together with the conclusions of the people of the outward and the inward. We desired to undertake this task in order to remain true to the condition imposed upon ourself at the opening of the book, namely that we undertake a comparison between the outer and the inner, for the station of joining between these two is the highest of stations and the ultimate goal. With this in mind we would quote the words of Allah: 'And if Allah had pleased He would have made you (all) a single nation, and they shall continue to differ, except those on whom your Lord has mercy; and for this did He create them.' It should be borne in mind that we are clarifying the meaning of the differences which exist in the realm of realities and substances — the differences existing in the essential realities of people and in their opinions and beliefs. Moreover, it should be noted also that this study has particular recourse to Allah's words, 'And they shall continue to differ.'

At this point a note of introduction is needed: substances and essences are, according to the belief of some, brought into existence by the Creator, while for others this is not so. The first belief belongs to the people of the outward, that is those scholars who demand that the common people imitate their example in the execution of religious duties. The second is that of the people of Allah, that is the men of gnosis, those who affirm the all-encompassing Oneness of God and certain of the philosophers. As for the first group, they quote the fact that Allah is All-Knowing and Wise and that He does not act except on behalf of what is good and beneficial and in accordance with His knowledge and wisdom; they also quote that 'He cannot be questioned concerning what He does and they shall be questioned.' Thus, in the light of this approach, the differences in the substances and the essences exist in relation to His knowledge and wisdom; likewise, the bringing into being of these substances and essences in the outer realm and their creation in the world of vision and witnessing spring from His knowledge of them from before eternity: thus the act whereby He brings into being any creational form corresponds to that which is contained in His knowledge. This is referred to in His words: 'He does what he wishes' and 'Allah orders what he desires.'

At this point, however, we should note that many dispute the validity of this argument; their disagreement lies in the fact that any substance or essence may protest with a voice issuing from a station of spirituality or with the voice of outer learning saying 'Why have You brought me into being in such and such a form?' or 'Why did You not create me in that form?' Thus the unhappy person — with respect to the happy and fortunate person — will say: 'Why did You create me in an unhappy state? Why did You not create me in a happy state?' The same might be said by the ignorant person with respect to the one of knowledge, the poor person with respect to the rich person. They would, in effect, have an argument against Allah — and not Allah against them — although Allah Himself says: 'Then Allah's is the conclusive argument.' Moreover, there is no escape from this accusation and there remains nothing to be done in this state of affairs but to submit and to be content with what has been decreed: one must accept that the matter depends on His knowledge and wisdom and things depend wholly on His will and desire. There is no doubt, however, that this belief is neither reasonable nor acceptable. It is for this reason that He says: 'Do not put questions about things which, if declared to you, may trouble you.' In truth, then, their belief is not consonant with the facts.

As for the people of the second group, they says that the realities, the substances and the essences are not brought into

being by the Creator — rather they are part of His knowledge
from before eternity. It is not permitted that these knowledges
be brought into being because, if these knowledges were 'created',
then either knowledge of what becomes known would be necessary prior to this within a specific time, or lack of knowledge of
these knowledges would be implied — before He brings them
into existence. Both ideas, however, are totally fallacious. The
only possibility left is that His knowledges are not in-time creations on His part. Moreover, it has been established in the principles of logic that knowledge depends upon or 'follows' what is
known: thus, the existence of a dependent thing, namely knowledge, without the existence of the thing upon which it depends,
namely the thing known, is impossible. Knowledge is not affirmed
as a knowledge except if it is corresponds to that which is known.
If this is not the case, then it is called ignorance — may Allah
be exalted above this. Thus, their aim in saying this is to establish
that knowledge must be in accordance with what is known, since
any knowledge which does not correspond to the known in the
realm of the outward is ignorance. Based on this premise, therefore, it is not permitted that His knowledge from before eternity
be part of His creation, or be conceived of as having been brought
into being by Him; if this is not the case, then His knowledge
cannot be affirmed and imperfection of knowledge is imputed
to Him as we have seen above.

The commentator of *Al-Fusus* says: 'Since pre-material forms
and realities are conceived in the realm of imagination, they
cannot be described as creational or brought into being; what
is imagined does not have existence in the phenomenal world
and only something which is created or brought into being can
be existent. Likewise, something pictured in the imagination, or
the mind's eye, through one's knowledge of that thing cannot
be described as having been brought into being as long as it is
not seen to exist in the phenomenal world; otherwise impos-
sibilities would also be capable of being brought into visible
existence.'

The commentator mentions a still more striking example when
he says: 'Know that the names possess rational forms in the
knowledge of Allah — since He is knowledgeable by His very

essence of His own Essence, His Names and Attributes. Thus those rational forms existing in the realm of knowledge are actually the Source and Essence itself, made manifest by their establishment in the realm of specificity; the latter is also called the realm of the pre-existent source-forms, irrespective of whether these forms are of a general or particular nature, according to the terminology of the people of Allah. According to the theorists, however, the general or universal forms are called substances and realities and the particular are called essences. Thus the substances are the universal forms defined through the names residing in the Presence of His knowledge — and as such these forms flow out from the divine source by an outflowing on the level of sanctity and purity; they emanate from the First Manifestation by means of the essential Love and through a seeking of the keys of the unseen whose outward manifestations and perfections are only known to Him.

This divine overflowing may be divided into two types: that is, the overflowing from the greater sanctity and that emanating from the lesser sanctity. From the first arise the pre-material forms and from the second the phenomenal manifestations of the forms with their relative qualities and characteristics. This theory is based on the premise that the doer and the one who receives the actions are one and the same: there is nothing in existence except Him and His perfections; thus, He is the Doer from one aspect and the One who receives from another — just as the philosophers have said that the intellect, the one who uses that intellect and the notion conceived of by that intellect are in reality one thing, although described in different ways. Likewise this could be said of love, the lover and the loved one. The Great Shaykh (Ibn 'Arabi) has also referred to this in *Al-Fusus* when he says: 'It is impossible to admit of another equal to Him in respect to the divine laws: all bodies receive the divine spirit by way of Him and by means of His breath; this is nothing other than their gaining the capacity of receiving the constant, never-ending outpouring of divine manifestations while existing in those forms.' The receiver can only exist by this very outpouring of purity and sanctity. Thus everthing from the beginning to the end is from Him, everything returns to Him just as it began from Him.

With this in mind, it is not permissible to say that the pre-material forms, the substances and the beginnings are created by the Creator — if we suppose that the Creator and the Receiver of the created forms are one and the same and if we suppose that the Doer is His Essence and the Receiver is His Names and Attributes. If we call the first the Absolute Essence and the Reality and the second the dependent existence and creation, if we call the whole a manifestation of His Names, His Attributes and Actions, if we accept that the pre-existent forms, the substances and the realities are images of His pre-eternal primal knowledge, then this Existence would not bring something into being which was dependent and related to His Essence and Perfections — for He has always been the same and how, one may ask, could He becomes otherwise? Change is not possible, in particular with respect to the Necessary of Existence. Indeed, there is nothing whatsoever which brings itself into being — and this applies equally with respect to His essential Perfections and those particularities associated with His Names. Besides, no thing can be devoid of both aspects: either it is necessary by its essence or possible by its essence. If it is necessary by its essence, then His perfections, His particularities and everything based upon these things come about by the essence: thus it cannot be that they are ever brought into being, in time. If it is possible, then its substance in the realm of knowledge and its pre-existent form in the realm of rationality are not brought into being in time by Him or any other, rather, they arise out of the pre-eternal divine knowledge, as has already been established.

As for the possible, it is nothing but the 'request' — in the terminology of the people of spiritual stations — for outward existence in accordance with that thing's capacity, a request which is made to the Real Actor and in accordance with existence in the realm of knowledge. This, then, is the aim of our study. Thus He says: 'And He gives you of all you ask Him' meaning with the tongue of your capacity and receptivity and in accordance with existence in the realm of knowledge, that is uncreated and out of time. If we accept this, then He does not bring anything into being from that Existence, but from the existence in the outward, as we have already made clear; moreover, it is not true to say that anything is 'brought into being' except within the sphere of this outward existence. Understand this point well — it will be of great benefit on many occasions on reading this book.

The subject of our study contains secrets of the greatest order with respect to the question of predestination; it is therefore necessary at this point that we investigate further into this matter and we shall begin with some appropriate examples, which will increase understanding and clarify the matter. Know then that a simile of the possible pre-existent forms and possible substances within the realm of the Real's knowledge is that of the pre-form and source-form of the letters in the mind of the writer: their establishment in the mind is not because the writer brought them into being — the writer has only knowledge of their existence and their essences, that is their existence in the realm of knowledge and their essences and various shapes as mental pictures. It is clear that knowledge itself has no influence over that which is known. Thus, from this aspect, these letters are not brought into being by the writer, although it is true that they are brought into being by the writer when he brings them into outward existence (by the act of writing) in accordance with what is in his mind. This same metaphor may be applied to the Real: if He brings something into outward existence, in accordance with what is in His knowledge from before eternity (and which is obviously prior to the existence of that thing), then it is called 'created' or 'brought into being.' If, however, it was in His 'essential' knowledge from before endless-time and part of His primal knowledge, then it is not called created or brought into existence. Thus we arrive at the desired conclusion, namely His knowledges from before eternity are not brought into being; 'And (as for) these examples, We set them forth for men, and none understand them but the learned.'

There is also another example worthy of mention: it is that the pre-material source forms and substances are related to the never-ending perfections hidden in His Essence, which are also known as Attributes and Names. These expressions are similar in their metaphorical nature to the branches, leaves and fruits which are all 'perfections' of the tree itself, which in its state (while in the realm of knowledge) within the essence of the seed is not called by the name tree and is not called 'an existence' in the outward. Rather this knowledge is called the knowledge of the seed together with its essential perfections and its inherent degree of 'treeness'. Likewise knowledge, with respect to the seed, for example — together with details of its essential perfections in the forms of its leaves, branches, flowers and fruits — is not related to the action of its coming into being. Similarly, knowledge of the Real, together with details of His essential perfections in the form of His names, attributes, actions, manifestations and emanations, does not presuppose its creation in time. Thus He Himself says: 'When He intends anything, He says: "Be, so it is", meaning that if He wishes to bring something into outer existence from those things existent in the realm of knowledge, then He indicates this by making it manifest in existence after its non-existence, thereby making visible that which was hidden. As He Himself says in the Qur'an, 'And His are the most exalted attributes in the heavens and the earth.' His words: 'Shall I guide you to the tree of immortality and a kingdom which decays not?' seem to indicate the Absolute Tree of existence, which is the world with all its ramifications, since its branches, leaves and flowers are the dependent existent beings: anyone who witnesses this tree together with its perfections, names and attributes will be in a 'kingdom which decays not.' This same meaning is also expressed in the language of the scholars of this science inasmuch as they relate existence in the realm of knowledge to the pre-material source forms and existence in the outward realm to the various manifest creations. Moreover, they relate the first to the first emanation of the Essence and the second to the second emanation of the Attributes. They affirm that the first emanation is the essential emanation, that is the emanation of the Essence alone within its own essence — and this is the presence of Oneness — there being no attribute or form within this realm, since the Essence (which is the Absolute Existence of the Real) is pure Oneness. Any existence other than this is nothing but absolute non-existence, namely, pure nothingness. Thus the Essence in its oneness is in no need of singularity or specificity to distinguish it from another essence nor has it any need to distinguish itself from anything else at all. Indeed its unity is its essence and this unity is the source of its singularity and uniqueness. It is essence by itself and of itself and thereby I mean that it is not dependent on anything; the Absolute encompasses its own being, there being no thing co-existent with it: this is in effect complete singularity. The realities in the essence of singularity are as the tree within the seed, hidden within the hidden. The second emanation makes manifest the pre-existent source forms which are the very workings of the Essence; this is His reception of form in the world of creation. The Real descends by means of this emanation from the Presence of Singularity to the Presence of Uniqueness through His relationship to the Names. It should be noted that this notion is in complete accord with the direction of our discourse above.

The aim of using quotations and supporting examples from the works of the distinguished saints of Allah is twofold: the first is to reassure the heart of the reader and to aid him in removing doubt; the second is to repulse the sayings of the ignorant and those who reject the people of Allah, as far as we are able. If this objective is not met, then there are many other studies one may refer to; it is not fitting, however, that we reproduce them here.

The aim of this introduction is to comment upon the meaning of Allah's words: 'And they shall continue to differ.' Given that this is understood and accepted as a principle, then we must also realise that these words are an indication of the essential differences in the realm of inner meaning with respect to the source-forms within the Presence of the Unseen and with respect to those of His knowledge. They are at the same time an indication of the differences in outward form which correspond to those differences in the Presence of the Unseen and the Sphere of Witnessing. Moreover the meaning of these words presupposes that the source-forms and related substances are pre-eternal and not created. As for His words: 'Except those on whom your Lord has mercy,' they refer to those known by your Lord to be people of guidance and kindness who have remained faithful to their own harmonious being and to their finer, subtler creational form. It refers then to the people who keep away from the people of argument, misguidance and perversion and take no part in their disputes. In truth the whole of the matter rests on the exigencies of the essence of the being in question. Allah has, in His own way, knowledge of what is to be in the future. But as we have seen knowledge itself has no influence in the matter. His words, 'And for this did He create them' means in fact 'for by reason of these differences did He create them'— they are as diverse in image, shape, opinion and belief as they were in their essence, substance and primal reality. He gives them outer existence in accordance with their existence in the realm of knowledge such that His knowledge does not contradict His action and His hidden unseen aspect does not contradict His witnessing. Moreover, there is no one who objects saying 'Why did you create me in such and such a manner?' This state of affairs is as it is because the Actor does not give existence to the receiving creational forms except in accordance with their true natures. This existence is 'sought' by means of the speech of spirituality from the Actor. This same meaning has already been referred to with the metaphor of the writer, the writing and the letters (and their existence both in the mind and the concrete world).

These source-forms and substances are non-existent in the phenomenal world but they exist in the realm of knowledge and are constantly seeking outer existence by the tongue of spirituality and their own capacity. The Actor, for His part, requires from His Essence a constant outpouring of existence, by means of the substances and source-forms. He is the One of Absolute Generosity and so the constant Outpourer of Good, be it in the realm of existence, of attribute, of knowledge, of speech or action. Thus, if one of the source forms demands of Allah, the true Actor, by the language of spirituality that it be given outward existence, then the Real has no option but to bestow on it that required existence in accordance with the capacity and receptivity of that particular source form. The Absolute Actor does not, therefore, govern the receiving form in an absolute manner but rather in accordance with the aspect of that receiving form. There is a similar relationship between the One of absolute Generosity and the creational form which requests existence from Him in that He can only bestow the most complete and perfect form on the created being; I mean by this that He bestows existence on it to the full extent of its capacity without any withholding on His part — for withholding would imply meanness, which is an impossibility with regard to His Presence, may He be exalted above such a notion. He bestows on them outward existence exactly in accordance with their capacity — no more and no less. If He were to bestow something which was above their capacity, they would not be able to accept it and so this bestowal would be futile — and such futility is impossible with respect to Allah. Likewise, if He were to bestow less than their capacity, then they would also not be able to accept it and the bestowal would again be in vain. Thus there can never be any objection on the part of any of the existent beings — no matter what the circumstances. No being could say: 'Why did You create me in such and such a manner,' because it knows in truth that such an objection would be unjustified; it knows that its existence is in accord with the source-form and the reality and that Allah has decided by its very nature that it be created in such and such a way. Likewise, as we have seen in the example of the letters, neither the 'a' or the 'b' or any other letter would demand of the writer that they be set down otherwise.

This notion is supported by Ibn al-'Arabi when he says: 'He does not rule over us except by us, nay, rather we rule over ourselves, albeit in Him.' It is for this reason that He has said: 'Then Allah's is the conclusive argument', that is, against those who are veiled when they say to the Real: 'Why did You do such and such a thing to us?' When something does not accord with their aims and the matter becomes difficult for them. As for the gnostics, the matter is clear for them. Moreover, the veiled think that the Real has not acted in the way they asked Him to act; this notion is of their making, however, and they only know as much as their particular creational form permits them to know, thus their argument is untenable and the conclusive argument which is Allah's remains. The famous saying of the Arabs is particularly relevant here: 'Your arms are for leaning on and your mouth is for speech.'

Thus any existence which manifests, be it in the realm of action, speech perfection or imperfection, be it beautiful or ugly, is dependent upon the source-form in accordance with the essence. Thus it is not directly dependent on Allah nor on other than Allah — although it does depend on Allah with respect to His bestowal of what was asked of Him; by this I mean that the existence of that thing is from Allah and by virtue of that 'request' made to Him. This is referred to when He says; 'Every one acts according to his manner' and also in the words of the Prophet, 'Everything lives and develops in accordance with what it has been created for.' These two statements are supported by the words of David: 'I said to my Lord: "O Lord, for what have You created the creation?" He replied, "For that which they have been created," ' meaning, for that particular capacity or receptivity, that perfection or imperfection inherent in their creation. Again Allah's words are sufficient in this matter, 'And for this did He create them', since this statement is the complete answer for the gnostic.

We have seen that the term 'creation' means the bringing into being of something: What is indicated, as we have seen on many previous occasions, is that Allah brings them into being in accordance with their source-form in the world of essences and substances; if there are any differences in the essences, then there are also differences in the attributes; if there are differences in the essences and attributes, then there are no likenesses or similarities between them in the totality of the states. Thus he who has said that 'There does not exist any resemblance between things at all except by the Necessary of Existence' has spoken the truth and in accordance with what he has actually witnessed.

It has been established as a principle by the scholars of the science of unity that the divine manifestations are not repeated and that the Real never manifests twice in the same way, neither in the realm of form or meaning — so it has been from before eternity and so it will be to eternity. He is the One who continues from pre-endless-time and He is the One who is in constant annihilation. If we now consider the basic premise that there is none but Him in existence, and nothing but His Names and Attributes, and that All is Him, by Him, from Him and to Him, then we realise that His perfections are never-ending and yet without repetition. Indeed all existence is a never-ending manifestation of His perfections. We realise that resemblance and equality with regard to all aspects of a thing are not possible under any cicrcumstances; we realise, too, the meaning of His words, 'And they continue to differ' and the hidden meaning indicated in 'and for this did he create them.' And Allah is more knowing and of acuter judgement in all matters.

The following saying of the Prophet is also relevant: 'Whoever finds good, then let him praise Allah, and whoever finds other than this, then let him blame no one but himself;' so also are the words of Imam 'Ali ibn Musa al-Rida: 'Generosity on the part of the creature is to carry out what is incumbent; generosity on the part the Creator is in both His giving and His withholding;' this is a subtle statement containing secrets of great value, secrets which may only be understood by the elite, for these secrets issue from the secrets of destiny, the divulgence of which is forbidden to other than those who are worthy of them. This idea is contained in the words of Allah when He says: 'Surely Allah commands you to make over trusts to their owners.' It is as if Allah is referring to this when He says: 'I have prepared for the righteous of my slaves something that the eye has never beheld, what the ear has never heard and what the heart of man has never perceived.' This 'something' is a special secret of the elite of the friends of Allah and the great prophets. We have dwelt long on this question because it is one of the most important in the science of divine unity; it is a principle containing precious jewels and costly pearls of wisdom which may only be gained by those who are purified from the pollution of greed and craving and from anything which prevents them from attaining the stations of divine unity. May Allah sanctify their purified souls and bestow on them the divine illumination; may Allah grant us the light which is reflected from their perfections and emanations, after seeking help from Him for He is the Generous, the Noble.

If the reader has understood the ideas we have expounded to him — ideas which merit being written with a pen of light on the cheeks of the maidens of Paradise, or being placed as amulets around the neck so that they may live through the ages — if he has imprinted them on his mind with the inward eye, if he has placed them in the store chests of his memory and perceiving intellect, then we shall now return to our original topic. Know then that all the different levels of mankind, both the common and the elite and the elite of the elite are three in number; by these I mean the beginning, the intermediate and the end. Even if these levels do not contain individual characteristics and details, they encompass with respect to type and universal groups. Thus the *shari'ah* is the name of the Divine Code and the prophetic pattern of behaviour, and is also the beginning; the *tariqah* by its name and meaning indicates the intermediate stage; and the *haqiqah* by its name and meaning indicates the final stage. No level falls outside these three. Moreover the first, the *shari'ah*, encompasses them all (as we have already discussed above); this is because it encompasses the first level, namely that of the common people, the second, that is that of the elite, and the third, the elite of the elite. The Muslims as a body — who by their acceptance of Islam take upon themselves the duties of the religion — together with the men of intellect are not outside these three levels; the levels embrace the whole and are subject to the demands of the whole — in that each level possesses laws distinct unto itself. Thus, it is not permitted to deny the validity of any of these levels, nor to reproach any of the people (who follow them). The model of prophetic behaviour, Muhammad, can only be followed to perfection when these three levels are respected.

Allah speaks about the differences of capacity and receptivity within creation when He says: 'For every one of you did We appoint a law and a way and if Allah had pleased He would have made you (all) a single people, but that He might try you in what He gave you, therefore strive with one another to hasten to virtuous deeds; to Allah is your return, of all (of you), so He will let you know that in which you differed.' By Allah, by Allah, if this were the only *ayah* in the Qur'an, it would be sufficient proof of what we are saying, without even considering the fact that a third of the Qur'an is laden with such examples and without having recourse to the body of authentic traditions related from the Prophet. If we investigate further, we realise that submission, faith and certainty are the prerequisites of these three levels — and also an inherent part of these three levels. The same could be said for the three states of revelation, inspiration and unveiling, for prophethood, message and *wilayah* (spiritual guardianship), for knowledge of certainty, experience of certainty and reality of certainty, and finally for the triad of words, actions and states — all of which exist according to the three states of *shari'ah, tariqah* and *haqiqah*. All existence is contained in these levels, the three-tiered division being necessary, given the multiplicity of creational and metaphysical realities. We see this in the three levels of knowledge, the knower and the known — that is the three-tiered division of manifest individuality, the Presence of Singularity and the Divine Uniqueness with respect to the worlds of the unseen. We see also the three divisions of knowledge, command and will with respect to the created worlds and their corresponding forms of receptivity, namely the known, the commanded and the object of one's will. Further, we witness the existence of the *mulk* (the kingdom), the *malakut* (the realm of angelic forms) and the *jabarut* (the realm of His Absolute Dominion), and then the world of the intelligences, the souls and the senses. There exists too the three-tiered level of the Muhammadi aspect — referred to when he says: 'There are three things which are dear to me in this world of yours, perfume, women and the coolness of the eye which comes from prayer' and everything else in creation accords with these classifications.

Thus it is not permitted to deny the sayings of the prophets, nor those who speak or deliver the prophetic message, particularly with respect to the people of *shari'ah* and the people of beginnings. Moreover, it is not permitted to deny the actions of the prophets, nor those who take upon themselves the prophetic attributes and act accordingly, particularly with respect to the people of *tariqah* and the people of the middle or intermediate path. Finally it is not permitted to deny the states of *haqiqah*, nor to reject those who have taken on the corresponding qualities of this level together with those of the ending or final level.

In short, it is not permitted to reject any of the people of the *shar'iah, tariqah* or *haqiqah*. The Prophet's words 'I have been given all the names and have been sent to perfect good behaviour' is an indication of just what we have been indicating: creational realities are not such that they may be completely contained in any one level or station; rather they are as diverse as their capacities and receptivities and each must be given its rightful place in accordance with this capacity and receptivity. Thus it is that we are commanded to talk to the people in accordance with the capacity of their intellects.

You may say that according to the above argument it is claimed that each group, with its own particular way of worship, its opinions and beliefs, is correct, but by the nature of things, each and every one cannot be right. I would say, in reply, that whoever is living according to the *shari'ah*, the *tariqah* and *haqiqah* (as defined above) and who carries out what is demanded of him in accordance with the respective levels of each, then he has the truth, is on the straight path and his religion is correct. Allah's words 'That is the right religion, but most people do not know' are another indication of this same meaning. Anyone who is not as we have described is astray, in error and a rejector of the truth. It is obligatory to avoid such people and this is a rule of behaviour which is always observed amongst the people of spiritual realisation; indeed all the principles and branches of the religion are founded on this rule Allah indicates this when he addresses the Prophet saying: 'This is my way: I call to Allah, I and those who follow me in certainty.' The words of those who have described the shaykhs of instruction also testify to this fact: 'The shaykh is the man of perfection with regard to the sciences of *shari'ah, tariqah* and *haqiqah;* they have reached the limits of perfection in each by their knowledge of the diseases of the self and the corresponding cures — provided of course the self is willing to accept this cure in the form of spiritual guidance.'

A similar division may be seen in the description of the levels of knowledge of the knower, namely in terms of the husk, the shell and the kernel. Each indicates a level of knowledge together with a corresponding awareness of the demands and claims of each level. Thus it has been said that the husk refers to any outward knowledge which protects the inner knowledge, namely the kernel, from harm: the *shari'ah*, therefore, stands in a similar relation to the *tariqah* as the *tariqah* to the *haqiqah*. Whoever does not protect his spiritual state and path by the *shari'ah* will destroy that state and cause harm to his path, whether by desire, folly or Satanic whisperings. Whoever does not attain the *haqiqah* by means of the *tariqah* and does not protect the former by the latter will cause harm to his *haqiqah* and resort to heresy and disbelief. The shell is the intellect which is illuminated by the light of sanctity and purified of the obscurities caused by fantasy and imagination. The kernel is the very stuff of divine and sacred light from which the intellect seeks help in order to rid itself of the above-mentioned obscurities; thus the heart which is attached to this world, shut off from understanding and veiled by official learning, is not able to comprehend the higher sciences by virtue of the good which has been pre-determined for him by Allah: 'Surely (as for) those for whom the good has already gone forth from Us, they shall be kept far off from it.'

Know too that the laws of the *shari'ah constitute the divine code and social order: it is incumbent on the prophets and the friends of Allah to establish this order together with its 'pillars' and to command the Muslim nation to respect and fulfil its demands. By this I mean that they are not permitted to omit any of the three levels, for this would imply an omission or deficiency with respect to their obligations, and this is impossible given that they are prophets and as such are protected from any wrong or hateful action; indeed nothing of this nature may happen at their hands. That they have always respected these three levels is clear from their various shara'i'* (divinely-inspired codes of behaviour) and ways of worship which have been given to all the prophets from Adam to Muhammad. Again we refer here to the (above-mentioned) words of our Prophet: '*Shari'ah* is my words, *tariqah* my actions and *haqiqah* my states.' The meaning of these words is also reinforced by the instructions given by Abraham to his people in the *surah*, 'The Cattle', which features the story of the star, the moon and the sun. The first instruction is for the guidance of the common people, the second for the elite and the third of the elite of the elite — in line with the three distinctions of *shari'ah, tariqah* and *haqiqah.*

The first symbolises the light of goodness which belongs to the people of *shari'ah*, the people of the outward and the common people in their search for the truth and in their going beyond. This is so because the star of this world is like the light of goodness in man. The second symbolises the light of the intellect and those of this station who are searching for the truth and the journeying beyond are the people of *tariqah*, the people of the inward and the elite. This is because the moon in this world is like the light of the intellect in man. The third symbolises the light of sanctity, known as the light of Reality, and those who are seeking the Real and the journey beyond are the people of *haqiqah*, the people of the inward of the inward and the elite of the elite. This is because the light of the sun in this world is like the light of sanctity in man — in accordance with the words of Allah: 'What! Is he whose heart Allah has opened for Islam so that he is in a light from his Lord (like the hard-hearted)?' Thereafter, there must follow a going beyond: by this I mean a going beyond the light of the Real. This is because the one who sees, the seen and the connecting light between them are three distinct things which would mean multiplicity. Vision and witnessing in the realm of divine unity does not admit of this; rather there must be a crossing beyond to a point where unity is attained. This point is reached by the annihilation of the knower in the known and the witnesser in the witnessed.

As for the opinion of some commentators, namely that Abraham was at the time a small child and was not able to distinguish between the star, the moon, the sun and his Lord, then it is a total falsehood, indeed a complete heresy — may the stations of the prophets and Friends of Allah be exalted above such words. This is so because the prophets and Friends of Allah are infallible and their infallibility necessarily extends throughout their whole life, from childhood to old age — with regard to their words, actions, states, religion, beliefs and all other aspects of their character whether visible or hidden. No heinous act whatsoever could possibly issue from their hand, neither from an unintentional mistake, human error or conscious oversight. Moreover, the opinion of others — chiefly the rationalist scholars — that Abraham was then at the beginning of his path and at the outset of his intellectual and gnostic awareness is also incorrect. This we know because this incident happened during the period of his prophecy when he was calling his people to Islam; it was thus during the period of his perfection, with respect to his intellect, his gnosis and his perspicacity. How, may one

ask, can such opinions be expressed when prophecy, messengership and the associated knowledges are not things which are
acquired and are not theoretical in nature; rather they are out-
right gifts from God, pure acts of giving without cause or reason,
on the part of the Lord, and not acquired through any action
on their part. This is indicated when Allah talks about our
Prophet saying, 'He has taught you what you did not know, and
Allah's grace on you is very great,' or when He says to Solomon,
'This is Our free gift, therefore give freely or withhold, without
reckoning,' or when Jesus says, 'Surely I am a servant of Allah;
He has given me the Book and made me a prophet; and He has
made me blessed wherever I may be, and He has enjoined on
me prayer and the poor-rate so long as I live,' or when He
addresses John the Baptist, 'O Yahya! Take hold of the Book
with strength, and We granted him wisdom while yet a child.'
Let these examples suffice as an indication of our meaning, although there are numerous other examples in the Qur'an.

Know too that the laws of the *shari'ah* constitute the divine
code and social order: it is incumbent on the prophets and the
friends of Allah to establish this order together with its 'pillars'
and to command the Muslim nation to respect and fulfil its
demands. By this I mean that they are not permitted to omit
any of the three levels, for this would imply an omission or
deficiency with respect to their obligations, and this is impossible
given that they are prophets and as such are protected from any
wrong or hateful action; indeed nothing of this nature may happen at their hands. That they have always respected these three
levels is clear from their various *shara'i'* (divinely-inspired codes
of behaviour) and ways of worship which have been given to all
the prophets from Adam to Muhammad. Again we refer here to
the (above-mentioned) words of our Prophet: '*Shari'ah* is my
words, *tariqah* my actions and *haqiqah* my states.' The meaning
of these words is also reinforced by the instructions given by
Abraham to his people in the *surah*, 'The Cattle', which features
the story of the star, the moon and the sun. The first instruction
is for the guidance of the common people, the second for the
elite and the third of the elite of the elite — in line with the
three distinctions of *shari'ah*, *tariqah* and *haqiqah*.

As for the words which testify that the incident involving
Abraham took place during the period of his prophethood and

his calling of the people to Islam, then the following *ayah* is one
of several where this is mentioned in the Qur'an: 'And the people
disputed with him. He said: "Do you dispute with me respecting
Allah? And He has guided me indeed; and I do not fear in any
way those that you set up with Him, unless my Lord pleases;
my Lord comprehends all things in His knowledge; will you not
then take heed?" And this was Our argument which we gave to
Abraham against his people; We exalt in dignity whom We
please; surely your Lord is Wise Knowing.' May Allah's witnessing be enough for us. If this had not been during the time of
his prophecy and calling, Allah would not have said: 'And the
people disputed with him.' It should be remembered that some
of his people were worshipping and prostrating to the stars, while
others worshipped and prostrated to the moon, and yet a third
group worshipped and prostrated to the sun and other idols.
Abraham would guide them according to the laws of the *shari'ah*
together with teachings about the Oneness of Allah, the Creator
and Originator of all existence; he would also instruct them in
the science of the inward and in the witnessing of the Oneness
in all existence, in witnessing the One who brings all into existence and the manifestation of Him as the Unique God. This
we may see from his words: 'Surely I have turned myself, being
upright, wholly to Him, Who originated the heavens and the
earth and I am not one of the polytheists.' He also asks, 'Is this
my Lord?' on three different occasions — not as a genuine in-
quiry but rather as a question whose reply is implied to be
negative. Thus the complete utterance might be: 'Is it possible
that this created and phenomenal event, namely the manifestation of the setting of the star, the moon and the sun be my Lord
and the Lord of all things? No, by Allah, it is not possible: it is
neither my Lord nor the Lord of all things, rather it is a created
thing fashioned by Allah'; or he might say: 'Is it by the light of
this created and phenomenal thing, by this light which is the
light of goodness, the light of the intellect or the light of sanctity
or the combination of these that I know my Lord? Is it possible
to gain knowledge of Him by means of these three lights? No,
by Allah, it is not possible: rather it is only possible by crossing
beyond them and ascending above their levels.' Arrival at true

knowledge of Him and direct witnessing of His essence is only possible by Him and by His light of Reality. This is referred to in the words of the Prophet when he says: 'I have known my Lord by my Lord.' One of the gnostics of his people has also said, 'By God one cannot arrive at Him except by Him.' Every gnostic knows that it is only possible to see the orb of the sun and its rays by the very light of the sun.

The people of *shari'ah* who seek gnosis of the Real by way of the light of goodness are like the person who seeks to see the orb of the sun in the darkness of the night by the light of the stars; as is obvious, he will never be able to catch sight of it. The · people of *tariqah* who seek gnosis of the Real by way of the light of the intellect are like the person who seeks the orb of the sun in the darkness of the night by the light of the moon; as is clear, he will never catch sight of it. The people of *haqiqah* who seek gnosis of the Real by means of the light of sanctity are like the person who actually sees the sun: it is clear that he can see it, although his seeing is that of the witnesser and the witnessed, not the seeing of pure divine unity. The subtlety of meaning expressed here is that just as anyone who sees the light of the sun by means of the light of the sun is only able to arrive at a witnessing of the sun after establishing a connection based on purity, light and perfect nobility between himself and it, so too the person who sees the Real is only able to arrive at this witnessing after establishing a connection based on the liberation of the self from other than Him, by means of contentment and affirmation of His absolute sanctity and exaltedness above creation. Such a connection means the taking on of His characteristics, as is demonstrated by the words of the Prophet when he said, 'Make your character the character of Allah,' and by Allah's words in a sacred *hadith* (spoken directly by Allah, albeit on the tongue of the Prophet and in the latter's words): 'I was his hearing, his sight, his tongue, his hand and his foot.' It is for this reason that the gnostic has said: 'It is not everyone who sets out who arrives, and not everyone who arrives attains, and not everyone who attains attains, and not everyone who attains separates, and not everyone who separates arrives, and not everyone who arrives arrives.'

The Commander of the Faithful ('Ali) explains the relationship (between Allah and His slave) in the following way: 'Allah possesses a drink which is reserved for His intimate friends *(awliya')*: when they drink they become intoxicated, when they become intoxicated they become joyful, when they become joyful they become sweet, when they become sweet they begin to melt, when they begin to melt they become free, when they become free they seek, when they seek they find, when they find they arrive, when they arrive they join, and when they join, there is no difference between them and their Beloved.'

Allah describes the lack of any distance or separation in His relationship with the Prophet when He says, 'And you did not smite when you smote (the enemy), but it was Allah Who smote.' The Prophet has also said, 'Whoever sees me has seen the Truth.' Others have said, 'Praise be to me, how great is my affair!' and 'I am the Truth' and other similar expressions. This station is called the station of annihilation in unity, by this I mean the station of annihilation of the knower in the known, the lover in the beloved and the witnesser in the witnessed — by way of the disappearance of phenomenal duality and the removal of egotism which is the obstacle to arrival at Him. The following verse also refers to this:

> Between myself and You is individual existence following from me.
> So, by Your grace, remove this individuality from between us.

The prophets, messengers, intimate friends and gnostics have all reached a point of annihilation in Him and then a continuing in Him; thus their contact with the ordinary world still exists despite the fact that they were spiritually annihilated in Him. It is necessary to understand this point well, for the annihilation of the Prophet in Allah did not prevent him from eating, drinking or getting married. His words 'I have moments with Allah which include no one, not even His most intimate of angels, nor messengers but myself' are an indication of this state of annihilation. Moreover his words 'I am a man like the rest of you' is an indication of the station of continuing in the world. Allah's words, 'And as for these examples, We set them forth for men, and none understands them but the learned' and 'Everything is perishable but He; His is the judgement, and to Him you shall be brought back' and 'Everyone on it must pass away. And there will endure for ever the person of your Lord, the Lord of Glory and honour' are all further indications of the same meaning.

If the meaning of the annihilation of the slave in his Lord is still unclear, then we would describe it metaphorically as the disappearance of the light of the stars in the light of the sun when the latter rises on the horizon, or as the constant breaking and disappearance of the waves in the sea. This idea has also been expressed in the following verse:

> The sea is the same sea as it has been of old;
> The events of today are its waves and its rivers.

Thus it has been said that the one who continues (after annihilation) into eternity and the one who is annihilated is in a state of annihilation which has not yet finished. Knowledge of certainty, experience of certainty, and truth of certainty are terms which describe the three gnoses. The truth of certainty is particular to the station of annihilation and the disappearance of the slave's features in his Lord (as the quotation above indicates). Indeed the establishing of the station of truth is in the disappearance of these individual features; if a person does attain to this kind of annihilation, then he annihilates his existence in the existence of the Truth, his essence in His Essence and his attributes in His Attributes; if he obliterates his form, then his name falls away from him like the disappearance of the light of the stars in the light of the sun. If he witnesses the truth, by the very Truth itself, in the manifestations of its perfections and attributes, he realises the meaning of 'Everything is perishing but Him.' If he understands the secret of His words, 'Therefore whither you turn, thither is Allah's purpose,' if he understands why the gnostic said, 'When poverty is perfected, then that is Allah' and why he said, 'Glory to myself, how great is my affair!' and why he said, 'Who is there like myself and is there anyone but I in the two worlds?' and Allah's words, 'Our Lord! Make perfect for us our light, and grant us protection, surely Thou hast power over all things' — if he comprehends all this, then it is as a guidance which will enable him to see this light that annihilates the darkness of his own existence and brings him to his Lord by a link of spirituality, illumination and purity, by stripping away other-than-Him and liberating him from dependency on the world of form. It is for this reason that Allah says in reply to them, 'It shall be said: Turn back and seek a light.' This means: 'Return back to the original state of non-existence and to the necessary annihilation of the essences of possibility and contingent existences, leave behind the seeing of the physical eye, and extricate yourselves from the darkness of egotism and otherness, and then take hold of the light of truth — it will allow you to go on for ever and ever and will cause you to enter into the Garden of the Essence, the Arena of the Attributes and the worlds of never-ending divine emanations.'

If we examine the Qur'anic *ayah:* 'Allah is the light of the heavens and the earth; a likeness of His light is as a niche... ,' we realise that it is alludes to the witnessing of this light according to the three levels of consciousness. The niche refers to the world of the *mulk* (the phenomenal world) and it corresponds to the *shari'ah.* The glass refers to the world of the *malakut* (the world of angelic and spiritual form) and corresponds to the *tariqah.* The lamp refers to the world of *jabarut* (His dominion) and corresponds to the *haqiqah.* The tree refers to His Presence of Power and corresponds to Absolute Existence from which all dependent form issues. This interpretation is correct because by common agreement, light is existence and darkness is non-existence. Allah's words, 'Light upon light. Allah guides to His light Whom He wills' is an indication of the light of the hereafter — and the cause of witnessing and arrival and is also the means to the connecting relationship between Him and His slaves. Thus Allah says immediately afterwards, 'Allah sets forth parables for men' as an exhortation to His slaves to realise that attainment of the light of witnessing is dependent upon removal of the darkness of their existence (existence which is contingent and a mere reflection of the true existence).

In this *ayah* and others before it are secrets beyond the compass of the heavens and the earth. Thus, for example, He says: 'If the sea were ink for the words of my Lord, the sea would surely be consumed before the words of my Lord are exhausted, though We were to bring the like of that (sea) to add thereto.' This *ayah* and the other examples above demonstrate the validity of what we are describing concerning the attainment of this light and the witnessing; they demonstrate too the importance of the removal of the duality of the phenomenal world and the way in which the Prophet guided his people to this very light. Thus he says in one of his supplications: 'O Allah, place light in my heart, light in my hearing, light in my sight, light in my flesh, light in my blood and light in my bones, light in front of me, light behind me, light beneath me, light above me, light to the right of me, light to the left of me and light in my grave. O Allah, increase me in light and bestow on me light and give me light, by the truth of Your Reality, O most Merciful of the Merciful.'

It is by these examples that we recognize the prophets' and messengers' respect for these three levels of consciousness, and we see how they commanded their respective peoples to also respect them and to carry on the duties incumbent on them — whether it be by the *shari'ah*, the *tariqah* or *haqiqah*. Therefore it is obligatory for every person of sane mind to carry out these duties as far as he is able. Moreover, it is obligatory to strive to attain perfection and bliss in each of these three levels after complete submission to the Lord: this is the belief of the people of Allah, their elite, the masters of divine unity and the chosen amongst them. Happy indeed is the slave who follows in their footsteps. 'All praise is due to Allah Who guided us to this, and we would not have found the way had it not been that Allah had guided us.'

Having established that the *shari'ah, tariqah* and *haqiqah* are all terms which describe the One Truth, the Divine Code, and that there exists no contradiction between the different levels, we shall begin the second aspect of our study, namely the superiority of one level over the next.

2

The Second Aspect:

Description of the people of *haqiqah* (the inner truth) and how their station is higher than that of the people of *tariqah* (the way); and how the people of *tariqah* are higher than the people of *shari'ah* (the law)

Know that although *shari'ah*, *tariqah* and *haqiqah* all describe one truth, *haqiqah* and its people are higher than *tariqah* and *tariqah* and its people are higher than *shari'ah*. *Shari'ah* is the level of beginnings, *tariqah* the intermediate stage and *haqiqah* the final level. Thus, just as perfection of the beginnings lies in the mean and the intermediate, so the perfection of the intermediate lies in the end; and just as the intermediate is not attained without the beginning, so the end is not attained without the intermediate. By this I mean that just as existence of that which is above is not possible without that which is below it — while the reverse is possible — so too existence at the intermediate level is not possible without the beginning, nor existence at the final stage without the intermediate — although the reverse is possible. Thus *shari'ah* is possible without *tariqah* although *tariqah* is not possible without *shari'ah*; likewise, *tariqah* is possible without *haqiqah*, but *haqiqah* without *tariqah* is not. This is because each is the perfection of the other. Therefore, although there is no contradiction between the three levels, the perfection of *shari'ah* is only possible through *tariqah* and that of *tariqah* only possible through *haqiqah*. Accordingly, the perfection of perfection is the joining together of all three levels, for the sum of two things, or two states when joined together, must be better and more perfect than the two when separate: the people of *haqiqah* are therefore superior in relation to the people of *shari'ah* and *tariqah*.

Our Prophet was the greatest and noblest of the prophets since he brought all three levels together, as his words attest, 'I have been given all the names.' We are familiar with the hidden meanings of these words, but there remains one aspect we have not considered, namely that the station of joining — which is particular to the Prophet and those of his people who are seekers of *haqiqah* — is the most sublime and most noble of stations. The words of the Prophet: 'My *qiblah* (the direction of prayer,

namely Makkah) is between the East and the West' also indicate
the station of joining — for the East was the *qiblah* of Jesus and
the West that of Moses and between the two was the *qiblah* of
the Prophet. The Prophet joins the two, that is to say, the stations
of the two. At the esoteric level the East is the world of souls
and spirits and the West is the world of material bodies and
corporeality: between these two states is the joining isthmus, the
stations of the Prophet with regard to both the form and the
inner meaning. Thus the station of the Presence of Singularity
is the station of both Reality and Form; this is like the state of
man who joins the two worlds which are inherently manifest in
him. There is likewise the state which encompasses the joining
of all the meanings of the prophets and messengers, or the state
which joins all the forms of the various external codes and
methods of worship. Thus the perfection of Moses and his people
was in their perception of the realities of the world of materiality
and corporeality together with their different degrees and levels;
the perfection of Jesus and his people was in their perception of
the realities of the world of the souls and spirits together with
their different degrees and levels; the perfection of Muhammad
and his people was in their perception of both the realities of
the world of spirit and those of the world of materiality. It is for
this reason that Allah refers to His Truth and Light (or Reality)
as being 'neither of the east nor the west.' Allah has also said
of His people: 'And thus We have made you a middle nation
that you may be the bearers of witness to the people... .'

Moreover, there exists similarity between the two worlds and
between the west and the east at the levels of form and meaning.
The east with regard to the realm of form refers to the place of
rising of the sun, the diffusion of its light and the illumination
of the sensory world; with respect to the realm of inner meaning,
it refers to the rising of the sun of reality and the diffusion of its
light (meaning here the spirits and the souls) in the darkness of
the world of corporeality so that the bodies and forms come to
life and continue in this light of reality. This state is referred to
by Allah when He says, 'And the earth shall beam with the light
of its Lord.' The Imam has also said: 'It is a light which shines
of a morning from before eternity, its effects appearing in the

realm of divine unity.' The two states referred to in the *ayah* and the saying of the Imam are thus connected in meaning. The same is true of the west: at the formal level it refers to the place of setting and eventual disappearence of the light and orb of the sun; at the level of meaning, it refers to the setting of the light of the sun of reality and disappearence of its rays (meaning here its spirtis and souls). Allah thus says, '(the sun) going down into a black sea' and 'Most surely in the creation of the heavens and the earth and the alternation of the night and the day there are signs for the men who understand.' There is also a relationship between them in the sense that the light of our Prophet is not solely from the world of the souls and not solely from the world of forms. As Allah has said: 'Neither of the east nor the west;' thus he is neither of the people of the senses nor of the people of the intellect, rather he is other than these two and above them, by countless degrees. He is not absolutely of the station of prophets, which is concerned with external authority, and not absolutely of the station of the intimate friends, which is concerned with internal authority: rather he is other than these two with respect to their spiritual stations and above them with respect to his gathering and encompassing these differences. The truth of this statement is manifest in the existence of the various legal systems and methods of worship which have been brought by the different prophets: thus Moses came to perfect the different aspects of the law, adding to this the perfection of some inward elements — this is established in the Torah which sets out the code of laws. Jesus came to perfect the inward, adding to this the perfection of some aspects of the outward — this is established in the Gospel with the exposition of the divine secrets and mysteries. Our Prophet Muhammad came to perfect both aspects and to join the two levels; hence his words, 'I have been given all the names' and 'My *qiblah* is between the East and the West.' This truth is also established in the Qur'an, by the latter's inclusion of both the laws and the secrets. In truth the very name of the book — al-Qur'an — is significant: linguistically *qara'a* can mean a picking up or gathering together. The Commander of the Faithful ('Ali) has said: 'I am the Qur'an speaking and I am the Book of Allah which unites.' He is the one who unites the two levels and the two states of the outward and the inward.

One of the gnostics has composed the following lines:

> I am the Qur'an and the seven oft-repeated verses,
> and the spirit of the spirit and not the spirit of empty
> vessels.

He is referring here to this all-encompassing station of joining which is the Muhammadi state. Another gnostic of excellence has expressed this same meaning in his writings: 'Just as the perfection of Moses was an absolute perfection of a specific kind, so he inclined to the perfection of the most inferior part of man, namely the body; it is for this reason that the Torah is full of references of use to man in his daily life and his means of subsistence. Since Jesus was of a greater perfection than him, his perfection lay in a part of man more noble than the body, namely the soul: thus it is that the Gospel is full of references to the Day of Resurrection and the Day of Judgement. Since Muhammad attained absolute perfection of a specific kind, his absolute perfection was in the human side of his character. As for his composite perfection, it is the perfection of all matter and form, and this is the path of excellence — this is precisely the hidden meaning contained in the abolition of monasticism in his religion. Thus the *fuqaha'* (those trained in jurisprudence) and the Muslim scholars are similar to Moses in their perfection of the outward dimensions whereas the Muslim philosophers and their like amongst the intellectuals are similar to Jesus in their perfection of the inward dimensions; the gnostics and men of realisation are similar to Muhammad in their perfection of both the inward and the outward dimensions and by their acting according to the three levels mentioned above *(shari'ah, tariqah* and *haqiqah)*. This idea is reinforced by the words of the sultan of the gnostics, the Commander of the Faithful: '*Shari'ah* is a river and *haqiqah* a sea: as for the *fuqaha'*, they keep to the banks of the river; as for the philosophers, they dive for pearls in the sea; as for the gnostics, they ride in boats to safety.' If this is understood, then the reader will realise that the peoples of the *shari'ah, tariqah* and *haqiqah* correspond to each of these three levels: the people of *shari'ah* are like the *fuqaha'* and those of their states; the people of *tariqah*

are like the scholors and philosophers and those of their stations;
the people of *haqiqah* are like the gnostics and those of their
station. Similarly Moses and his people, Jesus and his people,
and Muhammad and his people each correspond to one of these
stations. Thus the station of joining is particular to the gnostics
and men of realisation from amongst the people of Muhammad
— namely the people of reality. These people are higher, greater,
nobler and more excellent than the other two levels. Moreover,
here lies the core of our investigation. The gnostics are at times
in the arena of Allah and His angels — in accordance with His
words, 'Allah bears witness that there is no god but He, and (so
do) the angels and those possessed of knowledge, maintaining
His creation with justice' — and sometimes in the arena of
Allah alone — in accordance with His words, 'and none knows
its interpretation except Allah, and those who are firmly rooted
in knowledge.' It is for this reason that they are classed as the
elite of the elite, the intimate ones and those who go before. It
is they who are referred to in the last of each of the following
(three-tiered classifications), namely, 'the common people, the
elite and the elite of the elite,' 'the people of the right, the people
of the left and the intimate' and 'the oppressor of his self, the
one of moderate temperament and the one who goes ahead doing
good works.' Further proof of their elite position is to be found
in Allah's words, 'We believe in it, it is all from our Lord; and
none of them is mindful except those with understanding.' Those
who thus say 'everything is from our Lord' are the ones of realisation and are no other than the elite referred to above; in contrast
the Ash'arites, who believe in absolute predestination, veil themselves from this station.

Witnessing that all is from the One True Lord is realisation
that imperfection on His part is not admissible since His sanctity,
incomparability and exaltedness over anything created are connected with the concept of pure divine unity. This unity is totally
removed from the duality of the phenomenal and may be described as the unity of action, of attribute and of essence. No
persons other than these attain to this degree although the
Ash'arites do not believe in it. Allah's words, 'and none do mind
except those having understanding' is further proof that this

meaning is intended — namely that this vast and noble secret is only known, as is fitting, to those of His slaves who have understanding.

Thus, having demonstrated that the stations of the people of *haqiqah* are higher than the people of *tariqah* and *shari'ah* in all respects, let us begin with our study of the third aspect, which is a description of how the divine code is dependent upon the intellect and how the intellect is dependent upon this same code and how each is dependent upon the other. It will be a demonstration and proof which will prevent the ignorant man from imagining that the divinely revealed laws contradict the intellect and that the methods of reasoning are opposed to this divine code. Many have made this mistake, with the result that they have themselves gone astray and have also led astray many other servants of Allah who were devoid of knowledge. This is referred to by Allah when He describes them and their adversaries during the difficult moments of the Day of Judgement: 'Our Lord! Show us those who led us astray from among the jinn and the men that we may trample them under our feet so that they may be of the lowest.' There are many examples of this nature in the Qur'an — and Allah is more knowing and of greater wisdom. He it is Who declares the Truth and Who guides to the right path.

3

The Third Aspect:

the need of the intellect for the divine code of laws and the dependence of the latter on the intellect

Know that this study necessitates a passage of introduction, namely a description of how all the prophets and intimate friends or saints are doctors of the self and healers of the heart, in the same way as the doctors and physicans are all healers of the ailments of the human body. By this I mean that just as the doctors of the human body know how to get rid of physical diseases from their patients by their skill in healing and their use of potions and drugs, so the doctors of the self or the soul know how to remove the psychological and spiritual ailments of their patients by their skillful guidance and their use of knowledge and gnosis derived from the realm of reality. Thus we read the following description of spiritual treatment in a language specific to its domain: 'Spiritual treatment is by knowledge of the perfections of the heart, by knowledge of whatever mars these perfections through illness, and by knowledge of that which cures this illness. Likewise, it is knowledge of the methods of maintaining good health and even temperament and prevention of further "infection" with this disease.' We read too of the spiritual doctor in similar terms: 'The spiritual doctor is the shaykh, the person who has gnosis of the treatment and who is capable of giving guidance and perfection.'

As we have already seen, it has also been said: 'The shaykh is the perfect man with regard to the *shari'ah*, the *tariqah* and the *haqiqah*, having reached the limits of perfection in each by his knowledge of the diseases and illnesses of the self and the corresponding treatment and medicine and his capacity to cure. The perfect man gives guidance to the self if it is ready for that guidance and agrees to be guided.' Just as it is not permitted for the one who is physically sick to object to the method of treatment nor the nature of the medicine given by the physician, so the person who is spiritually or psychologically sick is not permitted to object to the spiritual doctor, nor to his methods of guidance, his imposition of spiritual exercises or difficult physical tests. Indeed, objecting to any doctor, whether of the physical or the spiritual, only increases the sickness of the sick person. If the physically sick person objects to the physician, then the latter will abandon him and the course of treatment; this will result in a worsening of his illness, sudden death or a long, drawn-out, painful end. Whatever happens, the result is undesirable and may lead to loss of life. Similarly, if the spiritually sick person objects to the spiritual doctor, then the latter will abandon him and the treatment (that is the guidance) and the spiritual illness will increase (that is, he will go further astray and Allah refers to this when He says: 'There is a disease in their hearts, so Allah added to their disease') and they will die the death of meaning or the death caused by disbelief and hypocrisy which Allah refers to when He says: 'Is he who was dead then We raised him to life and made for him a light by which he walks among people, like him whose likeness is that of one in utter darkness whence he cannot come forth?' Either result is undesirable: it causes eternal distress and never-ending misery. Thus, just as a physically sick person who wishes to regain perfect health is obliged to take bitter-tasting medicine from the physician, willingly or unwillingly, without objection or remonstration, so the spiritually sick person who desires perfect health is also obliged to drink a bitter medicine, namely to accept the imposition of arduous tasks of varying degrees of severity from the spiritual doctor — willingly or unwillingly and without objection or remonstration. Allah refers to this when He says, with respect to the Prophet Muhammad: 'But no! By your Lord! They do not believe (in reality) until they make you a judge of that which has become a matter of disagreement among them, and then do not find any straitness in their hearts as to what you have decided and submit with entire submission.'

Our aim in this introductory study is to demonstrate to the reader the truth and validity of the principles and precepts outlined herewith, with particular regard to the *shari'ah, tariqah* and *haqiqah*. We also wish to show how each level is just as it should be, and that no one from any one level should object to anything from another level, or say that that thing contradicts the intellect or the narrated body of traditions. It is clear that something

which is contrary to one person's intellect is not necessarily
contrary to another person's intellect, particularly in the case of
the intellects of the prophets and saints — their intellects are
the most perfect of intellects, just as their souls are the most
perfect of souls: there is manifestly a great distance between the
two and whoever denies this is in sheer folly and in haughty
disregard of his intellect. We are not, however, addressing such
persons.

The situation is similar with regard to the body of the narrated
traditions: it is not possible that one can have heard or understood
all the traditions which exist. By the nature of things we do not
become aware of many of the traditions and we thus cannot be
expected to comprehend them all. Allah refers to this notion
when He says: 'I have prepared for My righteous slaves what
the eye has not seen, what the ear has not heard and what the
heart has not yet awareness of.' It is also clear that the majority
of the laws and prohibitions of the divine legal code are beyond
the compass and perception of the intellect and sensory awareness. Nevertheless, it is not permitted to object to any of them,
since the prophets and saints would not have been commanded
to enact these laws if they had not have been in accordance with
their intellect; indeed, anything which is in accord with their
intellects is in accordance with all intellects. It may be that the
conclusion drawn in a particular subject is contrary to one person's intellect or contrary to others of like intellect, but this does
not mean that it is irrational and contrary to the intellect: most
intellects are incapable of understanding the divinely appointed
code of laws. Moreover, most of the profounder meanings of the
laws and judgements lie outside the framework of human understanding. The Messenger did not allow the people of outward
dimension to ask about the precise nature and purpose of certain
things — questions, for example, concerning the reason why
the midday prayer should consist of four cycles, the sunset prayer
of three and the morning prayer of only two. The same applied
to the rest of the basic pillars of the legal code. As for the incapacity of the intellect to comprehend the more profound meanings
of the divine system, we may cite its inability to understand the
secret of the Angel of Death: the intellect does not have the power

to see how one angel is able to seize the souls of hundreds of thousands of persons or animals from the four corners of the earth in one instant. Likewise, it cannot perceive the secret of Gabriel and how he descends in one instant from the seventh heaven and from the Throne to the earth, how he reveals the revelation to a prophet and then returns in the same instant or a few moments later. In the light of these events, the best a thinking Muslim can do is to submit to the divine commands and laws; the best he can do is to affirm and believe in them without enquiring into their substance and inner reality. There is nothing in the divine code which is contrary to the intellect and, on investigation, one realises that the whole system of legal duties and ordinances with all its details and ramifications is based on the intellect and is within the true grasp of the thinking man.

Indeed, all the workings of existence are based on the intellect and the understanding of the man of intellect: it was within these parameters that existence came into being and so will it end with the annihilation of existence. Thus it has been said: 'Glory to the One Who brought existence into being with the intellect and sealed it with the man of intellect. It has also been narrated in a *hadith* of the Prophet: 'The first thing which Allah created was the intellect. He thereupon said to it: "Come closer" and it came closer. He then said: "Go back" and it went back. He then said: "By My power and My glory, I have not created any creation more beloved to Me than you: By you I take and by you I give, by you I reward and by you I punish." '

The likeness of the divine code and the intellect and the dependence of each on the other is also the likeness of the soul and the body and the dependence of each on the other: I mean by this that just as the workings of the soul and the manifestation of its attributes and perfections is not possible except by means of the body (by way of its physical strength and the various limbs), so the workings of the divine code and the manifestations of its various levels are not possible except by means of the intellect and by means of the different levels and stations of the intellect.

The different levels of the intellect comprise what is called the material intellect, the intellect of action, the faculty of intellect, and the acquiring intellect. The whole of the divine code is based on these different levels: the first and the second are the levels of the common people, the third is that of the elite, and the fourth that of the elite of the elite from amongst the prophets and saints.

The object of this study is to show that the divine code is not independent of the intellect, nor the intellect independent of the divine code. Most scholars, gnostics and philosophers, among them the perfect shaykh Abu'l-Qasim al-Husayn ibn Muhammad al-Raghib al-Isfahani, agree with this. In his book *Tafsil al-Nash'atayn fi tahsil al-sa'adatayn,*[1] Shaykh Raghib mentions this subject in detail saying: 'Know that the intellect never guides except by the divine code and that the divine code will never be understood except by the intellect.' The intellect is like the foundation and the divine code is like the building: the building cannot be firmly established without a foundation. Moreover, the intellect is like the faculty of sight and the divine code like the rays of light: sight is of no use without light. It is for this reason that Allah says, 'Indeed there has come to you light and a clear Book from Allah; with it Allah guides him who will follow His pleasure into the ways of safety and brings them out of utter darkness into light by His will.' Similarly, the intellect is like a lamp and the divine code the oil which fuels it: if there is no oil, then the lamp will not burn, and without the lamp, there will be no light. Allah has indicated this to us with His words: 'Allah is the light of the heavens and the earth... Light upon light.' What is referred to in the latter portion of the *ayah* is the light of the intellect which is above the light of the divine code — for the former will not shine without the latter. Besides, the divine code is the intellect from without and the intellect is the divine code from within: indeed the two are mutually supportive, indeed, united.

As the divine code is the intellect in its outward aspect, so Allah has stripped the name intellect from the disbeliever on

---

[1] (A detailed Exposition of the Two Lives of this World and the Next with respect to the Obtaining of the Two Happinesses)

more than one occasion in the Qur'an, like, for example, when He says: 'Deaf, dumb (and) blind, so they do not understand.' As the intellect is the divine code in its inward aspect, Allah has said: 'The nature made by Allah in which He has made men: there is no altering of Allah's creation; that is the right religion, but most people do not know.' In this *ayah* Allah relates knowing and the intellect to *din* — religion as a complete way of life. Allah also refers to the union of the intellect and the divine code when He says, 'Light upon light' meaning here the light of the intellect and the light of the divine code. Thereafter He says, 'Allah guides to His light whom He wills' referring to these two lights as one single light. If the intellect is missing, then our worship is deficient, for the divine code does not cover in detail all aspects of belief and worship; likewise, if the divine code is missing, then the intellect is incapable of dealing with many of the details of belief and worship. This is because the divine code is as the eye and the intellect as the light or vice-versa: neither of the two can do without the other.

One should realise too that the intellect of itself is hardly enough: it can perceive the universality of things, but it cannot cope with the details. It realises the benefit of belief in the truth, in speaking the truth, in behaving well towards others, in acting justly, in being chaste and so forth, although it may not comprehend the details of these matters. The divine code encompasses both the fundamentals of belief and worship together with the details of these matters; it describes in detail man's obligations and how to conduct one's affairs in an equitable manner. Thus the intellect does not know of itself, for example, that pork, blood or wine are prohibited, or that one should abstain from eating at specific times, or that one should not marry someone who is closely related, or that one should not have sexual intercourse with a woman during her period of menstrual bleeding. The only way of finding out these things is to refer to the divine code since it is a system of correct belief and correct behaviour: it is a means towards the best of this world and the next and whoever abandons it goes astray. Allah indicates that there is no option for the intellect but to accept and realise this fact when He says, 'We do not chastise until We raise an apostle' and also,

'And had We destroyed them with chastisement before this, they would certainly have said: "O our Lord! why didst Thou not send to us an apostle, for then we should have followed Thy communications before we met disgrace and shame." ' On another occasion Allah refers to the intellect and the divine code in terms of grace and mercy: 'And were it not for the grace of Allah upon you and His mercy, you would have certainly followed Satan, save a few' — by the word 'few' Allah is indicating the elite.

As we have already seen, Allah shows that a person who does not devote himself to the divine code and worship of His Lord is neither a true man nor a person of intellect — if he is called a man, he is supposed to be a thinking person. Shaykh Raghib has said that 'man, because of his human nature, either becomes a true man by means of his intellect or he loses his human qualities when his behaviour is no longer connected to this faculty; in fact he is reduced to being a mere shadow of a man and becomes in reality like a mindless brute.' As we have seen above, the intellect is not perfected except after having taken on the guidance of the divine code. In several places in the Qur'an the disbeliever is regarded as devoid of intellect because he has failed to heed the prophetic words of guidance. Acceptance of this guidance, this divine code, is in fact worship of Allah. Therefore the true man is the person who recognises the truth of the message and thereby worships his Lord: it was for this very purpose that he was created. Allah says, 'And I have not created the jinn and the men except that they should serve Me' and 'And they were not enjoined anything except that they should serve Allah, being sincere to Him in obedience, upright, and keep up the prayer and pay the poor-rate.'

Anything which has been brought into existence for a specific task is as if in a state of non-existence if it does not fulfil that specific task. Thus, in a similar way, people discard a thing's very name if that thing is not fulfilling the function for which it was created. When they see a worthless horse, for example, they might say, 'That is not a horse;' likewise of an abject man they might say, 'That is not a man;' again they might say of someone 'he has no eye' or that 'he has no ear' if that persons's eye or ear have ceased to function properly, although there may be still a trace of hearing or sight left. Allah refers to this when He talks about those who do not use their faculty of intellect: 'Deaf, dumb (and) blind for they do not understand.' Likewise man only attains to his human nature to the extent that he attains to the worship for which he has been created: whoever worships in the correct manner perfects thereby his humanity; whoever refuses to worship is stripped thereby of his humanity and becomes the worst of beasts. Allah refers to these disbelievers when He says, 'They are as cattle, nay, they are in worse errors' and also, 'Surely the vilest of animals, in Allah's sight, are the deaf, the dumb, who do not understand;' thus not only does He describe them as beasts and animals but also as the worst of their kind. Indeed, He describes their speech as non-human: 'And their prayer before the House is nothing but whistling and clapping of hands,' likening them to the birds that whistle and clap their wings. Again Allah elaborates on this theme when He declares that man is not a man except by way of his religion: 'The Beneficent God, taught the Qur'an, He created man, taught him how to express himself.' It should be noticed that the two halves of the statement are not joined by an 'and'; one would have thought at first that in describing man Allah would have said, 'He created man, He taught him how to express himself and then taught him the Qur'an,' but Allah begins by mentioning the Qur'an and thereafter says that He created man, since he is not considered to be a man if he does not apply himself to the Qur'an. Allah demonstrates hereby that the true capacity to articulate thoughts is attained only through knowledge of the Qur'an. Allah demonstrates these meanings in a particular order and leaves out the joining word 'and' in between, making each phrase take the place of the one preceding it. Thus the words indicate a certain progression and are not merely placed one after the other as mere additional information.

Again, in order to emphasize this point, we would repeat that man cannot be considered to be a man as long as he has no knowledge of the various acts of worship required of him, and his speech is not considered speech unless his words are uttered in accordance with the demands of the divine code. We are not denying that the unbeliever is a human being in a general sense, but rather that, with respect to the exigencies of the intellect and the divine code, it is not fitting to call him human except in a superficial way as there appears no sign of these two things in his actions. If, however, he is called a human being for the sake of classifying him with a general name, then there is no objection to this. It is clear that many words are used in this way: knowledge of the divine code shows that some words do not in fact mean what they appear to mean. The Arabs use the word *ghinan* to mean abundance of wealth, but a narration of the Prophet demonstrates that this is not so: *'ghinan* is not abundance of wealth, but rather it indicates self-sufficiency and contentment of the self.' Allah Himself has said, 'Whoever is rich, let him abstain altogether' and here uses the word according to its usual meaning. In short, if a wise person uses a word of praise, it is understood as such, although the word may either be used to describe something praiseworthy or despicable, for example, if someone says someone is well-known, it can carry either a positive or a pejorative implication depending on the circumstances.

Thus it might be said that everything is described or praised in terms which are related to the nature óf that thing or its kind; it is said, for example, 'such and such a person is a human-being' or 'this sword is a sword.' In an analogous manner it is said that the absolute human being is the prophet of his time. One scholar has said that the person who says that man is a living being, endowed with speech and doomed to die, is correct, but the real or inner meaning of this statement is not as many people imagine. He does not live or die in the same way as animals and his speech is not the mere faculty of expressing words; rather, what is meant is that the life of the one referred to in His words 'He taught him the mode of expression' and the subsequent death of such a person is the life and death of the man who has overcome the forces of desire and anger by means of the *shari'ah*. Thus death is here the death of the will and life is the true and natural life of the balanced man. This notion has also been expressed in the phrase 'Die the death of the will and you will live the natural life of a balanced man;' the Prophet has also indicated this kind of death with His words, 'Die before you die.' The Commander of the Faithful ('Ali) has also said in this respect: 'He has brought his intellect to life and has killed his self *(nafs)* such that his splender manifests and his coarseness is refined; there then appears a shining radiance which lights up the way for him; he travels along that way, propelled from gate to gate until he reaches the gate of peace and the abode of rest; his step is firm and his body is tranquil, enclosed in safety and ease — and this by virtue of how he has used his heart and satisfied his Lord.'

Examples such as these are many and the reader is advised to research the matter in the appropriate books — and Allah is more Knowing and Wise; He it is who declares the Truth and guides to the right path.

Thus we conclude our investigation of the *shari'ah, tariqah* and *haqiqah* and the need of the intellect for the divine code and the need of the divine code for the intellect; we have treated the matter in such detail and depth as befits a matter of such importance. We shall now begin another investigation which follows on from, and is a necessary complement to, the two other subjects; indeed our research cannot be completed in a fitting matter except by recourse to this third domain of investigation which is concerned with what may be called the two principles and the two rules. The first principle concerns the general duty incumbent upon the prophets, the messengers and the saints which is the duty to instruct and guide creation to the straight path.

4

The First Principle:

the general precepts of the prophets and messengers in their instruction
and guidance of mankind to the straight path

Know that the general precepts and the body of laws established
by the prophets, messengers, saints and Imams from Adam himself to our Prophet Muhammad and from the latter to the Mahdi
are the means of conveying every man to his own particular state
of perfection in accordance with his capacity and receptivity.
Moreover this body of laws is a means of bringing him out of
his state of deficiency and ignorance in accordance with his
strength and striving. This is indicated by Allah when He says:
'Even as We have sent among you an Apostle from among you
who recites to you Our communications and purifies you and
teaches you the Book and the wisdom and teaches you that which
you did not know.' Indeed Allah's purpose in bringing creation
into being is just this, as He indicates on another occasion: 'Allah
is He Who created seven heavens, and of the earth the like of
them; the decree continues to descend among them, that you
may know that Allah has power over all things and that Allah
indeed encompasses all things in His knowledge.' Moreover in
a sacred *hadith* He also says, 'I was a hidden treasure and
I desired to be known and so I created the world.' Furthermore
He says, 'And were it not for Allah's grace upon you and His
mercy, not one of you would have ever been pure' meaning if it
were not for Allah's generosity in revealing the Book and His
mercy in sending down the messengers, none of you would be
purified of their ignorance and their disbelief. The reason for
this is that something which is in a state of potentiality must
finally, of necessity, emerge into a state of actuality. Perfection
is potential in all created beings: if the prophets and messengers
had not existed and perfected the twin forces of knowledge and
action, which reside in man as potentiality, then no one would
ever have been able to rise above imperfection to perfection. The
words of the Prophet, 'I have been given all the names' and 'I
have been sent to perfect good conduct' are indications of this.
What the Prophet is saying is that 'I have been sent to perfect

the good conduct which has been established by the prophets before me and the perfection of this good conduct is dependent upon my being sent into the visible world of creation: in truth, all the prophets and messengers of the visible and invisible worlds were my caliphs, my vicegerents and manifestations of my own manifestation.' The Prophet has also said, 'Adam and those after him are beneath my banner' and 'I was a Prophet when Adam was between the water and clay.'

At this point there is need for an introductory discourse in order to explain what is meant by these notions in rational terms; thereafter, we will return to our original subject. One should realise that the speaking or rational self possesses two powers of knowledge and action and each has degrees of perfection and imperfection. The most perfect degree is what is called the acquiring intellect and it is concerned with attaining knowledge which may be learned — knowledge related to both the realm of pure knowledge and to the realm of action. The acquiring intellect is also concerned with knowledge of the correct path, namely, the path which leads to attainment of these knowledges without causing confusion or doubt with regard to one's belief and without, causing one to go astray through error. It is concerned too with the blessings of Allah, despite their boundless, basically incomprehensible nature.

There are different degrees of perfection with regard to the intellect and its knowledge. The highest of these is the level of certainty in belief within the domain of religious fundamentals: anyone who reaches this level is released from eternal torment and achieves eternal blessing and riches.

It should be realised from this that Allah acts according to a specific purpose and not in jest, may He be exalted high above any such notion. We know that Allah has no such frivolous intent since it is impossible to impute frivolity to Him: the Qur'an speaks of this saying, 'And were it not for Allah's repelling some (bad) men with others (who are good), the earth would certainly be in a state of disorder' and also, 'And We did not create the heaven and the earth and what is between them for sport.'

Now we should pause to reflect upon two matters: the first is that *lutf* or divine grace and kindness is obligatory on Allah;

likewise, the dutiful Muslim is closest in obedience as long as
he himself possesses kindness, since kindness is related to His
wisdom, generosity and mercy. By saying that kindness is 'obligatory on Allah' we mean no more than this. Anyone who
requires something of someone knows that the best transactions
are those performed with kindness and so he will naturally act
accordingly to achieve his aim — that is as long as he has the
capacity. If he does not act with kindness, then this would contradict his purpose. Similarly, a contradiction with respect to
the All-wise is impossible: the very revelation of the Book and
the sending of the messengers is *lutf* and the imposition of the
religious duties is also a kindness. It is in this way that such
things are 'obligatory on Allah', that is, when we ourselves consider the matter rationally for His action cannot be at odds with
His overall purpose. This is the very meaning of Allah's words
when He says, 'And I have not created the jinn and the men
except that they should serve Me.'

The second point is the fact that Allah has created desires in
man and has enabled him to fulfil these desires. The intellects
of many men do not discriminate between what is good and
what is bad behaviour; since ignorance reigns over most of them,
this also facilitates bad behaviour and discourages praiseworthy
behaviour. Indeed, by investing man with sexual desires and the
means to fulfil these desires, the very fabric of society as a whole
is easily exposed to destructive influences. However, mankind is
protected from corruption and brought closer to righteousness
by means of the revelation of the Book, the sending of the messengers and man's very obligation to obey these messengers — it
is this too which is encompassed by the term divine *lutf*. Thus
it is obligatory on Allah in the sense that if He were not to act
in this way, then He would be abandoning good action and
committing bad action, and the two are both impossible with
respect to Allah: He is of necessity kind and concerned for His
slaves since to forego this kindness and concern would cause
them to become corrupt in their actions.

It is absolutely necessary that we become fully acquainted
with this kind of knowledge for it forms the basis of our present
investigation. Most of this knowledge is contained in the body

of reported traditions, in the books of the people of the outward and scholars of the Prophetic narrations, and is in complete accord with the aims of the people of the inward.

We shall now return to our original subject. Know, therefore, that perfection and deficiency with respect to each individual being and each kind will be explained to the reader in its proper place. As for absolute perfection, it is found in gnosis of Allah and in the performance of the different acts of worship; moreover, this absolute perfection corresponds to the various degrees and levels inherent in this gnosis and in such worship. As for absolute deficiency, it is that which stands in direct opposition to this gnosis, that is, imperfection in its various degrees and levels of intensity. Since attainment of these various degrees of perfection and freeing oneself from the different levels of imperfection can only be achieved by the perfection of the twin forces of knowledge and action, all creation's striving is directed towards the perfecting of these two forces and the attainment of the two fundamental principles indicated above, namely, the roots and branches of the religion. All parameters of mankind's behaviour, from the divine commands to the divine prohibitions, are contained within these two principles. If one investigates we are left in no doubt or ambiguity as to the truth of these statements. Indeed the one who said that all commands and prohibitions of Allah are contained in the two sayings of the Prophet, 'Respect and reverence for Allah's command' and 'Compassion for Allah's creation' is in total agreement with what we are saying. Anyone who acts in accordance with these two sayings — and all that they imply in the way of command and prohibition — is in fact carrying out the whole divinely inspired code of laws. Likewise, anyone who acts correctly, in accordance with the above-mentioned roots and branches of the religion, is also carrying out the totality of Allah's commands and prohibitions and attains thereby his own specific perfection in accordance with his own capacity.

Allah's purpose in all this is attainment of the ultimate aim inherent in His creation and His imposition of the code of duties (known as the *shari'ah*). None of this has been done in jest and without design — for this would be incompatible with the perfection and wisdom of Allah; indeed, it would be an impossibility as we have shown above.

Just as all people are contained within the three different levels, namely the beginning, the middle and the end, so their different levels of instruction and guidance are all contained within the three levels of *shari'ah, tariqah* and *haqiqah*. With respect to the essences and substances, they are likewise not restricted to one level; rather they vary in accordance with their capacity and receptivity. The wise care of Allah for His creation demands a harmonious system which allows each element to be brought to its own specific perfection. Such a system permits the raising of each element out of its state of imperfection; by means of the force and vigour inherent in each element, it then manifests (in that subsequent form).

Thus the demands and imposition (made by Allah on His slaves) vary according to each group or rather according to each species or individual — despite the fact that as a whole they are governed by one law. The duties of each of the above-mentioned groups differ from each other with respect to the law and their branches but not with respect to the pillars and fundamental principles of the religion. By this I mean that the duties and knowledge of the state of perfection of the people of *shari'ah* are different from those of the people of *tariqah*. Similarly, the state of perfection and the knowledge of the people of *haqiqah* are different from those of the people of *tariqah*. The reader will become aware of this when reading the detailed description of each of the three groups; he will see how one is superior to the other, although they are all united in their overall purpose. In the light of this hierarchy within Allah's creation, we see that the duties of the prophets, the messengers, the saints and the inheritors of the spiritual teaching are other than those of the rest of creation: although the former still take part in the duties of the latter, the latter do not share in the knowledge of the former. This is referred to when Allah says, 'Continue then in the right way as you are commanded' and in the words of the Prophet when he says, 'The *surah* of *Hud* caused my hair to grow white.' From these two quotations we learn of the importance and high status of the prophets and messengers with respect to the rest of creation.

We now should consider two further points. The first is why one particular group of persons has a higher status than others and secondly, why more duties are imposed upon the group of a higher status and of a greater position of honour. As for the first, we must realise that Allah has created the creatures and has imposed specific duties upon them, without them having prior knowledge of these duties. Thus it is incumbent upon Allah to teach them about these duties so that they are able to fulfil them, keep to the covenant between them and Allah, and in doing so, attain the purpose which Allah has foreseen for them since, as has been demonstrated above, Allah never does anything in jest. This teaching is called grace by the people of the outward and providence by the people of the inward. No creature has the capacity to receive these duties from Allah by himself because there is no direct relation between him and Allah; moreover there exists, by the very nature of creation and the nature of Allah, a distance between them which separates the two. This is expressed in Allah's words, 'And it is not for any mortal that Allah should speak to him except by revelation or from behind a veil, or by sending a messenger and revealing by His permission what He pleases; surely He is High, Wise.' It is for this reason that the intellect esteems that it is incumbent upon Allah to designate a group of persons with whom He establishes a specific relationship. Such persons are responsible for transmitting these duties by means of the revelation or divine inspiration; they convey these duties to those of Allah's slaves upon whom such duties are incumbent. Thus Allah says, 'And if We had made him an angel, We would certainly have made him a man, and we would certainly have made confused to them what they make confused.'

The prophets and the messengers are the original recipients of Allah's message, and the saints and the spiritual inheritors follow behind and continue the task begun by the former. Allah refers to this when He says: 'Surely We have revealed to you as We revealed to Noah, and the prophets after Him, and as We revealed to Abraham and Ishmael and Issac and Jacob and the tribes, and Jesus and Job and Jonah and Aaron and Solomon and We gave to David Psalms. And (We sent) apostles We have mentioned before and apostles We have not mentioned to you; and to Moses Allah addressed His word, speaking (to him): (We sent) apostles as the givers of good news and as warners, so that people should not have a plea against Allah after (the coming of) the apostles; and Allah is Mighty, Wise.'

One might remark that this is an explanation of the reason for the need of a group of persons who provide a link between Allah and His creation and who transmit the duties incumbent upon the latter, and that it is not a description of the particular qualities of the group which makes them suitable for such a task. However, this question will be explained after our discourse which shows how they take on Allah's qualities — referred to when He says, 'I become his hearing, his sight, his tongue and his arm' and 'You did not smite when you smote (the enemy) but it was Allah Who smote.'

One might ask who obtained this essential relationship for them or, indeed, in what manner it came about. We would reply that there are two aspects to the answer. The first aspect is from the point of view of the people of the *shari'ah* and the outward, namely that this special relationship issues from the care and concern of Allah and His bestowal upon them of this particular station of spirituality. Thus He says, 'He gives it to whom He pleases; and Allah is the Lord of mighty grace' and 'He cannot be questioned concerning what He does and they shall be questioned.' The second aspect of the answer is with regard to the way of the reality and truth, namely that the cause is seen to be in terms of the state of search (towards manifest forms) inherent in substances and essences; moreover the matter is also considered with respect to whether or not these substances are brought into being by the Creator. We have already discussed above how attainment of a manifest rank or level issues from the relevant essences and substances — which in turn are determined by Allah's foreknowledge of them. This is because knowledge is dependent upon what is known and the known only exists in the aspect which has been determined for it (in the created or phenomenal world). The many interpretations and obscure secrets attached to this subject are known only to the scholars of these sciences. We have in fact clarified the majority of these matters in the opening chapters of this work: they concern the stations of knowledge which the prophets, the spiritual guardians and the saints have warned against divulging and these stations are among the secrets of destiny.

The Sultan of the Saints and Gnostics, the Commander of the Faithful, says the following about destiny and Allah's decree: 'Destiny is one of the secrets which are guarded and protected by Allah, which are raised high behind the veil of Allah, hidden from creation and sealed with the seal of Allah's foreknowledge, removed from the knowledge of His slaves and elevated above their vision; their intellects are prevented from attaining this secret by being unable to reach it — either by the truth of Lordship or by the everlasting Power, either by the splendour of Majesty or by the force of Oneness — for this secret is an overflowing sea which belongs entirely to Allah. Its depth extends from the heavens to the earth, its breadth from the east to the west, a sea as black as the darkest night, abounding in life and fishes, alternately ebbing and flowing. At the bottom of his sea shines a sun. It is not fitting that anyone catch sight of it but by the One on Whom all depend; whoever attempts to see it is setting himself up as a rival to Allah in His wisdom, is challenging His sovereignty and is threatening to reveal His secret: He indeed becomes deserving of Allah's wrath, and his abode is hell; and an evil destination shall it be.'

There is nothing more to be added to this — and how could it be otherwise since these words are spoken by the Lord of the Friends of Allah, the Seal of the Spiritual Guardians, by he who encompasses all their stations and by he who gives them these stations in the world of light, despite his coming after them in the visible world. According to his words, it is thus impossible to envisage criticism of those upon whom such ranks have been decreed; what is indicated is that it is an obligation upon Allah to appoint such persons and single them out for special treatment, in accordance with His knowledge and wisdom; this is emphasised by His words, 'Surely We purified them by a pure quality, the keeping in mind of the (final) abode. And most surely they were with Us, of the elect, the best.'

We should now examine the actual relationship between them and the Real on the one hand, and between Him and the creation on the other. As for the first, it has two aspects: that with regard to the intellect and that with regard to the revelation of the Qur'an and the body of traditions (*ahadith*). The sound intellect is capable of perceiving, for example, that if there is no relationship between two essences or two persons, then it is not possible to imagine that any love exists between them: the first condition for the presence of love is the existence of an essential relationship — and thereafter an incidental relationship. Such a love takes many forms and they are outlined in the books of philosophy (under the sections entitled 'love') and also in the books of the devotees of divine unity. Some of the philosophers have even gone so far as to say that it is not permitted for Allah to love anyone or for anyone to love Him since love of its nature implies a correspondence of generic state. They argue that the 'Necessary of Existence', having absolutely no correspondence of kind with the 'possible of existence', is not permitted to associate Himself with love at all. This argument has no basis of truth: we are merely mentioning it as a warning that their theories are invalid of their system of belief. In short, there must exist a relationship of love, be it essential or incidental. This relationship is explained in the language of the people of Allah in the following way: 'Original love is the love of the essence itself for itself, a love which does not depend on any extraneous matter: this kind of love is the origin of all the other kinds of love.' Thus any link between two things is either the relationship of their two essences or a uniting on the level of attributes, spiritual states or actions. Their relationship with Allah is with respect to their sanctification (of Him) and their rising above the impurity of mankind and the polluting influence of the incidental and possible; it is also with respect to their embuing themselves with the qualities of their Lord and with divine behaviour. If they remained in the sphere of mankind and the law of the natural world, they would not be able to achieve this relationship. The Prophet has said, 'I have a station with Allah which is reached neither by the most intimate of the angels nor the messengers sent to man.' It is thus necessary that they divest themselves of the world of man and that they take on the divine qualities in order to establish this relationship.

It has been recorded in an authentic *hadith* that if the Prophet were connected only to the world of man and had no relationship with the divine, he would not have been able to receive the revelation. Thus it is that the Prophet had need of Gabriel (who appeared to him in the form of the companion Dahiyah or in other forms so as not to alienate him from the world of the senses or unduly disturb him) in order that he might receive the message, transmit it and then call and guide the people to Islam: on several occasions he would faint after receiving the revelation and say to 'Aishah 'Speak to me Hamira,' in order that he might return from that (spiritual) world to the world of the senses and that he might deliver the message he had been commanded to deliver. An indication of this is also contained in the station of Moses which is described by Allah when He says, 'And Musa fell down in a swoon.' His swooning was a result of his state and the fact he was a mortal and of the natural world of creation: Allah spoke to Moses while the latter was divested of his physical senses. The true relationship (between Allah and man) is thus established by the witnesser who is able to perceive the divine: it is at the moment of witnessing that he is able to speak with Allah. Moses did not attain this station until Allah asked, 'And what is in your right hand, O Musa' He said, 'This is my staff: I recline on it and I beat the leaves with it to make them fall upon my sheep and I have other uses for it.' Likewise, the Prophet was taken from the world of mankind during the *mi'raj*, the night journey, until Allah says: 'And He revealed to his servant what He revealed.' This revelation took place at the moment when the Prophet was stripped (of the creational world) and it occurred by way of the divine relationship with the Essence — without the mediation of any angel or Gabriel. It has been narrated that Allah revealed thirty thousand secrets in an hour or less. Gabriel says of this station, 'If I had stretched out the tips of my fingers they would have burned;' this is an indication of the nobility of man and his superiority over the angels and other creatures.

If we consider the matter with respect to the Truth, the Real Himself rather than the messengers, then the following *ayah* suffices: 'So when I made him (man) complete and breathed into him of My spirit, (the angels) fell down making obeisance of him.' These words indicate two things: firstly, the relationship between Allah and his slaves and secondly, the nobility and superiority of man over the angels. This is reinforced by a saying of one of people of gnosis: 'The essential relationship between the Real and His slave may be considered from two aspects: either that the laws govening the phenomenal-transient world of the slave together with the manifestations of multiplicity inherent in the slave's life in the created world do not impinge upon the laws of the Necessary of Existence and His unity — rather, that the slave is influenced by the latter and the darkness of his multiplicity is embued with the light of His unity and Oneness — or that the slave takes upon himself the qualities of the Real and attains to a realisation of all His Names. If these two aspects are in conjunction, then the slave has attained the goal and has reached perfection. If only the first aspect is realised by the slave, then he becomes the beloved and intimate of Allah. The attainment of the second aspect without with the first is impossible. Moreover, both aspects contain many different levels within them. As for the first aspect, there must be a total overwhelming of the multiplicity and its inherent transient frailty by the light of Oneness and the domination of the laws of Necessary Existence over the laws of human existence and over man's inherent weakness. As for the second aspect, there must be an attainment of the station of realisation through all and not just some of the Divine Names. There are numerous works on this matter by past and latter-day Mu'tazilite and Ash'arite scholars of the science of divine unity; this is not however the moment to elaborate on this subject and the reader is advised to make further investigations of his own.

As for the second part of our investigation, namely with respect to the Qur'an and the narrated body of traditions, then we should refer to the words of Allah: 'Then Allah will bring a people, He shall love them and they shall love Him, modest before the believers, mighty against the unbelievers;' we should also take into account the sacred *hadith*, 'Truly the righteous long passionately for their meeting with Me and surely I am even more passionately longing for My meeting with them' and His words,

'I was a hidden treasure and I desired to be known, so I created the world;' these words bear witness both to the love of the Real Himself and the love of the slave. Moreover this love, as we have already explained, is only attained after the establishment of a specific relationship and degree of intimacy with the divine. The words of the Prophet, 'I have a station with Allah which is reached neither by the most intimate of angels nor the messengers sent to man' refer to this. Such a station is evidently only possible after the annihilation of his qualities in those of the Lord and the annihilation of his existence in His existence, like the merging of a drop of water in the sea or a lump of ice in water.

If the nature of these different aspects of the relationship with the divine are still unclear to the reader, then we shall give another example which will clarify this matter beyond any doubt. It is the likeness of fire: fire is light, illuminating and transparent; it may be used to cook food until it is tender and it may be used to provide light. Charcoal and firewood, on the other hand, are dark and darken by their very presence; moreover, they do not yield the benefits of fire — indeed, by their nature, these materials are cold, opaque and dry. If, however, they come into contact with fire, then they too take on the qualities of light, illumination and transparency and, in turn, become themselves the fire itself. Furthermore, one may also obtain from them all the benefits of cooking and lighting which one may obtain from fire. Connected to this likeness is the saying of the Prophet: 'Whoever sees me in a dream has truly seen me,' and the words of one of the *awliya'* who said: 'Praise! for how vast is my affair!' and the words of another: 'I am the Truth' and 'I am from my Passion and my Passion am I — we strike such likeness for the people but only the knowldgeable comprehend them.'

Up to this point we have been considering the relationship established between the prophets and the Real, may He be exalted. We shall now consider the relationship which is established between the prophets and creation. This relationship may also be considered from two angles, firstly, with respect to the intellect, and secondly, with respect to what has been narrated in the Qur'an and the *ahadith*. As for the first, it is as we have already seen, namely, a question of the intellect's perception of the possible-incidental in relation to the transient-phenomenal, the state of mankind (as opposed to divinity) and the creation. All persons, indeed all beings, are alike in their sharing of these characteristics — for all existence is contained in the Necessary (of existence) and the possible (of existence). Moreover, the Necessary of Existence is by common accord one, that is, the One; there remains, therefore, only the possible. As scholars of this science are well aware all possible things are alike, both with regard to their essences and substances.

As for the consideration of the relationship of the Prophet with creation, with regard to the Qur'an and the narrated traditions, then we should keep in mind the words of Allah: 'I am a mortal like you, it is revealed to me that your god is one God' and His words: 'What is the matter with this Apostle that he eats food and goes around in the market.' Both these verses indicate the human aspect of the Prophet; his relationship to creation is based on human qualities and natural patterns of behaviour.

Know too that there is also a relationship between them and the angels and likewise a relationship between Allah and the angels. The following words of Allah refer to it in a general way: '(As for) those who say: Our Lord is Allah, then continue in the right way, the angels descend upon them', and again in a more particular way: 'The Lord of Mighty Power has taught him, the Lord of Strength', and likewise the words: 'The Faithful Spirit has descended with it upon your heart.'

As for the relationship between Allah and the angels, it is established by their elevation above the baseness of corporeal realities and the natural abjectness of animals. This is demonstrated in Allah's words when He says of them, 'We celebrate Thy praise and extol Thy holiness.' The angels express these words in accordance with their essential being and their station, as the following words of Allah affirm: 'And there is none of us but has an assigned place.' Again this is demonstrated in Allah's instruction of them when the Qur'an says: 'Glory be to Thee! We have no knowledge but that which Thou has taught us; surely Thou are the Knowing the Wise.' It is clear that instruction cannot effectively take place without a relationship between the teacher and the taught: thus Allah says to Adam, on seeing the relationship between him and the angels: 'O Adam! Inform them of their names.' Then when he had informed them of their names, He said: 'Did I not say to you that I surely know what is unseen in the heavens and the earth and (that) I know what you manifest and what you hide.' In the light of this *ayah* we should also consider the saints and the spiritual guardians — for they receive knowledge without any intermediary. This is demonstrated when Allah says, 'We granted him (one from among Our servants) knowledge from Ourselves' and also when He speaks of all men saying, 'Read and your Lord is Most Honourable, Who taught (to write) with the pen, taught man what he knew not' and also when he says, 'The Beneficent God, taught the Qur'an, He created man, taught him the mode of expression.' There are many other examples with respect to this subject; and Allah is More Knowing and More Wise.

As for the second matter, it concerns their not being overburdened by their duties, given the honour and nobility of their standing. There are also two aspects to this matter. The first concerns their capacity which is theirs from before eternity and which has been acquired through no causative reason or action on their part; this is based on the judgement of Allah when He says: 'Surely (as for) those for whom the good has already gone forth from Us, they shall be kept far off from it (the torment of hell)' and His words: 'This is Our free gift, therefore give freely or withhold, without reckoning' and His words: 'That is the grace of Allah: He gives it to Whom He pleases, and Allah is the Lord of Mighty Grace.'

The second aspect of this matter concerns the intensity of their striving and their excercise of physical and spiritual restraint in the performance of their acts of worship and in their seeking after the satisfaction of Allah. This is expressed in Allah's words: 'And whoever does this seeking Allah's pleasure, We will give him a mighty reward.' The Prophet's excercise of spiritual discipline and his striving, together with his war on the unbelievers and his endurance of their torments are familiar to everyone. He himself has said, 'Never has a prophet been tormented as I have been tormented.' We should remember in particular too that Allah says in the Qur'an, 'We have not revealed the Qur'an to

you that you may be unsuccesful...' and the *hadith* related by
'Aishah, 'He would rise in the night to pray the *tahajjud* prayer
and continue until his feet became swollen from standing.'
'Aishah then said: 'O Messenger of Allah, has not the *ayah* been
revealed about you that "Allah will forgive your past faults and
those to come?" ' He then replied to her: 'Should I not be a
grateful slave?' Detailed accounts of the self-restraint and struggle
of the other prophets may be known from the books (that were
revealed to them) and a more general picture is available from
the Qur'an. Muslim scholars know that the Qur'an is the best
witness and the best proof of the veracity (of a story) — and
may Allah suffice as a witness; He it is Who says the truth and
guides to the correct path.

Although there are many other areas of investigation let us
content ourselves with the point we have arrived at so far and
begin now to consider the second principle. This second principle
is concerned with Allah's designation of a (certain) perfection
for each being and with the development and progression of this
being with respect to the realm of form and to the realm of inner
meaning and in accordance with their station of perfection.

5

The Second Principle:

Allah's designation of a specific perfection to each existing thing whether
spiritual or corporeal — in both the phenomenal realm and the realm
of inner meaning.

Know that the search after perfection is not a feature particular
to man alone, but rather of all existent and created beings, be
they of a sublime or base nature: they are all making for the
object of their 'search'; both the Qur'an, the traditions and the
conclusions of the intellect bear witness to this fact. We may cite
the words of Allah: 'And there is no animal that walks upon the
earth nor bird that flies with two wings but (they are) general
like yourselves; We have not neglected anything in the Book,
then to their Lord shall they be gathered' and His words: 'Do
you not see that Allah is He Whom obeys whoever is in the
heavens and the earth, and the sun the moon and the stars, and
the mountains and the trees, and the animals and many of the
people...' and His words: 'He knows the prayer of each one and
its glorification, and Allah is Cognizant of what they do' and
His words: 'And there is not a single thing but glorifies Him
with His praise, but you do not understand their glorification.'
These four *ayat* are conclusive proof that all beings have had
duties entrusted to them by the Creator: they have all been
commanded to worship in accordance with their receptivity and
capability. The first *ayah* refers to the earth and its inhabitants,
the second to the heavens and the earth and all that is between
them, the third refers to all specific beings, and the fourth refers
to all beings in an absolute way. Thus all are facing and moving
towards Allah, engaged in a search for gnosis of Him.

The obeisance and prayer referred to in these *ayat* carry the
meaning of worship and gnosis — and not the prayer which is
familiar to us in the code of the *shari'ah*. Likewise, their prayer
and glorification are not like the praise and glorification of man;
if they were, then we would understand them. That we do not
understand their particular form of prayer or praise is shown in
the words of Allah: 'But you do not understand their glorification.' Thus the prayer, obeisance and praise of each being is in

accord with its state. When we examine the beings other than men, we realise that their ways of glorification are in fact the natural behaviour patterns of each. This is affirmed by Allah's words: 'Every one acts according to his manner.' What is desired and sought by all is the same thing, namely gnosis of Him and worship of Him. As to gnosis it is referred to by Allah in the sacred *hadith*: 'I was a hidden treasure and I desired to be known so I created the world.' As for the aspect of worship, it is referred to when He says: 'And I have not created the jinn and the men except that they should serve Me.' Consider how the soul of man, his body, limbs and physical strength are in prostration to Him, obeying His command and submitting to His laws. This is the prostration and prayer of inner meaning. The relationship of the whole world with regard to the soul of man is the same as we have just described for the world in its totality is the body of cosmic man or macrocosm: all its components are analogous to the members of the body; all man's praise, prayer and prostration are acts of obeisance in relation to Cosmic Man in accordance with that He prohibits or commands. The prostration and glorification of both man and the cosmic man are in truth a glorification of the Real and obeisance to Him, since the individual soul of man is the caliph (or deputy) of Allah in the body and the absolute soul of man is the caliph of Allah in the world. As Allah Himself says, 'Whoever obeys the Apostle, he indeed obeys Allah' and 'And as for these examples, We set them forth for men, and none understands them but the learned!'

In connection with the above, we should mention what has been related by one of the Imams, namely that true gratitude is the employment of each limb of the body for that for which it has been created. It has also been said, 'Every existent being, be it of a sublime or base nature, stands in relation to the greater man and acts in accordance with that for which it has been created — except man.' What we mean by this is that there is no being which contradicts His command or prohibition, no being which refuses to obey and worship but man. Indeed, he is in a state of opposition to Allah; he is not in a state of complete obedience to His command — in the same way as we are not in complete obedience to our soul and intellect. This opposition, however, is in fact in compliance with the decree of Allah for it is in accordance with Allah's knowledge of it from before eternity to eternity. Thus one of the gnostics has commented on this matter saying: 'Whoever opposes the decree of Allah is not in fact opposing Him, and whoever opposes Him in that purpose for which he has designated is in fact in compliance with the general form in which Allah created him.'

The Commander of the Faithful has also indicated this in one of his sermons concerning Adam and his progeny: 'And Allah brought him to reside in His garden and made his food plentiful for him therein. He then warned him concerning that which He had prohibited: He taught him that if he were to approach (that which He had prohibited), he would be exposing himself to an act of disobedience and would consequently place his position in the garden in jeopardy. Adam did, however, approach what had been forbidden him — in accordance with Allah's forenowledge — and, after Adam had turned to Him in forgiveness, Allah caused him to descend from the Garden in order that he might fill the earth with his progeny.' The Commander of the Faithful said on another occasion: 'Know with certainty that Allah does not bestow on a slave more than what is intended for him in the foreknowledge of the Wise. Anyone who realises this and acts accordingly is one of those who attain to the greatest ease and benefit; whoever ignores this or doubts its validity is of those who work hardest towards their own harm. Thus many a time it happens that blessings are given to him, and great ease and affluence is accorded to him (despite the obstinacy of the person), and many a time he is tried and afflicted by care.

Thus, O you who enjoy your benefits, increase your thanks, restrain your haste and be content when your provision comes to an end.' The Prophet is reported to have said, in a similar vein; 'The pen has dried and with it (has been written) whatever exists in the cosmos' and 'The growth and development of all creation is towards that for which is has been created.' Similarly, Allah says, 'And everything they have done is in the writings.' We are not, however, attempting to affirm the doctrine of predestination, nor are we trying to assert as true the saying of the one who said, 'Everything which is to occur and which Allah knows will occur must occur, and everything which is not to occur and which Allah knows will not occur cannot occur.' Rather what we mean is that nothing happens in existence which is in opposition to the knowledge of Allah — whether it be in accordance (with the divine command) or in opposition to it. This then is just a tiny drop from the ocean of the secrets of the Divine Decree; it is forbidden to divulge this Divine Decree as we have already seen from one of the most excellent and pertinent of traditions on the subject, namely that of the Commander of the Faithful mentioned above. It is incumbent upon the reader to reflect upon its meanings and take note of the secrets hidden therein.

Know that just as it may be ascertained that every existent being has its own form of prayer, praise and prostration, so it may also be ascertained that every existent being has life, speech and knowledge — which in fact are expressions of the different degrees of perfection sought after by all. As for life, there is true life and superficial life. True life, as has been established is knowledge and gnosis of Allah and this, as we see from the following words of Allah, is possessed by all existent beings, 'And if you asked them who created the heavens and the earth, they will certainly say: Allah.' This *ayah* affirms the divinity and One-ness of Allah — and these words alone suffice to demonstrate how man is endowed with inherent gnosis (of his Lord). The following *ayah* also affirms this: 'And there is not a single thing but glorifies Him with His praise.' Glorification of something is naturally preceded by knowledge of that thing: glorification without knowledge of what one is glorifying is impossible — whether this knowledge be inherent in man's faculty or whether it be acquired.

As for the superficial life: it has been established that each existent being possesses life of itself and the following words of Allah testify to this: 'And We have made from water every living thing.' Moreover, it is one of the elements of the phenomenal world, for the elements and form of every compound contain water and water itself is contained in and makes up the human body. Allah Himself says, 'And He it is Who created man from the water, then He has made for him blood relationship and marriage relationship.' If we assert that it is of the simple elements, then this refers to the universal matter upon which the Throne stood before the bringing into being of the cosmos and all it contained. Allah speaks of this when He says, 'And He it is Who created the heavens and the earth in six periods — and His dominion (Throne) extend over the water — that He might manifest to you which of you it best in action.' In short, everything possesses life in accordance with its state. One may, if one wishes, call this (condition of life) knowledge of gnosis, or, if one wishes, elemental water or, if one wishes, universal matter: there is no dispute as to the general applicability of these terms.

As for speech, there is superficial or apparent speech, and true speech. Apparent speech is referred to by Allah when He says, 'Allah, Who makes everything speak, has made us speak' and by the Prophet when he says, 'Everything on earth, both green and dry, bears witness to the caller of the call to prayer *(adhan)* and all things, including even the fishes of the sea and the birds of the sky, asked forgiveness of Allah for the seeker of knowledge.' Thus these two statements are both evidence that everything possesses speech: indeed, an even clearer example of this is the occasion when the small stones in the hands of the Prophet praised Allah. These pebbles may be said to represent the mineral kingdom. As for the plant kingdom, there is the example of the sighing of the tree and the occasion when the burnt arm spoke: all existent beings are therefore contained in these three kingdoms. As for the real or true speech, it is the understanding of the intellect as an absolute or pure process. Moreover, this process of understanding on the part of the essence of anything and of the Essence of the Creator of that thing is true speech. Besides, the proof that they know and glorify Him is that if they did not know Him, they would not be able to glorify Him — something about which one is ignorant can never the praised or glorified by anyone.

As for gnosis, there is likewise real gnosis and apparent gnosis; I mean by this an inherent or naturally created gnosis, on the one hand, and an acquired or sought-after gnosis, on the other. Inherent or real gnosis is referred to in the following *ayah:* 'And should you ask them who created the heavens and the earth they would most certainly say: "Allah" ' and also His words: 'Am I

not Your Lord? They said: Yes!' If the reader were to object
that it is the progeny of Adam who are being referred to here
and not to all existent beings then we would reply that this is
correct; however, Adam himself encompasses the greater and
lesser man and, in this *ayah,* what is being referred to is the
greater/cosmic man or Macrocosm, that is, the cosmos and all
the existent beings contained therein. That all is descended from
this cosmic man is shown by the following *ayah:* 'O people, be
careful of your duty to your Lord, Who created you from a single
being and created its mate of the same (kind) and spread from
these two many men and many women.' What is meant here by
men and women is the male and the female which exist in all
created beings both of the highest and lowest orders. This is also
indicated in another *ayah:* 'He has made it in two kinds', the
two kinds referring to the male and the female. As for the statement of the one who said: 'In everything there is an *ayah* — or
a sign — of Him which demonstrates His Oneness', it also demonstrates the validity of this explanation of inherent or created
gnosis.

Acquired or manifest gnosis is something which is particular
to men, angels and jinn — notwithstanding their inherent gnosis
which precedes it. It has been established by the people of Allah,
and supported by a consensus of opinion from amongst most of
the men of intellect, that existence is one and that it is a cycle
which turns about the lover and the loved one, the knower and
the known, the seeker and the sought. This is affirmed by Allah's
words: 'Then Allah will bring a people, He shall love them and
they shall love Him' and also His words: 'Thus I desired to be
known.' We realise, on investigation, that the true Loved One
is only Allah and those who love Him are all things other than
Him — including thus the mineral, vegetable and animal
realms and men, jinn and angels. This is expressed in the following verse:

> The goodness of each elegant thing is derived from His
> beauty,
> A beauty which is loaned to it and to all charming things

and also in the following:

> Allow your heart to pursue its desire as it wishes,
> for love is nothing but for the First Lover.

Thus it is true to say that all things feel love for Him and are facing and moving towards His Presence.

On examination, we realise that the one loved and those who love, the seeker and the sought, the knower and the known are one. Merely expressing this principle presupposes otherness, multiplicity and the witnessing of something which is not Him and is thus in opposition to true divine unity. As our aim is nothing but realization of this unity, it is incumbent upon us to perceive one existence, albeit expressed in two different ways. Firstly, it may be considered absolutely inconceivable to admit of another together with Him — given the Presence of His Oneness, His station of Absoluteness and Unity — and secondly, that He exists together with His Names, Attributes and Actions and the corresponding manifestations of these, expressed as the worlds of the phenomenal.

With respect to the first it has been said:

> I was Time itself before the veil was raised.
> I was a brother to you — indeed a rememberer of you
> and grateful.
> So when the night lit up, I realised
> That You are the remembered, the remembrance and the
> one who remembers.

It has also been said that 'No one loves Allah but Allah and no one knows Allah but Allah and no One remembers Allah but Allah.'

With respect to the second, it has been said, 'There is nothing in existence except Allah, His Name, Attributes and Actions: thus all is Him, by Him, from Him and to Him.' He Himself has said, 'He is the First, the Last, the Outward and the Inward, and He is cognizant of all things.' He has also said, 'Is it not sufficient as regards your Lord that He is a witness over all things? Now surely they are in doubt as to the meetings of their

Lord; now surely he encompasses all things.' The following verse
refers to this matter:

> Your beauty pervades all realities;
> Indeed it only veils Your majesty.
> It radiates to the universe from behind its veil.
> And by being covered is revealed.

It has also been said:

> My Beloved appeared radiant to me from every aspect
> And so I witnessed Him in every meaning and form.

The import of all these words is one and the same, namely the
affirmation that all things contain inherent paths of development
and specific modes of conduct. We have thus drawn the general
outlines of this subject and we shall now begin to describe these
in a more detailed manner.

Know that for every existing thing there are two courses of
development: that of form and that of inner meaning. As for the
progress and development of form with regard to matter, it extends up to the level of the plant world in the form of coral — in
the latter we see that matter possesses branches and leaves like
plants and trees. As for its progression in the realm of inner
meaning, it becomes, in one way or another, part of the human
body — I mean, for example, in the form of food, drink or
potions.

Progression in the realm of form in regard to plants extends
to the level of animals as, for example, in the case of the date-palm
which possesses — like animals — a tendency and inclination
for reproduction with another date palm by the force of the
affinity which exists between the two. There are other aspects
of the date palm which affirm this relationship to the animal
world, namely the fact that it the head of the palm is cut, then
the tree dies and if it is submerged in water, then it also dies,
as would animals under similar conditions. As for its progression
in the realm of inner meaning, it is that it becomes part of the
human body — by becoming food for man, for example.

Progression in the world of form in regard to animals extends to the level of man and acquires the faculty of speech as, for example, in the case of the monkey or the parrot. As for the progression in the realm of inner meaning, it is that it becomes part of the body of man by one means or another. Indeed the whole secret is contained herein: the perfection of all existing things below man is in their arrival at man and the perfection of man is in his arrival at the Real; thus the totality of the different worlds are directed towards man both in the realm of form and inner meaning — both with regard to the greater and lesser man — so that they may attain to their specific perfection prescribed from before eternity. Man himself is constantly aiming for the Real in order to attain to his specific perfection. The following *ayah* indicates this: 'And he has made what is in the heavens and what is in the earth subservient to you.' Yet a clearer indication of this meaning is expressed in the words addressed by Allah to the Prophet: 'If it were not for you, I would not have created the planets' and here what is being referred to is the whole cosmic system and all contained therein.

As for the progression of man in the realm of form, it is that he becomes angelic, thereby acquiring purification and elevation above the outer form which clothes him and above the baser aspects of his sensory natural attributes. As for his progression with respect to the inner meaning, it is that he attains to the rank of prophethood, messengership and sainthood, arriving thereby to the station of Pure Oneness, which is the elimination of duality and multiplicity leading to the all-embracing unity referred to by Allah when He says, 'Then he drew near, then he bowed, so he was the measure of two bows or closer still.'

As for the progression in the realm of form with respect to the jinn, it is that they attain to an angelic rank by rising above the earthly and by their glorification of Him. Most people believe that the jinn are earthly angels and that they are called jinn because they are hidden from people's sight. Allah Himself says when referring to Iblis (Satan): 'He was of the jinn, so he transgressed the commandment of his Lord.' Some people, however, believe that they possess forms of fire, that their abode is the sphere of ether and that they also have access to the sphere of water, air and earth by virtue of their quality of tremendous diffusiveness. In the development of the jinn with regard to the realm of inner meaning they attain to the rank of man and to human gnosis and they believe in the code of the *shari'ah* and the Qur'an; this is expressed in the Qur'an itself: 'Say it has been revealed to me that a party of the jinn listened and they said: "Surely we have heard a wonderful Qur'an, guiding to the right way, so we believe in it and we will not set up anyone with our Lord" '.

As for the development in the realm of form in regard to the angels, they attain to the rank of proximity, of glorification of Allah and holiness. They reach the rank of cherubim by Allah's raising them above the rest of the angels; in this way He separates one particular kind of angel from the rest, in the same manner as Gabriel and Michael are brought to prominence from amongst the rest of the angels, or as man is distinguished from the general species of animal. In their development in the realm of inner meaning they come to a perception of some of the secrets of man which the latter has received from Allah. These are secrets which are particular to man and not shared by the angels: this is referred to by Gabriel when he says, 'If I were to reach out with the tips of my fingers extended I would certainly have burnt them.' It is for this reason that the gnostic believes man to be greater and nobler than the angels: the angels have no share in the development which is particular to man, indeed, they have never tasted of man's secret in this respect.

We have now come to the end of our study of the various ranks of perfection with respect to each existent being, both of the highest and lowest orders of creation. If you have understood this science and have realised that man's perfection is of a higher and more noble rank than that of all other beings, then you should strive to attain your own perfection and to realise fully your own rank. You should avoid what is other than yourself, even if it is an angel, for being occupied with the rank of others prevents you from attaining your greater happiness and your highest rank: 'And all We relate to you of the accounts of the apostles is to strengthen your heart therewith; and in this has come to you the truth and admonition and a reminder to the believers;' and Allah is more Knowing and more Wise, He it is Who says the truth and guides to the correct path.

II
Roots

1

The First Foundation:

the five roots of religion, namely divine unity (*tawhid*), divine justice *('adl)*, prophethood, imamate and the events of the hereafter *(ma'ad)* according to the three degrees of *shari'ah, tariqah* and *haqiqah.*

Know that the aim of the prophets and *awliya'*, as we have already explained above on various occasions, is to convey each creational reality to its own specific perfection, in accordance with its capability and receptivity, and to elevate them above the darkness of their imperfection and ignorance through their own measure of striving and exertion. The prophets and the saints are aware that achievement of their aim is only feasible by a perfection of the twin forces of knowledge and action in the roots of the religion *(usul),* on the one hand, and in the branches *(furu'),* on the other. They establish the roots to purify their inward life and to perfect their system of belief, and they establish the branches to purify their outward life and to perfect their actions. They inform the people of the roots and branches of religion by the twin blessings of the outward and inward on the command and with the permission of Allah. Allah refers to this in His Book when he says, 'and made complete to you His favours outwardly and inwardly' and thereafter 'And if you count Allah's favours, you will not be able to number them;' thus the slave realises that the blessings bestowed upon him by Allah are innumerable, both in this world and the next.

The meaning of inner purification is the purification of the impurities of manifest and hidden *shirk* (associating other than Allah with Allah). The polishing of the mirror of the self from the rust of disbelief and misguided actions is only possible with correct belief in the unity of Allah, in His justice, in imamate and the final day of reckoning. This is indicated in the words of the prophet when he says, 'Islam has been built upon five (pillars)' and the words of Allah, 'Surely Allah does not forgive that anything be associated with Him and forgives what is besides that to whomsoever He pleases.' Both the words of Allah and those of the Prophet refer to the two kinds of *shirk* which stand diametrically opposed to the two kinds of *tawhid* — namely the divine unity and the unity of existence, (which will be described later). The five principles are based upon these two kinds of unity and upon purification from actual or assumed impurity, including the cleansing of the body. But this purification is only possible by means of the five branches, namely prayer, fasting, *zakat* (payment of the purifying tax), *hajj* (pilgrimage) and *jihad*. Hence the Prophet's words: 'Islam is built on cleanliness,' and the words of Allah: 'Surely Allah loves those who turn much to Him and He loves those who purify themselves.'

The Commander of the Faithful has explained the meaning of purification: 'Allah has imposed belief (on the Muslims) as a purification from idolatry *(shirk)*, the prayer as a way of freeing oneself from pride, *zakat* (the alms-tax) as a means of provision, fasting as a test of sincerity, *hajj* as an act of worship which brings one closer to the *din* (complete life-pattern) of Islam, the *jihad* as a glorification of Islam, the enjoining of good for the benefit of the common people, the forbidding of evil as a restriction on the foolish, the maintaining of good family relationships as a means of increase in numbers, retribution as a means of sparing people's blood, application of the punishments as a means of maintaining respect for what is forbidden, abstention from drinking wine as a protection for the intellect, withholding from theft as a means of preserving one's integrity, abstention from adultery as a means of maintaining and protecting good lineage, abstention from homosexuality in order that man may go on multiplying, death as a martyr *(shahid)* to overcome the perverse and the rebellious, abstention from lying as a means of revering the truth, peace as a heaven from whatever inspires fear, imamate as a way of establishing order within the nation of Muslims and obedience as a mark of respect for the Imams.'

Thus, anyone who wishes to purify the outward and the inward in the way outlined above should establish these roots and branches and all they imply, within the framework of the three levels of *shari'ah, tariqah* and *haqiqah*. The roots and branches of the people of each of these levels differs from the next — as we have already explained and shall further explain by God's will. Therefore, in the light of this, we must first define the roots and then the branches according to the way of the people of truth and reality; thereafter, we must investigate how they are both applied and define the pillars or the foundation of knowledge and action; we must then explain how they are both contained in the three above-mentioned levels.

2

An Investigation of the Roots:
according to the way of the people of truth

Know that there are great differences of opinion concerning this matter: some believe that the roots of faith are two in number, that is, affirmation of Allah and His Prophet and certainty of belief with regard to the laws (and the fact that the Prophet ruled by these laws), while the people known as the Ash'arites withhold affirmation of that about which there is disagreement and ambiguity. According to others, the roots of the faith are three in number: affirmation with the heart, the manifestation of this belief on the tongue, and the actions of the limbs — and this opinion is shared by some of the Shi'ahs. The Shi'ahs say that the roots of the faith are three in number: affirmation of the Oneness of Allah in His Essence and justice of His actions, affirmation of the prophethood of all the prophets, and the imamate of the infallible Imams. Other Shi'ahs believe that the number of the roots of the faith are four in number: divine unity, divine justice, prophethood and imamate. According to the Mu'tazalites, the roots of the faith are five in number: divine unity, divine justice, affirmation of prophethood, the promised reward and retribution, and the enjoining of good and the forbidding of evil. Some of the later Shi'ahs also believe this, although they express their belief in (slightly) different terms, namely that the roots of belief are five in number: divine unity, divine justice, prophethood, imamate and *al-ma'ad,* the resurrection and return of man to his Creator to face judgement. This is in fact the correct system of belief: it is what I prefer and what is preferred by most of the scholars of the people of Allah.

The one who possesses a correct system of belief and perfect faith must also believe in the unity of Allah so that he may free himself from associating others (or other things) with Allah. Moreover, as well as belief in His unity, he must also believe that He is Just and Wise, that He does not commit any hateful action and that He is not negligent in carrying out what is incumbent upon Him; by this belief he frees himself from fatalism and the attributing of good and bad actions to Allah, for any such notion would imply oppression of the slaves on the part of

Allah — may He be exalted above such a notion. He Himself has rejected this when He says, 'And your Lord is not in the least unjust to His servants.' As these two beliefs are dependent upon the existence of the Prophet and the manifestation of his miracle (namely the Qur'an, in order that false belief may be distinguished from correct belief), it is also necessary to believe in the prophet and his prophecy.

The claim of certain people that knowledge of the roots need not be based upon the evidence of the Qur'an and the body of traditions, but rather that it is enough to acquire knowledge of them by means of the intellect, is not true: if the intellect were sufficient in acquiring knowledge of Islam and its roots, every man of sane mind would acquire correct belief and this is not the case. We should not, however, despise the Brahmins and the philosophers who believe only in the validity of the intellect and so do not take into consideration what has been transmitted by narration (from revelation). The way of the dutiful Muslim is to know the roots by means of his intellectual faculty, after having established the truth of these roots from the (sayings of the) infallible Prophet or Imam. Moreover, it is not necessary that in doing so he incline towards the way of the Isma'ilis or any other group since this is the true and valid method, the way of the infallible Imams and the early scholars (although not the later scholars). On his death a prophet of necessity leaves his religion and *shari'ah* in the hands of a perfected and infallible Imam who preserves the *shari'ah* and establishes its pillars either by coercion, by giving guidance or by instruction. These are referred to as 'those in authority' — in Allah's words: 'Obey Allah and obey the Apostle and those in authority from among you.' It is also necessary to believe in the Imam, just as the prophet is a source of grace for the dutiful Muslim, so the Imam is also a source of grace. Moreover, just as the sending of the messenger and prophet is incumbent upon Allah, so too is the appointment and establishment of the Imam incumbent upon Him in the sense that if He did not appoint someone it would imply deficiency on His part. These two roots are dependent upon Allah, that is, His appointment of the Prophet and the Imam; comprehension of these two roots is by reference to the

Qur'an and the narrated traditions — and not by means of the intellect, as we have explained above.

There are numerous works on this subject, but it is not appropriate that we discuss the matter any further in this study. These works are to be found in particular in the sphere of theological debate *('ilm al-kalam)* about the nature of life after death in the section dealing with the roots of religion *(usul al-din)*. The whole of this topic is nothing but an expression of the prophetic reminder to man of the Day of Return, of guidance for man so as to know how to prepare for the day of standing (before Allah) and of news of the promised reward and punishment. Thus it is necessary for him also to believe in the Day of Return and all that it implies of reward and punishment, which may also be expressed as attainment of perfection, on the one hand, or deficiency, on the other; he must believe in this so that he does not neglect any part of the roots or principles (mentioned above) or the branches (to be explained later). The roots are confined to these five and the dutiful Muslim has no need of any more than these. Moreover it is not permissible that he base his worship on less than these, and Allah is more Knowing and more Wise — He it is Who says the truth and He it is Who guides to the correct path.

We shall now begin to comment upon each of these roots within the parameters of the three levels, namely *shari'ah, tariqah* and *haqiqah.*

3

Divine Unity *(tawhid)*

The science of divine unity, *tawhid*, despite its various divisions and types, may be contained within two general divisions: firstly, the *tawhid* of the prophets and secondly, the *tawhid* of the saints or friends of Allah. As for the *tawhid* of the prophets, it is a divine *tawhid* which is contained in the realm of common or general knowledge; it is therefore the *tawhid* which is concerned with the calling of men to the worship of an Absolute God and away from worship of a limited and dependent god; it is the *tawhid* of calling man to the affirmation of One God and the rejection of many gods. The first kind of *tawhid* is referred to in Allah's words: 'Say O followers of the Book! Come to an equitable proposition between us and you, that we shall not serve any but Allah and (that) we shall not associate aught with Him, and (that) some of us shall not take others for lords besides Allah' and also His words: 'What! Makes he the gods a single god? A strange thing is this to be sure! The second kind of *tawhid* is expressed in His words: 'Surely your Lord is One God' and 'So know that there is no god but Allah'; moreover, the phrase *la ilaha illa'llah* — there is no god but Allah — has the same meaning, that is, it is a rejection of many gods and an affirmation of One God. The words of the Prophet also testify to this: 'I have been commanded to fight the people until they say 'There is no god but Allah'; indeed these words express the perennial mission to mankind of the prophets and messengers from Adam to Muhammad.

As for the *tawhid* of the saints *(awliya')*, it is a *tawhid* of His existence and of the inward: it is a *tawhid* of the elite and calls man to witness Absolute (Existence which belongs to Allah) rather than to witness limited or dependent existences. In other words, it calls to the affirmation of the One Existent, the True, the Necessary of Existence — by His Essence — and to the negation of multiple existences which are only possible by His Essence and are at the same time, by their nature, doomed to non-existence. This is referred to by Allah's words: 'Everything is perishable but He; His is the judgement and to Him you shall be brought back' and also by His words: 'Everyone must pass away. And there will endure for ever the Person of your Lord, the Lord of glory and honour.' The words of all the gnostics also reflect the same truth: 'There is nothing in existence but Allah, His Names, His Attributes and His Actions. Thus everything is Him, by Him, from Him and to Him' — such is the call of the Saints and the Imams from Seth to the Mahdi.

There are no other kinds of *tawhid* besides these two because idolatry or polytheism *(shirk)*, which stands in opposition to it, is also confined to two kinds: that is, manifest and hidden *shirk*. A person may either outwardly or inwardly associate others with Allah: if he or she does so outwardly, as in the worship of idols, cult-objects, stones, earth, the sun or the moon then it is manifest *shirk*, since it is so conspicuous to the people of the world. This is referred to by Allah when He says, 'And they have taken besides Him gods, who do not create anything, for they themselves are created and they do not in themselves cause any harm or profit, and they control not death, nor life, nor raising (the dead).' This *shirk* is the antithesis of divine *tawhid*. If, however, he or she inwardly bears witness to the existence of other-then-Him and outwardly affirms this — witnessing contingent existences such as the intellect, the self (or soul), the planets and heavenly bodies, the elements, the various mineral, vegetable and animal kingdoms — then it is called hidden *shirk* because of its inconspicuousness; it is referred to by Allah when he says, 'O my two mates of the prison! Are sundry lords better or Allah the One, the Supreme? You do not serve besides Him but names which you have named, you and your fathers' Allah has not sent down any authority for them; judgement is only Allah's. He has commanded that you shall not serve aught but Him; this is the right religion but most people know it not.' This *shirk* is the antithesis of the *tawhid* of existence: there is no other *shirk* besides these two.

Know that the appearance of all the prophets and messengers is only for the purpose of calling mankind to the divine *tawhid* and freeing him from manifest *shirk*. The appearance of all the Saints and Imams is only for the purpose of calling man to a *tawhid* of existence and of ridding him of hidden *shirk*. All those who set out for the Absolute God, leaving behind the dependent or finite gods all those who turn from worship of the creation to worship of the Creator and who utter the words of divine *tawhid*, 'There is no god but Allah' free themselves from manifest *shirk*, become, according to the *shari'ah*, Muslims, who believe and affirm the Oneness of Allah. Moreover, both their outward and their inward aspects become purified of the impurity of manifest *shirk*. This is referred to in the words of Allah when He says, 'The idolaters are nothing but unclean.' If he does not do so then he is a *mushrik* — guilty of *shirk* — an unbeliever and impure both outwardly and inwardly.

All those who set out in the direction of the Absolute Existent leaving behind the dependent and finite existence, all those who turn from witnessing of the contingency of existence to a witnessing of the Necessary of Existence and who utter the formula of the the *tawhid* of existence, namely that there is nothing in existence but Allah, rid themselves of hidden *shirk* and truly affirm the Oneness of Allah; they become gnostics and men of spiritual realisation. Moreover, both their inward and outward aspects become purified of the impurity of hidden *shirk*. This is in accordance with the words of Allah, 'And most of them do not believe in Allah without associating others with Him.' If a person does not do this, then he is inwardly impure. Some scholars, however, would say that such a person is both outwardly and inwardly impure and their opinion is supported by the words of Allah: 'Surely Allah does not forgive that anything should be associated with Him and forgives what is besides that to whomever He pleases.' This judgement applies to man in general and not to a particular group: thus anyone who is a *mushrik* or idolater, irrespective of whether he is guilty of manifest or hidden *shirk*, will not be forgiven. But this is an extremely difficult matter to come to terms with for only very rarely will someone be able to free himself of both types of idolatry. Allah Himself says, 'And very few of My servants are grateful' and 'And very few are they.' It is for this reason that a gnostic has said: 'Freeing oneself from manifest *shirk* is easier that freeing oneself from hidden *shirk*. Similarly, arrival at divine *tawhid* is easier than arrival at the *tawhid* of existence. This is because the one who commits hidden *shirk* reckons himself to be among those who affirm the

Oneness of Allah — and he reckons this because of his affirmation of divine *tawhid*. At the same time, however, he overlooks the hidden *shirk* which is veiling him from Allah. The Prophet alludes to this when he says, 'The creatures of *shirk* from amongst my people are more hidden than the black creatures of the ant world crawling over a hard rock on a dark night.'

It is clear that hidden *shirk* is particular to the *mu'minun* (the believers) and the *muslimun* (those who have submitted to the will of God); it cannot be ascribed to the hypocrites and the unbelievers. Hence the words of Allah 'And most of them do not believe in Allah without associating others (with Him)'. Moreover, the Prophet must have intended to ascribe this kind of *shirk* to his people because manifest *shirk* cannot co-exist with faith. The Qur'an refers to hidden *shirk* as 'low desire' when Allah says, 'Have you then considered him who takes his low desire for his god and Allah has made him err having knowledge.' Allah thus causes him to go astray from the path of knowledge since a person becomes an unbeliever, an idolater and a hypocrite by way of his low desire; it has been said, 'If it were not for "low desire", idols would never have been worshipped.' It has also been said; 'No god, other than Allah, has ever been worshipped that is greater than one's base desire.' This is because the unbeliever tends to the religion of his fathers and forefathers by way of his low desire — becoming thereby one of the idolaters. They are referred to by Allah when He says, 'They say: "We found our fathers on a course and surely we are guided by their footsteps." '

We have presented the above principles by way of a brief introduction; we shall now begin a description of each of the different kinds of *tawhid* particular to each of the three groups.

i)   According to the people of *shari'ah*

This *tawhid* is divine *tawhid*, that is, the rejection of many gods and the affirmation of one God (or to express it in other terms the rejection of finite gods and the affirmation of the One Absolute God). This kind of *tawhid* may be divided into two kinds: one kind which is connected to those of *taqlid* (imitation of others more learned than they in matters of religion) from amongst the common or ignorant people, and a second kind which is connected to those of perception and intellectual reasoning from amongst the elite and the scholars.

As for the first group, their way is to believe that God is One, that He has no associate to His divinity and no rival or equal in existence, that there is nothing like Him and that He is the One Who hears and the One Who sees. They hold strongly to their belief, aware of Allah's words: 'If there had been in them any gods except Allah, they would both have certainly been in a state of disorder' and His words: 'Say He, Allah is One. Allah is He on Whom all depend. He begets not, nor is He begotten. And none is like Him.' They also believe that He is the Living, the Knower, the All-Powerful, the One Who hears, sees and wills, the Possessor of speech and that 'not the weight of an atom escapes His knowledge in the heavens or in the earth and He is Cognizant of all things.' They also believe that any gods other than Him are mere idols ('They do not in themselves cause any harm or profit and they control not death nor life') and that the worshippers of these idols are unbelievers, *mushrikun*, and cursed wherever they be found. They believe too that it is obligatory to stay well clear of any association with such persons both in this world and the next — as Allah Himself has commanded with His words: 'O you who believe! Do not take your fathers and your brothers for guardians if they love unbelief more than belief; and whoever of you takes them for a guardian, these it is that are the unjust' and by His words: 'You shall not find a people who believe in Allah and the latter day befriending those who act in opposition to Allah and His Apostle, even though they were their (own) fathers, or their sons, or their brothers, or their kinsfolk.' People who have such a system of belief live within the protection of Islam in this world, they are safe from themselves, secure in their wealth and in their honour; in the next world their return will be to the generosity and mercy of Allah — truly Allah is the Possessor of vast bounty.

The perfect shaykh Abu Isma'il al-Harawi has indicated this in his book called *Manazil al-Sa'irin:* 'There are three aspects of *tawhid,* the first being the *tawhid* of the common people: this *tawhid* is made valid by the profession of faith *(shahadah)*; the second kind is the *tawhid* of the elite which is established by means of the spiritual realities; the third kind is the *tawhid* which has its source in pre-creational reality and is the *tawhid* of the elite of the elite.'

As for the *tawhid* of imitation *(taqlid)*, it is to bear witness that there is no god but Allah, that He is One and has no associate, that He is One and 'He upon whom all depend. He begets not, nor is He begotten and none is like Him.' This is the manifest *tawhid* which rejects the greater *shirk;* by it is established the *qiblah* (the direction of Makkah faced while praying) and the inviolability of life and property; by it lives and property are spared and by it the House of Peace is made distinct from the House of Disbelief; by it the worship of ordinary Muslims is made valid — even if their action and belief is not based on proofs and reasoning.

As for the *tawhid* of reasoning, it is to establish the Oneness of God by intellectual proofs, showing that to admit of the existence of more than one god is logically inadmissible. If there were two independent gods in existence, then each would be distinct from the other by their essence, while sharing in each other's attributes: each would therefore be compounded of one part which separates and discriminates (from the other) and one part which joins and shares (with the other part). Any compound, however, is a contingency because it is in need of its own part and the part of something else; and if this is the case then it would mean that the Necessary of Existence was a contingent being and this is false, for of necessity He is the One God. The people of this group are of the station of the *tawhid* of proofs and scholarly research and not of the station of unity through actual experience. It would be true to say that they are aware of the truth by certain of its aspects only; they will be of the people who are saved (from the Fire) and who will enter the exterior Garden, as promised (to the believers) on the Day of Resurrection. This *tawhid* is called the *tawhid* of action because they demonstrate the (existence of the) Actor by the action and the Creator by the creation. They have no greater aim or destination but this, for such are the limits of their knowledge: 'They know the appearances of this world's life, but of the hereafter they are absolutely heedless.'

ii) According to the people of *tariqah*

After arrival at this *tawhid*, the people of this group bear witness with the eye of inner vision that God is One, that there is no other than Him in existence and that there is no other Actor but Him. This is referred to in their words, 'There is no Actor but Allah' and 'There is no Actor other than Him in existence.' The people of this group cease to look to the causes and the chain of events arising from such causes; they rely on Him with a true reliance; they hand over their affair to Him entirely; they are pleased with what comes to them from Him and they are content with it. Hence Allah says, 'Allah is well pleased with them and they are well pleased with Allah.' In this way they attain to the stations of reliance, of submission, of contentment and the like. Allah refers to this when He says: 'And whoever trusts in Allah, He is sufficient for him; surely Allah attains His purpose; Allah indeed has appointed a measure for everything.' In this way they arrive at the rank of the *tawhid* of attribute after the *tawhid* of action; by it they merit the station of the garden of attributes and the station of contentment — which is the highest station in the *tawhid* of attributes. Allah Himself says, 'And the best of all is Allah's goodly pleasure' and the Prophet refers to this with the words, 'Contentment is the greatest of Allah's doors.' Shaykh Abu Isma'il al-Harawi has also referred to this, saying: 'As for the second kind of *tawhid* — namely that which is established by truths and realities — it is the *tawhid* of the elite; it is the *tawhid* of the abandonment of manifest causes, rising above intellectual arguments. This means that there is no bearing of witness based on rational proof, there is no seeking of causes for one's reliance on Allah and no seeking of means in the attainment of one's salvation. Thus the people of this group witness the supremacy of the Real in His Power and Knowledge; they bear witness to His placing of all things in their rightful place, His connection to these things by their longing for Him, and His invisibility with respect to them by virtue of their form and structure. This *tawhid* lends to the inner knowledge of causes and the abandonment of the phenomenal world.

The difference between this kind of *tawhid* and that of the people of *shari'ah* is that that of the latter is a *tawhid* of factual knowledge belonging to the common people and the former is the *tawhid* of actual experience belonging to the elite. The first allows one to rid oneself of manifest *shirk* and the second of hidden *shirk* — which is the greater and more difficult of the two. As for the vast difference between this *tawhid* and the *tawhid* of the elite from amongst the people of Allah, it is that the *tawhid* particular to the people of *tariqah* is based on reliance, submission and contentment, together with the attainment of the corresponding stations, the taking on of the character of Allah and the adopting of His qualities. This way is connected to the *tawhid* of attributes and this way implies a Giver of attributes, an object which may be described as possessing those attributes and the attributes themselves. Yet this notion in turn denotes multiplicity, or rather it is multiplicity itself. In the same manner the multiplicity may be seen in the notion of the Relied upon and the one who relies, likewise in the One who is content with and the contented. It is clear that between multiplicity and *tawhid* there is a great distance.

The *tawhid* of the elite of the elite is based on total annihilation, complete extinction and a passing beyond all stations, levels and all manifestations of the contingent or phenomenal world, even beyond existence itself and all that it implies. This is referred to by their words: '*Tawhid* is the abandonment of anything which is extraneous (to His sole existence).' What a difference then between this kind of *tawhid* and that! What a difference between the one who continues by himself and the one who is annihilated in his Lord: 'That is Allah's grace; 'He grants it to Whom He pleases and Allah is the Lord of mighty grace.'

In His noble Book Allah also speaks about 'the knowledge of certainty', 'the source of certainty' and 'the truth of certainty', thus indicating thereby these three kinds of *tawhid*. And they are indicated by the terms 'submission', 'faith' and 'certainty' or the terms 'companions of the left', 'companions of the right' and 'those who strive (by their good deeds) for His proximity'. The

Prophet has also referred to the people of these different levels when he says, 'This world is forbidden to the people of the next and the next world is forbidden to the people of this and they are both forbidden the people of Allah.' This means that the station of *taqlid* has placed the people of the first group among the people of this world: they do not go beyond it because of the greed with which they seek after this world and because of their miserliness and cupidity with respect to the material comforts of this world. Moreover, it is well known that 'love of this world is the source of all wrong actions.' Thus it is correct to associate the people of this group with this world — for this is the reality of their situation. Allah refers to them saying, 'They know the appearances of this world's life, but of the hereafter they are absolutely heedless.'

The station of realisation, the spiritual rank and the *tawhid* of experience — a degree superior to that of mere factual knowledge — places the people of the second group amongst the people of the next world: they have gone beyond outward appearances, witnessing the object of their desire — as it actually is — by the eye of inward vision. This is referred to by Allah Who says: 'Say: this is My way: I call to Allah, I and those who follow Me being certain.'

As for the people of the third group, their station of annihilation, their rank of the inward within the inward, their membership of the elite of the elite and their *tawhid* of the essence places them among the people of Allah and His chosen ones. This is because they have gone beyond the outward and the inward; by this I mean the material and angelic worlds, the world of the unseen and that of witnessing, and they have arrived at the goal by the Essence of all things — which is the Real, the Truth. They witness Him by His light, in a manner befitting (His majesty), and, like the gnostic, they say, 'Praise to the One, whom no one reaches except by Him.' Likewise they would say, like the Prophet, 'I saw my Lord by my Lord' and 'I know my Lord by my Lord.' As Salman was of this station, the Prophet said of him, 'Surely the Garden yearns more strongly for Salman than Salman for the Garden;' this is because the Garden is of the next world and Salman is of the people of Allah, who are many ranks above the people of the Garden. Thus it is not surprising that he does not yearn after that which is lower than him, for to descend from something higher to something lower indicates imperfection. This is referred to by the Prophet when he says, 'The good actions of the righteous are the wrong actions of the intimate.'

iii) According to the people of *haqiqah*

The arrival of the people of Allah at the station of the two kinds of *tawhid* mentioned above means that they do not witness other-than-Allah in existence and that in reality they know no other but Him: this is because His existence is true and essential and the existence of other-than-Him is contingent, phenomenal and exposed to destruction at any moment. Allah refers to this in His words: 'Everything is perishable but He; His is the judgement and to Him shall you be brought back,' and His words: 'Everything on it must pass away. And there will endure forever the Person of your Lord, the Lord of glory and honour.' This destruction and disappearance is not dependent upon a particular time or period — as some of those who are veiled from these realities have claimed — rather it has always been happening from before endless-time and will continue to happen to eternity in exactly the same manner — just as the waves disappear back into the sea and the drops of rain dissolve into the ocean despite our intellectual conception of them as distinct entities since, in reality, the waves and droplets have absolutely no separate existence; the true existence is only that of the sea and the waves are in a state of self-destruction and disappearance. Such a notion is entirely rational and may be understood by every sane person, indeed, it is also a phenomenon that may be perceived by the senses of everyone. The following lines of verse also express this idea:

> The sea is as the sea of old; truly the action of the waves and the rivers
> Does not veil you from their real form, for the very forms therein are veils.

Thus, just as the one who realises that in reality there is no existence but that of the sea (the waves and raindrops being non-existent and time-bound and thus doomed to extinction and disappearance), will say that there is nothing in reality nor in outward manifestations but the sea, so he who witnesses the Real, the creation and the creational manifestations for what they actually are, he who realises that the creation and all phenomena are in fact non-existent (since at any moment they are doomed to destruction and disappearance), is also permitted to say that, in reality, there is no existence save that of the Real. This is the meaning of their words, 'The one who continues (in Allah) continues forever and the one of annihilation is still in a state of annihilation.' Allah refers to this when He says, 'Yet are they in doubt with regard to a new creation.'

According to the gnostic, contingent existence is maintained by the Spirit of the Merciful, by the input from real existence at every moment (into the manifest world of disappearing forms) and by a corresponding moment by moment acceptance of this existence (on the part of the existences of this world).

The reality of this contingent existence is difficult to comprehend for it is of an extremely subtle nature. Allah refers to this when He says, 'And you see the mountains, you think them to be solid, and they shall pass away as the passing away of the cloud.' Contingent existence may be understood from the way in which fruits grow bigger at every moment although the senses are not able to perceive this growth (likewise the imperceptible coming into being of the fruit, its existence prior to ripeness and its eventual disappearance from the tree). There is a similar likeness in the way water moves to form waves: at every moment they are also in a state of disappearance; moreover, others like them are simultaneously coming into being by the power of Allah and the perfection of His handiwork. Every time contingent existence is in need of continuing its outward existence the Real extends existence to it from the Spirit of Mercy such that its existence outweighs its non-existence; moreover, this existence is in accordance with its own essence and not with that of its causer or bringer into being. This bestowal of existence manifests to sensory perception in the disappearance one form, its subsequent transformation by nourishment and food into another, and by the faculty of breathing. As for the mineral world, the celestial spheres and the domain of the spirits, the intellect judges them to be of continued unbroken life by the predominance of the existence lent to them. Man's inner vision, however, judges every contingent existence to be a new creation at every moment. Thus, in the vision of the gnostic who witnesses the Real or existence as it actually is, there exists nothing but the Real Himself.

This vision of the Real is sometimes expressed as existence and sometimes as essence. This notion is lent support by the consensus of the gnostics who say, 'There is nothing in existence but Allah, His Names, His Attributes and His Actions; everything is Him, by Him, from Him and to Him.' On investigation we realise that this same meaning is expressed in the words of Allah, 'He is the First and the Last and the Ascendant (over all) and the Knower of hidden things, and He is Cognizant of all things' and His words, 'Is it not sufficient as regards your Lord that He is a witness over all things? Now surely they are in doubt as to the meeting of their Lord, now surely He encompasses all things.' In other words, the person or thing which encompasses is in no way separate from that which is encompassed and that which is encompassed is not separate from the encompasser. Allah emphasizes this when He says, 'Any way you turn there is the face of Allah;' by consensus the 'face' referred to here is the essence and thus we may read: 'Anywhere you turn in the contingent phenomenal world, there is His essence and His existence.' This is evident since the encompasser only encompasses by the presence of the thing encompassed — 'And Allah encompasses all things.'

The *tawhid* of action means the removal from one's vision of any actor or action, such that one arrives at the One True Actor, the Originator of all actions. In this way one establishes the intellect in the unity of action. The *tawhid* of attribute is an expression of the removal of every attribute and object possessed of attributes from one's vision until one arrives at the One True Possessor of attributes — the Originator of all attributes and objects possessed of attributes. In this way one establishes one's inner vision in the unity of attribute. As for the *tawhid* of essence, it is an expression for the removal of any essence or existence from one's sight, such that one arrives at the One Absolute Existence, the Pure and Immaculate Essence, that is the Bringer into existence of all existences and the source of all essences. In this way one establishes one's spiritual vision in the unity of existence and essence — becoming thereby a perfected gnostic, a man of realisation and arrival, at the station of abode and firmness, above which there is no station. This station is referred to in their words, 'There is no other village after Abadan.'

The Prophet has referred to these three kinds of *tawhid* in his supplication, which is well known to the elite and the common people: 'O Allah I seek refuge from Your punishment by Your mercy, I seek refuge from Your wrath by Your contentment and I seek refuge from You by You.' The first part of the supplication refers to the *tawhid* of action, the second to the *tawhid* of attribute and the third to the *tawhid* of essence. The people of this science have also divided *tawhid* into three types, calling the person of the first 'the possessor of intellect', the person of the second 'the possessor of sight' and the third 'the possessor of intellect and sight.' This is because the third gathers and comprises the other two and takes precedence over them.

We shall finish this study by mentioning another of the gnostic sayings, namely: 'The possessor of intellect is he who sees creation in a manifest way and the Truth in an inward way, the Truth being for him a mirror of creation: by the veiling of the mirror with the manifest pictures it contains, the Absolute is veiled by limited and dependent creation. The possessor of sight is the one who sees the Truth in a manifest way and the creation in an inward way. Thus for him creation is the mirror of the Truth: by the appearance of the Truth in creation and the disappearance of the creation in the Truth, the mirror disappears by means of the picture. The possessor of intellect and sight is the person who sees the Truth in creation and the creation in the Truth. He is veiled from neither of them by the other, rather from one aspect he actually sees the existence of the Inventor of existence in a real way and from another aspect he sees the creation; he is not veiled by multiplicity from witnessing the aspect of the

Inventor of existence, the One, and is not disturbed from witnessing, in the multiplicity of the creational manifestations, the Oneness of the Essence which emanates from them. The perfect shaykh Muhyi al-Din ibn 'Arabi says in the following verse:

> Thus in creation is truth itself, if you possess sight,
> And in the truth is creation itself, if you possess intellect.
> If you possess both sight and intellect, then you see
> Nothing therein but One thing, albeit in different forms.

Since, as we have already indicated, there is no station above this noble station Shaykh ibn 'Arabi has also said in his *Fusus*; 'If you have tasted of this, you have tasted the goal above which there is no other goal for those of creation. Thus do not hunger or tire yourself out in trying to rise higher than this level, for there is absolutely nothing above it: there is only pure non-existence after it — may Allah bestow upon us and you arrival at this station, by (the blessing of) Muhammad and his noble family.' We shall now conclude our description of the three kinds of *tawhid;* and Allah is more Knowing and more Wise; He it is Who says the truth and guides to the correct path.

4

The Justice of Allah ('adl)

What is meant by 'adl is that Allah is incapable of committing an offensive action and that He does not fail to fulfil that which is incumbent upon Him. Offensive action is any action for which the intellect feels revulsion and which is not consistent with its judgement of how something should be — actions such as lying, oppression and theft. The intellect of a sane man feels revulsion for these things and never judges them to be favourable courses of action. As we have seen above, it is incumbent upon Allah, since it is He Who has created man and imposed upon him specific duties, to send someone from Himself to teach man the nature of these duties and to guide him to the correct path. Allah affirms this when He says, 'Certainly Allah conferred a benefit upon the believers when He raised an Apostle from among themselves, reciting to them, and teaching them the Book and the wisdom, although before that they were surely in manifest error.' If this were not the case, it would imply that He was negligent in teaching whatever was necessary for correct performance of the duties; this in turn would contradict His purpose and it is impossible for the Wise, the Perfect to contradict His own purpose. Thus it was incumbent upon Him to send someone to mankind to teach them their duties that they might fulfil the purpose for which He had created them. This He affirms with the words, 'And I have not created the jinn and the men except that they should serve Me' and His words in a sacred hadith, 'I was a hidden treasure and I desired to be known: so I created the world.' This is what is known as lutf (divine grace or kindness), which we have already explained above: the slave comes closer to His grace by his obedience and is distanced from it by his disobedience.

According to most scholars, the question of what is good and what is bad is a matter for the intellect and is not dependent upon what is mentioned on the subject in the Qur'an and the Prophetic traditions (ahadith). Some, however, believe the opposite to be true, that is, that this matter depends on the judgement contained in the Qur'an and ahadith. Thus disagreement has arisen in this matter: the Mu'tazalites and their followers believe that it depends on the intellect and the Ash'arites and their followers believe that it depends on the Qur'an and the *ahadith*. In fact the Mu'tazalites are correct. The Qur'an and the *ahadith* have no influence in this matter: if it depended on the Qur'an, the *ahadith* and the code of the *shari'ah,* then the unbelievers and idol-worshippers would not be able to dinstinguish between good and bad conduct. In fact, however, truth is considered good and lying bad, justice is considered good and oppression bad — and likewise for the rest of the qualities admired or abhorred by the intellect. Moreover, most men of intellect agree that the question of good and bad is something which is judged to be so by the intellect and does not depend on the evidence of the Qur'an and *ahadith.*

The Mu'tazalites and their followers have provided irrefutable proofs of the validity of what we are saying. We shall mention them here so that the reader may decide for himself between the truth of our claim and theirs. What they say is that our purpose in the creation of Allah is to be just and upright; in this way Allah does not commit any bad action (by His intent) and does not fail in what is incumbent upon Him. When judging what is good or bad according to the dictates of the absolute intellect (or conscience), we may argue in the following way: Know that when anyone (who is responsible for what he does in terms of the *shari'ah*) performs any action of his own choice, then that action will either be disliked by the intellect or it will not; if the former is the case, then it is an obligatory action. Again with regard to the second, either the doer of the action merits praise or he does not; if he does, then this is a meritorious action. Again with regard to the second, either it is better to do the action or it is not; if the former is the case, then it is a good action. Again with regard to the second, either it is better to avoid doing the action or it is not; if the first is the case, then the action is disliked. Finally there are actions which are allowed. There are no actions performed by a Muslim which fall outside these classifications. Thus, on investigation, we are left in no doubt that our intellect is either repulsed by certain of our actions (like oppression, lying, idle jesting, and evil scheming) or it is attracted to them (like acts of gratitude for the Bestower of blessings, the quality of trustworthiness and the prompt repayment of debts). Moreover, knowledge of good and bad may be obtained by every person of sane intellect himself: he has no need of the law of the *shari'ah* or the Qur'an or the narrated *ahadith*. Even those who reject divinely inspired legal codes (like the unbelievers, the brahmins and the scholars of other religions) are aware of this distinction (between good and bad). Whoever denies the validity of this argument is both arrogant and ignorant and is not worthy of being spoken to (on this matter). We shall now begin to explain the question of divine justice with relation to the three levels.

i)   According to the people of *shari'ah*

All that is contained in this section may be expressed in the notion that Allah does not commit any action which is odious (to the intellect) and He does not fail in fulfilling what is incumbent upon Him. Since He is aware of what (action) is repulsive and what (action) odious, and since He is aware of His being elevated above any dependence on such action, His awareness always safeguards Him from such action. Moreover, nothing urges Him to such action because He is devoid of need and transcends such action. Therefore, since there is nothing to urge Him to such an action and yet there is something which prevents Him from such an action, it is impossible that such actions issue from the All-Powerful, from the One Who elects.

As it is established that Allah never commits any odious action and never fails in what is incumbent upon Him, the existence of dangerous animals, poisonous plants, noxious substances and other harmful things together with the curelty of certain animals without apparent reason in the world of created phenomena is all for the good; whenever any action of oppression, lying or corruption, for example, occurs in the world, then it is because of other-than-Him and not because of Him. He never wills anything which is odious; indeed, the very desire for something odious is odious. Allah refers to this when He says: 'And when they commit an indecency they say: We found our fathers doing this and Allah has enjoined it on us. Say: Surely Allah does not enjoin indecency. Do you say against Allah what you do not know? Say: "My Lord has enjoined justice", and raise up your faces at the time of the prayer and call on Him, being sincere to Him in obedience as He brought you forth in the beginning, so shall you also return. A part has He guided aright and (as for another) part, error is justly their due; surely they took the devils for guardians beside Allah and they think that they are followers of the right way.' This *ayah* is the best of proofs for the validity of what we are saying. Another *ayah* is further proof, namely: 'And if benefit comes to them, they say: "This is from Allah". And if misfortune befalls them, they say: "This is from you". Say: "All is from Allah", but what is the matter with these people that they do not make approach to understanding what is told (them)? Whatever benefit comes to you (O man!), it is from Allah, and whatever misfortune befalls you, it is from yourself, and We have sent you (O Prophet!) to mankind as an apostle and Allah is sufficient as a witness. Whoever obeys the Apostle, he indeed obeys Allah and whoever turns back, so We have not sent you as a keeper over them.' These words bear witness to the fact that bad actions issue from the slave of Allah, as do good actions, albeit with the accord and guidance of Allah; thus any praise or criticism falls on the slave and no other person. However we interpret this matter, there is nothing to suggest any injustice or actions of an odious nature on the part of Allah. It is this that is meant by *'adl* by the people of *shari'ah* — in accordance with the judgement of the intellect and the relevant sources within the Qur'an and *ahadith*. This is referred to by Allah when He says: 'Whoever does good, it is for his own soul and whoever does evil, it is against it, and your Lord is not the least unjust to His servants.'

ii)   According to the people of *tariqah*

The justice of the people of *tariqah* is attained after their firm conviction that Allah has bestowed upon every created thing certain rights, perfections, inherent qualities, instincts, states and actions — in accordance with what is just and harmonious and without injury, loss, imperfection or negligence. This must be so since He is the One of Absolute Generosity and as such He not only bestows generously upon those created beings that are in a state of receptivity but he does so in the most perfect manner. If this were not the case, then He would not be described as Generous. Allah refers to this when He says, 'Our Lord is He Who gave to everything its creation, then guided it to its goal' and also when He says, 'And He gives you of all that you ask Him; and if you count Allah's favours, you will not be able to number them.' Allah's blessings are beyond the bounds of number. Moreover, His words, 'Say nothing will afflict us save what Allah has ordained for us; He is our Patron; and on Allah let the believers rely,' clarify the meaning of the above; they also demonstrate again that any action issuing from Him is always in accordance with justice, wisdom and equity. Thus it is the duty of Allah's slave to trust and rely upon the actions or words issuing from Him: it is his duty to act only in accordance with His command directives and not to pay attention to any other. He Himself has said, 'Is not Allah sufficient for His servants?' and 'And whosoever trusts in Allah, He is sufficient for him; surely Allah attains His purpose; Allah has appointed a measure for everything.'

In this way the people of *tariqah* and gnosis become estabished in the station of firmness and constancy, that is, they attain the station of trust, submission and contentment: this station is referred to by Allah with the words, 'Allah confirms those who believe with the sure word in this world's life and in the hereafter.' The slave of such a station cannot transgress the bounds (of this station): he realises that the All-Wise, the Perfect in His Essence, the One Who is Cognizant of all things both past and to come, does not act but in accordance with His knowledge and wisdom and that nothing issues from Him which is in opposition to what actually happens; thus there is no alternative but to trust in and be content with one's own actions — be they good or bad — since this station is within the knowledge of Allah.

Allah indicates that the contentment of the slave results in the contentment of his Lord with him: '(as for) those who believe and do good, surely these are the best of men, their reward with their Lord is gardens of perpetuity beneath which rivers flow, abiding therein for ever; Allah is well pleased with them and they are well pleased with Him; that is for him who fears his

Lord.' Again Allah refers to those of this station of contentment, submission and trust free of concern for the past or the future or for the affairs of this world when He says, 'Now surely the friends of Allah — they shall have no fear nor shall they grieve.' Such persons are free of grief and regret for what has passed or fears for what is to come because they know that it is all within the knowledge of Lord and that He does not do anything but in the most appropriate manner. The Commander of the Faithful ('Ali) says in this respect, 'I have found all renunciation of the world *(zuhd)* in just two phrases from the Qur'an: "So that you may not grieve at what escaped you, nor be joyous at what He bestowed on you." '

The aim of the slave of Allah is thus to attain to an equilibrium in all states irrespective of whether these states be liked or disliked, easy to deal with or difficult. He ('Ali) has referred to this in a still more direct way with the words, 'Know with a certainty of knowledge that Allah does not bestow upon the slave more than that which has been allotted to him in His Wise Remembrance, irrespective of the intensity of his efforts, striving and cunning. Moreover, He does not prevent a slave from reaching what has been allotted to him in His Wise Remembrance, irrespective of the slave's weakness, or lack of cunning. Whoever is aware of this and acts by his knowledge will be among those who enjoy the greatest ease and benefit. As for the one who abandons this course of action or doubts its validity, then he will be among those most active in bringing about harm to themselves. Many a time it happens that one person is blessed with a continual flow of bounty and many a time another is afflicted with trial and hardship. Therefore, 'O you who enjoy benefits, increase your thanks, make less haste and be content when your provision comes to an end.' These words are conclusive evidence of the truth of all we have said on this subject. We have mentioned this saying in order to lend weight and clarity to the matter in hand and although we have used this quotation earlier on in the work, we feel justified in the repetition, given the variety of interpretations possible at the different levels of our investigation.

It has been narrated that Ibn 'Abbas has said: 'I was riding mounted behind the Prophet when he said to me: "O youth! O my son! shall I teach you some words (of wisdom) which Allah will cause to be of benefit to you?" I replied: "Yes, O Messenger of Allah." He said: "Take care (to be aware) of Allah and He will take care of you; be mindful of Allah and you will find Him in front of you; if you come close to Allah in times of ease, He will come close to you in times of hardship; if you ask for something, then ask for it of Allah and if you seek help, then seek help from Allah — for the (writing of the) Pen has dried concerning what is to be until the Day of Resurrection. Even if men wanted to favour you in a way which Allah had not decreed for you, they would not be able to and if they wanted to harm you in a way which Allah had not decreed for you, then they would not be able to. Thus work for Allah with gratitude and certainty and know that there is great good in being patient in the face of those things you dislike; know too that victory comes with patience and relief after trial and that with hardship comes ease." '

It is clear that no one will be able to attain to this station unless he becomes aware of what we have mentioned above: namely that Allah is cognizant of things before and after their coming into existence and that actions undertaken by Allah are in accordance with His knowledge and wisdom. It has also been narrated that one of the great companions Jabir ibn 'Abdullah al-Ansari, afflicted by weakness and frailty in his old age, was visited by Muhammad ibn 'Ali al-Baqir. The latter asked him about his state and he replied, 'I am welcoming old age after (the passing of) youth, illness after health and death after life.' Al-Baqir then said, 'As for myself, if Allah were to place old-age upon me, then I would love old-age; if, however, He were to place youth upon me, then I would love youth; if He were to cause me to be ill, I would love illness and if He cured me, then I would love the cure; if He caused me to die, I would love death and if He caused me to carry on living, I would love carrying on living.' When Jabir heard these words he kissed his face saying: 'The Messenger was right when he said to me: "Surely you will meet one of my sons, his name will be the same as mine; he will penetrate to the depth of knowledge, just as the ox cleaves the soil (while ploughing)." '¹ From these words we realise that

Jabir was of the station of patience and that Muhammad al-Baqir
was of the station of contentment: between these two stations
the difference is manifest.

In short, these stations are only attained by way of the slave's
knowledge that his Lord is aware of his state and the state of all
creatures from before endless-time until eternity and by the
slave's knowledge that He is just in His actions and states, elevated above oppression or transgression, whether it be against
Himself or others. This is as He Himself has said: 'Surely Allah
does not do any injustice to men, but men are injust to themselves.' If you have grasped this, then you should learn and
acquire this belief for yourselves, together with the accompanying
states mentioned above — and Allah is more Knowing and
more Wise; He it is Who says the truth and He guides to the
correct path.

iii) According to the people of *haqiqah*

This station occurs after firm establishment in the two above-
mentioned stations of justice. It is the station of knowing that
Allah is just in His bestowal of existent on every existant being
and that He is just in His bestowal of a behaviour-pattern and
certain attributes on these beings after ascertaining the essential
capacity and inherent receptivity of each. This is so because
every existent being, irrespective of whether it is assigned to the
phenomenal world or not, has a specificity and reality in the
knowledge of its Lord before it actually comes into outward
existence. If He were to bestow an existence which was in opposition to its nature, then He would be guilty of injustice. Such an
action is not permissible coming from Him, since He is just in
His actions and His speech and equitable in His bestowal of
withholding of anything as we have already mentioned. Thus it
is incumbent upon Him to give existence to every existent being
in a way which is concordant with the state of that being in
itself neither adding to nor detracting from that specific measure of existence. This then is true justice since justice is the

---

¹ It is for this reason that he is called al-Baqir — meaning literally the one who
cleaves or seeks out the knowledge of past and later generations.

placing of something in its rightful place.

Many things have been related with respect to this matter, for example: 'Say: "Every one acts according to his manner." ' These words of Allah mean that everyone acts according to his outward manner and physical form and these in turn are in accordance with his inward manner and his spiritual form. When David asked, 'O Lord, why have You created the creation?' He replied: 'For the very condition that they find themselves in,' meaning in the different states of receptivity and readiness. When seen in this light, one can understand why there is no one who raises his voice in objection to Allah and no one who demands to know why he has not been created in a different form. Each existent being knows that Allah could reply with the tongue of spiritual inspiration saying: 'I have not bestowed existence on you except in a measure concordant with your receptivity and your readiness and in accordance with your essence and substance, not in accordance with Myself. I am the Actor and you are the receiver, and receptivity is on the part of the one who receives, not on the part of the Actor. Rather your existence is in accordance with your own essence and receptivity; thus you are objecting to your own receptivity and readiness, not to Me: this is because the Actor has no influence over the one receiving, only over the measure of his receptivity. Now if you are aware that I am Cognizant of you, then (it should be remembered that) knowledge does not impinge upon what is known until the latter actually appears. Besides, conformity is a necessary condition in the relationship between knowledge and the known: this is so because knowledge follows from what is known, so what follows is not aware of that which precedes apart from being aware of that thing out of which it was created. Furthermore I am the Wise, the Just, the Knower and the Perfect, nothing issues from Me except in an aspect which is fitting. My words: "He cannot be questioned concerning what He does and they shall be questioned" demonstrate that I am the All-Knowing and the Wise and the actions of the All-Knowing and the Wise are not open to question, rather they will be questioned because of their ignorance of the truth and on account of their inability to place each thing in its correct place. If you, like Me, were cognizant of the realities of all things, both past and present, then you would not be of those whom are questioned about what they do. As for Myself, I am the All-Knowing, the Wise, the Perfect and as such it is not fitting at all that questions be asked as to My actions: this is because I do not do anything except in accordance with My knowledge and wisdom and in the manner which is most fitting. Thus it is that I have said: "Not a weight of an atom becomes absent from Him in the heavens or in the earth, and neither less than that nor greater, but (all) is in a clear book" and also "that is the decree of the Mighty, the Knowing." '

Thus we exhort the reader to reflect upon this matter for surely it will reveal to him all the secrets contained in the subject we are now considering. This is the highest of stations, there being no rank above it — and Allah is more Knowing and more Wise; He it is Who says the truth and guides to the correct path.

5

Prophethood

Prophethood is a term used to express the act of receiving the realities of gnosis and intellectual knowledge from Allah on the part of the Purified Soul by means of the essence of the First Intellect, known sometimes as Gabriel and sometimes as the Holy Spirit. It is also used to express the transmission of this gnosis and intellectual knowledge to those who listen and benefit thereby and to the followers of the prophets and messengers.

i) According to the people of *shari'ah*

The prophet is the man sent from Allah to His slaves: he is sent in order to perfect them by making them aware of the manner in which they need to worship Him and by teaching them about that which will safeguard them from any acts of disobedience. His prophethood is recognised by three things. The first is that he does not establish anything which is contrary to the rational workings of the intellect (like his saying, for example, that the Creator is more than one in number). The second is that he calls creation to obedience of Allah and to an abstention from acts of disobedience. The third is that, as a result of the call of the prophet, there appears a *mu'jizah* (miracle) and a corresponding challenge to his call. A *mu'jizah* is any action which breaks normal patterns and which ordinary human beings are incapable of performing and a challenge is that a prophet says to his people: 'If you do not accept my message, then such and such will happen to you;' his people then say exactly the same thing to him in disbelief of his message and they exhort him to do something that they may believe in his prophecy — like their calling on him to split the moon or make the stones speak. An (extraordinary) action which does not occur specifically in response to a challenge or a denial of a message (on the part of a prophet) is called a *karamah* — an act of wondrous proportions — and it belongs to the saints rather than the prophets.

The reason for sending a prophet or a messenger is because it becomes incumbent upon Allah — given His aim in bringing the slaves to their own specific perfection from before eternity in accordance with their essence and substance — to teach His slaves the manner of their duties and worship and the gnosis whereby they may attain to His purpose. We would clarify this by saying that Allah has, by their various sense faculties and physical strength and by their differences of judgement and opinion enabled them to commit evil action or righteous action. Thus it is incumbent upon Allah to send a prophet to them in order to direct them to the correct manner of behaviour and social contract (that is the code of the *shari'ah*). This *lutf* is incumbent upon Him as we have already mentioned above. Moreover, since Allah cannot be perceived by the senses, since not everyone has the power to receive this understanding from Him himself and since instruction of His slaves without an intermediary is not possible, it is incumbent upon Him to appoint a group of messengers as a connecting link between Himself and them. In this way the messengers take (instructions) from Him and deliver them to His slaves.

It is necessary too that the prophets or messengers who take on the pattern and qualities of Allah be infallible, that is, be free from any minor or major misdeed from the very beginning of their lives until the end. In this way, their words and actions gain the trust of the people. Thus it has been said that it is not permissible for the messengers to commit bad actions or to fail in their obligations, but that they still live in a manner which does not put them beyond the realm of free choice. In this way the intellect of the people are not alienated from them and they trust in that which is being brought by them as a kind of divine grace. This divine grace is an obligation on Allah and it is called (in this case) *'ismah* — or infallibility. No one sent from His Presence to the people will be believed unless he confronts opposition and challenges to his call with an action which breaks the normal patterns of reality. It is this that is known as *mu'jizah*, and by necessity it is incumbent (upon Allah) to make these miracles appear at the hand of the messengers. It is necessary so that their mission is not invalidated and so that they do not fail in the purpose which Allah has assigned for them. Allah refers to this when He says, 'Certainly Allah conferred a benefit upon the believers when He raised among them an Apostle from among themselves, reciting to them His communications and purifying them, and teaching them the Book and the wisdom, although before that they were surely in manifest error.' Such is the nature of this station with respect to the people of the *shari'ah*, and Allah is more Knowing and more Wise.

ii)   According to the people of *tariqah*

Prophethood for the people of the spiritual path means knowledge of the divine realities and secrets of Lordship. It may be divided into two types, the prophethood of instruction in knowledge and the prophethood of instruction in the code of laws. The first means a transmission of gnosis of the Essence, Names and Attributes, and the second means all of the aforesaid together with a transmission of the laws, inculcation of courtesy and moral behaviour, instruction of wisdom and the establishment of a political framework, which are covered by the term of *risalah* or divine message. We shall now comment upon this term in more detail.

Know that there is an outward and an inward aspect to the Real. The inward contains the Divine Solitude of Truth which is in the realm of the Absolute Unseen. Multiplicity is in the realm of knowledge and the pre-creational source-forms. The outward is always dependent on multiplicity and there is no way that it can free itself of this. This is because manifestation of the Names and Attributes is only possible when each is assigned its own particular form; thus, of necessity, multiplicity exists. Since each of these particular forms is seeking its own relevant manifestation, area of authority and code of law, there arises conflict and strife among these specific forms. For this reason a manifestation of wisdom and justice becomes necessary in the form of an arbiter to judge between them and to maintain order in this world and the next. The arbiter rules by its Lord (who is the Lord of all lords) over the various Names in a just way and brings each of the names to its own perfection, both in the realm of the outward and the inward. Such an arbiter is the Prophet of Reality, the Pole of pre-endless time, the first, the last. He is the Muhammadi reality mentioned by the Prophet Himself in his words: 'I was a prophet when Adam was (in a state) between water and clay', that is, in a state between knowledge and corporeal form.

As for the one who judges between the manifestations other than the Names, it is the prophet who attains to prophethood after his manifestation as the vicegerent of the Prophet of Reality. This prophet is sent to creation as a guide and a teacher who indicates the way to their perfection — a perfection which is prescribed beforehand with respect to each in the realm of knowledge and in accordance with the respective capacities of their pre-creational source-forms. This prophet is either one who brings and establishes a particular code of law or one from among the prophets of the tribe of Israel (who reaffirmed the already established code). The prophetic mission is an expression of the special treatment of man by God. This special relationship issues from Him by means of His revelation. This revelation is in the form of those divine emanations or unveilings which cause the bringing into being of the source-forms in the realm of knowledge; these emanations are also known as the most sacred divine outpourings. Since these outpourings, on becoming manifest, all seek by their nature to attain to the highest station — according to the natural law whereby things of like quality strive to outdo each other — Allah has elevated the rank of prophethood by means of the manifestation of miracles and supernatural events together with the corresponding challenge or opposition (from the opponents of the prophet) and has thus distinguished real prophethood from false prophethood. Thus the prophets are manifestations of the divine Essence by their authority over the other manifestations and by their standing in judgement between them.

Prophethood is particular to the realm of the outward; all prophets of necessity share the task of calling people to worship, guiding them and living among them. Prophethood is as a complete cycle which includes in it various finite cycles within the perfect enclosed space — like, for example, the *ulu'l-'azm* (those in authority) and the messengers and various prophets of the tribes of Israel within the enclosed dimensions which are not (in themselves) perfect. This then is the station of the people of *tariqah* with respect to prophethood, the message, the prophet and the messenger; and success is by Allah.

iii) According to the people of *haqiqah*

The station of this group occurs after establishment in the two above-mentioned stations. It is the rank of absolute divine caliphate, although it has different ranks according to the rank of the person who is the manifestation of this caliphate. We have already explained some aspects of these ranks and we shall now continue to comment upon the rest.

Know that the prophethood of this group is an expression of the good news or revelation from the divine: the prophet is the one who is informed of the Essence of Allah and of His Attributes, His Names, His laws and His wishes. The real and essential prophetic announcement is nothing other than that. The Greater Spirit was sent by Allah to the First Universal Soul and from there to the particular individual soul in order to inform it, in · the language of the intellect, of the Unity of Essence, the Attributes from before endless time, the divine Names, the illustrious laws and His revered will. Every prophet from Adam to Muhammad is a manifestation of the various manifestations of the prophethood of the Greater Spirit: the prophethood of the latter is essential and eternal; the prophethood of the various other manifestations is incidental and interrupted — except that of the prophethood of Muhammad whose prophethood is eternal and uninterrupted since his reality is the reality of the Greater Spirit and his form includes the various forms in which this reality manifests. The rest of the prophets manifest by means of some of the names and qualities: each manifestation is an emanation of one of the qualities, or one of the names, except that of the Muhammadi manifestation which emanates from the essence of the Greater Spirit and by means of all its qualities. Moreover, in this manifestation prophethood comes to a close. The Messenger, may Allah bless him and his family, preceded all the prophets with respect to the reality of prophethood, yet comes after them with respect to outward form. He himself has said: 'We are the last and the first' and also 'I was a prophet when Adam was (in a state) between water and clay.'

As for the description of the caliphate and the caliph, this has also been given in terms of the people of this station. When the authority of the eternal essence and that of the higher attributes demand an expansion of the divine kingdom and the unfurling of the banners of Lordship, it occurs by means of the manifestation of creational realities and their subsequent subjugation by the executing and management of (creational) affairs, by the maintenance of the various ranks of existence and the elevation of the stations of witnessing. The beginning of this whole affair issues from the original pre-creational Essence and is therefore far removed from creation because of the distance of the relationship between the might of original pre-creation and the abasement of the transient-contingent world. In order for all this to occur, the All-Wise commands a vicegerent to take His place in matters of action, governance, maintenance and care. This vicegerent possesses an aspect based in pre-creational existence whereby he gains assistance from the Real and an aspect in contingent creation whereby he is assisted by creation. Thus Allah makes him his vicegerent or deputy. He also invests him with the robe (the knowledge) of all His Names, empowers him by way of the authority of the caliphate with the governance of affairs and transfers rule of the people to him. He also hands over the execution of His commands within the spheres of His earthly kingdom and spiritual kingdoms and responsiblity for the subjugation of creation to His rule and dominion. He named man *insan* (from the Arabic word for human being, whose root implies intimacy and friendship) because of the possibility of intimacy between him and the rest of creation. He also placed in him, by virtue of His two names — the Outward and the Inward — an inner reality and an outward form which thereby enables him to act in both the earthly and spiritual worlds. His inner reality is the Greater Spirit and by it man merits the role of the caliphate: the First Intellect is his vizier and his interpreter and the Universal Soul his treasurer and bondsman; Universal Nature is his agent and the head of the natural forces. As for his outward form, it is the form of the world from the Throne to the surface of the earth together with all the simpler and compound elements contained therein. This outward form is also the Cosmic Man, referred to by the scholars when they say, 'The world is the greater man;' as for their words, 'Man is the microcosm,' they are here referring to man as an individual type and as the caliph of Allah on earth. As for the Cosmic Man, he is the Caliph of Allah in the heavens and the earth; the lesser man or microcosm is the selected copy of him, just as the son is the copy of the father.

The lesser man also has an inner reality and an outward form, the former being the individual spirit, the soul and the temperament and the latter a select copy of the form of the world: in it is contained in corresponding proportions every part of the world, be it of subtle or gross nature. Glory be to the One who made the whole in one of the parts. It has also been said: It is hardly something beyond belief if Allah were to gather the world in man — as a faithful reflection of the whole — and if he were to choose one particular person for this role. Indeed the forms of all persons result from the forms of Adam and Eve — and by this we imply that they too in turn have issued from the Greater Spirit and the Universal Soul. The Cosmic Man is a manifestation of the Evident Reality and the lesser man attains to this by the annihilation of his individuality and the obliteration of his dependent or limited nature. From this state it will then be correct for him to declare that which certain persons would find obscure:

> Even if I am known simply as Adam's son,
> Therein lies meaning for me, as witnessed by my forefathers.

The reader should pay particular attention to this point, for it is the source of many finer points which in turn lead to an understanding of many truths; and Allah says the truth and guides to the correct path. With this we conclude our study of prophethood and the message within the framework of the three levels; we shall now begin our investigation of imamate.

6

Imamate

In an absolute sense imamate refes to a religious governance which includes an exhortation to the common people to safeguard what is of benefit to them (with respect to their religion and their worldly affairs) and aims to protect them from that which might harm them.

i) According to the people of *shari'ah*

For the people of the *shari'ah* imamate is an obligatory matter both with respect to the intellect and in the light of the legal code, in the same way as prophethood is an obligatory matter for a person in a state of *fitrah* (the natural harmonious condition of man) and in the state of Islam, both from the point of view of the intellect and in the light of the narrated evidence. As for the obligation with regard to the intellect, it arises from the people's need of an Imam who is necessarily infallible and who preserves the laws of the *shari'ah* for them, exhorts them to respect these laws by means of the promised reward and the threatened torment, and who carries out the legally prescribed punishments in this world. This need is similar to their need for a prophet who discriminates between that which is permissible and that which is forbidden. Just as men were in need of the establishment of the *shari'ah* in the beginning, so they are also in need of its continued maintenance and preservation.

Likewise, if the sending of the prophet is a divine obligation — a necessary act of grace by the Deity and a necessary means of establishing certainty of faith — then so too is the establishment of the Imam: it is necessary so as not to invalidate Allah's proofs and demonstrations (which were made manifest originally by way of the prophetic message and revealed books). One may express this in another way by saying that the establishment of the Imam is a divine grace and grace is incumbent on Him. Thus the Muslim who chooses the way of obedience to the Imam possesses divine grace. If he does not choose this way, then there will be no grace for him, despite his firmness in both states;

moreover, by his choice of obedience, evil ceases to exist in his life. There is no doubt that when there exists a respected leader who unwaveringly carries out that which is necessary for correct governance, who aids the ignorant and the weak and treats the oppressed justly, then all corruption and injustice disappears (or at least the greater part of it). Thus it is necessary that his existence be full of grace just as others are full of such grace. We have said that this grace and kindness is incumbent upon Allah. If He were not full of grace, and the duties still remained in force then the dutybound Muslim would have no rational reason to comply: the Real would then be defeating His purpose and this is impossible with respect to Him. Since we have demonstrated the truth of the two premises, we have also shown that the establishment of the Imam is obligatory upon Allah — this with respect to the intellect and rational proofs.

If we now examine the narrated evidence, we may refer to Allah's words: 'O you who believe! Obey Allah and obey the Apostle and those in authority from among you.' These words may be used as proof — in the sense that Allah has commanded the Muslims to be obedient to those in authority, just as He has commanded to obedience of Himself and to His Messenger. If obedience to Himself and to His Messenger is obligatory, then obedience to 'those in authority' is likewise obligatory. Either this phrase refers to particular persons or it does not: the second of these two possibilities is invalid since, if it were true, then the term used would refer to all people and would thus be devoid of meaning. As for the first of the two, it either refers to all the nations of Muslims or to some of them. The first of these is necessarily false; the second stands and thus it must be that there exists within the nation of Muslims a particular infallible person, for whom it is not permissible to make mistakes and who is known as one of 'those in authority'.

We thus arrive at the point of our argument: that it is necessary that the imamate be an obligatory religious doctrine both with respect to the intellect and to the *shari'ah*. This, however, is in opposition to the majority of the Muslim nation. Most, because of their lack of understanding of religion and Islam, do not count imamate as one of the pillars of Islam. They claim that it is permissible for the person from 'those in authority' to be any person from among the sultans or kings of this world, even if they are known for their oppression and corruption. Moreover, this majority do not permit that this person be the infallible Imam from the family of the Prophet, despite the validity of the Imam's claim, supported as it is by textual evidence from the Qur'an and from the Messenger. They do not recognise that because 'those in authority' from among the sultans and kings rule by force and coercion, it is not then permitted for Allah to command His creation to absolute obedience of them: to command to obedience of an oppressor or evil person is in itself an act of oppression and evil, may Allah be exalted above such a notion. It is for this reason that the Imami sect believe that the prophet and the Imam must be infallible: if they were not, then the commanding of obedience to them would imply evil and oppression on the part of Allah, may Allah be elevated above such a description of Himself. We have clear evidence from both narrated sources and from the intellect that He is in a state of sanctity and holiness, far removed (from the impurities of creation).

It is necessary that the Imam be exempt of all wrong action, just as the prophet is infallible. This is so because the reason for the necessity of infallibility for the prophet and the Imam is one and the same: if the infallibility of the prophet is obligatory, then so too must the Imam be infallible; the reason for this has already been mentioned. It is necessary that the prophet be free of all wrong action, both minor and major, both before the beginning of his prophethood and after it (the question of whether an action is done knowingly or inadvertantly is therefore irrelevant); if he were permitted to commit wrong action, then the intellect would be repulsed from following him. Furthermore, it is not fitting that the Wise should make obedience necessary to someone disdained by the intellect. And the person who is known as being from 'those in authority' must be appointed and established in authority at the time of the Prophet — so the term is not applied to all: if the Imam were not appointed, then it would mean that Allah were deficient in that which was incumbent upon Him, as would the Prophet. Such a notion may not even be entertained according to the consensus of scholars. Indeed Allah has appointed him in clear terms when He says, 'Only Allah is your *Wali* and His Apostle and those who believe, those who keep the prayers and pay the poor-rate while they bow;' no other person but the Commander of the Faithful ('Ali) has given the poor-rate while bowing, according to the consensus of the commentators, thus it is he who is meant by 'those in authority' — by Allah's appointment of him and no other. Likewise, no others may become Imam but his infallible sons and progeny: infallibility is a condition of imamate and *wilayah* and there are no others but these who may be described as possessing infallibility, even according to their opponents. The Real has also indicated them when He says, 'Allah only desires to keep away uncleanliness from you, O people of the House! and the purify you a (thorough) purifying' and also His words, 'Then Allah will bring a people, he shall love them and they shall love Him, lowly before the believers, mighty against the unbelievers, they shall strive hard in Allah's way and shall not fear the censure of the censurer; this is Allah's grace, He gives it to who He pleases and Allah is Ample-giving, knowing.' These words refer specifically to the future and to no other time. Likewise His words: 'And we desired to bestow a favour upon those who were deemed weak in the land, and to make them the Imams and to make them the heirs:' none other than they merit the prophetic inheritance and divine gnoses. An indication of the truth of Allah's words is their weakness at the time of the Marwan and 'Abbasid dynasties and even up to the present day, in view of the number of their enemies and their lack of supporters. If the Mahdi did not fear his enemies, then it would be incumbent upon him to become manifest. If he were not to become manifest, then he would failing in his obligation; yet this is not possible as is explained in the books of theology.

Allah also mentions the Imams when he says: 'Surely Allah has bought of the believers their persons and their property for this, that they shall have the Garden; they fight in Allah's way, so they slay and are slain; a promise which is binding on Him in the Torah and the Gospel and the Qur'an; and who is more faithful to his covenant than Allah? Rejoice therefore in the pledge which you have made; and that is the mighty achievement. They who turn to Allah, who serve (Him), who praise (Him), who ·fast, who bow down, who prostrate themselves, who enjoin what is good and forbid what is evil, and who keep the limits of Allah; and give good news to the believers.' On examination we realise that the qualities referred to belong to no others but the Imams. There are numerous examples of this in the Qur'an and the body of Prophetic traditions and the reader should look for them in the appropriate places. Allah it is Who says the Truth and guides to the correct path.

ii)   According to the people of *tariqah*

According to the people of this station, imamate refers to the caliphate which issues from Allah and the Pole of the Age. The Imam is the possessor of that caliphate and is called the *wali*. There are two types of *wali*: there is the *wali* whose *wilayah* (governance) is real and essential and which issues from before endless-time, as such he is called the Absolute Wali; he is the Greater Pole. The other kind is he whose *wilayah* draws its power from the Absolute Wali, by this I mean an acquired *wilayah,* received by inheritance and incidental (with respect to the absolute): the *wali* of such a *wilayah* is called the dependent *wali*; he is the Imam or the caliph. Both types are dependent upon our Prophet and upon whoever of the people of His House inherits from him — that is the Commander of the Faithful and his progeny. In the light of this we may say that this station is recognised by three signs: the first, the designation of *wilayah,* the second, the appointment of the Absolute Wali and the third, the appointment of the dependent *wali*.

As for the first, *wilayah* is the act of living among created beings after annihilation in the Real and subsistence in Him: in reality, it is nothing but the inward dimension of prophethood whose outward manifestation is the bringing of news and whose inward is their imposition of the laws. Prophethood is sealed, since there are no new tidings from Allah and no prophet after Muhammad. Only *wilayah* continues among men until eternity; the souls of the *awliya'* (plural of *wali*) from the people of Muhammad are the bearers of responsibility for the execution of the *wilayah*; thus *wilayah*

is executed by them in creation until the Final Day or rather, forever without end. An indication of the authenticity of the *wali*
is that he outwardly confirms with the Prophet: both derive their
pattern of behaviour from one source, the *wali* being a manifestation of the behaviour of the Prophet. Some have spoken of
themselves as having the qualities of a prophet in a poetic sense:
they see themselves as descending upon the station of the prophet
in a divine way; thus Ibn al-Farid has said:

> I was sent from myself as a messenger to myself
> And my essence testified to myself by my signs.

Prophethood, in the exoteric sense, is a cycle which is composed
of a line of points marking the lives of the prophets. This line is
perfected by the Muhammadi point, since prophethood is like a
wall of bricks which is completed, except that it needs one more
brick, that brick being the appearance of the Prophet Muhammad. In a similar way *wilayah,* in the exoteric sense, is also a
cycle composed of a line of points marking the lives of the *awliya':*
this line is completed by the point which seals the *wilayah,* namely
the existence of Muhammad ibn al-Hasan, the master of the age,
also known as the Mahdi. One of the gnostics, after demonstrat-
ing the truth of this by means of the intellect, the Prophetic
sayings and unveilings, says, 'The station of the Greater Pole is
the rank of the pole of the poles and it corresponds to the inward
aspect of the prophethood of Muhammad; it does not exist but
by inheritance from him and by the fact that Muhammad is the
perfection (of the prophetic cycle). The seal of the *wilayah* and
the pole of the poles do not exist but by the inward aspect of
the seal of prophethood.' The same gnostic has also said, 'The
seal of prophethood is the person by whom Allah has sealed
prophethood: it is one person alone, namely our Prophet Muhammad. The matter is similar in the case of the seal of *wilayah:* by
it the good of this world and the next is brought to final perfection;
with his death the order of this world is plunged into disorder.
He is the Mahdi, whose return is promised for the end of time.'
Another aspect of the *wilayah* of the *wali* has also been described
in the following way: '*Wilayah* is the establishment of the slave

by means of the Real after annihilation of the self. This takes place by the turning of the Real to him and by His bringing him to the furthest station of intimacy and certainty. The *wali* is the person whose affairs have been taken over by the Real, Who safeguards him from disobedient action and does not leave him nor his soul until He brings him to the highest perfection in the realm of man.' Allah has said, 'And He befriends the good' and also, 'Thou art my guardian in this world and the hereafter. Make me die a Muslim and join me with the good.'

The Shaykh al-A'zam (Ibn 'Arabi) has divided the subject of *wilayah* into different sections; his own words on the matter provide a clearer description than any other: 'Know that *wilayah* may be divided into absolute and dependent *wilayah*, in other words common *wilayah* and *wilayah* of the elite. If we consider *wilayah* with respect to itself, then it is a divine attribute in an absolute sense; if we consider it as being related to the prophets and the *awliya'*, then it is dependent. Moreover, the dependent is fortified and given validity by the absolute and the absolute finds manifestation in the dependent: thus the *wilayah* of all the prophets and the *awliya'* is part of the absolute *wilayah*, just as the prophethood of the prophets is part of the absolute prophethood. Since absolute prophethood from the outset is particular to Muhammad and his reality, and this is a continuation of the original reality particular to the prophets and the messengers from Adam to Jesus (who are in fact different manifestations of the Muhammadi reality), so absolute *wilayah* is particular to 'Ali ibn Abi Talib and to his reality (by way of the essential and inherited spiritual legacy from pre-eternity) and thereafter (by way of a continuation of the original reality) to his infallible progeny. This spiritual line extends until Allah seals it with the Mahdi.'

The reason why 'Ali is singled out for the absolute *wilayah* may be found in the saying of the Prophet related with an authentic chain of narration by Akhtab Khawarazam and Ahmad ibn Hanbal, they being amongst the most eminent and trusted of the jurists *(fuqaha')* and narrators respected by the majority of the Muslims, 'Allah has created my soul and the soul of 'Ali ibn Abi Talib a thousand thousand years before He created Adam.'

Shaykh Muhyi al-Din ibn 'Arabi also refers to the Prophet after a long study of the matter in this *Futuhat*: 'He was the lord of the whole world and the first manifestation in existence; his existence was from the divine light, motes of dust and the Universal Truth; his very being came into being in these motes of dust as did the world in its entirety; the closest person to him was 'Ali ibn Abi Talib, the secret embracement of the secret of all the prophets.'

As for the second and the third of the above-mentioned divisions, that is, the appointment of the absolute seal of the *awliya'* by means of the absolute *wilayah* and the appointment of the seal of the dependent *awliya'* by dependent *wilayah*, these will be explained in the following chapter. It is thus necessary to recapitulate: the *wali* and the Imam according to the people of *tariqah* are the dependent *wali* and the Imam who follows the absolute *wali;* moreover, according to them, the prophet is both the dependent prophet and the messenger who follows the absolute prophet. Thus we reach the aim of this study, namely to establish the inter-relationship of the rank of prophethood with the rank of *wilayah* and the rank of the absolute with that of the dependent; and Allah is more Knowing and more-Wise — He it is Who says the truth and guides to the right path.

iii) According to the people of *haqiqah*

According to this group the Imam and the *wali* are the Great Imam and the Absolute Wali, also known as the Pole and the Imam of the Imams who is responsible for the ordering of existence, the establishing of the *shari'ah, tariqah* and *haqiqah*. The ranks of all, from the prophet, the messenger and the *wali* have their source in him. Shaykh al-A'zam (Ibn 'Arabi) has referred to him in his *Fusus:* 'This knowledge only belongs to the Seal of the Messengers and the Seal of the Saints *(khatim al-awliya');* none of the prophets or messengers imbibe it anywhere else than in the niche of the messenger who is their Seal. Again, none of the saints imbibe it elsewhere than in the niche of the saint who is their seal; indeed even the messengers only imbibe it, in so far as they do imbibe it, from the niche of the Seal of the Saints.'

Risalah — messengership — and prophethood (by this I mean the prophethood which is concerned with the establishment of the *shari'ah* and the corresponding message or calling of the people) are interrupted; *wilayah*, however, is never interrupted. Thus those sent as bearers of the message, being by nature saints *(awliya')*, do not imbibe this knowledge except from the niche of the Seal of the Saints or Walis. It is not surprising that those of the Saints beneath them imbibe less, despite the fact that, with respect to governance and judgement, the Seal of the Walis follows the *shari'ah* — namely that which is brought by the Seal of the Messengers. This does not imply any criticism of his station and does not contradict what we have been describing: from one point of view he is inferior and from another superior.

Thus he (Ibn 'Arabi) continues after a few words by saying: 'All prophets, without exception, since Adam to the last, take from the niche of the Seal of the Prophets: even if the clay of the latter was formed after them, he is no less present by his spiritual reality. It is for this reason that it has been said: "He it is Who bestows on all the prophets, messengers and saints, their stations in the world of light, the world of the souls and the world of forms." Hence the saying of the Prophet, "I was a Prophet when Adam was still in a state between water and clay" means that Adam and all the prophets were only prophets at the time of their mission. In the same way, the Seal of the Saints was a *wali* 'when Adam was still in a state between water and clay;' whereas other saints only became saints after having realised the conditions of saintliness *(wilayah)*, that is, when they had assimilated the divine qualities of Allah expressed in this Names, the Saint *(al-Wali)*, the Adored. Thus the relationship of the Seal of the Messengers to the Seal of the Saints is similar to that of the saints and the messengers with respect to him: he is simultaneously the saint *(wali)*, the messenger and the prophet. As for the Seal of the Saints *(awliya')*, he is the saint, the heir, who imbibes his strength from the source; he is the one who contemptlates all ranks, this contemplation being just one of the good qualities from among the bounty and blessings of the Seal of the Messengers, Muhammad, the leader of this group, the lord of the progeny of Adam and the one responsible for the task of mediation (on the Final Day).'

These words, occurring as they do after his demonstration of the existence of the Seal of the Saints and the truth of all that we have said on the matter, show that the absolute Seal of the Saints, is the Commander of the Faithful 'Ali: he is described with the same good qualities ascribed to the Lord of the Messengers. Such qualities as are mentioned by the commentator of the *Fusus* with respect to the Lord of the Messengers can only be ascribed to him. As we have now concluded our investigation of imamate with respect to the three levels, then we shall now begin our study of *ma'ad*, namely the last of the five principles outlined above; and success is by Allah.

7

Events of the Hereafter *(maʿad)*

Know that the Day of Judgement, in an absolute sense, denotes the return of the world and all contained therein to whence it came. This return is both with respect to the form and the inner meaning or spirit and also in relation to the three different levels of resurrection — that is the minor, the intermediary and the final. Moreover, they all take place at either a cosmic or an individual dimension; all told this amounts to a total of twelve separate days of resurrection, both with respect to the form and the inner meaning and containing the minor intermediate and final levels. This is arranged such that there are three days of resurrection of form and three of spirit with respect to the cosmic dimension; this is repeated with respect to the individual dimension and there is thus of necessity twelve days of resurrection in all. We shall now explain each in brief, as there is not space to go into more detail.

i) According to the people of *shariʿah*

According to the people of this group, the Day of Judgement is a term for the gathering together of the parts of the dead body, their recomposition into their previous form and the return of the soul to this body. This is also referred to as the assembling of the bodies (into one place). Such a thing is possible and Allah is capable of doing all possible things and is also cognizant of them; moreover, the body is capable of recomposition and so therefore He is capable of this — and this is the point of our argument. This point is based on rational premises: they are that Allah has created man and has bestowed knowledge, power, will, perception and various other capabilities upon him. He has also placed the reins of choice in his hands and has imposed upon him difficult duties; He has singled him out by His grace and blessings — both of a hidden and manifest nature — for a purpose related to this grace and these blessings. Since this world is the abode of hardship, it is also the abode of gain and acquisition, and He causes man to live therein for a length of time which allows him to attain his own perfection. He then goes to the abode of punishment and reward, known as the hereafter. All the prophets have given news of the gathering of the bodies — and this for the benefit of all. This news must be true by virtue of their infallibility and the impossibility of their telling any lies. Likewise the Garden and the Fire, which are both experienced by physical sensations and which they promise are to come, are true. They are true because they are possible and because there is trustworthy news of their coming.

Some have said that the return of something (essentially) non-existent is impossible: if this were so, if would imply entry into and disturbance of the one existence and would mean that the one was in fact two. To this the scholars (of this station) have replied: 'Since the gathering of the bodies is true, it is necessary that no part of the body or the souls of the Muslims become non-existent; rather they change their composition and nature. The passing away referred to by Allah in "Everyone on it must pass away and there will endure for ever the Person of your Lord, the Lord of glory and honour" is referring to this in a metaphorical way.' Some have also said that the reality of man is incidental or phenomenal, and to this they have replied, 'If man were an incidental-phenomenal existence, he would need a place which took on his qualities. Nothing, however, takes on the qualities of man of necessity, rather, he takes on the qualities of things other than him.' Thus he is an essence; if he were merely a body or some part of its limbs, then he would not be able to take on the qualities of knowledge. He does however of necessity take on these qualities of knowledge: he is an essence, possessed of knowledge, and the body and the rest of the limbs are the instruments of his actions. This essence is what is known as the soul in the divine *shari'ah;* it must be added, however, that there is a great difference of opinion with regard to this matter.

The Dahriyyah (whose god may be said to be Time) reject this belief and claim that man becomes non-existent at the time of his death and say that there is no return to existence for him. Those who say that the non-existent is actually something say that he becomes non-existent when he dies and then he returns to existence, whence he is either punished or rewarded. His non-existence is referred to by Allah with his words: 'Everyone on it will pass away;' as for his return and his inevitable reward and punishment in the hereafter, this is referred to in numerous places in the Generous Qur'an. But those who reject the belief that his being is corporeal say, 'His extinction and annihilation express the disintegration of the parts and evanescence of the limbs as a composite form and the return of all the parts of the body and all the bodily functions present before death.' This latter is the true statement from amongst the above-mentioned statements. Those who believe in the existence of the original parts and their necessary recomposition after a change in state and that the self is a simple essence are nearer to the truth than others since they free themselves of all ambiguity and contentious belief.

Most of these arguments have been taken from the works of Khawaja Nasir al-Din al-Tusi, from those sections dealing with the roots of the religion and other sections. In the course of his writings, he mentions the dubious nature of the beliefs of the philosophers. We shall conclude our study with his reply to those philosophers, who claim that the resurrection of the body is an impossibility: 'They argue that when the constitution of each body attains to a balanced harmony and is prepared, then it has a right to receive the emanations of the soul of the active intelligence; they claim that if the parts of the dead body take on the qualities of harmoney and disposition, they therefore have a right to a self or soul from the intellect and that its first self or soul would also be returned to him. This would imply the joining of two selves or souls in one body and that is impossible.' We too would reply to this that since we have established the existence of an Actor Who chooses of His own free will, we thus invalidate the very basis of the argument and we have no need to reply to this foolish talk; and Allah says the truth and guides to the correct path.

ii) According to the people of *tariqah*

Those of this group, as well as believing in the Day of Judgement

as mentioned above, understand it to be an expression of the
return of the manifestation of some of the Names to the manifestation of other Names; this is referred to in Allah's words: 'The
day on which We will gather those who guard (against evil) to
the Beneficent God to receive honours.'

Know that the Day of Resurrection, the Day of Final Return
is, as a general principle, an expression of the manifestation of
the Real in the form of the two Names, the Inward and the Last,
together with other Names such as the Just, the Real, the One
who brings to life and the One who brings death. The world
and the beginning of creation are expressions of His manifestations in the form of the two Names of the Outward and the First
together with the other Names such as the Bringer into being,
the Bringer into existence, the Creator and the Provider. In this
way He fulfils the claims of each of His never-ending Names.
His manifestation in an absolute sense by way of the forms of
the Names — which are also known by such terms as 'the creation' and 'the world' — is indicated in His words: 'I was a
hidden treasure and I desired to be known so I created the
world.' These words refer also to the fulfilment of the claims and
rights of each of His Names.

It has been established by the people of Allah and their elite
that when each of the individual and particular manifestations
of His Names is taken into account, then they are endless; if,
however, His Names are considered according to general kinds
and types of manifestation, then they are finite in nature. Of
necessity Allah is constantly manifest in the outward forms of
His Names and Attributes, irrespective of whether these be in
relation to this world or the next. It is for this reason that some
of the gnostics believe that this life and the hereafter are two
manifestations from amongst the rest of His manifestations; thus
it must be that they are constantly actual and 'happening', rather
than fixed and static at a particular time or period. It is impossible
to separate these manifestations from existence: this means that
resurrection on the Day of Judgement is an expression for the
constantly changing state of the exterior world and its constant
return to the interior world — just as this world is an expression
for the constant appearance of the inward by means of the out-

ward and likewise its continual return. Although the Names are many in number, they are all governed by just four: 'He is the First and the Last and the Outward and the Inward.' The First and the Last and all the related Names are associated with this world, and the various levels of beginning, the Inward and the Last and all the related names are associated with the hereafter and the various levels of ending.

This notion is permissible from one point of view, but not from another. The truth of this matter is that each of Allah's Names has specific laws and 'exigencies': thus, for example, the hereafter is a necessary implication of the Names the Subduer, the Alone, the One, the Eternal, the Single, the One who causes to return, the One who obliterates and the One who causes death. Similarly, this world is a necessary implication of the Name the Outward, the Originator, the First and the Bringer into existence. Each, however, on investigation is the same as the other, the difference being in their sphere of influence.

Allah, the Real — may His remembrance be made more splendid by this beginning and return, by the outward manifestation and inner dimensions, by the ascent and the descent, by the multiplicity and singularity, by this world and the hereafter — has talked about the Divine Command on various occasions in the Generous Qur'an. On one of these occasions He says, 'He regulates everything from heaven to the earth; then shall it ascend to Him in a day the measure of which is one thousand years' and on another, He says, 'To Him ascend the angels and the Spirit in a day the measure of which is fifty thousand years.' These numbers may be worked out in accordance with mathematical calculations such that the orbits of the planets are seven in number, some (of these orbits) being shared with others and some single and alone. For those single and alone, the orbit for each of the planets is one thousand years and for those shared with others, the span is seven thousand years: seven times seven is forty-nine — a figure which is completed by addition to it of the leap years, which amount during this period to one thousand years, to make fifty thousand years exactly. This latter is called the Greater Day of Resurrection; the seven particular to each of the individual stars is the intermediate resurrection; and the special span of a thousand years refers, in particular, to the Minor Day of Resurrection.

If you have understood this, then know too that the purpose of these investigations is to demonstrate that Allah has described the Divine Command governing the ascent, descent, appearance and disappearance, the bringing into being and the return to creation of all these cosmic phenomena in His words, 'Allah is He Who created seven heavens, and of the earth the like of them; the decree continues to descend among them, that you may know that Allah has power over all things and Allah indeed encompasses all things in (His) knowledge' and also in His words, 'Allah is He Who raised the heavens without any pillars that you see and He is firm in power and He made the sun and the moon subservient (to you); each one pursues its course to an appointed time; He regulates the affair, making clear the signs that you may be certain of meeting your Lord.' The decree and the affair (referred to in these two *ayat*) are always under His control because this world and the hereafter are two manifestations from amongst the totality of manifestations. Like the numerical relationship between a hundred or a thousand and the number one, the latter appearing in both the former, the number a thousand or a hundred count as some of the 'greater manifestations' of the number one. However, although the one is fully contained in each of the numbers as a whole, it is not contained when counted as a separate entity; in this case it is never ending and extends both forwards and backwards for ever and ever. The Real and His manifestations are similar because although this world and the next are among His 'greater manifestations', they do not contain all His manifestations. When seen in relation to these two manifestations (and others like them), then His manifestations are contained therein in a general way; when, however, we treat each of His manifestations in an individual way, then they are seen to be never-ending and continuing to eternity.

Whichever way we look at it, it must be that the manifestation returns to the outward in the countless abodes encompassed by this world and the next: this, in reality, is the *ma'ad* and no other; by this I mean the return of the manifestations to the outward and the encompassing to the encompassed. Allah refers to this with the words 'the ordinance' and 'the state': 'That is the ordinance of the Mighty, the Knowing' and 'Every moment He manifests Himself in a different state (of glory).' By these words Allah is indicating that every day of His 'divine' days — each lasting fifty thousand years, or every day of the days of this world, each lasting seven thousand years — He is occupied by this state or ordinance. In other words, He is occupied with fulfilling the 'rights' and 'claims' of each of His Names by means of one of His manifestations or one of His ranks in the various abodes of descent and ascent and stations of appearance and disappearance; this is so since the cosmos and whatever occurs therein are never-ending manifestations of actions, and actions are manifestations of the Attributes, and Attributes are manifestations of Names, and the Names are manifestations of the Essence and its essential Perfections.

Since it has been established that the actions, Attributes, Names and Perfections are never-ending, it may also be established that the return of these manifestations is also never-ending — that is, from the individual rather than the universal point of view. If, for example, the individual manifestion returns to the totality of manifestations or the compound returns to the state of simple elements, the return of the part to the whole and the compound to the simple element is permissible a second time without presupposing any idea of infinite pre-existence with respect to any phenomenal or incidental occurrences in the realm of the possible, or without presupposing any inconsistency in the laws of the *shari'ah*, or with respect to the Quran or *ahadith*. The amalgamation of some of the Names into others or some of the manifestations into others does not in any way cause this to happen: the One who goes on goes on for ever and the One in annihilation is still in a state of annihilation. In Allah's words, 'Most surely there is a reminder in this for him who has a heart or he who gives ear and is a witness' and his words, 'This is a day on which the people shall be gathered together and this is a day that shall be witnessed. And We do not delay it but to an appointed term. On the day when it shall come, no soul shall speak except with His permission, then (some) of them shall be unhappy and (others) happy. So as for those who are unhappy, they shall be in the fire; for them shall be sighing and groaning in it; abiding therein so long as the heavens and the earth endure, except as your Lord pleases; surely your Lord is the mighty Doer of what He intends. And as for those who are made happy, they shall be in the Garden, abiding in it as long as the heavens and the earth endure, except as your Lord please; a gift which shall never be cut off.' These *ayat* are irrefutable proof of the meaning (that we have expounded) and of the authenticity of the three kinds of resurrection (in the manner we have described above). This will only be understood by those who understand the meaning of Allah's words, 'As long as the heavens and the earth endure, except as your Lord pleases.' Many secrets are contained in these words but we have already mentioned the gist of their meaning.

If you have already understood these principles and have realised the meaning of the true return of the totality of Names, then know the following: The divine Names possess spheres of governance and influence and also cycles, states, dominions, beginnings and ends. An explanation of this is complex in character: the sound intellect judges that the sphere of influence of those Names which indicate injury and loss (to man) is other than that of those Names which indicate benefit and good (to man); likewise the sphere of influence of the Name 'the Giver of life' is other than that of 'the Bringer of death'; moreover, the dominion of the Names 'the One who guides' is other than that of the Name 'the One who leads astray' — the same may be said for 'the First', the Last, the Outward and the Inward and all the countless other names (with opposite meanings). Thus, just as this world is a necessary requirement of the Name 'the First' and 'the Outward' and their other related Names, so the hereafter is a necessary requirement of the Names 'the Last' and 'the Inward' and their other related Names. Likewise, just as the existence of this world and the appearance of its laws of influence and governance are obligatory by the nature of divine wisdom and in accordance with the requirements of those Names related to the world and its laws, so too the existence of the hereafter together with the laws of governance and influence are also obligatory by the nature of divine wisdom and in accordance with those Names which are related to the hereafter and its laws. From these general laws many other laws may be construed. Nevertheless we shall give the reader an example of what is meant which will facilitate a rapid understanding of this secret.

Existence and true authority in the realm of inner meaning occur according to the same pattern of superficial authority in the realm of form. I mean by this that just as authority in the exterior world is organised by means of sultans, viziers, amirs, armies, subjects and all other citizens (living within their jurisdiction), so real or true authority is also organised in the same way. Thus the essential Names correspond to the vizier, the names of Attributes to the amir, the names of action to the army and the result of compounding various Names corresponds to the subjects. Furthermore, just as each person from the court of authority, in the outward realm is delegated a particular role and task shared by no other, so too to each of the names of the real Sultan is delegated a particular role and task which is also shared by no other. Accordingly every existence in the outward is a manifestation of the Names of Allah and a locus of His influence and governance, and its return is only to that particuar Name, since the Name is the lord and the manifestation is the 'lorded over'. The following words of Allah testify to this notion: 'The day on which We will gather those who guard (against evil) to the Beneficent God to receive honours' and also His words: 'And that to your Lord is the (final) goal.'

With respect to the inner realm of reality and truth, the return of the totality of manifestations is only to Allah, just as on investigation (we realise that) each subject in fact is turning to the sultan (of the outward), despite the presence of the vizier, amir, chamberlain, representatives and the subjects who come to them. Again we would clarify this by giving the example of the person who comes to the sultan of the outward seeking a favour: of necessity this favour is actually bestowed by one of his treasurers. Likewise, the person who comes to him requesting authority to rule over a certain city deals not with the Sultan himself but with his wazir; similarly, the person who comes to ask for help in overcoming an enemy or oppressor only deals with one of his amirs. Countless examples such as these may be found with respect to the various assistant courtiers, armies and subjects: this is so because the affairs of authority and their organisation are all undertaken by such people. Thus the totality (of something) with respect to the totality (of its separate parts) can only function by means of this totality.

The same may be said for the real or true Sultan: if a poor man comes to Him or stands in His Presence saying 'O Allah' and seeks wealth, then of necessity he turns only to the Name 'the One of riches and independence;' likewise, the sick person who goes before Allah saying 'O Allah' and requests good health, then he of necessity turns only to the Name 'the One who cures'; likewise, the person who is astray who goes before Him saying 'O Allah' and seeks guidance, then of necessity he turns only to the Name 'the One who guides.' Countless other examples may be given with respect to the rest of His names. True Authority only functions in this way. This is reflected in the following verse:

> How much is everything in need, how much is all dependent!
> This is the truth, as we have said, so do not conceal, it
> Everything is mutually related, there is no separation from Him,
> So take what I have said from me!

On investigation we realise that this has the same meaning as that expressed by the gnostics when they say: 'Truly there is a secret to Lordship, which, if it became manifest, would invalidate Lordship.' This is so because lordship is a matter which only functions by way of two related aspects, the first being the Names and the second, the pre-creational Source Forms. The Source Forms are in fact non-existent, only existent by the existence accredited to them: thus anything which functions by means of a non-existent thing must in fact not be functioning in reality. This is because lordship is based on the lorded-over and the lorded-over are dependent on the Lord. If we assume the lorded-over (existence) to be non-existent, then there is no valid basis for lordship, despite the fact that the Lord exists; the reverse of this also applies, even if this supposition is in itself impossible. Some scholars have commented on this secret by saying that the secret of lordship is that it is based on the lorded-over. Since this matter implies a relationship between two things, there are of necessity two aspects, one of these being the lorded-over. Yet the Source Forms are in non-existence and that which is based on something non-existent is itself non-existent. Others have said the opposite of this, that is, that the secret of lordship is the appearance of the Lord by means of the (outward) manifestation of the Source Forms: He is the Lord Who is manifest by His maintenance of these outward manifestations, which only exist by His existence. As such these manifestations are lorded-over slaves and the Real, the Truth, is their Lord. In fact lordship is not attained except by way of the Real. By their very state, the Source Forms are non-existent from pre-endless-time, thus there is a secret of lordship which is revealed but which nevertheless does not invalidate it. Other subtle secrets are contained in this point and all are related to the point we have already mentioned, that is, the *Ma'ad*, the Final Day of Return, which is an expression of the return of each manifestation to the Name by whose rule and dominion it became manifest.

Despite the fact that the matter is as we have discribed, it should be noted that the Names possess cycles and spheres of dominion and influence and that it is permissible that some of the Names together with their respective spheres of dominion may dominate to the exclusion of others; thus the appearance of the Day of Resurrection is a result of the defeat of the Names connected to this world, and the victory of the Names connected to the next. The rest of the names can also be appraised in a similar manner, with respect to all the different periods and times (of divine reckoning). Some scholars have referred briefly to this matter in the following manner: Know that the Names of the divine actions may be divided according to their different spheres of influence and dominion. Of these, there are some whose rule and influence are never interrupted, from before endless-time to eternity — like, for example, the Names which have dominion over the purified spirits and the angelic souls and over that which is not of the age of created realities and yet which is nevertheless a part of (cosmic) time as a whole. There are also some whose rule is not interrupted with respect to eternity, although it is interrupted with respect to the age of before endless-time — like, for example, the Names which have dominion over the hereafter. That they and their rule are eternal is testified by the Qur'anic *ayat*: they do not extend to pre-endless-time by virtue of their non-manifestation; indeed, their manifestation only commences with the ceasing of the activity of this world.

All the Names have a sphere of governance in accordance with their manifestations and the appearance of their rule of influence. Indeed it is on these spheres of governance that the courses of the seven planets are based (each course lasting a thousand years); likewise, in the case of the different codes of law such that for each *shari'ah* there is a Name and the duration and sphere of governance of each *shari'ah* is dependent upon its Name, just as its authority lasts as long as that of the Name and is anulled on the disappearance of that Names. The pattern is analogous in the case of the emanation of the Attributes, such that when a particular Attribute manifests its sphere of influence, other Attributes below it become concealed.

Furthermore, each of the divisions of the Names calls up a particular manifestation in which the rule and influence (of this division of the Names) appear: this rule and influence is in fact (a manifestation of) the Source-Forms. If these latter are capable of receiving all the various spheres of rule and influence of the Names, then they appear, as in the case of the Source-Forms of man, as a particular manifestation and expression of one of their many activities. If they are not capable of receiving all the various spheres of rule and influence, then they are confined to some of the Names, as in the case of the Source-Forms of the angels. The duration of the Source-Forms in the outward (or the lack of duration in it with respect to this world and the next) is dependent upon the duration of the cycles of dominion connected to the Names (or their lack of duration). This matter must be understood well, and by Allah comes success. We shall now begin to classify the Final Day of Return, both in the realm of form and that of the spirit of inner meaning according to the people of *tariqah* and *haqiqah* and in the light of the triad of days of resurrection, namely the minor, intermediate and final.

The minor, intermediate and major days of resurrection in spirit for the people of *tariqah*

a)   The minor day

This particular day of resurrectioin describes the awakening and rising after the deliberate death of the will; it corresponds to the saying of the Prophet, 'Die before you die' and the words of the Wise Himself, 'Die the death of the will and you will live naturally (by your essence) as a result.' The words of the Prophet 'Whoever dies, then his day of rising up has arrived' affirms the above notion, both with respect to death both in the exoteric and esoteric sense.

   This death is divided into four types according to the people of this group: the red, the white, the green and the black. As for the death in an absolute sense, it is the removal of the desires of the self: the life of the self *(nafs)* is by means of these desires and the self does not incline to the passions and the demands of the body's natural instincts except by means of these desires. Whenever the self tends to this lower aspect, then the heart, which is the rational soul, withdraws to its centre and loses the true life of gnosis as a result of ignorance. If, however, the self dies by removal of its desires, then the heart moves naturally and by way of the original motion of love to its own world, namely the world of purity, light and essential life — which is totally incapable of 'receiving' death. Allah has referred to this life and death with His words, 'Is he who was dead then We raised him to life and made for him a light by which he walks among the people, like him whose likeness is that of one in utter darkness whence he cannot come forth? In other words, 'Is he who was dead by his ignorance, then We raised him to life by knowledge and made for him a light by which he walks among the people in a state of gnosis and perfection and full of eternal life, like him who is still in the utter darkness of ignorance whence he has not yet emerged?'

Ja'far ibn Muhammad al-Sadiq has said, 'Death is turning (for forgiveness to Him).' Allah has said (in the words of Moses), 'Therefore turn to your Creator in penitence and kill (or mortify) yourselves;' thus whoever turns for forgiveness, kills himself. This idea is also referred to by Allah when He says, 'And reckon not those who are killed in Allah's way as dead; nay they are alive (and) are provided sustenance from their Lord. Rejoicing in what Allah has given them out of His grace.' It is for this same reason that the Prophet, on returning from the *jihad* against the non-believers, said: 'We have returned from the lesser *jihad* to the greater *jihad.*' They then said, 'O Messenger of Allah, what is the greater *jihad?*' He replied, 'The *jihad* against the self which is opposing with its desires and demands.' It is also narrated that the Prophet said, 'The *mujahid* is the one who does *jihad* against his self, for whoever kills his desires comes alive by his dicovery of guidance (instead),' that is, by arriving at guidance and gnosis after being astray on the path of ignorance. It is this death which is known as the red death by the people of this science: it is one of the four above-mentioned deaths; it has also been called the death which gathers all other deaths, since if it occurs, all other types of death also occur. The following verse illustrates further this relationship of life and death:

> Kill me my trusted companions, for in killing me is my life
> And my death is in my life and my life is in my death.

It is called the red death for two reasons: the first is that blood, which is red, appears when someone is killed, and secondly, the face then turns red (after the killing) by the infusion of divine light.

As for the white death, it is an expression for hunger, for hunger illuminates the inward and whitens the face of the heart. Thus if the spiritual traveller does not eat his fill and remains in a state of hunger, then he dies the white death and thereby gives life to his intelligence. This is because gluttony kills sagacity: whoever kills the desire for gluttony gives life to his intelligence.

As for the green death, it alludes to the discarded patched robe. If the traveller is content to wear this as his adornment and covers his private parts and makes sure that his prayer, while wearing the robe, is acceptable, then he dies the green death. This is because he comes alive by his contentment and by the illumination of his face with the radiance of the Essential Beauty and by his having no need of the transient adornment of this world. The following verse emphasises this:

> If a man is not sullied by blame of his honour
> Then any robe he wears will be beautiful.

As for the black death, it alludes to the traveller's patient endurance of the injustice done by others. This is because he only becomes a truly beloved person in the eyes of Allah if he experiences pain and constriction caused by their injustice towards him. This person, however, finds delight in this time of trouble, knowing that it comes from the Beloved; everything which issues from the Beloved, be it good or bad, becomes a desirable thing (for as the people of this group say: 'All from the Beloved is beloved'). It has been said:

> In my passion for You I find censure pleasurable,
> And out of love for Your remembrance, may they reproach me with blame.
> I have become like my enemies and most beloved of them
> Because my portion from them was my portion from You.
> You disdain me, so I deliberately disdain myself;
> Whoever disdains You, is not treated generously.

In this way he dies the black death, which is annihilation in Allah by witnessing that the pain and trouble is from Him and experiencing the annihilation of actions in the action of his Beloved, or rather seeing himself and others annihilated in the Beloved. At this point he comes alive by the existence of the Real by way of the Real by way of His assistance which emanates from the Presence of Absolute Existence.

The garden attained by this resurrection after death is called the Garden of the Senses. Allah describes it saying, 'And as for him who fears to stand in the presence of his Lord and forbids the soul from low desires, then surely the Garden is the abode.'

He also says that 'therein shall be what their souls yearn after and (wherein) the eyes shall delight;' this is because it is a garden which is experienced physically: in it is overflowing food and drink which is to be enjoyed by the senses. It is for this reason that He says, 'And you shall abide there forever.' We ask Allah that He may grant us provision and bestow on us arrival at this garden, for it is a place of countless and boundless blessings: 'And if you count Allah's favours, you will not be able to count them.'

b) The intermediate day

This day of resurrection alludes to the death of man with respect to base behaviour, evil character and vile qualities and his coming alive by way of praiseworthy behaviour, generous and excellent character and fine qualities — all things which were at the very core of the Prophet's message and purpose. This is reflected in his words, 'I have been given all the names' and 'I have been sent to perfect good behaviour' and 'Make your qualities the Qualities of Allah.'

Know too that if there were a blessing greater than good behaviour and the taking on of the qualities of good behaviour, then Allah would have bestowed it upon His Prophet. As He Himself says, 'And most surely you conform yourself to sublime morality.' When one takes on the character of Allah and takes on His qualities, then this brings eternal happiness and causes one to arrive at the Enduring Presence. It is not possible, however, to arrive at these two things without a means to them and it is for this reason that He has commanded us to take on His Qualities. Proof of this is to be found also in His words, 'Neither the heavens nor the earth can contain Me but the heart of the believing slave (contains Me).' Thus it has also been narrated that 'The heart of the believer is the Throne of Allah' and 'The heart of the believer is the abode of Allah' and 'The heart of the believer is between the fingers of the Merciful.' All these sayings refer to the subject of our investigation, namely the taking on of the Qualities of Allah, and the only creature in existence capable of this is man. Man is, as it were, the heart of the world, and the very heart of man occupies a similar position within man as man's position in relation to the world as a whole. The truth of this first statement is testified by Allah's words, 'Surely We offered the trust to the heavens and the earth and the mountains...' and the second by his words, 'Neither the heavens nor the earth can contain Me... .'

The garden attained after this particular death is called the Garden of the Spirit: it is reserved for the spiritual inheritors from amongst His slaves. This is referred to by His words, 'Successful indeed are the believers, who are humble in their prayers and keep aloof from what is vain' and also 'These are they who are the heirs, who shall inherit the Paradise; they shall abide therein.' If man exchanges his baser behaviour for that which is praiseworthy and extricates himself from the dark depths of natural instincts, if he frees himself from mean and evil behaviour and takes on fine qualities so that he may be described as having a beautiful and harmonious temperament, if he takes on all these qualities by means of the Divine Qualities, and if, having attained all this, he establishes and maintains the duties of the *shari'ah* and the religion, then his soul will enter the interior Garden before entering Exterior Garden. Thus he becomes a lord of two gardens and two ranks. This is referred to by Allah: 'And as for him who fears to stand in the presence of his Lord, there are two gardens', that is the Garden of the Senses and Garden of the Spirit. We shall now describe this matter in more detail.

If we examine this subject from another angle, then we see that when the soul or self devotes its energy to true spiritual exercises which are based on real knowledge, then the person loses all of the viler features of his self — in particular, the seven most fundamental of them, namely vanity, arrogance, miserliness, envy, cupidity, excessive sexual desire and anger — and takes on all of the finer qualities — in particular, the seven most fundamental of these, namely, gnosis, wisdom, forbearance, humility, generosity, chastity and courage. In this way the self attains to the rank of harmony and evenness of temperament which marks for man the highest station of perfection on the path to Allah. It is with respect to the hierarchy of these stations that the Generous Book refers to the seven gates and ranks of

Gehenna *(Jahannam):* 'It has seven gates; for every gate there shall be a separate party.' These ranks are called (in order of descent): Jahannam, Ladha, Hatamah, Saqar, Jahm, Sa'ir and Hawiyah. It has been narrated that 'Ali (peace be upon him) was asked about the meaning of Allah's words, 'for every gate there shall be a separate party' and he said to his companions, 'Do you know what the gates of the Fire are like?;' they replied, 'Are they like these doors?' He answered, 'No, rather they are like this' and he placed one hand over the other. Allah has placed the different gardens in ranks one above the other; it is this which is referred to when He says, 'and a Garden, the extensiveness of which is (as) the heavens and the earth.' Similarly He has placed the different degrees of the Fire one above the other: the lowest is the Jàhannam of the hypocrites; above this is the Ladha of the idolaters *(mushrikun)* from amongst the Arabs; above this is the Hatamah for the Fireworshippers; above this is the Saqar for the Sabeans; above this is the Jahm for the Christians; above this is the Sa'ir for the Jews; and above this the Hawiyah for those believers who are rebellious. Thus it extends upwards to the different ranks of the Garden, and its eight abodes called the Jannat al-Na'im, the Jannat al-Firdaws, the Jannat al-Khuld, the Jannat al-Ma'wa, the Jannat al-'Adnin, the Dar al-Salam and the Dar al-Qarar, since the seven stations belonging to the base qualities all become spiritual gardens when they are exchanged for the seven stations belonging to the praiseworthy qualities. In this way there appears the rank of justice which encompasses the totality of stations and becomes in turn the eighth of these gardens.

Allah has referred to these spiritual gardens and their wealth and blessings in a *hadith* when He says, 'I have prepared for My slaves from amongst the righteous that which the eye has not seen, what the ear has not heard and what the heart of man has never conceived?' Likewise, the Prophet has described them with his words, 'Truly Allah possesses a garden in which there are no maidens and no palaces, in which there is no honey and no milk; rather therein our Lord manifests smilingly.' This is not the Garden of the Senses but rather the Garden of the Spirit:

the difference between the two is evident. He has also referred to this kind of garden with His words, 'By the One in Whose hand is the soul of Muhammad: truly the Garden and the Fire are closer to each other of you than the lace of your sandals'. Here He refers to the interior paradise and to the transience of the world in comparison with the world to come.

The Commander of the Faithful ('Ali) has also indicated all of these matters with his words: 'He has brought life to his intellect, and brought death to his self, until he has worn down his roughness and made smooth his coarseness and a great radiance of exceeding brightness has shone out, lighting for him the path so that he may journey by it; he is driven from gate to gate until he reaches the Gate of Peace and the Abode of Rest; therein his feet come firmly to rest and his body feels ease and security by virtue of that with which he busied his heart and contented his Lord.' These words serve our purpose in that they refer as a whole to the subject under discussion. His words, 'he is driven form gate to gate until he reaches the Gate of Peace and the Abode of Rest,' refer in particular to what we have in mind. In effect they show how, as we have said, the gates of Jahm, in the esoteric sense, become the gates of paradise with the transformation of the baser qualities into the good. In fact the totality of these ranks are based on the greater Gate, namely the Gate of Contentment which is referred to by the Prophet when he says, 'Contentment is the greater gate of Allah, as revealed in the Qur'an'. Allah has also referred to this rank together with its people with His words, '(As for) those who believe and do good, surely they are the best of men. Their reward with their Lord is gardens of perpetuity beneath which rivers flow, abiding therein for ever; Allah is well pleased with them and they are well pleased with Him; that is for him who fears his Lord.' He also indicates this Garden and the sight of it together with its delights and blessings when He says, 'And when you see there, you shall see blesseings and a great kingdom. Upon them shall be garments of fine green silk and thick silk interwoven with gold, and they shall be adorned with bracelets of silver, and their Lord shall make them drink a pure drink. Surely this is a reward for you and your striving shall be recompensed.' There are also many other *ayat* and Prophetic sayings on this same subject but we shall content ourselves with these and now turn to another matter; and by Allah is success and He it is Who says the truth and He it is Who guides to the correct path.

c) The major day

This day of resurrection expresses their annihilation in the Real and their biding by Him. This station is also called the annihilation in divine unity and the proximity which comes through supererogatory action. It is referred to in Allah's words, 'A slave does not continue to come closer to Me by his acts of supererogatory prayers unless I love him; if I love him, then I become his hearing and his sight and his tongue and his hand and his foot such that he hears by Me and he sees by Me and he speaks by Me and he walks by Me.' The result of this resurrection, after the annihilation described above — which is the real or true death — is the Garden of Witnessing. This garden is above the Garden of Inheritance and the Garden of the Soul.

Shaykh Muhyi al-Din ibn 'Arabi has indicated three interior gardens which result from these kinds of resurrection in his *Futuhat* saying: 'Know that there are three gardens: the garden which is particular to the divine, namely the garden into which go, among others, the children (who die and) who have not reached the age of action (from the time of their first cry to the end of their sixth year). Allah also gives to certain of His slaves (who desire it) whatever they wish for of this particular garden: these slaves are the people who belong (of necessity) to these gardens, namely the mad who are incapable of rational thinking, the people of gnostic unity and the people living between the ages of two prophets, including all those whom the divine message has not reached. The second garden is the Garden of Inheritance: it is attained by all those who are mentioned above together with the believers and those who are (rescued) from the Fire. The third garden is the Garden of Actions: the people of this garden take up residence therein according to their actions. Whoever surpasses others by the excellence of his actions has a greater portion of this garden.

Thus there is no good action without is a corresponding garden. Superiority in excellence between the people of this garden is in accordance with what is required by their stations.

Ibn 'Arabi then goes on to say: 'Know that the people of the Garden are of four kinds: the messengers or prophets, the saints or followers of the messengers who have a certainty of knowledge and clear evidence from their Lord, the believers or those who affirm the former and the scholars who declare, on the basis of rational proofs, that there is no god but Allah. Allah has said, "Allah bears witness that there is no god but He, and (so do) the angels and those possessed of knowledge." These are the scholars to whom I refer; Allah mentions them when He says, "Allah will exalt those of you who believe, and those who are given knowledge, in high degrees." '

Ibn 'Arabi continues: 'The ways leading to knowledge of Allah are two, not three in nubmer. Whoever affirms the Oneness of Allah, by means other than these two ways, then he is a *muqallid* (a person who imitates those more knowledgeable). The first of these is the way of unveiling: it is a knowledge which descends by destiny such that a person finds this knowledge within his self. It is a knowledge which admits of no doubt or ambiguity and which cannot be denied; however, the person knows of no proof for this knowledge save that which he finds within himself. The second of these is the way of reflection and evidence based on rational proof: it is a way which is inferior to the first for it may be that the person of investigation and rational proofs is exposed to a doubt which leads to a refutation of his argument — and it is here that the way of unveiling may take over the task found too burdensome by means of rational proofs. There is no third way since it is this very realisation within the realm of the Real which is the desired goal: thus the people of knowledge are those who bear witness to the unity of Allah by means of proofs and investigation. Any further knowledge of divine unity is by means of the *tawhid* of the essence and is not given to all of those of unveiling but rather to certain of them.'

Ibn 'Arabi continues: 'The four groups (mentioned above) are distinguished from each other in the Gardens of 'Adnin by their witnessing of the Real in the "proximity of whiteness". They exist therein according to four stations. One group are the lords of the raised platforms and they are of the highest level — that is, for the messengers and the prophets; the second group are the saints, the inheritors of the prophets by their speech, action and state — they have clear evidence from their Lord and they are the masters of the divans and throne; the third group are the scholars who demonstrate the existence and nature of Allah by intellectual proof — they are the masters of the footstools; the fourth group are the believers who imitate others more knowledgeable than they concerning the unity of Allah — they occupy different ranks on the Day of Judgement and take precedence over those of rational proofs. As for those outside these four groups, Allah knows best as to their state.' At this point the words of Shaykh Muhyi al-Din come to an end on this subject.

With the above in mind, we should point out that although this classification is correct and indeed is the best of its kind, other gnostics from amongst the people of Allah have given other definitions with regard to the totality of these groups. One of these is as follows: 'Know that the people as a whole are either non-believers or Muslims. As for the non-believers they are of three kinds: the worshippers of idols and cult objects (who are originally intended by the term non-believers), then the People of the Book, who believe in Allah, His Names and His Attributes, but who deny the Prophet and the revelations brought by him — like, for example, the Zoroastrians, the Jews and the Christians — and finally the Magians and those who possess scriptures resembling sacred books — like the fire-worshippers. These groups may also be divided according to the common, the elite and the elite of the elite, and their station in the Jahim is in accordance with their rank and the corresponding levels of the Jahim. These three groups may further be classified according to the high, the low and the intermediate: each of the levels corresponds to a particular group from among them; and Allah is more Knowing and more Wise. As for the Muslims, they are divided according to three types: the first being the prophets, the messengers and the spiritual inheritors who follow them, known as the saints *(awliya')*, from Seth to the Mahdi; secondly, those possessing knowledge of Allah either by unveiling or by rational argument, like the various ranks of the Sufi shaykhs and the scholars who establish and maintain jurisdiction according to the divinely inspired legal codes; and thirdly, the people of certainty of faith and imitation. All of these groups may also be divided according to the common, the elite and the elite of the elite. Thus their stations in the Garden are in accordance with their ranks (each occupy a corresponding level and chamber in the Garden). Likewise these three groups may be classified in terms of low, high or intermediate, each of these ranks and divisions having a particular group assigned to it; and Allah is more knowing and more Wise.'

It is with these words that the gnostic concludes this particular subject. It would not be fitting to include more on the subject in a work of this nature: it will be clear to those of knowledge and spiritual tasting that such divisions and classifications as have been described are correct; and 'All Praise is due to Allah Who guided us to this, and we would not have found our way had it not been that Allah had guided us.'

Here we conclude our discussion of the three days of spiritual resurrection with respect to the people of *tariqah*. As for the people of *haqiqah*, their resurrection occurs after the three stations mentioned above: it may be expressed as annihilation in the unity of action, attribute and essense, and their abiding in the Real, in accordance with their different ranks therein. This resurrection is also based on the three days of rising, namely the minor, intermediate and the major, in accordance with the three types of unity and annihilation therein.

iii) According to the people of *haqiqah*

The minor, intermediate and major days of resurrection in spirit for the people of *haqiqah*

a) *The minor day*

This day of resurrection expresses their annihilation in the unity of action and their arrival at the witnessing of the One Actor in all things. It is the station of those from whom the veil of actions is lifted by the opening of their inner vision. Indeed, the veil is lifted from all things such that they do not see any actions at all but that they issue from One Actor and One Governor — while taking care to respect the twin aspects of the decree and the delegation of trust placed in them by Allah and while preserving the twin aspects of submission to His will and free choice. Such persons become freed of any perception of otherness or awareness of their own actions such that they reach a level of witnessing whereby all actions issue from One Actor, namely the Real. In this way they become firmly established in the *tawhid* of action. Their witnessing takes place in the arena of the minor resurrection in His presence such that they are as dead persons being washed for burial. The signs of their station are reliance on Him, submission, the handing-over of affairs and the affirmation, by action rather than words, that there is no actor but Allah.

This subject has already been discussed with respect to the people of *tariqah*, although the two groups are not exactly the same. Whereas prayer, for example, is the same in its outward form, not everyone who prays is on the same spiritual level: there is a great difference between prayer which issues from knowledge, certainty and presence of mind and prayer which issues from ignorance, doubt and negligence. Allah refers to the first when He says, 'Successful indeed are the believers who are humble in their prayers and who keep aloof from what is vain... who are diligent about their prayers, these are they who are the heirs, who shall inherit paradise and shall abide therein' and with regard to the second: 'And their prayer before the House is nothing but whistling and clapping of hands.'

The result of this resurrection after annihilation in the above-mentioned manner is the Garden of Actions and its corresponding pleasures and blessings — that is the witnessing of the Real Actor in each of one's actions, whether physical or spiritual. The real esoteric garden reserved for this group also has three divisions: the Garden of Actions, the Garden of Attributes and the Garden of the Essence. The Garden of Actions, with respect to this group, is the first of these in the hierarchy of the gardens. Detailed descriptions of these gardens have been narrated and we shall now describe them in the language of the people of this group.

The Garden of Actions is the garden of form containing delicious foods and drinks and beautiful maidens — these things
are the reward for righteous actions. It is called both the Garden
of Actions and the Garden of the Self. At the esoteric level this
garden refers to the same place of foods and sensual pleasures
but as a result of witnessing the actions as issuing from the One
Actor, the Beloved by His essence. He is to this world as the
spirit is to the body. This is so since the contemplation of the
Actor in the unity of action is exactly the same as contemplation
of the reality of man in relation to his body and the movement
of its limbs. The prophets, saints and gnostics are all agreed that
the relationship of the Real to the world is analogous to the
relationship of the soul of man to his body and physical form.
This notion is supported by the words of the Prophet who says,
'Whoever knows himself knows his Lord' and the words of Allah,
'We will soon show them Our signs in the universe and in their
souls, until it becomes clear to them that it is the truth.' The
following verse also expresses this idea:

> All that you witness is one action alone, although con-
> cealed by veils.
> When the cover disappears, then you do not see other
> than Him,
> And nothing remains at any level of the different forms.

The Garden of the Attributes is the interior garden from the
divine emanations of the Names and the Attributes: it is the
garden of the heart (which has already been mentioned as the
station of the purification of behaviour and the heart's assimila-
tion of the Divine Qualities).

The Garden of the Essence is the witnessing of the Beauty of
Oneness in the totality of manifestations, be it with regard to
one individual manifestation or phenomena in general. This latter is the Garden of the Soul: it is attained by the unity of essence
and the placing of eye shadow on the eye of the soul with the
eye shadow of the solitude of the Real so that one never witnesses

anything but the Beloved. Thus the result of the annihilation of the slave in the unity of action and the minor esoteric resurrection is the Garden of Actions — in accordance with its various ranks and levels, and Allah is more Knowing and more Wise.

b) The intermediate day

This station expresses their annihilation in the divine unity *(tawhid)* of attribute and their arrival at a witnessing of the one attribute which pervades all things. In other words, whenever the veil of the totality of a⁺tributes is lifted from someone and the veil of witnessing other-than-Him disappears completely, then the person sees only one real attribute in the whole of existence like, for example, the perception of the attribute of life as pervading the body of man, or perception of the strength and capacity for action which pervades both man and animals — I mean by this that he witnesses this one attribute as an extension or addition to the Essence of Oneness which has authority over all things. Thus such a person sees all things as possessing this particular attribute; he sees this in the same way as one may see that every limb of the body possesses the attribute of life and strength. In this way one dies the real death and Allah's words, 'But We have remvoed from you your veil so your sight today is sharp' becomes a reality for him. The following has also been said:

> The eye is one and the forms are many,
> This is the secret revealed to the people of gnosis.

It has been narrated that Abu Yazid al-Bastami was asked, 'How are you this morning, O Abu Yazid?' He replied, 'There is no morning as far as I am concerned, for morning and evening are for those who are dependent upon form and attribute, and I possess no attribute.' These words are clear proof of the firmness of his establishment in the *tawhid* of attribute after that of action by way of unveilings and spiritual tastings. It is this that is meant by the gnostic's words, 'The essence is veiled by the attributes and the attributes by the action,' for all those from whom the veil of actions is not raised do not attain to the *tawhid* of actions; all those from whom the veil of attributes is not raised do not attain to the *tawhid* of attributes; and all those from whom the veil of the essence is not raised do not attain to the *tawhid* of essence. Moreover all those who do not attain to these different states of *tawhid* are not judged (favourably) with respect to their Islam and faith; indeed they are hardly considered to be human beings. This is attested by Allah's words, 'Surely the vilest of animals, in Allah's sight, are the deaf, the dumb, who do not understand' and also by His words, 'They are as cattle, nay, they are in worse errors!' What results from this witnessing in the minor resurrection is the Garden of Attributes (which we have already described above) and arrival at its pleasures and blessings — namely the witnessing of the attribute of the Beloved in the form of every single one of the lovers, be they spiritual or corporeal. One who has arrived at this station declares:

> The Beloved manifested to me from every direction
> And I witnessed Him in all meaning and forms.

Yet another declares:

> Every fine thing takes its beauty from His splendour.
> This beauty is lent to this thing, indeed to all fine things.

May Allah grant us and you arrival at this point of witnessing at the various levels of this garden, both by way of spiritual tasting and unveilings. It is from Him that all seek help and upon Him that all rely — He it is who utters the truth and guides to the correct path.

c) *The major day*

This resurrection expresses the abiding of all the essences in the Essence of the Real — after their annihilation therein. This annihilation is a gnostic annihilation and not an actual experiential annihilation: Allah refers to it with His words, 'Everyone (in creation) must pass away and there will endure for ever the face of your Lord' and His words, 'Everything is perishable but He; His is the judgement and to Him you shall be brought back.' This is the station of unveiling of the Essence of Reality, the unveiling of one's existence from the veils of divine splender and might, and the disappearance of the veil of seeing other-than-Him in any way whatsoever: the one of this station witnesses one single Essence which emanates in the various countless manifestations. Such a station is indicated in the verse which says:

Your beauty pervades all realities;
Indeed it is nothing but a veil of Your splendour.

This notion is also expressed in the gnostic's words: 'There is nothing in existence but Allah, His Names and His Actions; all is Him, by Him, from Him and to Him.' Thus he arrives at the *tawhid* of essence and comes to the arena of the major resurrection; he witnesses the meaning of Allah's words, 'To whom belongs the kingdom this day? To Allah the One, the Subduer (of all).' This is because by his unified gaze, by his belief in the judgement that there is nothing in existence but Allah, he subdues all the essences; he follows the adivce given by Allah: 'Say: Allah; then leave them sporting in their vain discourses' and 'And do not associate any other god with Allah.' This then is what is called the *tawhid* of essence, of the elite of the elite, above which there is no higher *tawhid*. This is expressed in the phrase: 'There is no village beyond Abadan and in Allah's words: 'He is the First and the Last, the Ascendant (over all) and the Knower of hidden things.' These words are an indication of this station of witnessing, since if it is established that there is nothing in existence but Him, then of necessity He is the First, the Last, the Ascendant and the Knower of hidden things; however, this does not imply that there is any change in His Essence or Attributes, since He is the First within the Last and the Last within the First, and likewise with respect to the Ascendant and the Cognizant (as we have already explained). The same may be said with respect to His words, 'Is it not sufficient as regards your Lord that He is a witness over all things? Now surely they are in doubt as to

the meeting of their Lord; now surely He encompasses all things,'
for these words are also an indication of this same station of
witnessing.

The sign of the witnessing and the mark of this *tawhid* is firm
establishment in the station of constancy and the perseverance
referred to in His words, 'Continue then in the right way as you
are commanded.' Firmness and constancy in real *tawhid* has been
described as a state awareness sharper than a sword, finer than
a hair and a station of the utmost difficulty. As the Prophet said,
'The *surah* Hud made my hair turn white.' As for the true meaning
of the above, it is that you continue on the straight path, which
itself is an expression for the point of balance between excess
and negligence — that is, a point where there is no further
tendency to either separation or convergence or to either manifest
or hidden *shirk*. This firmness and constancy is mentioned with
reference to the Prophet's spiritual ascent *(mi'raj)*, in His words,
'The eye did not turn aside, nor did it exceed the limit.' This is
so since if one's sight turns aside from the point of gathered and
balanced unity, which is a necessary basis for a truly harmonious
existence, then one is transgressing the bounds of truth. If these
bounds are not respected, then one goes astray from the straight
path and one enters into the company of those who associate
others with Allah — who are also astray from the real and His
path — and this applies equally to those guilty of manifest or
hidden idolatry *(shirk)*. His words 'the measure of two bows or
closer still' is an indication of this point. Allah's words, 'And do
not utter your prayer with a raised voice, nor be silent with
regard to it, but seek a way between these' is also an indication
of this. It means that 'you should not turn to your right or your
left when your attention is fixed on Us' and here what is being
referred to is this world and the next, on the one hand, and to
gatheredness and separation, on the other. This was the way
followed by your fathers and forefathers from amongst the
prophets, messengers, saints and spiritual heirs, and in particular
by Abraham and his sons. One of the gnostics has said, 'Beware
of merging and separation for the first causes heresy and the
negation of one's Islam, and the second rejection of the truth
that He (Allah) is the Absolute Actor; you should respect both

however, for the one who joins them is the one of true affirmation.'
Such a person has the highest of stations in return for his firmness
and balance and his avoidance of either of the two extremes.
There are numerous references to this state, especially in the
Qur'an and the traditions. The noble, however, will be content
with our indication of this.

The result of this esoteric resurrection is the Garden of the
Essence, which is the highet of stations; it is the garden reserved
for those who affirm the Oneness of Allah and who, by means
of thier *tawhid*, rise above any witnessing of otherness. It is they
who are mentioned in His words, 'Surely those who guard against
evil shall be in gardens and rivers, in the seat of honour with
the most Powerful King;' anyone who witnesses other-than-Him
in existence is neither of those who affirm His Oneness nor of
those who guard against evil. It is for this reason that Allah says:
'O you who believe! Be careful of (your duty to) Allah with the
care which is due to him, and do not die unless you are Muslims'.
The 'care which is due to Him' is nothing other than taking care
not to witness other than Him in the path of unification. Allah
emphasises this when He says, 'and do not die unless you are
Muslims' — that is, do not die the real esoteric death unless
you have submitted to this kind of Islam, namely the *tawhid* of
essence rather than the *tawhid* of attribute and action. Indeed
the testimony of Allah, His angels and those of knowledge from
amongst His slaves is sufficient: 'Say: May Allah be sufficient
as a witness between me and you and whoever has knowledge
of the Book.'

This is the last of the three days of spiritual resurrection particular to the people of *haqiqah*. We must now begin to consider
the six days of resurrection in the literal sense or the realm of
form with respect to the horizons — that is, the cosmic dimension. In this way the totality of stations will be twelve in number.
Since the divisions we have mentioned earlier are different from
this division, we should begin by mentioning the three days
related to form at the individual level in order that no contradiction should appear in our argument... .

The minor day of resurrection at this level expresses the liberation of the individual from the veil of the body and worldly

activity by the natural death, referred to in the saying of the Prophet, 'Whoever dies, than his day of rising up has arrived.' The intermediate day of resurrection expresses his exit from the world and his sojourn in the barrier or interspace known as the grave, referred to by Allah when He says, 'And before them is a barrier until the day they are raised' and the words of the Prophet, 'The grave is either a meadow from amongst the meadows of the Garden or a pit from amongst the pits of the Fire.' The major day of resurrection expresses the gathering of the people on the Great Day which is also known as the 'Day of Calamity' and their standing on the vast plain of the Day of Resurrection as attested by Allah in His words, 'And We will gather them and leave not any of them behind.' In this way each person arrives at that particular station reserved for him, be it in the Garden or the Fire; and Allah is more Knowing and more Wise. Let us now begin our description of the six days related to the cosmic dimension and their corresponding classification with respect to the realms of form and the spirit or inner meaning.

iv) The minor, intermediate and major days of resurrection in form with respect to the cosmic dimension

a) The minor day

This title expresses the destruction of the physical world and the compound material forms contained therein and the return of all this to the world of simple corporeal elements. This is referred to by Allah when He says, 'And when the mountains are made to pass away and when the camels are left untended and when the wild animals are made to go forth and when the seas are set on fire and when the souls are united.'

Some, however, consider that this title refers to the appearance of the Mahdi at the end of time when he comes to pass judgement over those living in his age. He is the Great Caliph of Allah and the Pole around which the whole world revolves; it is also by him that *wilayah* is sealed and all duties, divine codes of law, spiritual paths and religions are concluded; it is by him that the whole world returns to what it was before it was brought into existence; it is by him that the beginnings of creation are related to the Final Day and by him that the cycle of creation thus comes to an end. The following words of Allah attest to this: 'And on the day when We will gather from every nation a party.' If Allah had meant the Greater Gathering, He would not have said, 'a party from every nation;' rather He would say as He says elsewhere, 'And We will gather them and leave not one of them behind.' Moreover, He has also said, 'Say: The first and the last shall most surely be gathered for the appointed hour of a known day' and it is this 'known' day which is different from the above: thus we know that this minor day of gathering is a part and not the whole, that is, not the Greater Day of Gathering. Some of the Shi'ahs believe, however, that this particular day of gathering is called the day of *raj'ah* — returning to life after death — and they take the above mentioned *ayah* as their evidence. We do not wish to linger on the topic and the reader should pursue the matter for himself in the appropriate places. Indeed a whole book devoted to this question has been written entitled *Kitab al-Raj'ah* (The Book of the Return).

b) *The intermediate day*

This title expresses the return of the simple elements to the Universal Essence: the latter receives back all the forms of the world of material bodies, including the planets, the stars and the plant, mineral and animal kingdoms. This is affirmed in Allah's words, 'On the day when We will scroll up heaven like the rolling up of a writing-scroll; as We originated the first creation, (so) We shall reproduce it; a promise (binding on Us); surely We will bring it about' and in more detail in His words, 'When the sun is covered and when the stars darken... and when the books are spread, and when the heaven has its covering removed, and when hell is kindled, and when the Garden is brought nigh.'

For some, however, this title expresses the transformation of the tangible material world into the interspace prior to the Final Day of Return, not to the world of absolute beginnings. For these people it refers to the time spent therein and the pain or pleasure which is experienced by the inhabitants of this interspace, in accordance with what they are due. Thus some undergo the torment of the grave and some the blessings of the next world. This meaning is contained in the words of the Prophet, 'The grave is either a meadow from amongst the meadows of the Garden or a pit from amongst the pits of the Fire' and also in Allah's words, 'And most certainly We will make them taste of the nearer chastisement before the greater chastisement' and likewise His words, 'and before them is a barrier (interspace) until the day they are raised.' It is in this world that they are gathered together to proceed to the vast plain of assembly, the arena of the Great Day of Resurrection. Indeed neither of these two aspects can be denied by those who consider this matter with care and clarity.

c)   The major day

This title expresses the return of the forms of the spiritual worlds, that is, the return of the various intellects and souls to the First Essence, from which all these realities and forms were originally created by Allah. This is affirmed in the words of the Prophet, 'The first thing to be created by Allah was the Essence; He then looked upon it and it dissolved in awe of Him, such that half of it became water and half and of it became fire; from this water Allah created the souls and from the fire the bodies... .'

However, with respect to the language of unveilings and the way of those of spiritual tasting, this title refers to the material from which Allah opened up all the forms of the world: this material is sometimes called the primeval motes or particles and soemtimes the major elements. The wisdom of this meaning is contained in Allah's words, 'As We originated the first creation, (so) We shall reproduce it; a promise (binding on Us); surely We will bring it about.' Also, according to those of unveilings and tasting, it refers to the bringing into being of the form of the hereafter from that essential material, such that this continues uninterrupted and unchanged for eternity: this is expressed in Allah's words, 'remaining there for ever.' A likeness of this is the likeness of a lump of wax which may appear in different shapes — either of its own volition (as happens in the case of the growth point of the seed) or from other-than-itself (as in the case of outside influence from Allah, or the angels, or any of the various forces which manifest in nature). Then follows the disappearance of all these forms and the return to their previous state of receptivity and their appearance in corresponding forms in the worlds of the hereafter and the abodes of the Garden and the Fire. The truth of this is attested by the resurrection of man to the same physical form and with the same limbs as he possessed before his death: this is mentioned in Allah's words, 'Yea! We are able to make complete his very fingertips' and various other *ayat*.

We have already mentioned the belief of the people of the external law, from amongst the scholastic theologians (*mutakallimun*), who affirm that the individual or partial forms are the original forms and deny the possibility of the annihilation of anything in existence under any circumstances. They believe that this annihilation is rather a term for a change from one from to another. As rational proof, they maintain that existence, being existent cannot ever be non-existent, and that non-existence, being non-existent, can never become existence and that the bringing into existence or non-existence can only be applied to possible things — and this only in respect to an alteration of form or change of one form into another. They believe in the necessity of the return of all creation to the hereafter and the return is to the forms that they previously possessed which will continue in this manner in the Garden and the Fire; and Allah is more Knowing and more Wise and He it is Who says the truth and guides to the correct path.

v) The minor, intermediate and major days of resurrection in spirit with respect to the cosmic dimension

a) The minor day

This title expresses the return of the individual souls or selves to the Universal Soul such that they ascend towards it. This is stated in Allah's words, 'O soul that art at rest! Return to your

Lord, well pleased (with Him), well pleasing (Him), so enter among My servants, and enter into My garden' and also His words, 'And when souls are united.' This joining of the souls is the arrival of the individual souls at the Universal Soul.— from which they originally came, in the same way as Eve came originally from Adam. This is referred to in Allah's words, 'O people! Be careful of (your duty to) your Lord, who created you from a single being and created its mate of the same (kind) and spread from these two, many men and women.' Adam and Eve are counted as two separate forms; it is they who are our father and mother. They are also counted as two separate spiritual entities, since they are also our mother and father in the realm of reality and truth. The validity of this is affirmed by the application of the word fathers (in Arabic) to the planets and the celestial forms and the word mothers (in Arabic) to the various elements and terrestrial forms. Shaykh Muhyi-al-Din has indicated this in a verse from his *Futuhat* (at the beginning of the eleventh chapter):

> I am the son of the fathers of the purified spirits
> And of the mothers of the elemental souls.

These souls are an expression, in the first instance, of the celestial souls and thereafter of the angelic, jinn, elemental, mineral, animal and finally the human souls; from another aspect the human souls are the principal and most noble of the souls. Moreover each of these divisions may be further subdivided; an example (from among others too numerous to mention) is that of the human soul which may be classified into the commanding, reproaching, inspired and contented self (and other classifications besides).

All the various souls of the world together with the inhabitants of this world are charged with duties. This, however, is a separate subject and it would not be suitable to include it here; indeed the words of Allah are sufficient, 'And there is not a single thing but glorifies Him with His praise.' It is clear that whatever has been commanded to praise the Creator is of necessity charged with a specific duty. The import of the above *ayah* must be fully understood, for it includes the praise of the stones and the earth and not just the souls and the selves; and Allah is more Knowing and more Wise — He it is Who says the truth and guides to the correct path.

b) The intermediate day

This title expresses the return of the individual spirits to the Universal Greater Spirit: this return takes place by their spiritual ascent towards this Spirit, while remaining connected to the body which they use and direct. The Greater Spirit is mentioned in the *hadith:* 'The first thing created by Allah was the spirit.' And Allah says: 'And when I fashioned him and blew into him of My spirit.' It is also linked to Allah by relationship of possession when He says, 'My slave,' 'My abode,' 'My earth' and 'My sky'; but this link does not imply either separation or connection — may He be exalted above this. It has also been narrated that Allah created the spirits many thousands of years before the bodies: one *hadith* of the Prophet reports that 'Allah created my spirit and that of 'Ali ibn Abi Talib a thousand thousand years before He created creation.' Likewise, it has been narrated that the spirits are like mustered armies: those that come to know each other unite in harmony and those that have no knowledge of each other separate in discord.

The subject of these spirits is a vast one, and it is not fitting that we continue it here in a work of this nature. The reader is urged to pursue the matter in the appropriate texts. We would simply add here that the whole world is like one person, as is indicated in words of the gnostics, 'The world is the Great Man and the relationship of all beings to him is like the relationship of the limbs and bodily organs to man himself;' as the gnostics say, 'Man is a microcosm.' Man is entrusted with duties as are all his limbs and physical capacities. Allah refers to this when He says, 'And He did not create you or raise you up but as one soul' and also His words, 'Certainly the creation of the heavens and the earth is greater than the creation of men' and His words, '(So He said to the heaven and the earth): Come both, willingly or unwillingly.' If these duties had not been taught and imposed upon man at all, then it would not have been right to command, forbid, or censure him. The following words of Allah serve as a final reply to any questions that one may raise about this matter: 'And there is no animal that walks upon the earth nor bird that flies with two wings but (they are) creatures like yourselves; We have not neglected anything in the Book, then to their Lord they shall be gathered;' and Allah is more Knowing and more Wise.

c) *The major day*

This title expresses the return of all the intellects, by way of an ascent, to the First Intellect referred to by the Prophet in his words, 'The first thing created by Allah was the intellect; He then said to it: "Come forward" and it came forward; He then said to it, "Go back" and it went back; He then said, "By My power and My majesty I have not created a more noble creation than you; by you I give, by you I take, by you I reward and by you I punish... ." '

It is evident that there are various intellects and because of their number there exist differences between them. Most scholars from amongst the philosophers affirm that Allah is One in all respects and that from this One there issues another one and it is this which is the First Intellect. From this intellect issues another intellect and another soul together with a celestial sphere composed of a form and an essence: in this way (the chain) continues to the last celestial sphere (or planet). I mean by this that these philosophers have established the existence of an intellect, a soul, a form and an essence for each of these spheres; this also applies to the angels for they are the lords of the intellects, and likewise to the jinn and mankind, according to some.

According to the scholars of this particular science, every being possesses an intellectual perception in accordance with its own particular capacity. One may call this inspiration, perspicacity, intuitive awareness, revelation, or simply knowledge or, indeed, by any other name one wishes — for what is being referred to is one thing's perception of other things. It is for this reason that the subject of the intellect has been classified in four divisions: the essential intellect, the acquired intellect, the intellect of action (or the potential intellect) and the inferring intellect. The intellect possesses various names in Arabic, among them words meaning 'core,' 'acumen,' 'discernment' and 'mind.' This supports the view that some kind of correlation must exist between the cosmic and the individual dimensions.

In the light of the above, it may be shown that anything which may be assumed to exist with respect to the lesser man should (in this context) also be assumed to exist with respect to the Great Man himself. Indeed the whole of our commentary throughout this book (with respect to the three different aspects of resurrection) is based on the application of this principle. Thus, just as life, death and resurrection, both in the realm of form and that of inner meaning, are true for the lesser man so they are also true for the Great Man. Just as death, both literal and figurative, is a cause of happiness for the lesser man, both in this world and the next, so the destruction and death of the Great Man is also a cause of his happiness and his eternal life; his abiding is for ever and it is in the form which he has attained in the previous world; his death is his exit from the abode of annihilation to the abode of continuing forever, from the abode of darkness and obscurity to the abode of light and radiance. It is for this reason that the gnostic 'Ali, when struck by Ibn Muljam al-Muradi said, 'By the Lord of the Ka'bah I have gained victory;' it is for this reason too that he also said: 'By Allah, surely the son of Abu Talib is more intimate with death than the child with the breast of its mother.' Allah too addressing the slaves says, 'Then invoke death if you are truthful' for He knows that death results in their happiness and brings about arrival at their own perfection.

If one wishes, one may also consider the three days of resurrection, in the literal and figurative sense with respect to the cosmic dimension, as the return of the world of action, namely the world of Lordship, to the world of the Names and Attributes, namely the world of Divinity, and the return of the world of divinity to the world of the Essence and the Presence of Solitude. If we consider the matter in this way, then it is also accords with the above-mentioned classification; in this way all aspects are

given their due consideration — as is indicated by the following
verse:

> Our terms are various but Your beauty is One
> And everything is indicating that very beauty.

III
Branches

1

Minor Ritual Ablution *(wudu')*

i) According to the people of *shari'ah*

All, both the common and the elite, are familiar with the meaning of *wudu'*. It may be classified in three ways: obligatory, recommended, and meritorious. We have no need here to refer to the last two, but rather we shall consider the first, namely the obligatory, which may be divided into two aspects: the actions performed and the manner in which they are performed.

There are five obligatory actions: intention, washing of the face, washing of the hands, wiping over the head, and wiping over the feet. There are ten obligations with regard to the manner of their performance: the making of the intention at the time of the *wudu'*, maintaining the intention until completion of the *wudu'*, washing the face from the point of growth of the hair above the forehead to the lower point of the beard — from the top of the face to the bottom reaching those parts of the face which may be covered when the thumb and middle finger are outstretched — washing both arms from the elbow to the tips of the fingers, the wiping of the front part of the head just enough for it to be recognised as wiping, wiping both feet from the ends of the toes to the point above the ankles, in a specific order — that is beginning with the washing of the face, then the right hand, then the left, then the wiping of both feet, the performance of each action in a continuous motion, not allowing any significant time to elapse between the washing of each limb such that one does not allow the part previously washed to dry before going on to the next part — wiping the head and both feet using the wetness and drops of water which remain (and not using any further water). This method is that used by the people of the House of the Prophet. There are many differences of manner with regard to the *wudu'* of other groups, besides the Shi'ahs, but this is not the appropriate moment to enter upon a discussion of them; and Allah is more Knowing and more Wise.

ii)   According to the people of *tariqah*

The purification of this group occurs after their performance of the above-mentioned ablution; it is an expression for the purification of the self from any base aspects of behaviour, the purification of the intellect from the impurity of wicked thoughts or ideas of a dubious nature which lead one or other astray, purification of the inner heart and mind of envy or rivalry and the purification of the limbs from actions unacceptable to the intellect or the code of the *shari'ah*. The intention of this kind of *wudu'* is that the person intends with his heart and innermost secret not to do any action which would conflict in any way with the pleasure of Allah and to make all his acts of worship purely for Allah and no other; this is referred to in His words, 'Say surely my prayer and my sacrifice and my life and my death are (all) for Allah, the Lord of the worlds; no associate has He; and this am I commanded, and I am the first of those who submit.'

As for the washing of the face, it is that the person washes the face of his heart clean of any impurity connected to the world and that contained therein, for 'Surely the world is carrion and those who seek it are dogs.' It is for this reason that the Prophet has also said, 'Love of this world is the source of all wrong action and abandonment of the world is the source of all worship'. 'Ali, may peace be upon him, has said, 'O world! Go and deceive other than me for I have pronounced divorce on you three times and there is thus no possibility of a remarriage.' As for the washing of the hands, it refers to washing them free of whatever is in their grasp — of money and the like and of the world and the hereafter; indeed the reality of this purification is nothing but the dismissal of whatever is at their disposal. As for the wiping of the head, it means wiping over one's 'true' head, namely one's intellect or perceiving self, that is one inspects it to ascertain whether there remains any trace of love of this world (and all this implies of wealth and honour). As for the wiping of the feet, it means preventing them from walking anywhere that is not for the pleasure of Allah and in obedience to Him, whether outwardly or inwardly. As for what the two feet means according to the inner dimension, then, according to some, they symbolise man's per-

ceptive faculty and his ability to carry out actions; according to
others, they symbolise the sexual instinct and the power of anger.
The Prophet has referred to the person who performs this kind
of *wudu'* in addition to the previous *wudu'* when he says, 'The
performance of one *wudu'* on top of another is light upon light;'
that is to say, the radiance of the outward is added to the radiance
of the inward. In this way it is light upon light, namely the light
of inner perception on top of the light what is legally prescribed
and it is this which brings about the firm establishment of the
spiritual wayfarer in the straight way, both in this world and
the next. This is referred to by Allah when He says, 'Allah
confirms those who believe with the sure word in this world's
life and in the hereafter;' may Allah bestow on us the (station
of) joining between them and our firm establishement in both;
He it is whose help is sought and it is on Him that we place our
trust.

iii) According to the people of *haqiqah*

The *wudu'* of these people, which is expressed as a purification,
refers to the purification of one's inner secret from the witnessing
of other-than-Him — under any circumstances. As for the intention of this *wudu'*, it is that the spiritual traveller makes the
intention in his innermost heart not to witness anything in existence as other-than-Him and not to move in any direction but
that of Him; anyone who does aim for other-than-Him is a *mushrik*
(idolater, polytheist) and guilty of hidden *shirk,* as we have already explained above; this is referred to by Allah's words, 'Have
you not considered him who takes his low desire for his god' and
His words, 'And most of them do not believe in Allah without
associating others (with Him).' The *mushrik* is ritually impure
as attested by Allah's words, 'The idolaters are nothing but
unclean;' thus their purification can only come about with this
intention, an intention which rejects all kinds of *shirk.*

It is evident that freeing oneself of idolatry, be it manifest or
hidden, is only possible by means of a divine or existential unity
(tawhid). The washing of the face symbolises the purification of
the face of reality and the cleansing of the inner heart from the

vision of other-than-Him — such that one does not contemplate
anything but His noble face, referred to in His words, 'Any way
you turn to, there is the face of Allah'. Moreover this person
does not recognise anything but His encompassing Essence, indicated in His words, 'Now surely He encompasses all things.'
Allah has also referred to this kind of turning to Him when He
inspired Abraham to say, 'Surely I have turned myself, being
upright, wholly to Him Who originated the heavens and the
earth, and I am not of the polytheists.'

As for the washing of the hands, it symbolises one's lack of
concern for any of the comforts of this world or the next which
are at the disposal of one's hands — such as wealth, position,
family and children which are of this world and knowledge, doing
without, and obedience which are other worldly, including whatever appears as a result of the next world, like the reward, the
Garden, the maidens and the palaces. This is because undue
consideration and praise for one's acts of worship and obedience
is considered an act of disobedience by the people of Allah. Thus
it has been said, 'A bad action which causes you regret is better
than a good action which makes you conceited;' it has also been
said, 'The best of actions is a wrong action which causes you to
turn for forgiveness and the worst of actions is an act of obedience
which results in conceit.' The Prophet has also referred to this
when he says: 'This world is forbidden the people of the hereafter
and the hereafter is forbidden the people of this world and both
are forbidden the people of Allah.'

As for the wiping over the head, it symbolises the elevation
of one's secret and innermost heart — that it is the 'real' head
— above the impurity of egotism and otherness, which acts as
a barrier between him and his Beloved. One of the gnostics refers
to this matter in the following verse:

> Between me and You is individual existence conflicting
> with me,
> So remove individual existence by Your grace from bet-
> ween us.

It has also been said: 'Your very existence is a wrong action which is greater than any other wrong actions.' We have already established that anyone who sees other-than-Him is an idolater and that all idolaters are unclean; that for such people there is no access to the world of sanctity and the divine presence is testified by the words of Allah, 'Surely Allah does not forgive that anything should be associated with Him, and forgives what is besides that to whomsoever He pleases.'

As for the wiping over the feet, it symbolises the elevation of the two powers of action and knowledge above any undertaking other than by Allah, for Allah and in Allah. This is because they are as the two legs and feet of the outer: it is by means of them that one strives in search of the Real and it is by means of them that one reaches Him. On investigation one realises that Allah's words (to Moses), 'Therefore put off your shoes; surely you are in the sacred valley' is an indication of this too, meaning that if a person arrives at Allah, he should remove his shoes, for he will have no further need of them; this is evident since, on arrival, one must jettison everything in existence, especially physical strength, the physical senses and all that these imply. Some, however, believe that what is meant by the two shoes is this world and the next and some say that they refer to the world of the outer and that of the inner; still others say that they refer to the body and the soul, and in fact all express the truth. A sacred *hadith* refers to this state and this station: 'The slave continues to draw closer to Me by his supererogatory acts of worship until I love him; and if I love him, then I become his hearing and his sight and his speech and his hand and his foot; thus he hears by Me and he sees by Me and he speaks by Me and he strikes by Me and he walks by Me.' This *hadith* refers, in fact, to a way of acting by Allah which is the station of perfection just below that indicated by His words, 'Why should not then a company from every party from among them go forth that they may apply themselves to obtain an understanding in religion, and that they may warn their people when they come back to them to be cautious?'

As to the washing of the hands and arms, it expresses the station described in His words, 'And you did not smite when you smote (the enemy), but it was Allah Who smote.' There are other studies on this subject and secrets too numerous to mention, but this present investigation will be enough for the man of intellect and perception; and Allah says the truth and guides to the correct path.

2

Major Ritual Purification *(ghusl)*

i) According to the people of *shari'ah*

The *ghusl* of the people of this group is defined by the various
degrees of the legal code, that is, the obligatory, the recommended, the forbidden and the disliked actions. A description
of all these would be very lengthy so we shall confine ourselves
to the obligations, the performance of which ensures purification
according to the outer law of the *shari'ah*. These obligations are
six in number, three of them involving actions and three involving
the manner of performance of these actions. As for the actions,
it is the ensuring that all urine has been passed — in the case of
men, to make sure that the penis is free of the sperm of sexual intercourse — and to make the intention, that is, the pronouncement
on the part of the person in a state of ritual impurity, together
with an undertaking from his heart, namely: 'I am about to
perform the *ghusl* in order to remove the major ritual impurity
so that I may make the prayer, which is obligatory for me, and
I do this in order to draw closer to Allah.' Thereafter he washes
the whole of his body from head to foot such that water reaches
to the roots of the hair covering his body and his washing is so
thorough as to merit the name *ghusl*. The manner in which these
actions should be performed has three aspects: the intention
should be made immediately before the *ghusl* is performed; the
intention should remain in force throughout the *ghusl;* and the
appropriate order of performance should be respected, that is,
one must begin with the head and then with the right side of
the body and then with the left.

ii) According to the people of *tariqah*

The *ghusl* of this group refers to their performance of the above-
mentioned *ghusl* in order to purify themselves from the real state
of ritual impurity, namely that state which distances one from

Allah (rather than from the superficial state of ritual impurity, namely that arising from any of the legally specified physical causes of pollution). The real state of ritual impurity may be divided into two parts: the first relates to the people of this group and the second to the people of *haqiqah*. An explanation of the second will follow immediately after this section.

As for the first, it refers to the impurity which arises from love of this world: truly the world is like a woman who takes another husband every hour, as the Imam has indicated in his words, 'I have pronounced divorce on you three times and so there is no possiblity of remarriage.' It is evident that if the world were not like a woman, then the Imam would not have addressed it in these terms; thus anyone who keeps her company and who makes loves to her with the self, the soul or the heart becomes ritually impure in the true sense. This state of ritual impurity is, as we have said, distancing oneself from Allah, for anyone who loves the world in the manner we have described above will of necessity distance himself from Allah. Indeed, love of Allah and intimacy with Him is the very opposite of love of and intimacy with the world and the two can never be joined together. This is referred to in the words of Allah, 'Whoever desires the reward of the hereafter, We will give him more of that again; and whoever desires the reward of this world, We will give him of it, and in the hereafter he has no portion.' The Imam has also referred to this in his words: 'Truly this world and the next are enemies to each other and are two completely different paths: whoever loves this world and pays allegiance to it will anger the hereafter and make it an enemy of him;' the two are in fact as the east and the west, and whenever the person walking between the two comes closer to one, he will necessarily distance himself from the other — in fact they as far apart as wives in a plural marriage. Thus purification from this ritual impurity is attained by the abandonment of the world and all it contains, such that one is not even connected to it by so much as a hair's breadth. Even if so much as one hair remains untouched by water during the legally prescribed *ghusl,* then the whole *ghusl* is invalidated. Thus attachment to the world, however little, has the same effect, namely the invalidation of one's *ghusl*. This same notion is expressed in the phrase: 'Whoever is veiled is veiled, whether it be by one or a thousand veils.'

The manner in which this particular *ghusl* is performed is that the spiritual traveller washes first his 'real' or 'true' head, that is his heart in this instance, with the water of the gnosis of reality, which descends from the ocean of sanctity; he washes it clean of the impurities of worldly desires and empty opinion, which cause man to enter the Hawwiyah, that is (one of the levels of) the Fire. This is so since if the desires of the self gain the upper hand, then they draw the person concerned towards the worship of idols and cult objects, be it in his thoughts or his actions. The meaning of outward idolatry is evident and that of inner idolatry has already been discussed in the light of Allah's words, 'Have you then considered him who takes his low desire for a goal.' Anyone who obeys his low desire will of necessity enter the Fire, for as Allah says: 'And as for him whose measure of good deeds is of little weight, his abode shall be the abyss (of Hawwiyah);' what is meant here is that if one's measure of knowledge and righteous action (which both arise as a result of a sound intellect and perfected self) weighs little, then he will enter the abyss of Hawwiyah. The root cause of these desires is the 'soul which commands (to evil)' *(al-nafs al-ammarah)* and this soul or self stems from the animal instincts, physical appetites and anger; these are the armies and supporters of the commanding self. This abyss is 'the lowest of the low' indicated in Allah's words: 'Certainly We created man in the best image, then We render him the lowest of the low.' Allah takes man to the lowest world of natural desire by means of his actions, which cause the person to follow his desires and thus oppose the will of Allah. This is indicated by the speech of the people of the Fire: 'Had we but listened or pondered, we should not have been among the inmates of the burning fire.' Thus the people of Allah are always the people of true knowledge, righteous action and sound intellect and are described as those of tranquillity, honour and peace of mind. Allah Himself says of them, 'Then as for him whose measure of good deeds is heavy, He shall live a pleasant life' and he will be 'in the highest states of the garden.' The people of low desires and of innovation are described as being frivolous, of weak intellect and without peace of mind or honour; Allah says of them: 'like him whom the devils have made to fall down perplexed to the ground.' The reply to all questions related this subject may be found in Allah's words, 'And as for him who fears to stand in the presence of his Lord and forbids the soul from low desires, then surely the Garden is his abode.'

Thus the people of this station to this goal by constantly forbidding their soul from low desires and by always urging their souls to that which will bring them into the Garden, the true abode and the final refuge. 'Ali, may pace be upon him, has indicated the people of this station in his words: 'Disencumber your heavy actions, that is, your actions which arise from following your desires and from love of this world, and you will reach (the Real and the Garden), for surely the last of you will arrive by the example of the first.' Attainment of the Real and the Garden is dependent upon the disencumberance or removal of wrong actions. Allah refers to this in His words, 'Most surely this is the mighty achievement, for the like of this then let the workers work.'

Then he washes his right side, that is, he purifies his spirit and innermost secret, his love of the higher manifestations of the hereafter and the Garden, for the people of the hereafter are characterised as the people of the right and of the higher realities. This is indicated in Allah's words, 'And the companions of the right hand; how happy are the companions of the right hand! Amid thornless lote-trees and banana trees (with fruits), one above the other... and water flowing constantly.'

Thereafter follows the washing of the left side, that is, he purifies his soul and body (which are contained in the left side and are referred to as the physical realities) from love of base objects and selfish desires expressed as a totality by the term 'the world'; he performs this washing with the water of abandonment, stripping away and lack of concern. The world is the particular domain of the people of the left, just as the hereafter is the domain of the people of right, as is expressed in Allah's words, 'And those of the left hand, how wretched are these of the left hand! In hot wind and boiling water and the shade of black smoke.' It is by means of this purification that they merit entering into the Garden and are prepared to approach the Presence of His Power.' This is indicated in his words, 'Surely those who guard (against evil) shall be in gardens and rivers, in the seat of honour with the most Powerful King.' May Allah grant us attainment of these stations for surely that is a grace from Allah, He gives it to whom He wishes and Allah is of mighty grace.

iii) According to the people of *haqiqah*

Ghusl for the people of this group represents their purification from the real ritual impurity, that is, the witnessing of other-than-Allah in an absolute sense. As we have explained above, this impurity is the distancing of oneself from Allah: anyone who witnesses other-than-Him is far from the Real; it is not posssible to remove this distance but one may approach the contemplation of the Real as He actually is. Allah indicates this when He says, 'Allah bears witness that there is no god but He, and (so do) the angels and those possessed of knowledge, maintaining His creation with justice; there is no god but He, the Mighty the Wise.' We have already commented upon this kind of unified vision *(tawhid)* on several occasions.

The order of performance of this *ghusl* is that he washes his 'real' or 'true' head, that is his spirit, alone and stripped of all else, with the water of the *tawhid* of essence; he washes it clean of the witnessing of other-than-Him. Just as love of Allah is the duty of the inward and is expressed as the 'tranquil soul' *(al-nafs al-mutma 'innah),* knowledge of Allah is the duty of the heart and contemplation of Him is the duty of the spirit; moreover arrival is the duty of the innermost secret, which in turn is the inner dimension of the spirit. Ja'far ibn Muhammad al-Sadiq has referred to this in one of his supplications, namely 'O Allah, make radiant my outwardness by obedience to You and my inwardness by love of You and my heart by knowledge of You and my spirit by my witnessing of You and my innermost secret by my constancy in striving to join with Your Presence, O Possessor of Majesty and Nobility.' This *ghusl* is only possible by the annihilation of the knower in the known and the witnesser in the witnessed. This annihilation is expressed as the annihilation of unity *(tawhid)* and is attained by witnessing the Real as He really is, that is, the witnessing of Him alone and no other with Him; by this I mean that he does not witness anything in existence but His existence and One Essence, stripped of all the transient physical phenomena. As Allah says, 'Everything is perishable but He; His is the judgement, and to Him you shall be brought back;' 'And there will endure for ever the person of your Lord, the Lord of glory and honour.' (We have already investigated these two *ayat* on more than one occasion and it would not be appropriate to discuss them again here).

As we have already established, this kind of *tawhid* is the true and straight path which man has been commanded to in the words of the Prophet, 'Continue then in the right way as you are commanded;' it is the middle way, referred to by Allah in His words, 'And (know that) this is My path, the right one, therefore follow it, and follow not other ways for they will lead you away from His way; thus He has enjoined you with that you may guard (against evil).' We have also established that this way has two sides or borders, namely that of excess and that of negligence. Purification from the impurity of excess, expressed as that of the right hand border of the way, is attained by freeing oneself of the all-encompassing *tawhid*, while purification from the impurity of negligence, expressed as that of the left, is attained by freeing oneself of the *tawhid* of the individual parts.Thereafter one is able to persevere along the above-mentioned path, namely the middle way, which is attained by the joining of the two types of *tawhid* and is called the greater purification. It also necessitates that one cease to witness other-than-Him in any way whatsoever; rather one contemplates Him in the realm of gatheredness, and this is expressed as the oneness of the separate parts after the gathering together. Such a vision is extremely difficult and it is for this reason that the Prophet described it as being 'sharper than a sword' and 'finer than a hair;' Allah has also referred to it in His words, 'The eye did not turn aside, nor did it exceed the limit' and also 'So he was the measure of two bows or closer still;' these words indicate the gathered *tawhid* of Muhammad, a *tawhid* which encompasses all the other kinds of *tawhid*.

In short, ritual impurity in the spiritual realm is nothing but the witnessing of other-than-Him, in whatever form this takes; thus attainment of purification in the spiritual realm can only occur after freeing oneself from this vision of otherness. Thus it is that the poet has said:

> I was content with the whim of fancy that you evoked in me;
> But I was not content when I joined with you,
> For when a glace of Laylah fell from afar,
> It seized my inside from the heart to the bowels.
> Women say that the living yearn to see.
> O Laylah, your eyes have caused me to die from the sickness of yearning
> And how can you see Laylah when your eye sees
> Other than her and you have not cleansed it with tears?

There are numerous examples of this kind and the reader is advised to seek them in the appropriate places; and Allah is more Knowing and more Wise and He it is that says the truth and guides to the correct path.

3

Purification with Earth *(tayammum)*

i)   According to the people of *shari'ah*

Tayammum for the people of this group is purification by means
of dust; this is used when water is absent or when one is excused
its use. *Tayammum* takes the place of *wudu'* or the *ghusl* and is
only permitted according to the following three conditions: the
absence of water after having undertaken a search for it, or
absence of the means whereby one may reach it (not possessing
the price of the water, or a bucket, rope or the like), or because
one fears for one's health or one's wealth (because of its excessive
price) if one were to use it. *Tayammum* is not correct unless done
with earth or whatever is commonly called earth (thus it includes
the natural forms of dust, clay and stone).

As to the manner of its performance it is that the person
strikes the earth once with both hands. If it is being done
instead of the *wudu'*, he should then brush off the excess
dust and wipe his face with both hands from the point
where the hair begins to grow at the top of the forehead
down level with the nose; then he should wipe over the
back of his right hand with the palm of his left, from the wrist
to the ends of the fingers and then over the back of his left hand
with the palm of his right, likewise from the wrist to the ends of
the fingers. If the *tayammum* is done instead of the *ghusl,* then one
should strike the earth twice, once for the face and once for the
hands, the manner of performance being the same as above. The
same things which invalidate the *wudu'* and the *ghusl* also invalidate the *tayammum* (the only essential difference between the two
being the capacity to use water or not); likewise all acts of worship
permitted with *wudu'* are also permitted by means of *tayammum,*
the two being exactly equal as to their validity — and Allah is
more Knowing and more Wise and He it is Who says the truth
and guides to the correct path.

ii) According to the people of *tariqah*

Before beginning this section in detail we should first define the meaning of the water of reality and the earth of reality.

According to the judgement of the intellect and the judgement contained in the narrated sources (of the Qur'an and the traditions), the water of reality symbolises the divine knowledge and gnosis or 'the life of reality.' This is explained on examination of the words of Allah which affirm that the life of everything issues from water, 'And We have made from water every living things.'[1]

It is evident that the life of every thing does not come from the water of the form (with which we are familiar): the angels, the jinn, the celestial spheres and planets are all recognised as things although their life does not issue from water, that is, they are not made up of the 'water of form.' Likewise, although it may be said that all composite things contain a certain proportion of the water of form, the same may not be said about many other existent beings, like, for example, the simple elements and the higher, sublime realities. What in fact is being said is that just as the degree of perfection in knowledge differs in rank and quality, so too water varies in its degrees of saltiness and sweetness and in other specific qualities.

We have already mentioned in our investigation of *tawhid* that every existent being has speech, life and knowledge. What is meant by knowledge is knowledge of Allah, His Names, His Attributes and His Actions; indeed there is no existent being that is devoid of these different degrees of knowledge, for they are possessed in accordance with the capacity, merit and receptivity of each; this (as we have already explained) is indicated in Allah's words, 'And there is not a single thing but glorifies Him with His praise, but you do not understand their glorification.' Glorification of anything can only take place after gnosis

---

[1] It has also been said that this means that the life of all things is (by means of water); this however is not permissible with regard to the Arabic of the *ayah* for, if this were the case, then the word 'living' would be in the genitive case, yet it is in the accusative and describes 'thing'; thus the meaning of the *ayah* is that He created the creation from water. This is also affirmed by His words: 'And Allah has created from water every living creature.'

of that thing and affirmation of that thing's existence. Thus our statement that everything in existence possesses three things — knowledge, gnosis and life — is correct. According to most commentators, Allah's words, 'He sends down water from the cloud, then watercourses flow (with water) according to their measure' also reflects this meaning since the water here refers to knowledge, the watercourses the hearts and 'to their measure' to the capacity and capability to which every existent being may attains. Likewise Allah's words, 'And His Throne (dominion) extends on the water' also indicates this meaning, since there is no link or relationship between the throne of form and the water of form, either with respect to the legal judgements and the nature of existent beings or with respect to the dictates of the intellect. Thus the meaning of knowledge — which is a universal reality pervading all things in a measure specific to each thing — is referred to in His words, 'That is the decree of the Mighty, the Knowing.' This is the best and most accurate of explanations, since the Throne and other realities besides the Throne are not established except by means of life and real life is nothing else but knowledge. The throne is one of the mightiest bodies or entities and the closest of things to the highest celestial realities; thus if the mightiest of things is described as possessing some of those qualities shared by other things in general, then of necessity this principle is applicable to other things lower than it. This is affirmed in Allah's words, 'The Beneficent Who ascended the Throne (and established His power);' by His Power over the mightiest of things He of necessity has dominion over everything below. There are numerous studies of a rational and logical nature on the subject but it would be inappropriate to include them here.

The 'real' or 'true' earth is the antithesis of this water according to both the judgement of the intellect and that contained in the narrated sources: the 'real water' is spiritual knowledge and sacred gnosis and the 'real earth' tangible, acquired knowledge and speculative and cognitive gnosis. If every time it was mentioned, the meaning of earth were pure dust (as the meaning of the Arabic would imply on the first reading), then Allah would not have said of Adam, 'Surely the likeness of Jesus (Isa) is with

Allah as the likeness of Adam; He created him from dust'. Although the word dust is used, it is clear that Adam was not created purely from dust, rather he was created from this, together with other elements; thus the dust is just one part of the various component elements of his body, but the whole is referred to as dust because it forms the major part in comparison to the other elements. This principle also applies to the animals, indeed to every existent being. Iblis (Satan), for example, was not created from fire alone (despite his saying, 'You have created me from fire') but rather from the four elements. He describes himself as having been made from fire because it constitutes the major element of the different components (fire is the dominant element of composition of the jinn of which Saytan is a member). Thus what is meant by dust, with respect to the creation of Adam, is in fact earth, together with all the other elements commonly associated with earth. Similarly, it is the knowledge of the outer acquired through the senses, with the aid of the speculative faculty, that is referred to as true earth. Thus it is apposite to connect all knowledge whose source springs from the outward and inward senses with the dust, and all knowledge whose source springs from unveilings and divine outpourings — like the divine knowledge and gnosis (known variously as revelation, inspiration or knowledge from His presence) — to this water. Allah refers to this in His words, 'And if they had kept up the Torah *(tawrah)* and the Gospel *(injil)* and that which was revealed to them from their Lord, they would certainly have eaten from above them and below them and from beneath their feet.' What is here referred to as 'above' is an indication of the spiritual world and the knowledge which is revealed from this world; what is referred to as 'below' is an indication of the knowledge of the physical realm and all the other knowledge which may be acquired from this realm. What some commentators have said, namely that the eating from above refers to the rain and from below to the plants, is not true, however, since the water and the plants are obtained not only by those who abide by the Torah, the Gospel and the Qur'an but also by all other men and animals as well. Thus to infer that the obtaining of these two types of food is conditional upon the keeping up of the Torah,

the Gospel and the Qur'an is rationally untenable to anyone
who reflects upon this matter.

If the people of *tariqah* are not able to purify the inner with
the water of the gnosis of reality (because of the existence of
some kind of obstacle), then it is permissible for them to use the
above-mentioned knowledge of the outer in order to purify their
inner self — in a measure appropriate to the degree of their
outward knowledge. The knowledge of the outer is thus related
to the *shari'ah*, the knowledge of the inner to the *tariqah,* and the
gnostic knowledge (which occupies a position above these two)
to the *haqiqah.* Thus if the spiritual traveller is not able to obtain
purification, with respect to the *tariqah,* by means of the real or
true water, then he is permitted to purify his outer knowledge
by means of the *shari'ah.* This is because the gradual purification
of the outer leads to a purification of the inner; thus it is that
Allah refers in detail to the reason for *tayammum* when He says,
'And if you are sick, or on a journey, or one of you come from
the privy or you have touched the women, and you cannot find
water, betake yourselves to pure earth, then wipe your faces,
and your hands therewith. Allah does not desire to put on you
any difficulty, but He wishes to purify you and that He may
complete His favour on you, so that you may be grateful.'

Allah also refers to another aspect of this matter by His commanding the slave to purify the self by means of the element of
pure earth; in doing so He is commanding the person who is
unable to purify the self by means of the intellect to fulfil the
duties of the *shari'ah,* since the intellect corresponds to water in
its ability to purify in the realm of reality. Outer purity is a
necessary prerequisite of inner purity (as we have seen above).
Allah refers to this with His words, 'And your garments do purify
and uncleanness do shun;' here the garments indicate the body
and all its outward actions, 'do purify' the purification of the
shari'ah and uncleanness here indicates man's attachment to the
world and his becoming sullied by it. Thus it is permissible to
understand these words as words of guidance and instruction
for the spiritual traveller, telling him to return to the original
state of annihilation and non-existence. This state is here called
the dust on the one hand, since it is from this that man originally

comes, as is evident from his outward and physical existence, and water on the other, since he is also originally from water. Hence Allah says, 'He has created you from dust' and 'I created you before when you were nothing.' This means that if the spiritual traveller is not able to use the water of reality, he may use dust, the substance out of which he was formed and the basest and lowest of things, to attain to a state of total humility; by means of this state he may attain to a state of poverty and absolute submission, which in turn are the two prerequisites for entry into the Presence of His Power. This Presence of Power is also known as the Garden of the Essence as indicated in His words, 'I am with those who possess hearts of humility' and in the words of the gnostic slave, 'When poverty is perfected then that is Allah.' This station may also be expressed as a submersion in the ocean of the water of eternal life, whereby true purity is attained together with entry into the House of Allah, the al-Aqsa Mosque and Masjid al-Haram which are all forbidden of access to other than those in this state of purity.

Shaykh Muhyi al-Din has indicated the aspect connected to dust, poverty and humility in a section devoted to this topic in his *Futuhat:* 'The earth becomes the goal because by its nature it is in a state of humility. In an absloute sense it is this humility which is the aim of slavery and worship; thus the purification of the slave is by fulfilling that which is expected of a slave, namely humility, poverty, respect of His Lord's rites, laws and commands. If it is forgotten that one's worship takes place on the earth, then one is reminded again by the fact that *tayammum* can only be done with the dust which is a part of this earth, that man and his progeny is from earth and that he remains close to it of necessity by his poverty and neediness. This notion is reflected in the saying of the Arabs, "The hand of the man becomes dusty when he is in need." '

When the slave of Allah recognises that dust is the lowest of the elements and that it is part of his own origins, then he is purified of any impurity which might cause him to leave this station. But this only applies in the case when water cannot be found. Water, as we have said, is knowledge: it is by knowledge that the hearts are given life, just as it is by water that the body and earth are given life. This is like the state of the person who imitates the dictates of his intellect with respect to his perception of Allah. Just as the *tayammum* of the person who finds water, and is able to use it, is invalidated, so too, if the legal code of the *shari'ah* commands to something, is one's obedience to the intellect and one's reflection upon Allah's intent with respect to that matter invalidated. This rule applies in particular when the intellect is unable to find a sufficient proof: it is the intellect itself which demands that one turn back to the legal code for affirmation. In this case the intellect and the legal code work in harmony; when this is realised, then one benefits greatly with respect to one's understanding of the secrets of worship.

Shaykh Muhyi al-Din has also indicated how water may be sub-divided according to the various levels of knowledge of truth and reality. We shall not discuss this matter here for fear of making this section too lengthy and of incommodating the reader. The overall purpose of this discussion, however, is as we have outlined above.

It is obligatory for the spiritual traveller to do *tayammum* (as we have mentioned above) in order that he may be able to use the above-mentioned water, that is, attain to the knowledge of truth and reality. The manner of this *tayammum* is that the person first wipes his face with the above-mentioned dust. In doing so, he purifies his secret and his reality of any impurity arising from attachment to this world and from loving any other but Allah; he then adorns his outward aspect with acts of obedience in accordance with the prophetic laws; he then wipes his right side, that is his heart, in order to purify it from attachment to the next world and from all associated with it, whether it be the blessings of the Garden, maidens or palaces; he then wipes his left side, that is his soul, in order to attain purification from this world and all associated with it, be it wealth, position and general benefit. Moreover, purification of the right and left side is only obtained by abandoning this world and the next (as we have already explained above). It is for this reason that we must wipe over the back of the right hand with the palm of the left and the back of the left with the palm of the right — such that the person does not oppose or contradict his outer with his inner and his inner with his outer. Thus purification of the one is achieved by means of the other.

iii) According to the people of *haqiqah*

The *tayammum* of this group refers to their annihilation from the world itself and all contained therein, including all the simple elements and compounds; in this way they are purified from egotism and otherness, which of necessity accompanies their attachement to the world and all contained therein. This is so since the world of the outer, which is also called the *mulk* or kingdom is equivalent to dust and the world of the inner, called the *malakut* or spiritual realm, is equivalent to water. This is shown by the fact that when Allah talks of the kingdom, He usually does so by referring to it as the earth and when He speaks of the spirtual realm, He usually does so by referring to the sky. The earth is obviously related to dust by the density and opaqueness of its nature, indeed the earth is composed of dust itself. The sky is related to water by the subtleness and lightness of its nature, indeed the sky is composed of water itself, this is confirmed by the consensus of the people of *shari'ah* and by a comparison of the cosmic and the individual dimensions. We shall now enlarge on this in more detail.

The difference between the people of *tariqah* and the people of *haqiqah* with respect to this purification is that the former purify themselves from blameworthy behaviour and from base characteristics by taking upon themselves praiseworthy characteristics and good qualities; the latter, however, purify themselves from the ego and any traces of themselves that might lead to duality and (seeing) other-than-Him. This is affirmed in the words of the Prophet when he says, 'Surely it is a covering on my heart and surely I seek forgiveness from Allah seventy times every day and night.' This is also reflected in the words of the gnostic, 'Between You and me there is an individual existence which is in conflict with me so remove, by Your grace, this individual existence from between us.' The covering which is indicated in the saying of the Prophet is his return to the world of multiplicity in order that he may call and guide the people. This is indicated by his words in the Qur'an, 'Say: I am only a mortal like you' and also Allah's words, '(it is) only a delivery (of communications) from Allah.' The complete stripping away of the self and the utter solitariness which he attains at certain times is also an indication of this state. The Prophet's saying 'I have times with Allah that I do not share even with the most intimate angel or prophet' demonstrates that he was in the world of arrival at Allah and total intimacy; it is the station of abiding after annihilation, expressed in His words, 'Two bows' lengths or closer still.'

The shaking off of the excess dust from one's hands after striking them on the ground during performance of the *tayammum* is an indication of one's hands shaking off their attachment to the two worlds. This kind of purification is performed by the gnostic striking his hands — which here represent the intellect and the self — on the world of the outer and that of the inner and preventing them from 'paying attention' to these worlds in any way; he then shakes his hands to remove the sight of this total annihilation; he then wipes over his true or real face — which is sometimes expressed as the secret and sometimes the spirit — in order to ascertain whether there remains any trace of love of the two worlds or not; he then wipes the back and palms of both hands (which are also expressions of the intellect and self), using the back and palm of both hands, in order to establish whether in reality there remains any trace on them of attachment to the two worlds. If there is attachment to other-than-Him in any way, be it strong or weak, then he is prevented from attaining the true purification of reality, be it by means of water or earth. Thus the spiritual traveller must inspect his outer and inner at the time of their annihilation in order to see if there remains any trace in them of attachment to the two worlds. This notion is supported by the words of the Prophet, 'This world is forbidden to the people of the hereafter and the hereafter is forbidden to the people of this and both are forbidden to the people of Allah.

Love of this world and the next is a veil and is a kind of *shirk* of something else with Allah. The existence of a veil, or of *shirk*, renders attainment of purification impossible, since the person who is veiled or quality of *shirk* is unclean, according to

Allah's judgement: 'Surely the idol worshippers, are nothing but unclean.' It is evident too that purity and uncleanliness are two opposites which can never be reconciled. Thus it is necessary to remove uncleanliness before beginning the purification in the manner we have already explained. Allah has referred to this with His words, 'O you who are clothed! Arise and warn, and magnify your Lord, and purify your garments and shun uncleanliness.' The words 'and purify your garments' refer to the purification of the outer; the words 'and shun uncleanliness' refer to the purification of the inner by distancing oneself from the uncleanliness of idolatry, veiling and seeing other-than-Him.

There are many other examples of a similar nature in the Qur'an and the body of *ahadith,* and the reader is advised to investigate them in the appropriate sources. At this point we shall conclude our study of the three types of purification, namely *wudu', ghusl* and *tayammum,* in the light of this particular station; and Allah says the truth and guides to the correct path.

Knowledge of the *qiblah* (direction of prayer) and the time and place of the prayer should be sought in the appropriate books of jurisprudence, as it would not be fitting to continue the study thereof in a work of this kind (although we shall be obliged to discuss the matter in due course, as the reader shall see). We shall now begin a study of the nature of prayer.

4

The Nature of Prayer:
in the light of the intellect, the Prophetic traditions and the unveilings
of the heart

The reader should realise that all divine laws are based upon a
consideration of time, place and the duty to the brotherhood of
Muslims, be it in the realm of form or of inner reality. Examples
of time-related events are the prayers, the fasting, *zakat* (the
almstax), *hajj*, the *jihad* and the various times of the recommended
visits to graves and shrines and the social meetings incumbent
upon Muslims. As for the place-related events, there are those
which are set in Makkah, Madinah, the Haram Mosque and
the Ka'bah, the al-Aqsa mosque and its sacred rock, the mosques
of Kufah and Basrah, the graves of the prophets and saints, and
the places of martyrdom of the infallible Imams of the family of
the Prophet. The brotherhood of Muslims refers, for example,
to the prophets, the messengers, the saints, the spiritual guardians, the messengers 'endowed with constancy', the Imams of
guidance and the caliphs of Allah in both worlds and all the
companions and followers may Allah be content with them all,
the angels and in particular Gabriel, Michael, Isra'fil and 'Izra'il
and their like from amongst the angels and the righteous slaves
of Allah.

Time, when measured in respect to itself is one single entity;
however time becomes particularised with respect to the above-
mentioned acts of worship — such that the latter cannot be
performed except in relation to a particular time. This particular
time possesses superiority over the rest of time — as the prophet
or messenger was aware of by way of his special inspiration from
Allah. Thus the obligatory prayer, for example, is neither valid
before nor after its appropriate time. Indeed the same applies
to all acts of worship. The likeness of this is that of someone
who dies leaving to his sons some treasure hidden in a particular
place; he then tells them that they should take a certain number
of steps from a certain wall in order to determine the location
of the treasure. If the sons were to count one step more or one
less, then they would not find the treasure. Thus, in order to
find their treasure, they must respect the number indicated. The

same is true for the various acts of worship and the times prescribed for them. If they are performed outside their times, then
they are not accepted and the person who offers them will in no
way be rewarded.

The same principle may be applied to the notion of place:
with respect to itself, place is one single entity, but from another
aspect, each locality possesses certain features which distinguish
it from other places. Certain acts of worship are only acceptable
when performed in a certain place. The Ka'bah, the Masjid
al-Haram and the al-Aqsa mosques are examples of these special
places.

The same principle applies with respect to the concept of
brotherhood: with respect to itself, the notion of brotherhood is
an all-encompassing entity; from another aspect, however, certain brothers of the brotherhood are distinct from the rest. The
prophets, messengers, saints, spiritual inheritors and the like are
examples of this.

On investigation we see that the daily prayers, the Friday
prayers, the 'Id (feast-day) prayers and the *hajj* have been prescribed in order that these three aspects be joined. The daily
prayers are undertake by a group of people in a particular locality,
the Friday and congregational prayers in a particular town, and
the *hajj* and the visits to the sacred shrines in a site which attracts
people from a particular region or country. The *hajj* occurs in a
particular place, known as the House of Allah and the House of
His slave, and its prayers are performed at a particular time; its
rites join together the brotherhood of Muslims. In one event,
therefore, place, time and brotherhood are brought together. By
virtue of the hidden wisdom of this event, Allah grants whatever
blessing or benefit the slaves may request in their supplications;
He does this by His outpouring of divine grace on the souls of
the slaves, in accordance with the merit of each and in relation
to their essences and the various capacities with which they have
been endowed. Moreoever, His bestowal and granting does not
depend on the intensity of each individual's prayer but rather
on the event itself: every gathering possesses its own inherent
wisdom and benefit which is shared by no other event. We may
cite the theory of numbers as an example of this. Thus we see

that in the number three there is a particularity which is not shared by four and vice-versa. The same principle can be applied to all numbers, from ten to a thousand and any number between them. This principle, as some have pointed out, is a principle of existence in general and one which accords exactly with the Muhammadi reality — a reality which encompasses all these numbers and levels, both in the realm of form and inner reality. The Prophet refers to this when he says, 'I have been given all the names' and 'I have been sent to perfect good behaviour.' These words are in accordance with the triads of truths which form the dominent feature of his reality, like for example the triad of prophethood, messengership and saintliness *(wilayah)*, the triad of submission, faith and certainty, and that of revelation, inspiration and unveiling. There are also other examples which demonstrate this same symbolic pattern, such as his love of perfume, women and prayer, as we know from his words, 'I love three things of your world; perfume, women and the coolness of the eye in prayer.'

The nature of the essence of the prophet requires this gathering together of things and the establishment of intimacy and friendship between the various existent beings — in particular with respect to mankind as a whole. It is for this reason he established certain places and events in order to guarantee this friendship and intimacy, the ultimate aim of his mission and indeed that of all the prophets being nothing but this. It is clear that the gathering of a particular group, at a particular place, in a particular manner several times a day will of necessity result in an increase of love between the members of the group and an increase in their firmness and resolution — in accordance with their capacity and merit. Examples of this are the congregational prayers undertaken in a particular locality, the Friday prayers in the prescribed place in a town, and the *hajj* once a year in Makkah. There is no disagreement among persons of intellect that such gatherings increase love and friendship; the Qur'an also provides numerous examples in proof of our words. Thus, just as this friendship is established during the five gatherings of the daily prayers in each locality, so it is also established in the Friday gatherings of each town, on the various days of the prescribed feasts, and on the occasion of the visits to the shrines and amongst the people of the different countries during the Hajj. Indeed, these places and events have only been described with this in mind. Other benefits and advantages arise — other than that of the joining of the people in friendship — like, for example, the social, commercial and marriage contracts which are undertaken during these gatherings. These social gatherings and events contain matters of hidden wisdom which are worthy of investigation; suffice it to say that they are all based on this triad of realities, namely time, place and the brotherhood of Muslims.

We shall now discuss the ascent of the Prophet *(mi'raj)*, which expresses these above-mentioned realities; we shall examine this subject first in relation to the world of form and then in relation to the world of inner reality. It should be noted that there are many differences of opinion among the scholars, the common people and the philosophers concerning the matter.

5

The Ascent of the Prophet *(mi'raj)*

i) In the realm of form

The title of this section refers to the Prophet's will and intent to attain to this triad of gatherings in the realm of form — just as he attains to them in the realm of inner meaning (in the various stations of sublimity between the heavens and the earth). Thus his movement in the realm of form from the Haram mosque to that of Kufah, then to the al-Aqsa Mosque and then his ascent to the seven heavens, the Throne and the Footstool (as is related in the Qur'an) was for this purpose, namely for the three above-mentioned gatherings. Such gatherings are a means whereby the Prophet's perfections may flow out to the people. The Prophet in fact draws them out of their state of imperfection and allows them to attain their own specific perfection, in accordance with their receptivity and capacity.

This ascent is related in the various Prophetic sayings of the 'night journey' and is referred to in the Qur'an by Allah's words, 'Glory be to Him Who made His servant to go on a night from the Sacred Mosque to the al-Aqsa Mosque (or 'remote mosque') of which We have blessed the precincts, so that We may show you some of Our signs; surely He is the Hearing, the Seeing.' It has been narrated that all the prophets ask for this form of ascent from Allah — a form which encompasses all the above-mentioned gatherings. Allah has also commanded His Prophet Muhammad to this, namely a crossing and ascent to these heavenly places by means of his body, in the realm of form; it is even reported that during his ascent to the sky he wanted to take off his sandals, just as Moses had done when he went up the mountain of Tur and the angel said to him, 'O Prophet of Allah, do not take them off for surely we desire that the blessing of your sandals may reach our places (of abode).' Such things are by no means impossible for Allah, for He is the One Who renders everything possible and the One Who determines events.

Moreover, it has been established in the divine wisdom that the prophets, saints, perfected ones and spiritual poles possess

great power in both the earthly and spiritual worlds: when a
person becomes perfected and merits being the caliph of Allah
in His earthly and spiritual kingdoms, then he is able to do
anything he wishes within the realm of these two worlds — consider, for example, the way in which some of the saints, of Allah
are able to travel huge distances (within a space of time not
normally possible) and are able to rise people from the dead.
There is also the example of Asaf (Solomon's vizier) who was
able to cover a vast distance across the earth when he went to
fetch the Throne of Bilqis (the Queen of Sheba). Moses, too,
was able to separate the sea in order to drown the Pharoah and
save his own people. Solomon controlled the winds, riding them
and journeying where he willed (according to the Qur'an). Abraham was able to render the fire (into which he had been
thrown) cool such that he was untouched by its flames. The
Prophet himself, when desiring to demonstrate a miracle, was
able to wield power in the lunar realm when he split the moon
in the presence of the disbelievers and a number of other persons
who were Muslims. Sham'un (one of the spiritual inheritors of
Jesus) was able to wield power in the solar realm by moving the
sun from the east to another position of his choosing. 'Ali, on
whom be peace, also exercised authority in the solar realm when
he twice caused the sun to move back to the place of prayer,
once in Madinah and once in the region of Babul (as is described
in the books of both the Sunnis and the Shiahs). There is also
the example of Idris (Enoch) who ascended to the realm of the
heavens where he has remained until the present time. Jesus
himself also ascended to the heavens. It has been shown how
the angels and the jinn are able to take whatever form they desire
and that they are able to enter into whatever world they wish.
It is commonly agreed that man is more noble than they; indeed
the angels have been commanded to make prostration before
them and to serve and obey them in all matters. One may thus
ask the question why man is unable to do the things of which
the angels are capable. The truth of the matter is that man is
in fact more capable than they are. This is evident when we
consider the nature of the *abdal* (the spiritual guardians who
hold sway over the world), and the way in which they change

from one form to another, and how they may appear in more than one place at the same time. This is similar to the way in which the angel Gabriel appeared in this world in the form of (the Prophet's companion) Dahiya al-Kalbi on several different occasions, as did other angels (when they appeared, for example, in aid of the Prophet on the day of the Battle of Badr and that of Hunayn).

When we accept the truth of the above and we realise that man is the noblest of creatures, then it is difficult for us not to accept too that all perfected men are capable of expressing special powers (in the manner described above); it would be difficult, too, for us not to accept that the noblest of prophets and saints were likewise capable of this and of greater things. Muhammad's ascent to the heavens is, in fact, of a lesser dimension than his influence over events in the lunar and solar realms and over Gabriel (when he wished to begin the ascent). It is most important that one understands and believes in these matters for any attempt to explain them away is of no use.

ii)   In the realm of inner meaning

Most people agree that the ascent of the Prophet in the realm of inner meaning refers to his arrival at the Real during the time of the night journey and by means of the unification of essence (which is also known as the 'unity of the separate after the gathering'). It also refers to his perception of the reality of things; this is reflected in his words, 'We were shown things as they actually are' and 'During that night I learnt the knowledge of the first and subsequent (peoples).' This station is connected to that of Abraham for Allah says of the latter, 'And thus did We show Abraham the kingdom of the heavens and the earth and that he might be of those who are sure.' This special relationship between the Prophet and Abraham is affirmed by the Qur'an and may be demonstrated by means of other proofs.

It is clear that this ascent (and other similar spiritual events) has no need of movement in the realm of form or of any notion of physical distance. When we talk about the movement of a particular person, then we are referring to his going from one place to another in the phenomenal world; the *mi'raj* that we are discussing, however, does not imply this kind of movement. When we talk about the movement of ideas in the mind, then we are referring to the way in which one can rationalise from principles to conclusions by means of thoughts. According to the general consensus, however, such a way of thinking is a kind of veil. 'Ali has affirmed this when he says; 'I have come to know Allah by abandoning thought.' Thus this station of the *mi'raj* is only attained by abandoning both these approaches and by no longer considering anything which inherently implies other-than-Him as valid. It is for this reason that Ja'far ibn Muhammad al-Sadiq, who was the Pole of the Age and the Imam of his time, said, 'Whoever understands separation, as distinct from arrival and movement as distinct from stillness has reached a point of establishment in the vision of divine unity *(tawhid).*' What is here meant by separation is the first separation of multiplicity, necessary by the inherent nature of creation; by arrival is meant the joining or gatheredness which is antithetical to it; by movement is meant the spiritual wayfaring; and by stillness one's establishment in the source of solitariness of the Essence. This arrival is also expressed as the annihilation of the slave in the Attributes of the Real by his abandonment of the attributes of his self; it is the realisation of the station of the Names to which the Prophet refers with his words, 'Whoever can enumerate these names will enter the Garden.' The separation is also expressed as the veiling of the slave by his own attributes and those of creation and by his attaching an absolute reality to them; those who veil themselves by seeing the outer (and what is other-than-Him) are of necessity far from the Real and the contemplation of Him although they may claim to be established in the station of *tawhid*.

All are agreed that there are four kinds of travel in the realm of inner meaning. The first is the travelling 'to' Allah from the various stations of the self: it is the arrival at the 'clear horizon,' which is the final station of the heart and the beginning of the emanations of His Names. The second is the travelling 'in' Allah by assimilating His Attributes and His Names; this kind of journey leads to the 'higher horizon' which is the final point of the Presence of Oneness. The third is ascent to the source of gathered-

ness and the Presence of Solitariness: this is the station of the
'two bow's lengths' as long as duality remains; when duality is
removed then it is the station of 'or closer still' and the final
station of saintliness *(wilayah)*. The fourth is travel 'by' Allah
'from' Allah in order to achieve perfection: this is the state of
abiding after annihilation and separation after gatheredness.

Each of these different ways of travel has a beginning and an
end; the beginning of each is clear from the beginning and end
of each stage as we have described above. As for the end, that
of the first is the removal of the veils of multiplicity from the
face of Oneness. The end of the second is the removal of the
veils of Oneness from the various aspects of multiplicty in the
inner realm of gnosis. The end of the third is the removal of the
limitation or restriction of the duality of outer and inner, by
attaining to unity in gatheredness. The end of the fourth is the
return from the Presence of the Real to creation in the station
of constancy and perseverance; it is the station of reconciling
gatheredness and separation by witnessing now the Real manifests throughout the various levels of creation and how the creation eventually disappears into the Real. In this station one
sees the source of Oneness in the forms of multiplicity and the
forms of multiplicity in the source of Oneness.

There are no further ways of travel or spiritual destinations
beyond these four. Thus the *mi'raj* as a whole, be it with respect
to a prophet, a messenger, a saint or a spiritual inheritor, is
contained in the above four divisions. Any variations in the mode
of travel which occur are connected to the capacity and receptivity of each particular person. Moreover, a *mi'raj* may take place
during a whole night, a single hour or even a blink of an eyelid.
Indeed, it may occur after striving for forty years or even forty
thousand years since this kind of travel has no specific limits as
to its nature and no specific time; 'and that is the grace of Allah;
He bestows it on whom He wishes and Allah is of mighty grace.'

With this in mind, we should now examine Allah's words,
'Glory be to Him Who made His servant go on a night from the
Sacred Mosque to the remote mosque (of al-Aqsa) of which We
have blessed the precincts, so that We may show to him some
of Our signs; surely He is the Hearing, the Seeing' for they are

pertinent proof of the truth of what we are saying. The meaning of 'Glory be to Him, Who made His servant to go on a night' is glory be to Him Who made His real or 'true' slave, namely Muhammad, go by night, that is, during the night of the multiplicity of form in the realm of creational and phenomenal realities; the meaning of 'from the Haram Mosque' is from the heart of reality which is *haram*, that is forbidden to others to enter; the meaning of 'to the remote mosque' is to the Presence of the Spirit and the world of witnessing which is the furthest or highest level of witnessing; Allah's words 'of which We have blessed the precincts' refer to His bestowal of the blessings of gnostic realities; and the words 'So that We may show to Him some of Our signs' refer to Allah's showing him of his *ayat* — which all point to His Essence, His Attributes, His Names and His Actions, indeed to a contemplation of Him in His worlds of spirituality and corporeality. His words, 'He is the Hearing, the Seeing' refer to the fact that Allah is the only True Hearer of the servant's prayers and the only One Who sees that each is answered.

One may express this still more lucidly by saying that the Haram Mosque is his true or real heart which is forbidden of access except to the Real Himself. The heart is the abode or the station of Allah; this is affirmed in His words, 'Neither the earth nor the heavens can contain Me but the heart of the believing slave (contains Me).' This heart is connected to the Haram Mosque since the latter is the *qiblah* (direction of prayer) of the people of the earth and the former is the *qiblah* or focus for all the physical limbs and inner organs of man, as well as being the centre of man's capacity both in the realm of form and inner meaning or spirit. Moreover, the heart is the first thing to appear as the form of man takes shape from the sperm, the blood clot and the lump of flesh in the womb; similarly, the Ka'bah was the 'First House established for the people in the blessed place of Bakka.' The al-Aqsa Mosque which is his spirit which has been 'added' to him, as the following words of Allah testify: 'And breathed into him of My spirit.' The spirit in the station of al-Aqsa is in th highest station of witnessing and unveiling as the words of 'Ali affirm when he says, 'And my heart (lives) by my knowledge of You and my spirit by my witnessing of You;'

this is also affirmed in the words of his grandfather, 'If the veil were lifted, it would not increase my certainty.' This station is connected to the al-Aqsa mosque, which is the *qiblah* of the east for the people of Jesus; the spirit is also the *qiblah* of the heart of man, just as the heart is the *qiblah* of the whole body. The Ka'bah is related to the concept of the mosque just as the mosque is connected to the Haram, and likewise the body may be seen to represent the Haram and the heart the mosque and the spirit the Ka'bah. His words: 'of which We have blessed the precincts' is an indication of the spirit and that which surrounds it. We should understand from these words that Allah has blessed the area around it with the blessings of gnostic realities, secret wisdom and subtle intelligences.

The reason for the ascent and arrival at the Divine Presence is so that Allah may show him — from His signs within the realm of the individual self, rather than from within the cosmic dimension — a vision of His Essence and of His Qualities in the essence and qualities of Muhammad by way of an actual witnessing of the pre-creational Source-Forms; the reason too, is so that Allah may make him hear, or render him receptive to His words and His secrets and may make him perceive the meaning of His indications and His subtle hidden communications. This is because Muhammad is the caliph in Allah's *mulk*, or world, and in His *malakut*, or spiritual domain. It is he who fulfils Allah's command, both in His cosmic dimension and His realm of the self. The meaning of 'His is the judgement, and to Him you shall be brought back' is that Muhammad holds judgement over these two domains; he alternately works with or withdraws from the inhabitants of these two domains; it is they who turn to Him for their needs and problems, that is, for whatever is of benefit to them, with respect to their religion and their daily life in this world. The following verse seems to indicate the words of such a caliph:

> My pen and my table in existence are given life
> By the Divine Pen and the Guarded Tablet.
> My hand is the right hand of Allah in his spiritual domain;
> I carry out what I wish and the principles and duties are
> my pleasure and blessing.

A *hadith* of the Prophet reflects this idea: 'Allah created Adam in His image;' again the import of the words of the gnostic, 'I am the Truth and all those like me' and 'Is there other than me in the two abodes?' is not lost on those who understand this science. This concludes our study of the *mi'raj* with respect to the self and the realm of inner meaning.

6

Different Aspects of Prayer

We shall now return to our study of the various aspects of prayer. We have already explained that the five roots (or principles) and the five branches (or pillars of Islam) are established by the prophets and the messengers by the command of Allah, in order that what is deficient may be made up and that each may attain to its own specific (as specified in His divine knowledge). We have also explained how this is facilitated by a perfection of the twin forces of knowledge and action. We have further explained that, had mankind been in need of more than this in order to attain to this perfection, it would have been incumbent upon Allah to communicate this and the prophets and messengers would have had to expound it in more detail. Mankind, has, however, no need of more than this: thus Allah does not command to more than this, nor does He order His prophet to command to mankind to more than this. He is like the astute physician who gives only the amount of medicine needed by the sick person, neither more nor less. We have demonstrated how there may be individual differences of judgement amongst the physicians of the outer, but this is only in accordance with the varying circumstances of time and place; on investigation, we realise that there is a basic consensus and harmony; this notion is reflected in Allah's words, 'And if it were from any other than Allah, they would have found in it many a discrepancy.' The reader should also realise that the greater the prophet or messenger, the more intense is his inculcation of these roots and branches. By common agreement our Prophet Muhammad, peace be upon him, is the greatest and noblest of the prophets — and thus of necessity establishment of these principles is of the highest order. It is for this reason that his prayer encompasses the totality of the acts of worship stipulated in the *shari'ah* (and established by all the prophets and messengers); indeed his prayer encompasses all the acts of worship which have been made incumebt upon creation as a whole. This is affirmed in Allah's words, 'And there is no animal that walks upon the earth nor bird that flies with its two wings but (they are) creatures like yourselves; We have not neglected anything in the Book; then to their Lord they shall be gathered.'

At this point a more detailed explanation will be necessary to show that the person who is in a state of prayer is not only in prayer but also fasting, paying *zakat* (the almstax), performing the *hajj* (pilgrimage) and fighting *jihad*. This aspect of prayer is affirmed in the words of Allah, 'He knows the prayer of each one and its glorification, and Allah is cognizant of what you do.' Each existent being has its own prayer and glorification of Him; thus the person in a state of prayer is in harmony with the totality of existent beings and in accord with their different situations and obligations.

Up to this point we have been considering the prayer as supplication and an act of obedience. If we now consider it as a particular form of worship which embraces the various movements of standing, sitting, bowing, prostrating, together with the words of praise and glorification, and which all take place within a specific time, then it is also true to say that the person praying is in harmony with the totality of creatures and that by his worship he embraces all acts of worship. This is true since all creatures, both spiritual and corporeal, have their own specific forms of praise, glorification, bowing, prostration, standing, and sitting (as we have demonstrated above with an *ayah* from the Qur'an and we as have already explained at the beginning of this work). If we consider the standing in prayer, then this is in harmony with mankind in general since men's movements are in an upright fashion. If we consider the bowing and the movement towards the horizontal position, then this accords with the pattern of all animals since, as all agree, their movements are in a horizontal plane. As for the prostration and downward movement, then they accord with the pattern of all plants. There are no other kinds of movement, apart from these three, and all the composite existent things both of the plant and animal kingdoms, together with man, are encompassed by them.

One may, if one wishes, express this in another may by saying that the standing is in accordance with those angels whose duty it is to stand constantly, the bowing is in harmony with those angels whose duty it is to bow constantly, and the prostration is in accord with those angels whose duty it is to prostrate constantly. The same may be said for all the specific movements of the prayer. Allah has referred to this in its totality when He says, 'Do you not see that Allah is He to Whom make prostration whoever is in the heavens and the earth and the sun and the moon and the stars and the mountains and the trees, and the animals and many of the people... .' What is meant by prostration here is none other than the prayer itself: here the word refers to the whole rather than the specific part, just as when someone says a given person is prostrating, he means he is in a state of prayer, or when one says such and such a person is given to prostration, meaning he is constantly praying. It is also permissible to understand this word as meaning obedience or submission, since Allah says elsewhere, 'And the herbs and the trees prostrate to Him' meaning adore or do obeisance to His command and will. Moreover there are many instances of the use of this word in different ways both in the Qur'an and the language of the Arabs.

As for the saying of the *takbir al-haram* — the *Allahu Akbar* (God is Great) — at the beginning of the prayer, indicating one has entered the sanctity of the prayer and all else is excluded, then this applies to all in their worship and in particular to pilgrims and those making for the Haram, the House of Allah.

As for the intention, that is the goal which is, established in the heart, then this also applies to all in their worship, since all are aiming for His presence: if this were not so, then Allah would not have said, 'And if you were to ask them who created the heavens and the earth, they would certainly say: Allah...' and nor would He have said, 'And everyone has a direction to which he should turn, therefore hasten to (do) good works... .'

As for the praise and glorification of Allah, then this is in harmony with all existent things as the words of Allah testify: 'And there is not a single thing but glorifies Him with His praise, but you do not understand their glorification.' This praise accords in particular with the angels since Allah says 'And we celebrated Thy praise and extol Thy holiness.' The same applies to all the states of remembrance of Him, all supplications and associated movements and periods of stillness.

As for wishing blessings on the Prophet, then this is in harmony with Allah, with the angels and all the believers, as is stated in His words, 'Surely Allah and His angels bless the Prophet: O you who believe! Call for (divine) blessings on him and salute him with a (becoming) salutation.'

As for the number of cycles *(raka'at)* contained in the prayer, be it two, three or four, then this is in accord with the peoples of each of the prophets who came to establish a particular *shari'ah*. Thus it has been narrated that some of the prophets used to pray two cycles of prayer, some three and some four. It is said that Adam would pray two cycles, Noah three and Abraham four. This notion of number also accords with the prayer of the angels, expressed in the following *ayah* as 'flying on wings;' 'All praise is due to Allah, the Originator of the heavens and the earth, the Maker of the angels, messengers flying on wings, two, three and four; He increases in creation what He pleases; surely Allah has power over all things.' This perception of the nature of prayer is true since the prayer of every existent thing is in fact that very capacity or receptivity (which we have explained earlier) and which is indicated in Allah's words, 'Say: Everyone acts according to his manner' and 'He knows the prayer of each one and its glorification and Allah is cognizant of what they do.'

The wings, the mode of prayer of the angels, is the power that they exercise in both the higher and lower worlds. Mawla al-A'zam Kamal al-Din 'Abd al-Razzaq has referred to this in his interpretation of the Qur'an saying, ' "The Maker of the angels, messengers flying on wings" is an expression for their cosmic influence both in the spiritual or celestial sphere and in the earthly domain by means of these wings. Allah has made them messengers sent to the prophets with revelation, to the saints with inspiration and to others among mankind who have the capacity to direct and order their affairs; that which maintains this influence amongst these people or things is the medium of the wings. Thus every dimension is subject to the influence of a specific wing: the twin faculties of the intellect, the active and the perceptive, give the rational soul two wings; the understanding (or memory), the stimulant (of this understanding) and that which motivates action give three wings to the animal soul; the means of drawing sustenance, the impulse towards growth, re-

generation and a specific shape or form give four wings to the
vegetative soul. The number of wings of the angels is not restricted but rather corresponds to the various kinds of influence
that they possess. It is for this reason that the Messenger of
Allah has related that he saw Gabriel with six hundred wings
on the night of the *mir'aj;* it is also reported that "Gabriel bathes
morning and evening in the river of life, shaking off the excess
water from his wings when emerging; Allah then created countless angels from these drops." Allah refers to these numerous
wings when He says at the end of the *ayah,* "He increases in
creation what He pleases; surely Allah has power over all things."
These words also demonstrate that such a thing is possible and
that Allah is capable of it.'

Up to this point we have been discussing how the person
praying shares with the totality of creation every time he performs
a prayer. The way in which the person praying shares with the
Real in all aspects may be seen from a consideration of the *hadith,*
related from the Prophet who in turn relates it from Allah, which
says: 'I have divided the prayer between Me and My slave; one
half of it is for Myself and one half is for My slave, and My slave
receives whatever he asks for. When the slave says, "In the name
of the Beneficent, the Merciful", Allah says, I (too) praise My
slave. When the slave says, "Praise belongs to Allah, the Lord
of the Worlds", Allah says, "My slave has praised Me." When
the slave says "the Beneficent, the Merciful", Allah says, "My
slave has extolled Me." When the slave says "Master of the Day
of Judgement", Allah says, "I delegate the management of affairs
to My slave." When the slave says, "Thee do we serve and Thee
do we beseech for help", Allah says: "This is between Me and
My slave." When the slave says: "Keep us on the right path... ,"
then Allah says, "This is for My slave and My slave shall have
what he asks for." '

One of the gnostics has expressed the same notion; we shall
mention it here in order to expand our vision and to stimulate
our investigation of this matter. The mutual desire and harmony
which exists between the soul and the body necessitates the
ascent of the bodily form to the soul and the descent of the
spiritual form to the body. Reflection on the meaning of gnoses

and spiritual realities, mention of the Beloved, perception of His attributes of beauty and majesty, and the witnessing of His vastness and radiance cause the body to quiver by the force of its feelings and the trembling of its limbs. Similarly, mention of the enemy, of the stratagems he employs to his evil ends which are abhorred by the soul, stirs one to anger, causes one's face and eyes to flush red, swells one's veins, and causes one's body to heat up and one's movement to become uncoordinated. But the submission of the limbs, the humility of the body, the protection and purification of the latter from any evil influence, the remembrance, glorification and praise of Allah on the tongue, the harmony of the inner with the outer by means of one's intention, the avoidance of the pleasures of the senses, the remembrance of the states of the angelic realm and the domain of power, the approach of the bodily form to these two realms and to the most intimate of the righteous slaves of Allah, causes the ascent of the heart and the spirit to the Presence of Sanctity, a drawing near to the Real, an imbuing from the world of lights, attainment of gnoses and spiritual realities and sustenance from the angelic realm *(malakut)* and the domain of power *(jabarut)*.

Thus prayer is established as a form of worship which encompasses the postures of submission and humilty; the discomfort and hardship of the limbs which have been duly distanced and purified from evil, the determination to come closer to Him, the sincerity of one's intention, the acts of remembrance which evoke His blessings, which glorify and extol Him in a manner befitting His Presence, the extreme abasement before His might, and obeisance to His command and judgement are all part of the prayer.

This prayer is repeated each day and night the same number of times as the five senses. These senses are the means whereby the soul of man perceives the various states of the world of darkness; they are a means of exit away from the Real to the world of abasement. By these senses the soul gains entry to the forms of overspreading darkness existing at the material level and to the base corporeal states, impurities and ever-changing modes; by them the heart is darkened and polluted and it becomes veiled from the world of light. It becomes confused and its awareness of Him is broken off. The five prayers have therefore been established to counterbalance this and its times and its cycles have been specified in accordance with divine wisdom. The five senses are curbed during the prayer and the doors of physical perception are closed in order to restrict the influence of the darker aspects. The inner gate which leads towards the Real and the world of light is opened by means of presence of mind, by correct intention and focus of one's attention on the Real, as is affirmed in the words of the Prophet 'Prayer is not acceptable except when the heart is aware.' Allah has established the first of these prayers at midday, when the sun has just passed its zenith, as is affirmed in the words of Allah, 'Keep up prayer from the declining of the sun (till the darkness of the night).' The need for this prayer arises when man's spirit inclines towards the setting of the sun, when light disappears behind the veil of darkness. Ascendancy over the essential darkness and attainment of the original and natural form of man which Adam possessed in the Garden before his fall issues from the station of witnessing. It is the station of fulfilment of the contract with Allah whereby man enters the company of the lovers; he has no duty to fulfil in these circumstances — in this state, where the body's humours are deeply affected by its natural or normal rhythms, prayer is of no use.

Four cycles of prayer have been established, related to the four elements from which man originated. Just as the first stage of Islam is acceptance of the first principles of existence, so worship has been established as a way of giving thanks for Allah's blessings. This worship is Allah's first blessing on mankind. Gratitude issues from a recognition of the blessing from the Bestower of Blessings and it is an affirmation that it is from Him and not from oneself. Similarly, gratitude of the tongue is an affirmation that He is the Originator and Master of all things. This is reflected in the words of the person praying: 'Surely I have turned myself wholly to Him Who originated the heavens and the earth' and it is reflected in his obligatory reading of the opening *surah* of the Qur'an. The same applies to his limbs: in doing the prayer he is submitting to Allah's command and renouncing any power, capacity, will or knowledge on his part. It is only by renouncing his own will together with the whims and desires which cause him to act in accordance with his own particular nature and character that he is able to be obedient to that which Allah wants of him.

The afternoon prayer has been established as a four-cycle prayer by following on from the first principles by way of the four humours. The time of this prayer is closer to the sunset (than it is to the midday prayer): the nearer the body approaches darkness and comes to a point of harmony with the soul by its attraction to it, the further the soul is distanced from proximity with Allah and the world of light.

The sunset prayer, at the time of the veiling in darkness, contains three cycles: they are related to the three forces of the body which are fundamental to its continued existence, namely, the vegetal, animal and emotional forces. These forces appear when the soul 'sets' or disappears on the horizon of the body and becomes completely veiled from sight; it is for this reason that this particular prayer occurs at sunset.

The night prayer has four cycles in accordance with the four sense organs, which are the sources whence the other organs derive their strengths and capacities. These other organs, known as the major forces, are three in number, namely the brain, the liver and the testicles; they are the centres of strength on which the life of man is based and on which depends his and mankind's continued survival. By means of these three forces, his body attains to perfection, his dominion is established, and his authority and strength are reinforced. It is for this reason that the times of this prayer occur just at the beginning of darkness, during the darkness and at the times of sleep. The process of perfecting the body and its organs causes the spirit to sleep and to be submerged in the body. When the time of increase in strength of the body reaches its completion and perfection, then the authority of this prayer and station is completed; at this moment the spirit comes to the end of its period of submergence and of assisting the natural forces so that the body may reach perfection, and it then moves towards its own world and makes manifest the light of its intellect. Thereafter it begins to divest itself of the darkness and bodily domain, to awaken from its sleep and to manifest the heart which perceives the generality of things and to lead it away from perception of the parts. This awakening is like the emergence of the dawn of inner meaning by means of the sunlight of the spirit and its return to the eastern horizon.

The time of the morning prayer is the point of the joining between the night and the day: it consists of two cycles of prayer related to the spirit and the body — just as man before puberty was one entity, one natural body becomes two with the appearance of the intellect.

The principle and the form of this prayer have a specific order: the standing in the first cycle symbolises the natural state of man and the form of the rational soul, standing upright amongst the other existent beings; this is affirmed in Allah's words, 'Certainly We created man in the best image. Then We render him the lowest of the low'.

The bowing symbolises the station of the animal soul, since an animal is in a state of bowing. And the coming to the upright position again symbolises its becoming another type or kind of being by means of the light of rationality. This other type possesses particularities of uprightness and aspects of perfection by which it achieves harmony and takes on praiseworthy characteristics; in this way the qualities of superiority and excellence particular to man are acquired. The prostration symbolises the vegetative soul; this is so since the plants are in a state of prostration. The meaning of the raising of the head after prostration becomes clear in the light of the above-mentioned description of the standing straight and the bowing. The second prostration indicates that this particular soul, despite becoming a more noble species in man, and despite being superior to the rest of the plant species by its raising itself from the earth, contributing to the production of the four humours, does not attain to a higher degree than this; rather it remains in its own state, lacking perception and will, and concerned only with those activities which are natural to it as a plant. The standing in the second cycle symbolises the world of the intellect and its entry to the way of the *jabarut* (the domain of power) by the perfection of divestment from otherness obtained by a reasoning process. As for the bowing of this soul, it represents its entry to the path of the *malakut* (the angelic realm); this is obtained by a withdrawal from sexual desire, anger and any influence from the lower aspects of the soul. The raising up of this soul to the position of standing straight indicates an increase in its rank, by way of its readiness to receive saintliness *(wilayah)* and the perfection of gnosis. As for the prostration of this soul, it symbolises the nobility of the vegetative souls together with their bodily forms, which is referred to by Allah when He says, 'And the herbs and the trees do adore (Him).' The sitting up after the prostration is as we have described above. The returning to the position of prostration symbolises abiding in the state wherein it exercises influence over the corporeal world; it also symbolises the movement of this soul, in its nobility, towards this particular world. The saying of the *shahadah* (witnessing that Allah is One and that Muhammad is His Messenger) symbolises the soul's arrival by way of this true worship to the state of witnessing, that is perception and awareness of what is contained in the two worlds. It also symbolises final arrival at a position of intimacy and establishment in that which is arrived at; it is the state of fulfilling his desire by remaining obedient to the Prophet; it is the station associated with the words, 'May the peace and mercy and blessings be on you, O Prophet; and may peace be on us and on the righteous slaves of Allah.' The peace referred to here is an overflowing of Allah which emanates and sustains from the world of sanctity; it reaches these souls when they divest themselves of imperfection and sickness and array themselves in the perfections of divine character and attribute. By way of these emanations, these souls become manifestations of one of His Names in accordance with the capacity of each.

It is at this point that the words of the gnostic come to an end, may Allah sanctify and purify his spirit and the light of his grave. They demonstrate his attainment of total perfection and his station of unveiling such that he was able to discover the secrets of prayer. He has thus transmitted these realities of unveiling and subtleties of 'tasted' physical experience to the generations living after him. It was thus by means of him and others like him from among the perfected ones and the spiritual poles that these secrets became manifest and the veil surrounding them was lifted.

Up to this point we have been considering the wisdom behind the various conditions and stages of the prayer. We shall now consider prayer in relation to fasting and, in particular, the position of the person praying who in effect enters into the same state as the person who is fasting. We shall consider too the rest of the above-mentioned acts of worship. We shall do this by including them in a general explanation of why prayer takes priority and is preferred over all the other acts of worship; we shall also include them in our explanation of why the acts of worship, which are the branches of Islam, are five in number. This necessitates the establishment of another method of classification which contains and defines in a specific way all these points.

7

A Method of Classification:

the five branches (or pillars of Islam), the reason for the priority given
to prayer, how the person praying encompasses the totality of worship,
the reason why one act of worship takes preference over another

It should be realised that there are differences of opinion with
regard to the divisions of this subject. This is because some have
added the question of purification to that of the prayer, the
subject of *i'tikaf* (withdrawal into the mosque, in particular
during the last ten days of Ramadan) to that of fasting, the
subject of *khums* (a fifth part of wealth payed in tax) to that of
zakat, the *'umrah* (or minor *hajj* to Makkah) to the *hajj* (the major
pilgrimage) and the subject of *ribat* (withdrawal of the group for
the purpose of remembrance of Allah and physical training in
preparation for *jihad*) and 'the forbidding of evil and the enjoining of good' to that of *jihad*. These systems of classification are
not accepted by all; however, we shall begin by dealing with the
most famous and obvious of these, indeed with those points
agreed upon by the majority namely the prayer, the fasting,
zakat, hajj and *jihad*. The truth of the matter is that the branches
of Islam are contained within these five classifications and it is
not fitting that they be divided into any more or less.

Proof that they are contained within this number can be seen
in the fact that the religious obligations prescribed by law are
either related to the soul and wealth, like, for example, prayer
and fasting, or they are related purely to wealth, like, for example,
zakat, or they are related to the soul and wealth combined, like,
for example, the *hajj* and *jihad* (making five in all). Since the
Muslim has no need of more than this in order to attain to his
perfection and since it is not possible to achieve this perfection
with any less, then it must be that this number is correct — in
this way we may establish the proof of our argument.

At this point it would be desirable to introduce a fitting
metaphor: Allah is the Perfect Physician and the prophets and
the messengers, as we have already explained, are like doctors
of the soul and healers of the heart. The precepts and laws which
they prescribe by means of the *shari'ah* are comparable to the
potions and medicines given to sick persons and indeed anything

which is conducive to their health. If they had known of any cure for their sickness more effective than this, they would have commanded the people to use it and would have shown them what course of 'treatment' they should follow. This is so since it is incumbent upon them and indeed upon Allah Himself — by virtue of His kindness and grace. As we have explained on numerous occasions, it is inconceivable that the prophets of Allah should fail to be kind or should fail to bestow their grace on the people. Thus one realises that the 'cure', expressed here in the form of the five branches, is sufficient to dispel the sickness of ignorance, disbelief, doubt and hypocrisy, and 'this is the ordinance of the Mighty, the Wise.'

Just as it is not permitted to increase this number, so it is not permitted to reduce it. So, for example, if the medical doctor prescribes a potion or medicine to remove a physical illness, the sick person is not permitted to increase or reduce the potion or medicine in any way; if he were to do this, it would either aggravate the disease or would result in the death of the person concerned. Similarly, in the case of the spiritual doctor, that is the prophet, if he prescribes something in the form of a duty of the *shari'ah* or a divine law in order to get rid of some ignorance, disease of disbelief or hypocrisy, it is not permitted for the spiritually sick person to add anything to, or subtract anything from, what has been prescribed. If he or she were to do this, then it would only result in making the spiritual disease worse or would result in eternal torment and death. Thus it is useless to increase or reduce the roots and branches; any addition to them will only worsen the person's disease or will even result in this death; any reduction in them has similar results. The same also applies in the case when just one of these is added to them or subtracted from them; thus whoever prays five cycles for the midday prayer (instead of four) will receive no benefit as a consequence, this is because to do this would be to overstep the bounds stipulated by the *shari'ah*. The same rule may be applied to the rest of the roots and branches. This matter must be fully understood for it is of great importance; and Allah is more Knowing and more Wise: 'As for these examples We set them forth for men, and none understand them but the learned.'

We shall now discuss the reason why each of these branches has an order of priority and preference with respect to the rest; thus prayer has priority over fasting and the fasting over *zakat* and so on. This is so since the prayer, (unlike the other branches), encompasses all the other four acts of worship. Thus the person who is praying is also in a state of fasting, *zakat, hajj and jihad.* He is in a state of prayer as long as he is facing the *qiblah* (the direction of the Ka'bah) and engaged in the movements of bowing, prostration, standing and sitting. He is also in a state of fasting as long as he is praying since the latter state requires of necessity that he abstain from food, drink and anything which would result in a fast being broken.

As for the *zakat,* it is the giving of one's wealth or of anything one possesses, including one's physical strength and capacity: this is in accordance with the meaning of the Prophet's words, 'All of you are guardians and all of you are responsible for what you are guarding' and 'For everything there is a *zakat* and the *zakat* of the body is obedience.' Thus as long as the person is bowing, or prostrating, standing or sitting, reading the Qur'an or praising Allah, expressing the intention by a conscious determination of the heart to perform the prayer and make the various accompanying movements of the body and the limbs, then he is truly giving out *zakat.*

As for the *hajj* of this person praying: as long as he is facing the *qiblah,* in the direction of the *Ka'bah,* protected from any other action that might invalidate his prayer, as long as he has as his object the pleasure and obedience of Allah, as long as he is going round his own heart (like the circumambulation of the Ka'bah), making sure that nothing other than Allah enters it (in accordance with the Prophet's words, 'Prayer is not acceptable but by the presence of the heart'), then he is like the person performing the *hajj.* There is no disagreement about this, since the exterior *hajj* is the journey to the House of Allah, the Haram, in order to carry out the rites in the realm of form, while the person who is praying is also journeying to the House of Allah, namely the heart and its precincts, in order to fulfil the rites in the realm of inner meaning. Because of this he is counted as one of the true pilgrims rather than one of those confined to the superficial realm of appearances.

As for the *jihad* of the person praying, it is by virtue of the fact that *jihad* refers to the struggle against the enemies of Islam in order to make them submit to Islam and obey the commands and prohibitions of Allah. The person praying is also engaged in the struggle with his self, with the soul that commands to evil, and it is the self which is considered the real enemy and the true source of disbelief with regard to the true way of Islam in the realm of inner meaning. This is reflected in the words of the Prophet: 'Your worst enemy is your *nafs* (self) between the two sides of your body' since it is the self which obeys the person whose body it inhabits and which accepts his commands and prohibitions. This notion is also reflected in the words of the Prophet: 'We have returned from the minor *jihad* to the major *jihad.*' When he was asked the meaning of these words, he replied, 'The major *jihad* is the *jihad* against the self.' Thus anyone who is engaged in fighting his self or ego is undoubtedly one of those of whom it is true to say that they are in *jihad*. There are numerous other commentaries upon the meaning of *jihad*; what we have presented to the reader is a concise summary of these meanings. The reader is urged to pay great attention to this matter so that he may understand this secret — a secret which is under the protection of Allah.

The reason for the preference of fasting over the paying of *zakat* is that the former is above all connected to the soul and *zakat* is connected above all to wealth, and the soul is nobler than wealth. It is for this reason that Allah says, 'Fasting is for Me and I am its reward' since it is an action in which doubt, ambiguity, vanity and conceit have no part. Indeed, it issues from the purest sincerity; if this is not the case, then the person fasting is not really fasting. Thus we realise that it is from his fear of Allah and his desire for His pleasure that he is undertaking this action. It is obligatory to give preference to this action because it is based on the soul, rather than on wealth.

Zakat is given preference over the *hajj* because it is dependent only on the giving of wealth and because it is repeated every year, indeed every hour, and because of the continual process of the business of buying and selling. The *hajj*, on the other hand, is only obligatory once in a lifetime, and only then on condition that one is able. It is thus obligatory to give preference to something which is obligatory every year, even every hour, over something which is obligatory only once in a lifetime.

Hajj is given preference over the *jihad* since the former necessitates great expense and is obligatory on all who are able: it is possible that the *jihad* may not be obligatory on every person and may not involve great expense. *Jihad* is bound by many conditions; when these conditions are not fulfilled, then the *jihad* is not realisable and nor, in this case, is it obligatory. If, however, what we mean by *jihad* is the true *jihad* (mentioned above), then this *jihad* is given priority over everything, even the prayer — since anyone who does not struggle against his self (or the whims of the ego) will not even be able to get up in order to perform the *wudu'* and the prayer. It is simply a matter of awareness: any person who uses his intellect will see the truth of this. Many studies have been made on this subject, for it contains illuminating secrets of wisdom, hidden to all but the people of this science. Most of these secrets will be explained individually later in this work.

Up to this point we have been examining the matter from the point of view of the people of Allah and spiritual realisation. There is, however, another viewpoint which we must also take into consideration, namely that of the people of the outer and of imitation. According to the latter, the reason why priority is given to the prayer over the fast is that prayer is obligatory on all persons (in the Muslim community) and in all circumstances, whereas fasting is not like this, being rather a special kind of worship occurring at a particular time. Moreover, the prayer is obligatory on every Muslim of sane mind who is capable of performing it; furthermore, it is obligatory in health and in sickness, on the person who is bed-ridden, or who is obliged to lie down, or the one who can only do the prayer in a sitting position; it is also obligatory in war, on land and at sea, remaining obligatory whatever the place or events. The fast, however, is excused those advanced of years, those who suffer from excessive thirst, pregnant women who fear their milk will be decreased as a result of the fast and women at the time of menstruation. Another reason for this preference is that the prayer is repeated five times every day, whereas the fast is only performed once a year.

The reason why the fast is given preference over *zakat* is because the *zakat* is obligatory on wealth; moreover, not everyone possesses sufficient wealth for it to become obligatory on him. Everyone, however, possesses a soul on which the fast is obligatory and it is for this reason, because of its application to all people, that it is given priority.

The reason why the *zakat* is given priority over the *hajj* is that the *zakat* must be paid on several occasions throughout the year by those who are not obliged to calculate the payment on a yearly basis and once a year by those who are. The *hajj*, however, is only obligatory once in a lifetime, on condition that one is able, and for this reason that *zakat* is given preference.

The reason why the *hajj* is given priority over *jihad* is that the *hajj* is obligatory on every person, whereas the *jihad* is obligatory on the Muslim community as a whole (although it is fulfilled for the whole by the action of just some of its members). There is clearly a great difference between the two. Moreover, *jihad* is only obligatory when the infallible Imam is present, or when he gives the order to fight. Understanding of the meaning of this condition is usually lacking and this is particularly evident in our times. Thus the *hajj* is given preference by its more general applicability.

There are many other secrets with regard to this particular subject since it is possible to interpret the matter from other angles. We shall however conclude here our explanation of the branches of Islam and the reason why one is given preference over the other. Allah seems to refer to these five roots and five branches when He says, 'These make ten complete.' It is by means of these ten that eternal happiness in the Garden is obtained. We ask Allah to bestow upon us arrival there by means of Muhammad, peace be with him, and his chosen family.

We have now come to the end of our study of the roots and the branches together with introductory explanations of these two matters; it has included a study of the wisdom contained in the nature and circumstances of the prayer and *mi'raj* (both in the realm of appearance and reality) together with the reason why one branch may be given priority over another; finally this study has considered other matters of a subtle and hidden nature. We shall therefore now begin an investigation of the prayer with regard to the three groups, namely the people of the *shari'ah, tariqah* and *haqiqah* and then go on to the rest of the branches in the same manner.

8

Prayer

i) According to the people of *shari'ah*

According to the people of this group, the prayer is composed
of three sub-divisions, namely actions or movements, the method
of their performance and those things from which one should
abstain. Each of these sub-divisions may be further divided into
two aspects, namely the obligatory *(fard)* and the strongly recommended *(sunnah)*. The total number of combinations of the above
amounts to five thousand three hundred and sixty-three; we are
not in a position to enumerate them all here. We shall, however,
describe these divisions and aspects in relation to what is demanded of the Muslim in just one of the cycles of the prayer
and with respect to just the movements and their manner of
performance. The rest may be deduced upon a moment's reflection.

The obligatory movements in the first cycle of the prayer are
thirteen in number: the standing, when able (or another position
which takes its place when one is unable), the intention, the
saying of the *takbirat al-ihram (Allahu Akbar)* which signals the
beginning of the state of the prayer, the reciting of the Qur'an,
the bowing, the first prostration and the *tasbih* during it proclaim-
ing the glory of God (the saying of the *subhan Allah...)*, the raising
up of one's head, the second prostration and the remembrance
of Allah during it, and finally the raising of the head again. The
manner and aspects of the performance are eighteen in number:
the making of the intention immediately before the *takbirat al-
ihram* and the keeping in mind of this intention until the end of
the prayer, the correct pronunciation of the words *Allahu Akbar*
(God is Great), the reading of the *al-Hamd surah* (the *Fatiha* or
opening) together with another *surah* (if one is able to recite one)
of one's choosing, the reading aloud when the recitation should
be done aloud and the reading silently when it should be done
silently, the remaining at ease for a moment during the bowing
and the like when standing up straight again, the prostrating in

such a way that one is touching the ground with seven points of the body — the forehead, both hands, both knees and the toes of both feet — the remaining at ease for a moment in the first prostration and the straightening up after it, the like for the second prostration. In this way the total number of movements and aspects amount to thirty-one.

The second cycle of the prayer is the same except for the making of the intention and the *takbirat al-ihram*, together with the manner and aspect of the performance of these two, which are four in number — leaving twenty eight for this cycle. This number together with the number for the first cycle makes a total of fifty-eight different movements and aspects of performance. To this number, six things are added, namely the sitting for the saying of the *tashahhud* (the witnessing that Allah is One) and the being at ease in this, the two (the bearing of witness that Allah is One and that Muhammad is His messenger) together with the sending of blessings on the Prophet and his family. Thus, with the above-mentioned the total becomes sixty-four movements or actions. If the prayer is that of the morning, then the saying of the *taslim* or salutation is added to this; if it is the midday, the afternoon or the evening prayer, then the like is also added. The reading of another *surah* apart from the *al-hamd* is also omitted, thus leaving sixty actions and aspects of performance. The total thus becomes one hundred and twenty-four actions and aspects of performance. This is the nature of the prayer according to the people of the *shari'ah*, with respect to the way of the Shiahs and with regard to the exoteric. The inward dimension is connected to the people of *tariqah* and will now be considered.

ii) According to the people of *tariqah*

According to this group, the prayer is proximity or a drawing near to the Real. It has been reported that the Prophet has said, 'Prayer is the sacrifice whereby every believer comes closer to Allah.' What is meant here is the proximity of spiritual station rather than the proximity of physical place. It has also been narrated that 'the prayer is service and drawing closer and joining; the service is the *shari'ah* and the drawing closer is the *tariqah* and the joining is the *haqiqah*.' It has also been said that 'The *shari'ah* is that you worship Him, the *tariqah* that you come into His presence and the *haqiqah* that you witness Him.' The coming close to the Real requires real prostration which is the station of prayer known as annihilation — either by way of the annihilation of the attributes in those of the Real, this being particular to the people of *tariqah*, or by way of the annihilation of the essence in that of the Real, this being particular to the people of *haqiqah*. Allah refers to this when He says, 'And make obeisance and draw night (to Allah)', that is, 'Annihilate your essence and your existence in the Essence and Existence of the Real and abide with Him for ever and ever; and this is the station of the people of *haqiqah* (which we shall describe immediately after this section). We shall now consider what one of the gnostics has said with respect to the 'form' of the prayer before returning to the question in hand.

Know that the prayer has been given a specific form by the Lord of Lords, just as He has given a specific form to the animals. The soul or spirit of the prayer is the intention, sincerity, and awareness of the heart; the various actions or movements represent the body of the prayer; the original or basic 'limbs of the prayer' are the pillars or principles and the 'limbs of perfection' are the parts or divisions. Sincerity and intention are analogous to the spirit; standing and the sitting are analogous to the body; the bowing and the prostration are analogous to the head, the hand and the legs; the bowing and prostration are perfected by the stillness of the heart and limbs; the words of remembrance and glorification prescribed in the prayer are analogous to the organs of perception.

Know that your drawing nearer to Allah in the prayer is comparable to the approach of some attendants of the sultan to offer him a young servant lad. Thus the lack of intention or sincerity in prayer is like offering a servant who lacks the breath of life: the gift of a dead person would be an insult to the sultan and would merit the death penalty. Omission of the bowing and the prostration is analogous to the lack of limbs; omission of the pillars or principles is analogous to the loss of both the servant's eyes and truncation of his nose and ears; lack of awareness of the heart and the paying of no heed to the meanings of the Qur'anic recitation is like the loss of the faculties of sight and hearing, although the eye socket and ears remain. The reader is hardly unaware of what would happen to the person who gives a lad of such a description to the sultan. Know then that prayer which is deficient is not acceptable as a means of drawing closer to Allah and of obtaining the noblest of spiritual ranks; indeed the one who offers such a prayer would almost certainly be refused or hindered in his goal. Moreover, the basis of the prayer is veneration and respect of the Real Sultan; neglect of the courtesies of prayer contradicts the nature of veneration and respect. How can a person's prayers be accepted and how may that person draw closer and attain a spiritual rank of distinction if these things are neglected? Thus it is incumbent upon every person to perform the prayer as we have indicated above, that is in such a way as to preserve the spirit of the prayer. In other words, sincerity and awareness of the heart should be maintained throughout the prayer and the heart itself should take on the very qualities mentioned in the Qur'anic recitation. Thus no prostration or bow is made without the heart of the person praying being humble and submissive, in harmony with his outer reality. What is desired is submission of the heart rather than of that which contains the heart. The person praying should not say *Allahu Akbar* while there still remains something greater than Allah in his heart; he should not say 'I have directed my face... unless his heart is fully facing Allah and turned away from that which is other-than-Him; he should not say 'Praise belongs to Allah' unless his heart is overflowing with gratitude for His blessings on him and full of happiness on account of these blessings; he should not say 'Thee alone I worship and Thee alone do I ask for help' unless he feels his own weakness and incapacity and that neither he himself nor anyone else is of consequence. This is referred to by Allah when He says to His Prophet: 'You have no concern in the affair.' One should thus be in a similar state for all the words of remembrance and the movement of the prayer; 'Allah does as He wills; He cannot be questioned concerning what He does and they shall be questioned.'

If the above has been fully understood, then the reader should also realise that what is meant by the prayer of the people of this group is that they first direct their hearts to the real *qiblah* and the Ka'bah of inner meaning; these latter are in fact expressions for the real or true heart, which is also called the House of Allah or the Haram. Allah refers to this in His words, 'Neither the earth nor the heavens can contain Me but the heart of the believing slave;' likewise the Prophet said: 'The heart of the believer is the House of Allah.' Perfect spiritual awareness is mentioned in the words of the Prophet, 'Prayer is only acceptable when the heart is aware;' Allah also refers to this when He says, 'Now surely, sincere obedience is due to Allah (alone)' and further with His words, 'Say: surely my prayer and my sacrifice and my life and my death are (all) for Allah, the Lord of the worlds.'

The person praying then says the *takbirat al-ihram*, thereby forbidding his self from doing anything which might conflict with the command of Allah or go beyond the bounds of His pleasure, be it in speech or in action. He then begins the reading of the Qur'an, namely 'All praise is due to Allah, the Lord of the Worlds;' with these words he gives thanks for His blessings and favours by making fitting praise of Him; he is also thereby affirming his duties of worship — in all their different forms — and affirming Oneness in the station of gatheredness, neither straying to the way of excess nor to the way of negligence. The words 'Thee alone do we worship' express the unity of action and 'Thee alone do we ask for help' express the unity of attribute. It is for this reason that following these two statements are the words, 'Guide us to the straight path, the path of those You have blessed': blessings are here associated with the prophets and saints, indeed with all who follow the way of Islam — and this is perfection of real unity in Allah *(tawhid)*. This straight path of those blessed by Allah, namely the prophets and the messengers, is emphasized by contrasting it with the way of those with whom Allah is angry and those who have gone astray. It has been said that these words refer to the Jews and Christians; this is correct in the first instance, but they also apply to all those who are astray from the straight path, which is the middle way, neither tending to excess, on the one hand, nor negligence on the other. It is the middle way because it is based on the principles of wisdom, chastity, courage and justice. If these words did not mean 'Keep us firmly established... on the straight path we are now on', then they would be devoid of meaning and even flippant, since all are in agreement that the prophets and the saints are on the straight path, as are all the believers and Muslims who follow them. This is affirmed in the words of Allah, 'And We chose them and guided them into the right way.' If these words referred to a request for guidance towards the straight path, it would necessarily imply that they were already astray and this would inevitably lead to a fallacious interpretation. This, however, is not permissible with respect to the prophets and messengers and so we are left with the above-mentioned explanation.

The person performing the prayer then makes the bow, thereby indicating his submission to Allah; in doing so, he also returns to his self with humility, submission and need. This is because the bowing is a return backwards to his original state of non-being and its essential contingency: the horizontal movement is associated with the animals just as the standing position is associated with man. It can mean nothing other than a return backwards to his original creational form. Thereafter follows a more pronounced movement downwards, namely that of prostration, since this latter is associated in particular with the plant kingdom, the plants of their nature always inclining downwards. This downward inclination is an indication of the return to origins. Thus the person praying descends from uprightness and the movement associated with man to the station and movement of the animals and finally to the station and downward inclination of the plants. This is so since in the world of form, man has ascended from the plant to the animal and finally to the station of man. This is referred to in Allah's words, 'Certainly We created man in the best image. Then We render him the lowest of the low.' The 'best image' according to the consensus of opinion is the true form of man and the 'lowest of the low' is the return to the level of the animals and then to that of the plants. This return is also referred to in His words, 'Turn back and seek light.' The light mentioned here is situated 'backwards', because perfection is only attained after a return to its source, both in the realm of form and inner meaning. The following words of Allah bear witness to this, 'O soul that art at rest! Return to you Lord, well pleased (with Him), well pleasing (Him).' Man is reaches this station by witnessing of the self's dependency and humility, through annihilation in the outer and inner.

Thus when the person witnesses the grandeur of the Creator and the baseness of his self in comparison, he sets about magnifying the glory of Allah to the utmost degree — both by his spiritual state and in his outward speech saying 'Glory be to my noble Lord and all praise is His.' The fruit of this glorification, after witnessing his humility and submission and his original state of non-existence, is firmness and uprightness. He witnesses his state with the Real and the state of the Real with him through an exchange of his qualities with those of the Real and by a refinement of his behaviour by His influence. This station continues until the person says 'Allah hears the one who praises Him' which signals his witnessing of the Real together with all created beings; thus Allah hears the speech of all things without let or hindrance — especially speech addressed to Him. He Himself hears the words of this person praying in the same way as the person praying hears Him, as in the saying of the Imam: 'I would repeat the *ayah* until I could hear the One who had said it;' the words of the Prophet, 'Whoever knows Himself knows his Lord' clearly bear witness to this mutual contact.

There are other secrets concerning this direct relationship between man and Allah, although it would not be fitting to mention them here. Suffice it to say that Allah has described this matter in His Generous Book: 'Is it not sufficient as regards your Lord that He is a witness over all things? Now surely they are in doubt as to the meeting of their Lord; now surely He encompasses all things' and it is expressed in a *qudsi hadith:* 'I was his hearing and his sight and his tongue and his hand and his foot... .' This notion is in no way far-fetched in the light of the words of Allah, 'And We are nearer to him than his jugular vein.' When we consider that this mutual communication was permitted the bush of form — in His words, 'And when he came to it, a voice was uttered from the right side of the valley in the blessed spot of the bush, saying: O Moses! Surely I am Allah, the Lord of the worlds' — we realise that this bush and blessed spot are none other than man and his essential form. This meaning is also contained in the words of the Prophet, 'Whoever sees me has seen the Truth;' this is because witnessing the Truth in a fitting manner is not possible except in the form of man. Shaykh Shibli with his words, 'I say and I hear and is there anyone in the two worlds besides me?' thereby affirms that he too was in this station. The words of the gnostic Ibn al-Farid also bear witness to this:

> If my state were as low as the point of the (Arabic letter) 'ba'
> I would have risen to a point never reached by you despite your skill.

These words indicate annihilation and return to the original state of non-existence and then arrival and abiding in the world of sanctity, also known as the Divine Presence, which is described in His words, 'Surely those who guard (against evil) will be in gardens and rivers, in the seat of honour with a most Powerful King.'

The person praying then prostrates, that is, he returns again to his origin in a backward descent until he reaches the rank of the plant world. The prostration involves the covering of the noblest and most exalted part of man, namely his face, with the basest of things in existence, namely the earth; this covering in dust indicates the breaking of the prostrating self and its humility. The submission and humility of the second spiritual level is annihilation of the annihilation after the annihilation: the first annihilation was of the attributes and human characteristics, but this annihilation is of existence and the essence. Just as the drawing close in the realm of Truth is dependent upon the annihilation of attribute, so arrival in the realm of Truth is dependent upon the annihilation of the essence — which is particular to the people of *haqiqah* as we have already indicated. As long as the spiritual traveller remains in the station of multiplicity, witnessing the outward manifestations of the Attributes, then he is distant from Allah; he is worshipping Allah in a restricted sense, rather than worshipping Him, the Absolute. When, however, he arrives at the Unity of the Essence, he frees himself of this and says with the tongue of the spiritual station, 'Glory be to my Lord, the Sublime and all praise is due to Him.' The word 'sublime' here indicates his worship of a Lord higher than the Lord worshipped in a restricted sense. It is evident that this notion of restricted Lords is dependent upon the Absolute Lord. It is for this reason that Allah says to His Prophet, 'And that to your Lord is the goal.' Thus, in reality, his Lord is none other than the Absolute Lord, the goal of all other lords and the goal of all things. This is so because the Absolute Lord is the manifestation of the name Allah, which itself is the Greatest Name; it follows, therefore, that the manifestation of what is the greatest must be the greatest. This point must be carefully considered and understood: if this were not the case, then it would not be true to say that He was 'the Lord of the lords' nor the 'Best of Creators.' Other studies of this matter have been made and may be investigated with respect to the Names and their manifestations.

The person praying then says the *taslim* or salutation, thereby surrendering the whole affair to Allah and moving on from an advance of his self to an advance in Him; this is the station of abiding which is obtained by contentment and submission and by joining the unity of action with that of attribute. The Real Himself indicates this with His words, 'But no! By your Lord! They do not believe in (reality) until they make you a judge of that which has become a matter of disagreement among them and they do not find any straightness in their hearts as to what you have decided and they do not submit with entire submission.' The following verse also bears witness to the truth of this matter:

> I have handed over all my affairs to the Beloved.
> So if He wishes, He may give me life, and if He wishes,
> He may destroy me.

Consider also the words of Allah: 'And it behoves not a believing man and a believing woman that they should have any choice in the matter when Allah and His Apostle have decided a matter' and His words: 'You have no concern in the affair.' Further proof of the validity of this notion is found in the words: 'And all We relate to you of the accounts of the apostles is to strengthen your heart therewith; and in this has come to you the truth and an admonition and reminder to the believers;' and Allah is more Knowing and more Wise; He it is Who says the truth and guides to the straight path.

iii) According to the people of *haqiqah*

The prayer of the people of this group refers to the station of arrival and witnessing in the realm of truth. This station is higher than that of drawing near mentioned above. We have already shown this to be the case in the classification of the people of this science which states that 'the prayer is service, intimacy (or drawing close) and arrival.' We have shown too that service is analogous to the *shari'ah*, intimacy to *tariqah* and arrival to *haqiqah*. There is also a still clearer definition of these three divisions, according to the language of the people of this science: they divide worship in three ways and attribute to each group a particular way, namely 'Worship is utmost humility for the common people, it is servitude for the elite who have made good their relationship with Allah by the sincerity of their journey along His path towards Him, and it is bondage for the elite of the elite who have witnessed themselves as existing only by Him in their worship.' The latter worship Him in the station of the 'Oneness of separation after the gathering' and are the people of *haqiqah* in the station of bondage rather than servitude — a term reserved for the people of *tariqah* who are among the elite and the people of the middle way.

There is obviously a great difference between the people of servitude and the people of bondage and between the elite and the elite of the elite. Briefly, the prayer of the people of this group refers to their contemplation of the Beloved with the eye of the Beloved Himself and no other. This is affirmed in the words of the Prophet, 'I saw my Lord with the eye of my Lord and I knew my Lord by my Lord.' When the Prophet was asked about the meaning of *ihsan* (beneficence), he replied, ' *Ihsan* is to worship Allah as if you see Him, for even if you do not see him, He sees you.'

One of the gnostics has spoken about the real meaning of the prayer and the attainment of the station of witnessing thereby; since it is relevant to this station, we shall mention it before going on to other matters: 'The words of the Prophet: "I have been given coolness of the eye in prayer" refer to divine contemplation . This is because the prayer is a spiritual dialogue between Allah and His slave, as His words "Therefore remember Me and I will remember you" affirm. Moreover, the prayer is an act of worship which is divided between Allah and His slave; this is referred to in the authentic *qudsi hadith* mentioned earlier, namely "I have divided the prayer between Me and My slave, one half being for Myself and one half for My slave and the slave is given what he asks for. When the slave says, 'In the name of Allah, the Beneficent, the Merciful,' Allah says, 'My slave is making remembrance of Me.' When the slave says, 'All praise is due to Allah, the Lord of the Worlds,' then Allah says, 'My slave is making praise of Me.' When the slave says, 'The Beneficent, the Merciful,' Allah says, 'My slave is extolling Me.' When the slave says, 'Master of the Day of Judgement', Allah says; 'My slave is glorifying Me.' When the slave says, 'Thee alone do we worship and Thee alone do we ask for help,' Allah says, 'This is between Me and My slave and My slave shall be given what he asks for.' " Thus there exists in this *ayah* an interrelationship which is not present in those preceding it which are purely directed to Allah. When the slave says; 'Keep us on the straight path. The path of those upon whom Thou has bestowed favours. Not (the path) of those upon whom Thy wrath is brought down, nor of those who go astray,' then Allah says: 'These are for My slave and my slave shall be given what he asks for.' Thus these *ayat* are reserved for the slave just as the first are reserved for Allah. It is because of this that the reading of *al-Hamd* is understood to be obligatory; whoever does not recite it, has not performed the prayer which is shared between Allah and His slave. Since the prayer is a dialogue it is also a remembrance; whoever makes remembrance of the Real keeps company with the Real and the Real keeps company with him. There is an authentic *qudsi hadith* in which Allah says: "I am sitting with the one who remembers Me." Thus whoever sits with the One he is invoking and is keen of sight will see the One with whom he is sitting; this seeing is witnessing and vision. If, however, the person is not of keen sight, then he will not see Him. It is in this way that the rank of the person praying is known — on the basis of whether or not he sees the Real during the prayer.'

The gnostic goes on to say: 'In the words, "I have been given coolness of the eye in prayer" we learn that the Prophet is being given this coolness and does not give it to himself; indeed this emanation of the Real within the person praying is dependent upon Allah and not upon the person praying. Allah does not specifically mention that this quality of coolness emanates from him since the Prophet is commanded to perform the prayer irrespective of whether he receives this emanation from Allah. Thus just as this emanation is a gift from Him, so too the witnessing is obtained in the same way. His words "I have been given coolness of the eye in prayer" refer to nothing else but the contemplation of the Beloved by the eye of the lover who draws near in the stillness of prayer. On seeing the Beloved, the eye too becomes stilled and it ceases to look at anything other than Him in all things. It is for this reason that the person praying is forbidden to turn away (from the *qiblah*) during the prayer: it is during this turning away that Satan (Shaytan) is able to furtively steal away the heart of the slave who is praying and thus prevent him from witnessing his Beloved. Indeed if the lover were heedful in the prayer, he would never turn his face from the *qiblah.*

'Every man knows his own state: he knows whether or not he is of this spiritual rank and station. Man is surely aware of his own self "even though he presents excuses (to the contrary)." Thus the person praying is aware when he is being sincere or not within himself — indeed no existent being is unaware of its own state — and the state of the person praying is that of spiritual tasting.'

The gnostic then goes on to say: 'Know that the seeing, hearing and witnessing of the Real on the part of the slave in prayer can occur by virtue of the strength of his faith and certainty. His certainty may be so clear that it resembles the faculty of sight and hearing. It can also occur by the sight of the heart, that is by the light of insight or discernment and understanding, or by the light emanating from the Divine Attributes within the heart such that knowledge becomes actual and experienced. It can also occur by vision of physical perception whereby the Real appears to him by emanation and is witnessed with his own eyes; when this happens the Real also shares the prayer between Himself and His slave. We have knowledge of these various states by way of the narrations telling of the divine emanations on the Day of Resurrection and how they vary in accordance with the belief of each believer.'

The gnostic then says: 'Examine the exaltedness of prayer and where it may lead the person praying; anyone who does not attain to the rank of vision in prayer has not reached its final goal and has not felt the coolness of the eye.' This is because he does not see the One with Whom he is having the spiritual dialogue. Whoever does not hear what the Real is communicating to him during the prayer is not of those "who lend an ear." Thus whoever is not present with his Lord during the prayer — inasmuch as he neither hears nor sees Him — cannot in any circumstances be considered to be in a state of prayer, nor is he of those "who lend an ear while he is witnessing." The Real Himself has indicated this kind of witnessing with His words, "Is it not sufficient as regards your Lord that He is a Witness over all things. Now surely they are in doubt as to the meeting of their Lord; now surely He encompasses all things." The Prophet has also referred to it with his words, "You will see your Lord as (clearly as) you see the full moon at night." The Commander of the Faithful ('Ali) likewise indicates this station of witnessing when he says; "Should I then worship something I cannot see?" and with his words, "The Truth is clearer and more manifest than that which is seen by the eye," then with his words, "And he shall be of a certainty as (clear as) the light of the sun" and with his words, "Even if the veil were lifted, it would not increase my certainty." '

Thus it is true to say of them that in such evident states of witnessing and in a state of true prayer, they are witnessers during their prayer. This is because on investigation we realise that continuous prayer is nothing but the witnessing of the Real in the above-mentioned manner, namely the prayer particular to the greatest of the slaves and the elite of the saints *(awliya')*. We ask Allah by His generosity to make us one of them for it is He who has gathered all these states in the perfect slave, the slave of Oneness. Therefore we ask Allah to bestow upon us arrival at the rank of these slaves and pray that He join us with those of His slaves upon whom he has bestowed other, even greater perfections.

Having established that what is meant by the prayer of the people of *haqiqah* is a witnessing of the Beloved, we shall now begin a study of the order of their prayer and the nature of its principles, in the light of their special rank.

Know that their prayer — given that they establish the prayer of *shari'ah and tariqah* — refers to the gnostic carrying out that which he has been commanded to do, namely to persevere upon the path of uprightness in the realm of divine unity *(tawhid)*. This is referred to in Allah's words, 'So persevere (upon the straight path) as you have been commanded.' This perseverance and uprightness in the station of perfection and the journeying by Allah after completion of the journey to Allah and the journey in Allah — that is the oneness of separation after the gathering — is a sign that he has moved on from the presence of action and attribute (called the Presence of Oneness and the Presence of Lordship) to the Presence of the singleness of Essence which is the *qiblah* of the gnostics and the Ka'bah of the man of realisation.

The *takbirat al-ihram* (uttering the words *Allahu Akbar*) means that he is forbidding himself from approaching any door but His door and from doing any action without His pleasure. This is referred to in His words, 'Say, surely my prayer and my sacrifice and my life and my death are (all) for Allah, the Lord of the Worlds; surely I have turned myself, being upright, wholly to Him Who originated the heavens and the earth, and I am not of the polytheists.'

He then reads the *al-Hamd* in the manner we have indicated, namely with the awareness that the prayer is shared between Allah and His slave. During the recitation he should also see with the clear witnessing, indicated in Allah's words concerning Abraham and other prophets, 'And thus did we show Abraham the kingdom of the heavens and the earth that he might be of those who are sure.'

He then makes a bow — that is he humbles himself before Allah — and in doing so the *mulk* (the earthly realm) and the *malakut* (the spiritual or angelic realm) humble themselves with him, since man is entrusted with the caliphate of Allah in both these realms and everything in existence needs, and indeed follows, him by virtue of the perfections contained within him.

He then makes a prostration, and in doing so the existence of all existent and created beings together with his own creation is annihilated. This very annihilation is brought to annihilation when he actually witnesses the meaning of: 'Everything (in creation) must pass away and there will endure for ever the face of you Lord, the Lord of glory and honour.' He then magnifies Allah with praise and reverence in the above-mentioned movements, thereby elevating Him above all imperfection. In doing so he actually witnesses the meaning of 'Glory be to my Lord, the Almighty, and to Him all praise is due', in the first movement and the meaning of 'Glory be to my Lord the High' in the second.

He then performs the *shahadah,* or profession of faith, attesting that the Absolute Essential Oneness and Pure Solitary Existence necessarily negates all phenomenal and contingent existences. This is in accordance with Allah's words — and those of the most perfect of His slaves — 'Allah bears witness that there is no god but He, and (so do) the angels and those possessed of knowledge, maintaining His creation with justice, there is no god but He, the Mighty, the Wise.'

He then submits to this vision of unity from his heart and his spirit in accordance with the words of Allah, mentioned above, 'And they do not find hardship in themselves concerning that which You have decreed and they submit with a total submission' and His words, 'Surely Allah and His angels bless the Prophet. O you who believe! Call for (divine) blessings on him and salute him with a (becoming) salutation.' Submission to Allah is only valid by means of a submission of His Prophet. Likewise, submission to His Prophet is only valid by submission to His deputy or *wali* referred to in the Qur'an as one of those in authority: 'Obey Allah and obey the Apostle and those in authority from among you.' Allah refers to the Prophet in the words, 'Say: if you love Allah then follow me, Allah will love you.' A great deal more space would be needed to enumerate all the secrets connected with this subject. However we shall restrict our study to the above and trust others will discover the rest of these secrets from the people of Allah — for surely such secrets are not hidden from the people of Allah.

Thus there is a group of people whose belief in the roots and branches of Islam is of the intensity we have been describing to the reader. It should be realised that their perception and understanding of divine realities is truly to a most profound degree and their establishment of the *shari'ah*, the *tariqah* and *haqiqah* is to a most elevated level. How, one may ask, can one possibly attribute to them any lack of belief with respect to the roots and branches? How can one attribute to them any lack of observance of the divine ordinances and prophetic laws? May they be elevated above such a notion! Such an idea has in fact come about because the majority of the scholars of the exoteric and all those of imitation amongst the common people have only to listen to the ignorance Sufis talking about unrestricted licence and the neglect of religious duties for them to believe that this is also what the people of *tawhid* believe; on hearing such things, they immediately think that anyone who arrives at Allah is exempted the duties of the *shari'ah* and the acts of worship prescribed in Islam. May Allah protect us from such things; we seek refuge in Him from attributing such things to these people.

All are in agreement that anyone who arrives at Allah or to a certain rank within His presence possesses a greater degree of obedience and his worship is sublimer and his striving correspondingly more intense, as was the case with the Messenger of Allah. This is evidence from the narration of 'A'ishah which demonstrates that the Prophet would rise in the night and pray until his feet become swollen from standing. 'A'ishah said, 'O Messenger of Allah, has it not been revealed to you "that Allah may forgive your past faults and those to follow?" ' The Messenger then replied to her saying, 'Am I not then a grateful slave?' meaning "If Allah's blessings on me are so great, then surely I should be a grateful slave." ' The words of *Surah al-Muzzammil* 'O you who have wrapped up in your garments! Rise to pray in the night except a little... or lessen it a little' were only revealed to the Prophet as a result of struggle and spiritual striving, standing in prayer, enduring thirst and rising before dawn. Moreover, it will be well known to the reader that the spiritual stations of the other prophets and messengers were similar.

If we now consider the matter with respect to the saints *(awliya')* and spiritual inheritors, then we may understand their station by considering that of the Commander of the Faithful. The latter would immerse himself in prayer and in the witnessing of the Real during the prayer. So intense was his state that if his children wanted to draw an arrow-head from his leg, they would wait until he was engaged in prayer before drawing it; although they would pull it (hard), he would feel no pain, so deep was his immersion. Again, on three occasions, the sun was brought back from its position of setting in the west — twice in Madinah and once in the region of Babul — in order that he might perform the prayer at the right time. To this day there exists a Mosque dedicated to him called the mosque of the Sun. The sun was also sent back for Sham'un, the spiritual inheritor of Jesus. It is clear that were it not for the great importance they attached to the prayer, they would not have possessed this extreme degree of yearning to perform it and Allah would not have accepted their supplication to the degree He did. It has been narrated that one the progeny of 'Ali, the infallible imam Zayn al-'Abidin used to pray a thousand cycles of prayer every day and night and used to say, 'I would be content if all these prayers equalled just two cycles of prayer of the Commander of the Faithful.' The like has also been narrated from every single one of his progeny.

Up to this point we have been discussing the matter in relation to the saints; if we now consider the matter in relation to the shaykhs of the people of Allah and their elite, then the reports about them may be divided into two categories: namely with respect to their speech and with respect to their actions.

As for their speech, then some have said that the perfect person is he who does not extinguish the light of his gnosis by his scrupulousness; his direction is towards complete perfection, namely that attained by combining true gnosis and total scrupulousness. It is absolutely necessary for the one of perfection to combine these two for it is only by doing so that he achieves perfection. Whoever arrives at complete gnosis, and then goes astray because his light burns up his knowledge, is not a man of perfection, nor has he fully realised perfection or the light of gnosis. In this way the light of scrupulousness, obtained by carefully avoiding that which Allah has forbidden, is extinguished by the light of gnosis. The same applies to anyone who relies on the light of scrupulousness to the detriment of the light of gnosis: if he abandons gnosis for the perfection of scrupulousness — without arriving at the realities of witnessing — he is also not one of the perfected, nor has he attained to the station of perfection. The secret of this combination derives from the coordination of the outer and the inner and the knowledge obtained as a result of this joining. This procedure which has been expounded by the gnostic whose words we have already cited, demonstrates the falsehood of the accusations levelled at the people of this science.

The gnostic goes on to say, 'The final point of arrival at Reality is abandoning any perception of action.' The gist of his words is that the one who arrives at Reality does not recognise any action as his own nor any Actor other than Allah. This does not mean that action must be avoided, for the gnostic's perception of non-action does not negate the actions of others. It would not be appropriate to go into details at this point; and we have deliberately omitted them for fear of overburdening the reader. However, one should pay great attention to this idea since by it all the false claims of the libertines and the heretics may be rejected.

Concerning the actions of the saints, it has been narrated that Shaykh Junayd has said, 'Uncertainties have vanished and all signs have disappeared; the only thing of benefit to us is the prayer we perform in the depth of the night.' It has been reported that the perfect Shaykh Sa'ad al-Din al-Hamawi would pray each day and night a large number of cycles of prayer; the truth of this may be known from his famous *awrad* (litances of invocations) performed at the end of each prayer. The same is true of Shaykh Shihab al-Din al-Kabir al-Suhrawardi and Abu Yazid al-Bastami, who was a cup-bearer in the house of Ja'far ibn Muhammad al-Sadiq. The same is also true of Shaykh al-A'zam Muhyi al-Din 'Arabi who would pray two cycles of prayer for every prophet and saint, after performing all the obligatory cycles of prayers. He would also do this during his visits to the shrines of Morocco, Sham (Syria, Lebanon and Palestine), Egypt (and in particular) Alexandria, Makkah, Madinah and the al-Aqsa Mosque; this we know from the section entitled 'The secrets of prayer' in his work *Al-Futuhat*.

Our aim in all this is to show that the people of this gnostic science are in no way like the scholars of the exoteric and the ordinary people of imitation suppose. In fact those who make false accusations about them are the descendants of men from the time of the Messenger of Allah who would make fun of the people of Allah and the masters of divine unity and Qur'anic exegesis. Such people would wink at each other in jest at the people of Allah; they would deny the validity of their way, in those days as in the present age. This is affirmed in the Qur'an when they say 'Surely we found our fathers on a course and surely we are followers of their footsteps.' We seek refuge in Allah from them and from those like them. This is most pertinently expressed by the poet of the following verse:

> If you knew what I was saying, you would excuse me;
> If you knew what you were saying, I would rebuke you.
>
> You are not aware of what I am saying, so you rebuke me;
> And having discovered that you are unaware, I excuse you.

One of the gnostics has noted that anyone who is devoid of a certain quality of excellence will not even admit the existence of that quality, rather he will firmly deny it. The people of Allah are in the station of perfect adherence to the Prophetic exemplar, indicated in His words 'Certainly you have in the Apostle of Allah an excellent exemplar.' By its nature the notion of an excellent exemplar does not admit of any difference of opinion: thus how one may ask can anything come pass by the hand of the people of Allah, that is in opposition to this exemplar? And how is it that the ignorant and common people suppose the things they do about them? — 'And that was as a result of your evil thoughts which you entertained about your Lord that you tumbled down into perdition, so are you become of the lost ones.' On investigation we realise that the relationship between these people of Allah and this particular group is analogous to that of Abraham with the people of Moses and Jesus — since the latter claimed that Abraham was one of them and not of the Muslims. Allah, however, rejects their claims saying: 'Abraham was not a Jew nor a Christian but he was an upright man, a Muslim.'

Some people associate such gnostics with deviation, disbelief and heresy, while others associate them with belief in incarnation, union with the divine and the ascription of human characteristics to Allah. The truth of the matter, however, is that they are far removed from such false assumptions and lying fantasies — just as Abraham was far removed from the assumptions and fantasies of the Jews and Christians. The words of Allah in the *qudsi hadith* 'My saints *(awliya')* are hidden beneath My dome, no one knows them but Myself' allude to these gnostics. They are also referred to in Allah's words, 'Then Allah will bring a people, He shall love them and they shall love Him, modest before the believers, mighty against the unbelievers, they shall strive hard in Allah's way and shall not fear the censure of any censurer; this is Allah's grace, He gives it to whom He pleases, and Allah is Ample-giving, Knowing.' Again they are referred to in the saying of the Commander of the Faithful, 'O Allah, surely the earth will never be without those who maintain (living) proof of the (truth) of Allah, either in a manifest way and known amongst the people or hidden for fear (of the injustice of men).' They exist in order that Allah's proofs and guidance — as expounded in the Qur'an — be protected from corrupt interpretation or negligence.

How many are they and where do they exist? By Allah these people are few in number and vast in rank; by them Allah preserves His proofs and words of guidance, until they in turn entrust these proofs and words of guidance to men like them-

selves, implanting this knowledge in their hearts. It is by way
of them too that one may grasp the true meaning of reality; they
possess the spirit of certainty and find easy what those living in
ease and luxury find difficult; they gain intimacy and friendship
with that which arouses horror in the ignorant; physically, they
keep company with the world while spiritually, they are connected to the higher realm; they are the caliphs of Allah on His
earth who call others to His way.

The poet has said the following about them:

> To Allah beneath His dome of glory belongs a group of
> men Whom He has hidden from the eyes of others out of
> reverence to them.

> They are the sultans in tattered garments
> Who have drawn apart from the kings of the earth.

> They have accepted other clothes and abstained from food,
> Moving with humility across this green sphere.

Not even the prophets or messengers of Allah have escaped
from the tongues of the detractors. The latter have accused them
of being, amongst other things, poets, magicians, soothsayers
and madmen: 'Said he: Most surely your Apostle who is sent to
you is mad' and also: 'This is most surely a manifest enchanter.'
Thus it is not surprising that the gnostics have failed to escape
their criticism. Indeed the prophets are also exemplars in this
respect for as those of this science have pointed out, 'Trial is a
part of (the life of the) prophets, of the saints and also of those
like them.' This idea is also expressed in following verse:

> No one, not even the purified Prophet, can escape their
> tongues.
> Thus if a person is courageous, they call him reckless.
> If a person is generous, they call him wasteful.
> If a person is quiet, they call him dumb;
> And if he is loquacious, they call him a prattler.
> If a person stands in prayer at night while fasting,
> They call him an exhibitionist and reject him.

If a person stands in prayer at night while fasting,

They call him an exhibitionist and reject him.

Thus do not worry if the people rebuke you or praise you but rather fear no one but Allah for Allah is greater than all.

Thus we come to the end of our study of the prayer with respect to the three groups. We shall now begin on the subject of fasting with respect to these same groups; and by Allah is all security and success.

9

Fasting

i) According to the people of *shari'ah*

What is meant here is abstention from certain things for a specific
period of time. Among the conditions of fasting is that of the
validity of intention: if the fasting is for a specific period, then
it is necessary under all circumstances — like, for example, the
month of Ramadan and fasting undertaken when a specific vow
has been made. It is sufficient, however, that an absolute intention covering the whole period of the fast be made in the case
of Ramadan rather than the individual, daily renewal of intention; all fasting other than that of the month of Ramadan, be it
supererogatory or obligatory, must be accompanied by an intention
to perform a specific fast. When undertaking a fast purely with
the intention of coming closer to Allah, it is permissible to make
the intention some time before the fast; the intention for a specific
fast, however, must be made at the same time as the beginning
of the fast. If the time passes through forgetfulness, such that
morning breaks, it is permissible to renew the intention up to
the time of the sun's zenith. If, however, the sun has passed its
zenith, then such an intention is no longer valid. If this happens
during the fast of Ramadan, then one should fast that day and
make up a day instead.

Various conditions and laws govern the fast, classified according to whether it is recommended, as in the case of a specific
vow, or whether, for example, it is performed for a non-specific
reason. However we do not have room to deal with all these
questions here. We shall restrict ourselves to a discussion of what
necessitates the making up of the fast and the payment of the
kaffarah (expiatory compensation) and of what necessitates the
making of a fast but without payment of the *kaffarah*. There are
nine things which render the making up of the fast and the
kaffarah obligatory: eating, drinking, intercourse in which penet-
ration takes place, deliberate emission of semen, submersion in
water (according to some), deliberately allowing thick dust to
enter the throat, such as particles of earth or flour, deliberately

waiting until the sun has risen before rising when one is in a state of ritual impurity, or relapse into sleep after having awoken twice previously, such that the sun has time to rise. The *kaffarah* for this is to free a slave or fast for two consecutive months or to feed sixty poor people — and one may choose as to which of these three one performs.

As for those things which make the making up of the fast obligatory without *kaffarah*, they are nine in number: eating, drinking or indulging in sexual intercourse instead of watching for the dawn (in the case when one is able), not accepting that the sun has risen when someone says so and when in fact it has, the imitation of others in assuming that the sun has not yet risen when one is capable of looking out for it oneself and when in fact it has risen, the imitation of others in assuming that the night has fallen while being able oneself to watch for it, and breaking the fast when in fact the night has not fallen or breaking the fast because of something which happens to darken the sky (although it subsequently becomes clear that the night has not in fact begun), the relapse into sleep after waking once (before doing the *ghusl* and in the case when one does not wake again until after the sun has risen), water entering the throat of someone taking it into his mouth in order to cool himself (although this does not apply to the rinsing of the mouth prior to the performing the prayer), and finally the injection of fluids into the body. The above is the fasting of the people of *shari'ah* according to the way of the Shiahs.

ii) According to the people of *tariqah*

The fasting of the people of this group, after they have performed the above-mentioned fast, refers to their abstaining from anything which might be in opposition to Allah's pleasure, command or prohibition, be it in speech or by action, be it in the realm of knowledge or the application of that knowledge. We have already mentioned these points above and we shall now discuss the matter in more detail.

Know that the Messenger of Allah has narrated from Allah Himself: 'For every good deed there are ten similar to it (in reward from Allah) or up to seven hundred times in number, except, that is, the fasting, for the fast is for Me and I am its reward.' The Prophet has also said, 'Everything possesses a door and the door of worship is the fast.'

The point of describing the fast in this particular way and in attaching such importance to it is for two reasons: the first is that the fast requires abstention from the forbidden things and prevention of the self *(nafs)* from indulgence in desire and passion — thus the fast is a hidden act seen only by Allah, unlike prayer, *zakat* and the other acts of worship which are seen by others and therefore may cause vanity and conceit to enter a person's worship. Moreover, vanity and conceit are two of the major reasons for making prayer invalid and bringing acts of obedience to nought. Hence Allah's words: 'Therefore whoever hopes to meet his Lord, he should do good deeds and, he should not, in the service of his Lord, join any other with Him.' What is meant by 'joining in service,' according to the consensus of the commentators is the performance of any action for the sake of being seen. But the Prophet has said, 'The creature of *shirk* (idolatry or associating another with Allah) is more hidden than a black ant on a smooth rock in a dark night.' According to the scholars of the esoteric, the *shirk* referred to here and in the *ayah* quoted above is the seeing of otherness with the Real. Imam 'Ali has also said, 'The subtlest form of *shirk* is the performance of actions for the sake of others;' this type of conceitedness is only possible when one deliberately lets others witness one's worship. We have already investigated this matter in the sections concerning *tawhid* and *shirk* (and the corresponding subdivisions of manifest and hidden *shirk* and divine and existential *tawhid*).

The second point about the fast is that it is a means of overwhelming the enemy of Allah. In truth Satan (Shaytan) is the enemy. His strength lies in his use of man's desires. Hunger, however, destroys all those desires which are Satan's instruments to lead man astray. When no such means exist, then he is incapable of action. It is for this reason that the Prophet has said; 'Truly Shaytan courses within the son of Adam as the blood courses, so therefore curb his coursing by means of hunger.' In this lies the secret of the Prophet's words, 'When Ramadan begins, the Garden is opened, the gate of the Fire are closed, Shaytan is bound in chains, and a caller calls: "Come forward, O you who desire good and retreat, O you who desire evil!" ' What is meant here is that Satan, the cause and source of evil, is weakened together with his supporters. Thus it is up to the reader to strive towards good deeds and avoid evil actions, desires and passions.

Abstention during the fast may be classified in two ways: the first aspect relates to the outer and the second to the inner. As for the outer, the first kind of fasting concerns that of the tongue from superfluous speech and from anything which is contrary to the pleasure of Allah and His will with respect to His commands and prohibitions. Allah, with respect to the fast of Mary (Maryam), only commands her to abstain from speech: 'Say: surely I have vowed a fast to the Beneficent God, so I shall not speak to any man today.' The truth of this is shown from His words, 'And shake towards you the trunk of the palm tree, it will drop on you fresh ripe dates.' Since this latter *ayah* is commanding her to eat and drink and the former to avoid superfluous speech, we realise that the greater of fasts is keeping silent and avoiding superfluous speech. If this were not so, then the Prophet would not have said, 'Whoever keeps silent gains success.' The hidden wisdom of this is that this abstention from outer speech produces an inner utterance, that is a speech of the inner soul. Thus when Mary keeps silent with her tongue, Jesus speaks words of clear meaning in the cradle and claims to be the caliph of the Merciful.

One must reflect well upon this matter for it is subtle in meaning: by it one may understand the secret of the words of the Prophet, 'The springs of wisdom will appear from the heart on the tongue of the one who devotes forty mornings purely for Allah.' The following has also been narrated from the Prophet: 'If speech turns to the nature of Allah, then refrain.' What is meant here is that one should refrain from any speech, word, allusion or indication of Allah for none of these can adequately express Him. Since words do not correspond to the reality of Him, there is no use in talking about Him with the tongue; indeed to do so would be harmful, as, for example, in the case of the inexpressible sciences of spiritual tasting. Thus the Prophet has said on another occasion, 'Whoever knows Allah curbs his tongue from speaking about Him or expressing Him, since this kind of knowledge cannot be contained in speech.' For example, a person may be incapable of describing honey even after having tasted it. It has been narrated from the Prophet that he said, 'When the stars are mentioned, then refrain from speech and when my companions are mentioned, then refrain (from speech).' Thus realisation of the secret of the cosmic decree is a matter of spiritual tasting and witnessing, just as the secret of his companions was a matter of taste, witnessing and inner awareness. The Prophet has also said, 'Is there anything that pitches the people on their noses into the Fire more than the harvest of their tongues?' What is usually understood by 'the harvest of the tongue' is superfluous speech. The Prophet has also said, 'Whoever increases his speech increases his anger, and whoever increases his anger diminishes his modesty, and whoever diminishes his modesty diminishes his scrupulousness and whoever diminishes his scrupulousness will enter the Fire.'

All of the above is summed up in the words of Allah: 'And were it not for Allah's grace upon you and His mercy in this world and the hereafter, a grievous chastisement would certainly have struck you on account of the discourse which you entered into, when you received it with your tongues and spoke with your mouths about that of which you had no knowledge, and you deemed it an easy matter while with Allah it was grievous. And when you heard it, why did you not say: It does not beseem us that we should talk of it; glory be to Thee! This is a great calumny. Allah admonishes you that you should not return to the like of it ever again if you are believers. And Allah makes clear to you His communications and Allah is Knowing, Wise.' By Allah, by Allah, if there were only these *ayat* in the Qur'an on this subject, it would be sufficient proof of the need to keep silent rather than make superfluous speech or talk when one has no knowledge about what one is saying. Furthermore, whoever truly believes that each person has two angels watching over him, assigned to him by Allah in order to record everything he does, be it good or bad, will not speak except when necessary and will not say anything but good. The truth of this is affirmed in the words of Allah: 'And when the two receivers receive, sitting on the right and on the left.' When the reader realises this, when he knows he must hold his tongue and refrain from superfluous speech — for he knows that there is more harm than good in it and the evil it works is worse than any good which might come out of it.

The second kind of fasting is to abstain from looking at what has been forbidden and to refrain from looking at what is permissible, except of necessity; this is because scrupulousness and piety do not lie in mere abstention from the forbidden things but also in avoiding that which is permissible — except when one is obliged to look at something through force of circumstance or need. Allah has indicated this in His words, 'Say to the believing men that they cast down their looks and guard their private parts.' What is meant here is that one must, of necessity, lower the eyes in order to protect the private parts: when one does not see something, the self does not demand that thing and feels no inclination towards it — like, for example, the blind person who has no concern for colours because he does not distinguish between them, rather he is concerned with the realm of hearing and listening. This matter may be intuitively perceived and understood by the intellect. Thus the lowering of the eyes is of great significance, since not to do so leads to all kinds of evil and corruption. Allah speaks of this, saying that those who guard their private parts will be caused to enter the Garden with the company of the righteous and God-fearing amongst His slaves: 'Successful indeed are the believers, who are humble in their prayers and who keep aloof from what is vain and who pay the poor-rate and who guard their private parts, except before their spouses and those whom their right hands possess, for surely they are not blameworthy, but whoever seeks to go beyond these transgresses the limits;' moreover, His words, 'except before their spouses,' indicate the truth of what we have said above with respect to that which is permissible, namely that it should be in case of necessity only.

The third kind of fasting is to refrain from listening to that which is forbidden — like, for example, listening to someone backbiting another Muslim, listening to singing and music of a forbidden nature, listening to the words of misguided people, and the evil speech of the people of innovation, all of which might lead someone away from the straight path. This is affirmed in the words of Allah, 'And when you see those who enter into false discourses about Our communications, withdraw from them until they enter into some other discourse' and also His words, 'And when they hear idle talk they turn aside from it.' Indeed Allah's words 'Surely the hearing and the sight and the heart, all of these, shall be questioned about that' comprehends these meanings. The heart referred to above is not an outward organ of perception, rather it is a mode of perception from the realm of reality and all true perception is dependent upon it since most faculties of perception have no feelings or sensitivity in themselves; rather they are instruments of the self, which is sometimes referred to as the heart, sometimes as the intellect and sometimes as the soul. Thus the heart is the true or real source of perception. The faculty of sight, for example, has no capacity of itself to see that the orb of the sun is in fact so many times bigger than the sphere of the earth and that even the smallest of the stars in the heavens is many times larger than the earth. The faculty of sight can only perceive in respect to its capacity and perceives the star as a small orb or shield-shaped sphere. This phenomenon is explained in detail in the books dealing with this science and those interested in this subject may investigate the matter further therein.

The fourth kind of fasting is to refrain from smelling anything, be it odious or sweet. It is evident that one is naturally repelled by any odious smell; indeed such a smell produces a bad effect on the liver, the brain and heart and may even lead to what is sometimes referred to as 'the sudden death.' One should also refrain from smelling even pleasant odours since they stimulate desire, be it forbidden or otherwise — like the perfumes musk, ambergris and amber. It has been narrated that the Prophet used to dislike the smell of garlic and onions and like the smell of the rose and the narcissus.

The fifth kind of fasting is to refrain from taste, for whoever tastes something is drawn towards the realm of desire and loses the sharpness of his intellect. An example of this is the tasting or consumption of the orphan's wealth or usury. The first is referred to in Allah's words, 'And do not approach the property of the orphan except in the best manner' and the second in His words, 'Those who swallow down usury cannot rise except as one whom Satan has prostrated by his touch' and 'Eat and drink and be not extravagant; surely He does not love the extravagant.' This latter *ayah* of Allah's also indicates that one should be moderate in one's eating and drinking, such that one neither exceeds the limits nor neglects to respond to one's bodily needs for to err in either of these directions is blameworthy in all circumstances. This is described in the saying of the Prophet as erring to the right or the left: 'The right and the left are both ways of error and the straight path is the middle way.'

The sixth kind of fasting is to abstain from the sense of touch which leads one to forbidden and blameworthy things, or to excess in what is permissible and to that which is outside the limits of moderation. This is referred to in Allah's words when He talks about this and the other senses: 'And you did not veil yourselves lest your ears and your eyes and your skins should bear witness against you... and they shall say to their skins, "Why have you borne witness against us?" They shall say, "Allah Who makes everything speak has made us speak" ' and also His words: 'On that day We shall set a seal upon their mouths and their hands shall not speak to Us, and their feet shall bear witness of what they earned.'

The Prophet has mentioned that these senses are under the guardianship of each person: they are, as it were, his helpers, actions and speech, and a means to attainment of perfection: 'Everyone of you is a guardian and everyone of you shall be questioned about that which you are guarding.' What is meant here is that every man is a gurdian, a ruler and sultan in relation to his subjects which are his senses and faculties of perception and that each man will one day be made to account for the way he employed them. If he employs them in the manner for which they were created, then he will be reckoned amongst the people of justice and equity and he will be of those whose final end is the Garden and Allah's mercy. If, however, he employs them in a manner for which they were not created, then he will be re-

ckoned one of the people of oppression, injustice and tyranny
and he will be of those whose final end is the wrath and punishment of Allah in the hell fire. Oppression and injustice are the
placing of something where it does not belong, just as justice is
the placing of something in its rightful place; thus anyone who
employs his bodily organs and limbs in a manner for which they
were not created is unjust, and he who is unjust is cursed and
merits the punishment of the fire.

Allah — may He be exalted — has prescribed the purification (by *wudu'*, *ghusl* or *tayammum*) in order to cleanse the senses
and in order that they be properly employed: 'O you who believe!
When you rise up to prayer, wash your faces and your hands as
far as the elbows, and wipe your heads and your feet to your
ankles... .' Allah orders His slave to do this so that he does not
neglect the duties of purification, in accordance with the outer
law and the inner meaning, as we have explained earlier. Allah
wishes that His slave should employ every bodily member in the
purpose for which it was originally created so that he may be said
to be amongst those who place things in their proper place and
hence amongst the people of justice and equity — in words,
deeds and knowledge. In this way such a person will enter into
the path of the people of Allah, His angels and those amongst
His bondsmen of knowledge. This is affirmed in His words,
'Allah bears witness that there is no god but He, and (so do)
the angels and those possessed of knowledge, maintaining his
creation with justice; there is no god but He, the Mighty, the
Wise. Surely the (true) religion with Allah is Islam... . And I
am of those who bear witness to this.'

Up to this point we have been considering the matter in relation
to the five outward senses. In one respect, the tongue should not
be included amongst them since it is specifically for the purpose
of expression and speech and hence not directly to be included
with the senses; but if we consider it in a more general way, it
is evident that it has a bearing on the subject of taste. Thus it
can be said that from one aspect it is included in this subject
and yet from another it is not (in which case the senses may be
treated as one subject and the tongue as another); and by Allah
comes success.

The first fast with respect to the five inner or psychic senses is to abstaining from using the faculty of thought for useless matters or for that which is detrimental to the return of the soul and the final reckoning after death. The faculty of thought has only been created so that men may progress from the beginnings of things to general conclusions: it is the practice of 'theoretical examination' in the language of the theologians. Thus it is better and more beneficial that one employs this faculty for that purpose for which it was created. If someone were to use it for other than that, then one would necessarily have to describe him as unjust; and we have already examined the nature of the unjust person and how he is cursed and refused entry to the door of Allah. The power and capacity of the faculty of the intellect is shown in Allah's words: 'Most surely there are signs in this for a people who reflect' and in the Prophet's saying: 'Reflection for a moment is better than action for seventy years.'

The second kind of inner fast is to abstain from employing the faculty of memory except for that for which it was created. Since the faculty of thought has only been created to reflect upon divine gnosis and intellectual knowledge and the like, things other than these should not exist in its storehouse. Indeed it is forbidden for the faculty of memory to retain other than these things — such that those in possession of such a faculty are referred to by Allah as 'those who keep the limits of Allah.' The best way to keep these limits is to employ each faculty in the proper way; and Allah is more Knowing and more Wise.

The third kind of inner fast is to abstain from employing the faculty of imagination in that for which is was not created. This faculty is employed, for example, in fixing in the imagination the form of a particular person, that is, his outward physical form and colour. But just as the faculty of conjecture is employed in the supposition of the existence of enmity or love between particular people, so the faculty of imagination projects within the person in whom this faculty resides, at every moment, numerous pictures of particular persons and various imaginative constructs. In this way it prevents the person from employing his imagination for that purpose for which it was created. This is demonstrated in Allah's words: 'Then lo! their cords and their rods — it seemed to him on account of their magic as if they were running.... . So Moses conceived in his mind a fear.' If the faculty of imagination had the capacity to perceive the meaning of this event, he would not have imagined that they were serpents, rather he would have realised that it was mere magic and that it was not real or true. On investigation, we realise that this faculty has only be created to exhibit the ideal world, also known as the world of absolute imagination. The truth of this may be seen if we compare the cosmic dimension with that of the individual souls in the light of Allah's words, 'We will soon show them our signs in the Universe and in their own souls, until it will become quite clear to them that it is the truth.'

The shaykh of divine knowledge, Shams al-Din al-Shahruzi (author of the *al-Shajarat al-ilahiyya* or the Divine Tree) has referred these matters in his treatise saying: 'One should realise that everything in the sublime and spiritual realm has a reflection in the lower realm. Thus the light of the sun is symbol of the divine light of Lordship. Allah has said: "And His are the most exalted attributes (or symbols) in the heavens and the earth" — meaning here the sun. The light of the moon is analogous to the light of the intellect, mentioned in the Prophet's words, "The first thing created by Allah was the intellect." The light of the stars is analogous to the light perceived by the senses — as is shown in Allah's words, "Surely the hearing and the sight and the heart, all of these shall be questioned about that." ' The Shaykh then goes on to demonstrate the truth of what we were saying in the first instance, saying, 'Know that the thickest veil which blinds the self from its own essence is that of the faculty of imagination — by its projection of images, on the one hand, and of interpretation, on the other, and its positing of an amalgamation and joining of the two in addition to this. Furthermore, by its constantly presenting all these things to the self never letting up either in sleep or in the waking state, the self becomes engrossed in them instead of reflecting on its essence and becomes veiled from its essence. However its essence is not veiled from the reality of its own essence, the divine manifestation, since the means of manifestation cannot veil Manifestation of Him; 'yet it does veil the person from reflection and real perception such that he becomes engrossed in other things.'

The shaykh's words, 'by its projection of images, on the one hand, and of interpretation, on the other, and its positing of an amalgamation and joining of the two in addition to this' does not accord with the words of some of the religious scholars and the majority of the philosophers since the latter are of the belief that the projection on the part of the faculty of imagination is of images only and the projection of the faculty of conjecture is concerned solely with meaning; it is the imaginative faculty of *sensus communis* which is concerned with image and meaning together — as the word clearly indicates. Thus it appears that the shaykh has confused the faculty of the *sensus communis* with that of the imaginative faculty; indeed this is perfectly possible on his part, man being human and as such exposed to error — just as it is possible on our part. Only Allah knows the unseen and 'Allah is more Knowing and more Wise; He it is Who says the truth and guides to the straight path.'

Shaykh al-A'zam Muhyi al-Din 'Arabi, the master of unveiling and pole of those of arrival, says something in his account of the way Divine Commands impinge on the realm of man which contradicts the words of Shahruzi: 'Know that the eye, the ear, the tongue, the hand, the stomach, the private parts and the feet are the faithful agents of man entrusted with the discharge of their duties; each of them is the ruler and the keeper of the particular part of man's wealth. The chief and leader of these senses is that upon whom all the other senses depend and this chief sense is subject to the authority of the imagination. The imagination, containing as it does both the good and evil aspects of projection, is subject to the authority of memory and memory is subject to the authority of reflection and reflection is subject to the authority of the intellect and the intellect is the vizier or man and man is the supreme head, known as the sacred spirit.' We mention this in particular because of his words, 'The imagination is subject to the authority of memory and memory is subject to the authority of reflection,' since, if imagination were able to influence the interpretation as well as the projection of images, it would not have been subjected to memory and reflection — 'And as for these examples, We set them forth for men, and none understand them but the learned.'

The fourth kind of inner fast is to restrain the faculty of conjecture from the projection of forms inimical to the self at one moment and things beloved of the self at another, since this only prevents the self from progressing along the straight path. This path, the *tawhid* of reality, prevents the perception of enmity and love, the enemy and the beloved — for such things are the business of the soul or self which commands to evil, with the support of the twin forces of anger and passion. The person whose soul is content is allowed to return to his Lord after death free of this and other similar things, since he is in the station of witnessing the Beloved and His actions. Whatever the Beloved does is beloved of him, and so he feels no enmity towards anyone and he is not bound by the love and the things beloved of men for he is in the realm of the absolute and the witnessing of the existence of the One, the Absolute and such a realm is devoid of all such things. Allah's words, 'Say Allah, then leave them sporting in their vain discourses' specifically refer to this and other similar circumstances. Thus the person who is truly fasting must be in possession of a tranquil soul and not a soul which commands to evil — in order to merit a return to His Lord: 'O soul that art at rest! Return to your Lord, well-pleased (with him), well-pleasing (Him), so enter among My servants and enter My garden.' The command to enter amongst the slave is only possible for a person in the station of serenity and tranquillity. Therefore Allah says, 'The fast is for Me and I am its reward.' Such a reward is only possible by means of a contemplation of His manifestation in the cosmos and in the individual soul. The Prophet has indicated this when he says, 'You will see your Lord as you see the full moon at night.' Some of the gnostics have spoken about the secrets of fasting which also belong to this station.

There are three levels of secrets with respect to the fast, the lowest being an abstention from that which would break the fast without restraining his bodily limbs or organs from that which is disliked; this is the fast of the common people and it is known as temperance or moderation. The second level is when there is added to this the abstention of the bodily organs: thus one prevents the tongue from backbiting, the eye from looking with doubt or suspicion, and likewise for the rest of the organs. This is the fast of the elite amongst the people of Allah. The third level is when one adds to the above the safeguarding of the heart from excessive thought and evil whisperings and the rendering of the heart submissive to the remembrance of Allah and the witnessing of Him in His manifestations; this is the fast of the elite of the elite and this is perfection and the sought-after goal. There are numerous other other descriptions of this nature and the reader is urged to study them from the appropriate sources; and Allah is more Knowing and more Wise.

The fifth kind of inner fast is to refrain from taking notice of the *sensus communis* which combines conjecture and imagination and which is constantly projecting form and meaning on to the soul. This *sensus communis* prevents one from advancing on the spiritual path, since anyone who is engrossed in form, as perceived of by this sense, veils himself from the spiritual form and anyone who is engrossed in meanings in the realm of conjecture veils himself from the inner meanings in the realm of reality and the intellect. Besides anyone who is veiled is veiled, be it by one single veil or a thousand. Thus it is obligatory upon the one fasting to abstain from this 'combined sense' so as to rid himself of such veils and so as to witness the Beloved in the manner we have described.

The people of Allah and their elite have established that the soul is like a tree possessing ten branches. Each branch takes water as required from the trunk of the tree, which in turn takes up water from the earth. This is a natural and self-evident phenomenon. If we then suppose that nine of the branches be cut, then of necessity their strength and the water consumed by them will go up the one remaining branch, which will then grow, become bigger and produce better, sweeter, finer and more beautiful fruit as a result. The same principle may be applied to the soul of man and his ten branches or senses: if one of these branches is cut off — by severing its attachment to the world — then the remaining branches are bound to grow bigger as a result and its fruit will be sublimer, profounder, finer and nobler: 'And certainly We have set forth to men in this Qur'an similitudes of every sort that they may heed.'

iii) According to the people of *haqiqah*

Having established the two above-mentioned kinds of fasting, then the people of this group establish this particular fast which is the fast of the gnostic who abstains from witnessing other than the Real whatever the circumstances — in accordance with the judgement of the men of this science: 'There is nothing in existence but Allah, His Names, Attributes and Actions; all is He, by Him, from Him and to Him.' This is because anyone who does not prevent his soul from witnessing other-than-Him in all circumstances is one who associates others with Allah *(mushrik)*; and neither fasting nor prayer are accepted of a *mushrik*. The basis prayer is purification from the impurity of associating others with Allah by means of the water of divine unity *(tawhid)* and the light of faith. Just as the prayer and most of the other acts of worship are only valid with this kind of purification together with the more familiar kind of (physical) purification, it is also evident that the prayer and the other acts of worship are not only invalid without this physical purification but are invalidated when offered by a *mushrik* or an unbeliever *(kafir)*. Moreover, the same applies to the fasting and so that fast of the *mushrik* is invalid irrespective of whether his *shirk* is manifest or hidden. Every *mushrik* is an unbeliever and every unbeliever a *mushrik;* this is affirmed in the words of Allah, 'And whoever associates anything with Allah, he indeed strays off into remote error.' This is the basic principle of the path of *tawhid* and the masters of *tawhid* and it is not permissible to talk openly about it except to the people of this science; this is in accordance with the words of Allah: 'Surely Allah commands you to make over trusts to their owners' and the Prophet's words: 'Do not give wisdom to other than the people of wisdom for you will be doing the wisdom an injustice, and do not prevent the people from obtaining it and so do them an injustice.' The poet has also said:

> Whoever bestows knowledge on the ignorant is throwing it away,
> And whoever denies it of those who merit it is being unjust.

The words of Jesus, 'Do not hang pearls around the necks of swine' are also an indication of this meaning.

Just as *shirk* may be manifest or hidden, the same is true of *tawhid*, the two being related to each other. Thus neither the prayer or the fast of the person of manifest *shirk* — which is the antithesis of divine *tawhid* — nor the fast or the prayer of hidden *shirk* — which is the antithesis of the *tawhid* of existence — is valid. Allah has indicated the person of hidden *shirk* with His words: 'Therefore whoever hopes to meet his Lord should do good deeds and, in the service of his Lord, he should not associate any other with Him.' If this were an indication of the persons of manifest *shirk*, He would have said simply, 'and do not associate anyone with his Lord'; since, however, He has said, 'in the service of his Lord,' we realise that it refers to the person of hidden *shirk*. Allah's words, 'And most of them do not believe in Allah without associating (others with Him)' also refer to the person of hidden *shirk*.

It has been narrated that, 'the *tawhid* of a moment destroys the unbelief *(kufr)* of seventy years and a moment's unbelief destroys seventy years Islam.' This is true since their coming together is something impossible and unimaginable, both with regard to the intellect and with respect to the sources of the Qur'an and the *ahadith*.

Thus it is the duty of the gnostic, in the first instance, to refrain from witnessing any action that is from other-than-Him, whatever the circumstances, so that he may arrive thereby at the station of the *tawhid* of action. It is likewise his duty to refrain from witnessing the attributes of other-than-Him, whatever the circumstances, so that he may arrive thereby at the station of the *tawhid* of attribute. It is then his duty to refrain from witnessing any existence other than Him, whatever the circumstances, so that he may arrive thereby at the station of the *tawhid* of essence; that is the absolute object and goal of the spiritual wayfaring or rather, of the whole of existence. When this is achieved, then the person may truly be said to be undertaking the real fast and abstaining from all things which would invalidate the reality of this fast. This is the fast mentioned in the *hadith:* 'Every good action will be rewarded by its like — up to seven hundred times

over — except the fast, for this is for Me and I am its reward,'
since no other kind of fast would merit Him as the reward. The
reward of the two previously mentioned fasts is the Garden and
its blessings, the maidens and palaces or the drawing close to
Allah, arrival at Him, unveilings and witnessing. However, this
fast's reward is Him and no other, and so it is greater and of a
higher order than the other two. This is because the greater the
action and exertion, the greater the reward. There is no greater
fast than this and so there can be no other reward but Him. It
is this which is referred to in the *ayah*, 'Most surely this is the
mighty achievement for the like of them, so let the workers work.'
It is also mentioned in Allah's words, 'Whoever does this seeking
Allah's pleasure, We will give him a mighty reward.'

The difference between the fast of the people of *tariqah* and
that of the people of *haqiqah* is that the former results in the
refinenement of behaviour and the taking on of the Attributes
of Allah (affirmed in the words of the Prophet: 'Make your
character the character of Allah'), while the second results in
the annihilation of Allah's slave and his abiding with the Real
in the station of pure *tawhid*. This station is also known as the
annihilation in *tawhid*, referred to in the sayings of the gnostics
and also in the *qudsi hadith:* 'Whoever seeks Me, finds Me, and
whoever finds Me, comes to know Me, and whoever comes to
know Me, loves Me, and whoever loves Me, then I kill that
person, and whomsoever I kill, then I must pay the blood money,
and to whomsoever I owe the blood money, then I am the recompense for the blood money.' All these words are an indication
of the annihilation of the slave in Him and his abiding in the
station of pure *tawhid*, also known as the joining of the separate
after the gathering — and referred to in His words: 'And you
did not smite when you smote (the enemy) but it was Allah Who
smote' and in the words of the Prophet: 'Whoever sees me (in
a dream) has seen the truth.' 'Glory be to Him and how great
is His affair.'

The people of Allah and their elite have given a striking
metaphor in reply to the ignorant, who suppose their words to
be untrue: 'Imagine the fire with the properties of light and heat
and the capacity to burn and cook food, for example, and then

imagine some charcoal which is dark and black and lacks heat and the capacity to cook food; then imagine that this charcoal is slowly brought closer to this fire such that it acquires all the properties of the latter and itself ends up by becoming fire with the capacity to do all that the fire does. Thus the one becomes the other. Is it not permissible for the charcoal to say, "I am the fire?" just as the gnostic said, "I am the Truth." ' Evidently it is permissible for him to say this if he is sincere in what he is saying. It has also been said, 'I am from my passions and my passions are from I,' and consider the words of Allah: 'And (as for) these examples, We set them forth for man, and none understands them but the learned.' It is not permissible to disclose any more of these secrets and Allah it is Who says the truth and guides to the correct path. Having concluded this section on fasting in relation to the three different groups, we shall now begin in the same manner on the subject of *zakat*.

10

Zakat (purifying tax)

i)   According to the people of *shari'ah*

According to the people of this group, *zakat* is obligatory on nine things: camels, cows, sheep and goats, gold, silver, wheat, barley, dates, and dried grapes; it is not obligatory on anything other than these. These nine may be divided in two ways: the first division includes those things for which the *zakat* is paid on completion of the full year, and the second when this does not apply. Those things for which the elapse of a full year is a condition are the first five commodities (that is, not including the grain crops and fruits), and those things for which the elapse of the year does not apply are the four latter commodities (namely the grains and the fruits).

There are two conditions with respect to those things governed by the elapse of a year, one dependent upon the owner and one dependent upon the commodity itself. The condition dependent upon the owner is of two types, the first being the condition of obligation and the second relative to his liablity (*daman*). The condition of obligation is of two divisions: that the person be a free man (and this applies in the case of all five commodities) and of sound intellect, in all except the cattle which are evaluated; this is so since those who are not of sound or mature mind (such as mad persons or children) are still obliged to pay the *zakat* on their cattle. The condition of liablity (on property or animals owned, rented or held in security or trust) are two in number: that the person be Muslim and that he has the ability to pay the *zakat*. There are two conditions with respect to the commodities themselves: the elapse of the year and the reaching of the *nisab* (or prescribed minimum levels at which the *zakat* is payable.

With respect to those things for which no account is taken of the elapse of the year, then the conditions are two in number, the first being dependent upon the person upon whom the *zakat* is obligatory and the second dependent upon the commodity itself. As for the condition dependent upon the person, it is only that he be a free person   *zakat*   on grains is not obligatory for someone who is not of sound mind, although there is no liability on the wealth of someone who is not of sound mind). As for the condition dependent upon the commodity itself, it is that the full *nisab* is reached. There are numerous other studies of the laws governing each of these different divisions; we have no need for further explanation of this in a work of this nature; and Allah is more-Knowing and more Wise.

ii) According to the people of *tariqah*

The *zakat* of the people of this group — after the giving of the above-mentioned *zakat* — is the obligation upon them to purify the soul from the baseness of miserliness and to cleanse the heart from the filth of meanness. This is indicated in the words of Allah, 'And whoever is saved from the greediness of his soul, these it is who are the successful.' He also indicates how this *zakat* increases the fruits of one's knowledge, realities and gnoses and makes them grow and become full of blessings: 'The parable of those who spend their property in the way of Allah is that of a grain growing seven ears with a hundred grains in each ear; and Allah multiplies for whom he pleases.' The meaning of this requires some more explanation: it refers to the spiritual wayfarer who, by removing the qualities of miserliness and meanness and planting in their place the qualities of magnificence and generosity, obtains other qualities whose branching fruits of gnoses and realities are countless in number, the least of them being deliverance from the baser qualities and blameworthy deeds which cause a person to enter the interior Gehanna. The comparison to the grain and the ear of corn is fitting in that every quality acquired by the spiritual traveller, be it praiseworthy or blameworthy, is also accompanied by other acquired qualities too many to enumerate, indeed, as numerous as the grains in an ear of corn — thus if one grain of corn falls to the ground, many ears of corn are produced, each containing so many grains.

With respect to the *zakat* of wealth, the following has been said: 'The secret of man's duty to pay *zakat* — over and above the benefit to the country as a whole, to the individual slave and to those in difficulty and need — is that wealth is loved by mankind and mankind has been commanded to love Allah and has been invited to do so with the same intensity. This wealth has been established as a measure of their love and as a test of their sincerity with respect to their claim of love, for any lover spends on the one most beloved to his heart.' It has also been said, 'The one who gives should be careful not to reproach or be patronizing towards the one who receives.' It is patronizing to look upon yourself as the generous benefactor of the person. The sign of this is that you expect thanks from him, or you feel dislike for him because of his lack of reverence for you, or because of his affection for an enemy of yours — to such an extent that your dislike increases far beyond any feeling of disgust that you may have previously had for the poor person. The reason for this is that you consider yourself more excellent than him. Therefore Allah warns, 'Do not make your charity worthless by reproach and injury.' The cure for this is to realise that in fact the poor person is doing a kindness to you in accepting what Allah has made a right for him from you.

Among the secrets of *zakat* is that it cleanses the heart and purifies it from miserliness and the degradation of meanness. If, however, you cleanse the heart of these qualities but render it full of conceit and haughtiness and thereby cause harm to others, then it is as if you have not cleansed it of anything; rather you have increased its degradation and impurity — and we seek refuge from Allah from such a state. Thus the *zakat* is His means of purification since by it purification is attained; it is as if the *zakat* is a means of *ghusl* or greater purification, whereby the major impurities are washed away from the inner dimension of the person concerned. It is for this reason that the Messenger of Allah and the members of his family receive *zakat*. Indeed it has been reported, 'Surely it *(zakat)* is the filthiest of people's wealth.' Thus if the poor man receives it from you, your purification is the excess received by the poor man from you. Have you not noticed that when you have a vein bled and the blood which you fear will cause you worldly harm flows out, was there not an unnecessary excess of blood within you? Thus that which draws out meanness together with the harm it would cause in the next world is even more of a noxious excess than the blood.

Up to this point we have been considering the matter with respect to the outer realm. If we now consider the matter with respect to the inner, since the people of *tariqah* do not possess any wealth on which to pay *zakat*, their *zakat* is paid by the purification of their selves of blameworthy and despicable characteristics and thereafter by their giving out, in the way of Allah and for His pleasure, that which is most beloved to them, namely the self. This is affirmed by Allah when He says: 'By no means shall you attain to righteousness until you spend (benevolently) out of what you love.' It is evident that the dearest thing to man, indeed to all creatures, is his soul or self; thus it is obligatory for him to give charity in the way of Allah so that he obtains the real purification of *zakat* and the complete cleansing mentioned above. This is affirmed in the words of Allah, 'And reckon not those who are killed in Allah's way as dead; nay they are alive and are provided sustenance from their Lord; rejoicing in what Allah has given them out of His grace.' The meaning of this *ayah* is that one should not think that those killed in the way of Allah are non-existent and without reward; rather the one who has been killed in the realm of form receives in the next world a reward and portion of the Garden, its blessings and palaces, and intimacy and honour with Allah. The one who has been killed in the realm of inner meaning is in a similar situation since he possesses wisdom, knowledge, fine behaviour and courtesy in this world as well as unveilings, witnessings and awareness of the realities of the spiritual domain and the realm of power. In short, he witnesses the Real in His manifestations on the horizon and in the self, that is, he experiences the highest level of witnessing and he also gains the Garden with its blessings and palaces in the hereafter. Above all this is the arrival at the Beloved and at the ultimate goal and attainment of what no eye has seen, no ear has heard and what the heart of man has never thought of.'

Allah refers to the persons of this station when He says, 'Surely those who guard (against evil) shall be in gardens and rivers, in the seat of honour with a most Powerful King' and also his words, 'It is not righteousness that you turn your faces to the east and west, but righteousness is this that one should believe in Allah and the last day and the angels and the Book and the prophets, and give away wealth out of love for Him to the near of kin and the orphans and the needy and the wayfarer and the beggars and for (the emancipation of) the captives and keep up the prayer and pay the poor-rate; and the performers of their promise when they make a promise, and the patient in distress and affliction and in time of conflicts — these are true (to themselves) and these are they who guard (against evil).' The above *ayah* refers to all the persons of this group and in particular defines the nature of righteousness which is the goal of this station.

Another aspect of this station concerns the fact that *zakat,* according to the law of the *shari'ah,* is payable with respect to the mineral, vegetable and animal kingdoms, the gold and silver belonging to the realm of the mineral, the wheat, barley, dates and dried grapes to the realm of the vegetable, and the camels, goats and sheep to the realm of the animal. The Prophet has said, 'For everything there is a *zakat;* the *zakat* of the body is obedience.' Thus every slave who acts in obedience to his Lord, in accordance with what he has been commanded to do, is in effect paying his *zakat* (and thereby purifying himself in the manner we have mentioned). This is so since the people of Allah and their elite, in their comparison of the macrocosm and the microcosm, remember that the bones in their body are analogous to the realm of the mineral, and that their hair and nails are analogous to the realm of the vegetable, and that their animal self and inner and outer senses are analogous to the realm of the animal. Whoever acts in obedience to his Lord of necessity brings fatigue to his limbs, organs and the other physical components of his body; on investigation, we realise that this fatigue is a kind of *zakat.* The fruit of fatigue in this world is that one becomes purified of filth and one rises above natural impurities and baseness of character, in accordance with the words of Allah, 'O you who are clothed! Arise and warn, and your Lord do magnify and your garments do purify and uncleanness do shun.' Then the mirror of his heart shines bright such that the lights of the angelic *malakut* and the traces of the *jabarut* or realm of power manifest therein; indeed his soul becomes an inhabitant of these two realms — which denote the two realms of the pure intelligible substances and the purified souls (or as they are also known according to the *shari'ah:* the realm of the intimate angels, indicated in the Qur'an as 'the sublime abode'). It is for this reason that the Messenger of Allah would always say the following in his supplications: 'O Allah, place light in my heart and light in my hearing and light in my sight and light in my flesh and light in my blood and light in my bones and light in front of me and light below , me and light in my grave, O Allah increase me in light and give me light by the truth of Your reality, O most Merciful of the Merciful.' The secret of this prayer is that it removes any darkness, obscurity, impurity and stain from him and gives light, clarity, purity, refinement and courtesy in their place; by means of this prayer he becomes of the people of the *malakut* and *jabarut* — by the strength of the spiritual link — and he attains to what the inhabitants of these abodes attain to, namely direct witnessings and unveilings. We have already mentioned this supplication once before; the reader should not imagine that its inclusion here is mere idle repetition, rather it is important as an example of the Prophet's guidance and instruction for the rest of his people out of his concern that they should also share such stations. If this were not so, then this supplication would have no meaning, given that the Prophet is infallible and free from all impurities.

The above remarks may also be applied to the three kinds of soul rather than the body and its physical members. Just as there exists in man the three kingdoms on a cosmic level, so there also exists the soul of the mineral realm, the soul of the vegetable realm and the soul of the animal realm. The *zakat* of these three kingdoms may be extracted of these three souls by the expulsion of the baser and blameworthy qualities of behaviour from each of them and their replacement with the finer attributes of good behaviour. The soul is one reality and multiplies in accordance with contingent phenomena. For every quality the soul acquires there is a corresponding name: by its detachment, it is called the human soul and by its attachment to the body, in the first instance, it is called the plant soul, and in the second, the animal soul, and in the third instance, the selfish soul. The *shari'ah* and the Qur'an have described the four souls or selves as self-accusing, commanding to evil, the tranquil soul, and the inspired soul. As to the soul which commands to evil, it is referred to in Allah's words: 'Surely man's soul is wont command (him to do) evil.' As for the self-accusing or self-reproaching soul, it is referred to in His words: 'Nay I swear by the day of resurrection; nay I swear by the self-accusing soul.' As for the inspired self, it is referred to in His words: 'And the soul and Him who made it perfect, then He inspired it to understand what is right and wrong for it.' As for the soul at rest it is referred to in His words: 'O soul that art rest! Return to your Lord, well pleased (with Him), well pleasing (Him). In the first instance the soul, because of the weakness of its intellectual power and its lack of will to prevent it from doing what is harmful, takes command over the body, its physical forces and the like. If, however, the self-accusing soul dominates by the power of the intellect and prevents it from doing what is blameworthy, then it reproaches the soul such that it turns away from what it is engaged in. When this quality of self-reproach becomes an inherent part of the soul, then the soul becomes inspired, and thus merits inspiration from Allah with regard to its actions and states. In becoming the inspired soul, it becomes aware of the difference between what is good and what is bad, what is beneficial and what is evil. When this quality becomes an integral characteristic of the soul, it thereby witnesses the world of the unseen. In this way it merits a witnessing of its Lord and becomes tranquil and is able to return to its own world. How good is the *zakat* whose fruit is such a return; and Allah is more Knowing and more Wise.

iii) According to the people of *haqiqah*

The *zakat* of this group is established after their fulfilment of the two above-mentioned types of *zakat*. Their particular *zakat* refers to the removal of the awareness of limitation from everything in existence and causing each to arrive at the world of the unrestricted or absolute, such that it becomes purified of the stain of otherness and the impurity of duality. Every imaginable existence is in fact Absolute Existence in a particular state of limitation. The manner in which the limit or restriction is removed from the three realms (of vegetable, mineral and animal) is, in the first instance, by the elevation of each realm above the restriction of composite elements so that it arrives at the purely simple elemental state. In the case of these simple elements, the limitations of this particular state are overcome by removing the restriction of simple individual elements and causing it to arrive at the celestial plane of the heavens and the planetary bodies. The limitations of the latter are removed by releasing it from the restriction of the celestial and planetary and by causing it to reach the universal body of natural forms. The latter is released from the limitation of its corporeality such that it reaches the level of universal substance. The latter is released from its own restriction of substance by its arrival at the level of universal nature. The latter is released from its restriction of nature and caused to arrive at the level of the simple or pure soul. The latter is released from its spiritual particularity and caused to arrive at the level of the the sacred souls and that of the universal souls which is the level of the pure intelligences. From these latter it is caused to arrive at the Presence of Oneness and Absolute Existence or Reality. This releasing from limitation and particularity is the true purification and the universal *zakat* in relation to every existence from among the existent beings in the realm of the possible.

We have already shown how the perfection of the mineral is its arrival at the realm of the vegetable, and the perfection of the vegetable is its arrival at the station of the animal, and the perfection of the animal is its arrival at the station of man, and the perfection of man is his arrival, in the first instance, at the station of the earthly realm *(mulk)* and then to that of the divine caliphate, and then to the station of pure creation. This is a kind of *zakat* in that it purifies man and indeed all existent beings of the impurity of limitation and the stain of specificity which, as we have seen, is a kind of hidden *shirk*. It is this that is the true *zakat* and the true goal, since there is no other kind of purification which is greater than this. Purification of the existent beings from the restriction of limitation and contingent phenomena is the greatest and sublimest of purifications; indeed it is the ultimate purpose of Allah's imposition of *zakat* on His slaves. We ask Allah to give us success in arriving at this station of *zakat* and similar stations; He it is from Whom the slaves seek help and on Whom they rely.

11

Hajj (pilgrimage)

i) According to the people of *shari'ah*

According to the people of this group, the word *hajj* refers to the journey towards the actual goal of the *hajj* itself. According to the law of the *shari'ah*, it specifically refers to the journey towards the House of Allah, the Haram, in order to perform the prescribed rites at the prescribed time; and there are two legal divisions to the term: the obligatory and the recommended.

The obligatory is of two types, the absolute and the restricted. As for the absolute, it is the pilgrimage of Islam, which is obligatory when eight conditions are fulfilled: that the person has reached puberty, is of perfectly sound mind, is a free man, is healthy, that the provision (for the journey) is available, that the means of conveyance to and from the place of pilgrimage exist together with adequate funds or means of support from one's own industry or profession, the absence of obstacles on the route and the possibility of travel. When any of these conditions is not fulfilled, then the *hajj* is no longer obligatory, although the judgement of the *hajj* as a recommended or desirable act of worship remains in force. Among the things which make for the perfection of the conditions is that it is obligatory to perform it at least once in a lifetime; any more than this is desirable, and this obligation demands that it be performed as soon as the conditions are fulfilled. As for the restricted type of *hajj* it becomes obligatory for specific reasons. Thus it becomes an obligation after the making of a vow or a contract with Allah, and it should be undertaken in accordance with the number of vows made. Thus if once, then one pilgrimage is made and if many, then many; two pilgrimages which have become obligatory may not be exchanged when one, for example, seems more important, so that if two are to be performed then the performance of one does not do for the other as well. It has, however, been narrated that if a person performs the pilgrimage with the intention of fulfilling a vow, then this may be counted as the Islamic *hajj* (or the main *hajj*, obligatory once in a lifetime); the first of these judgements is surer as a precautionary measure. A vow should not be made except by a free person of perfectly sound mind; the rest of the conditions, however, need not be fulfilled.

There are three kinds of *hajj: tamattu'*, *qiran* and *ifrad*. The *hajj tamattu'* is obligatory on whoever has no family resident in the proximity of the Haram Mosque. The *ifrad* and *qiran* pilgrimage are an obligation on persons residing in the proximity of the Haram: the prescribed distance is twelve miles between the person's residence and the Haram Mosque, extending in all four directions from the House; this is equivalent to four *farasikh*, each *farsakh* (parasang) being four thousand cubits and each cubit being of twenty-four inches.

There are two types of action undertaken during the *hajj*, those which are obligatory and those which are *sunnah* — after the example of the Prophet. There are two divisions to what is obligatory: that which is a pillar and that which is not, and they apply to all these above-mentioned kinds of *hajj*. The pillars of the *tamattu'* *hajj* are ten in number, four of them being for the *'umrah* (or minor *hajj*) and six for the *hajj* itself. As for those belonging to the *'umrah,* they are the intention, the donning of the *ihram* (two pieces of seamless white cloth) at the prescribed limits and the prescribed times, the *tawaf* (the circumambulation of the Ka'bah) of the *'umrah* and the running between Safa and Marwah. As for those belonging to the *hajj*, they are the intention, the standing at 'Arafat, the standing at the place of the rites and sacrifice, the *tawaf* of *hajj*, and the running between Safa and Marwah. The things which are not pillars are eight in number: the pronouncing of the *talbiyah:* 'Here I am at your service' four times when possible, or doing whatever takes its place when one is incapable of the above; the two cycles of prayer for the *tawaf* of *'umrah;* the cutting of hair after running between Safa and Marwah; the pronouncing of the *talbiyah* when donning the *ihram* for the *hajj*, or when donning whatever may take its place; the sacrifice of an animal, or whatever takes it place (that is the fast) if one is unable to slaughter; the two cycles of prayer for the *tawaf* of *hajj;* the *tawaf* of the women and the accompanying two cycles of prayer. As for the pillars of the *qiran* and the *ifrad* pilgrimages they are six in number: the intention, the donning of the *ihram*, the standing at the places of the rites and sacrifice, the *tawaf* of the visit (to the Ka'bah) and that of running between Safa and Marwah.

The things other than the pillars with respect to these two types of *hajj* are four in number: the *talbiyah* or whatever takes its place — when the animal is garlanded at the prescribed rites and sacrifice — and the two cycles of prayer for the *tawaf* of the visit and the *tawaf* of the women together with its accompanying two cycles of prayer. The *qiran hajj* is distinguished from the *ifrad* by the driving of the sacrificial animal. It is desirable in both these kinds of *hajj* to renew the *talbiyah* while beginning each *tawaf*. The things which are *sunnah* are many in number and may be learned from the appropriate books; and may peace be on those who follow the guidance. Herewith we conclude the section the *hajj* of the people of *shari'ah* according to the manner of the Shiahs.

ii) According to the people of *tariqah*

The *hajj* of this group occurs after the establishment of the above-mentioned *hajj;* this *hajj* refers to journeying towards the real House of Allah and the inner Ka'bah by means of spiritual wayfaring. According to this group, the House of Allah has different dimensions: there is that of the cosmos and that of the individual souls. As for the cosmic Ka'bah, it refers to the heart of the Great Man, also known as the Universal Soul and the *Bayt al-Ma'mur* (the House in heaven above the Ka'bah) or the Guarded Tablet; as for that of the individuals souls, it refers to the heart of man as the microcosm, also known, for example, as the rational individual soul. The first is related to the people of *haqiqah* since it is their *qiblah;* the second is related to the people of *tariqah*, for it is also their *qiblah* (We shall consider the journey of the people of *haqiqah* after our present discussion).

To understand the manner of journeying towards the *qiblah* of the people of *tariqah*, which is their journeying towards their own heart, a preliminary introduction is necessary. It has been narrated that the first house to extend over the water and to appear on the surface was the Ka'bah and this happened before

the earth and all centres of civilisation. This is affirmed in the
words of the Prophet: 'The Ka'bah was the first house to appear
on the surface of the water during the creation of the heavens.
Allah created it a thousand years before the earth. It was like a
white foam on the surface of the water, and the earth was laid
out beneath it.' The following words of Allah also bear witness
to the truth of these words: 'Most surely the first house appointed
for men is the one at Bakkah, blessed and a guidance for the
nations. In it are clear signs, the standing place of Abraham and
whoever enters it shall be secure, and pilgrimage to the House
is incumbent upon men for the sake of Allah, (upon) everyone
who is able to undertake the journey to it; and whoever disbelieves, then surely Allah is Self-Sufficient, above any need of the
worlds.' Our intention in quoting the saying of the Prophet and
the Qur'anic *ayah* is to demonstrate to the reader that there exists
a Ka'bah of the phenomenal realm and a Ka'bah of the noumenal
realm. Moreover, each may be classified in two ways: as for the
former it may be divided firstly into the phenomenal mosque,
also known as the House of Allah or the Haram, and secondly,
the phenomenal heart, also known as the House of Allah, or the
Haram. As for the latter, on the one hand it is the heart of the
Great Man, also known as the Universal Soul and, on the other,
the heart of man as the microcosm, also known as the rational
individual soul. Just as the saying of the Prophet and the *ayah*
apply to the first two divisions, so they also apply to the latter
two divisions — since the first reality which appeared within the
world of the soul from the soul of the Great Man was his true
heart (which is also known as the Universal Soul) and is referred
to in Allah's words, 'O people! Be careful of (your duty to) your
Lord, Who created you from a single being.' Likewise the first
form to appear in the world of corporeality, also known as the
earth, was the outer form of Bakkah; this is referred to in Allah's
words, 'Most surely the first house appointed for men is the one
at Bakkah, blessed and a guidance.' The first reality to appear
in the world of the soul from the soul of the lesser man or microcosm — referred to by Allah in His words: 'So when I made
him complete and breathed into him of My spirit' — was his
true heart in accordance with Allah's words, 'Nothing in the

earth and the heavens contains Me but the heart of the believing slave (contains Me)'. The first form to appear in the world of corporeality, that is the body of man, was the form of the heart, referred to by Allah as the breast: 'Have We not expanded for you your breast?' Just as one demonstrates the existence of the noumenal Ka'bah, that is the heart of the Great Man, by the phenomenal Ka'bah, so one may demonstrate the noumenal Ka'bah within the heart of the lesser man. This is affirmed in Allah's words: 'We will soon show them Our signs in the Universe and in their own souls until it will become quite clear to them that it is the truth.' Up to this point we have been considering the matter in a general way: we shall now look at it in more detail.

The Universal Soul, which is known as the Greater House of Allah, occupies a position above that of all other things. Allah's words, 'And He it is Who created the heavens and the earth in six periods and His throne (dominion) extends on the water' also demonstrate that the Throne *('arsh)* occupied a position above the spiritual spheres of the intelligences and souls, before the creation of the heavens and the earth in the corporeal realm — assuming that the throne is understood to refer to the noumenal Throne, the First Intellect. If, however, what is meant by the throne is the phenomenal Throne, which is the greater sphere of the *Atlas,* the ninth sphere, then what is meant by water is the phenomenal water, according to one of the commentators, namely Nasir al-Din Baydawi; this, he says, is because since there is no obstacle between the throne and the water, it is possible to say that it is above or on it.

If we now consider the matter from another point of view, then it can be said that water is the divine knowledge on which everything has always been firmly established — and will continue likewise forever. It is specifically referred to as the Throne because of its vastness and might. Thus if we assume, with regard to the realm of form, that this water on which the Throne rests is the sperm of the Great Man, as has been determined by the people of Allah, then it refers to the water of form and the sperm from which the whole form of the world came existence. The people of the outer law are in agreement that the world began from water and they base their judgement on the saying of the

Prophet, 'The first thing created by Allah was matter. He then looked upon it and it melted away in modesty (or because of the force of the gaze, according to a different narration), half of it becoming fire and the other half water. He then created the heavens from the water and the planets from fire, or He created the Garden from water and Hell from fire, or He created the spiritual realites from the water and the corporeal realities from the fire' (the basic meaning is the same, despite the difference of terms). The proof of this is the correspondence between the cosmic world and that of the individual souls. The beginning of the microcosm and its creation in the realm of form was from water, that is the drop of sperm, and the microcosm is a model for the macrocosm in all aspects. Thus it follows that the latter must also have been created from water.

The Prophet's words: 'during the creation of the heavens' is an indication of the priority of the spiritual realities over the corporeal realities. His words, 'a thousand years before the earth' is an indication that Allah created the Universal Soul, that is, the Ka'bah of the spiritual realm a thousand years before the bodily forms, that is, the earth and all contained therein. Moreover, what is meant by a thousand years is the two complete ages, first that of the Intellect and then that of the Soul — since they both precede the souls and bodily forms by a long period; that is by two cycles of the orbits of the seven planets, since each planet has an orbit particular to itself which lasts for a thousand years, and an orbit which it shares with the others lasting six thousand years. Thus the world of bodily forms was created two complete cycles — in term of the orbits of the seven planets — after the creation of the souls. It has been established that during the period of Saturn's orbit the earth was still a wilderness. It was during the beginning of Jupiter's orbit that it became inhabited, and it was during the final stage of this orbit that the animals appeared, culminating in the appearance of man. Thus what is meant by a thousand years is the cycle of these two planets in the manner we have described — or the two ages of the Intellect and the Soul — and in our opinion, this latter notion is closer to the truth. The priority of the souls over the world of bodily forms is so clear and evident that there is no need of any further explanation, especially given the fact that there are *ahadith* and *ayat* from the Qur'an which testify to the truth of this matter. The words, 'And it was a white foam on the surface of the water' is an indication of the purity of the Universal Soul and its transparency and subtlety in relation to the other realities of the angelic realm (*malakut*) — which lies beneath it and is referred to as the water. This is so since everything which is of a higher position, whether it is spiritual or corporeal, is finer and subtler.

As for the correspondence of the House of Allah to the lesser man in the light of the above-cited *hadith,* the appearance of the Ka'bah on the surface of the water may symbolise the attachment of the soul to the sperm in the creation of man, otherwise the words may be interpreted at the literal level. The creation of the Ka'bah 'during the creation of the heavens' refers to the creation of the soul of man or the heart, as it is also known, before the animal soul, which is also known as the heavens; 'a thousand years before the earth' symbolises the creation of the soul of the lesser man two complete ages before his body. The words, 'white foam' symbolise the purity of its substance and its subtlety before its attachment to the body, that is the earth. The words, 'on the surface of the water' symbolise the sperm which is the original matter making up the body and the general form of man. What is meant here is the attachment of the soul when it was created and made manifest in the world of the unseen and the world of the Divine Command. The words, 'then the earth was laid beneath it' alludes to the body: what is meant here is that when the soul is directed to the sperm, the body extends in accordance with the judgement and command of the soul until the station of man's form comes into being as a result of the joining of these two.

The bodily limbs and parts all turn in the direction of the heart so that they may attain to their goal and the knowledge appropriate to them. The blessed Bakkah in the above-cited *ayah* symbolises the breast which surrounds the heart in the same way as Makkah encompasses the Mosque and the Ka'bah; this is because the Ka'bah is analogous to the heart, the breast to the mosque, and the body to the Haram or Makkah. The words 'blessed' indicates the blessing obtained from the heart in the way of divine gnoses. The words, 'and a guidance for the nations' indicate that the House is a guidance to the various groups around it — that is, the twin forces of the spirit and body for example, or the human, animal and vegetative souls. The words, 'in it are clear signs, the standing place of Abraham' are an indication of the presence of the acquiring intellect, that is, the presence of sanctity and the station of drawing close; this is one of the greatest of Allah's signs and one of the sublimest. The words, 'whoever enters it shall be secure' imply that whoever enters this house, that is the heart, in a fitting manner, will be secure from the Satanic guiles of the soul which commands to evil, from the Satanic guiles of the demon imagination, from seizure by the armies of false conjecture and from the influence of brigand jinn and men. The meaning of the words, 'and pilgrimage to the House is incumbent upon men for the sake of Allah, (upon) everyone who is able to undertake the journey to it' is that the pilgrimage to the house is incumbent upon those whom we have mentioned above who should journey to it and circumambulate it so that they may perceive its signs, secrets and realities and so that they may arrive by means of it to Allah, to His Gardens and to His Presence. The meaning of everyone who is able 'to undertake the journey to it' is everyone who is able to follow this spiritual path and to persevere in constancy along it, that is. by means of the provision from the realm of reality, through the knowledge of certainty and total annihilation and the death of the will. The above is true, since anyone who does not possess this capacity is no longer obliged to perform this *hajj*, as has already been determined in the case of the *hajj* of the *shari'ah* law. Whoever denies the truth of this *hajj* and disobeys the command of Allah, whoever strays from its path and from fulfilment of its rites, then 'surely Allah is Self-Sufficient, above any need of the worlds'. Anyone who relies solely on Allah in his travelling along this path and who progresses thereon with complete devotion will be guided to the straight path in the direction of the inner House of Allah.

Up to this point we have been examining the *hajj* of spiritual travel in relation to the self; we shall now begin on the subject of the *hajj* of the cosmic realm and the perception of the realities of the angelic realm *(malakut)* and the realm of Absolute Dominion *(jabarut)* and the circumambulation of them. Know that whoever wishes to undertake this *hajj* and to travel to this House, then it is incumbent upon him, in the first instance, to don the *ihram* or invest himself in the state of prohibition. What this means is that the person must forbid himself any indulgence in the sensual desires, be they of a forbidden or permitted nature; that is, he should only permit himself what is absolutely necessary in accordance with Allah's words, 'And whoever is driven to necessity, not desiring, nor exceeding the limit'. It also mean that the person refrains from harming any animal or human being, be it through his action or intention, so that he may witness his own state. In this way he may attain to knowledge and gnosis. Moreover, it is incumbent upon him in this state to busy himself with the four *talbiyas* and their meaning, which is that his Lord has no need of his obedience or his worship, or indeed of the obedience or worship of any person; rather he realises that every existent being is in need of Him, by reason of their essence, their very existence and their strength. The person then faces Allah saying the *talbiyah* 'Here I am at your service' in the tongue of the state rather than by actual speech, such that the reality of slavery becomes clear to him. He then enters into the mosque of the breast, that is, the Mosque of the Haram around the heart, which in turn is the Ka'bah of the realm of reality. He than circumambulates it seven times, that is, he examines it seven times so that he may know his own state and so that the veils may be lifted from him. These veils are the blameworthy qualities of behaviour and his base actions, for the seven veils corresponding to the number of the gates of Gehenna, namely conceit, pride, envy, greed, miserliness, anger and excessive sensual desire. These seven things are removed by the making of the seven *tawaf*, each of the latter being the cause of removal of one of the former. These seven *tawaf* are also the cause of the heart's taking on the corresponding praiseworthy qualities, namely knowledge, wisdom, chastity, courage, justice, generosity and humility. The person then prays the prayer of gratitude at the station of Abraham in the realm of the intellect and is thereby brought to this station, by the purity of spiritual capacity and the vision which opens to him from his fear of Allah.

The person then runs between Safa and Marwah, that is, he travels between the world of the outer and that of the inner in order to witness his Beloved in them both and to examine the signs contained in them both, in accordance with Allah's words, 'Is it not sufficient as regards your Lord that He is a witness over all things?' Now surely they are in doubt as to the meeting of their Lord; now surely He encompasses all things.'

. He then cuts his hair at Marwah, that is, he causes to fall from his head any remaining trace of I-ness or duality; in doing so, he comes out of the state of *ihram* (ritual purity) and the actions of the *'umrah,* (the lesser pilgrimage) which are analogous to the ablution and the prayer, and all things which were previously forbidden to him then become permitted. This is so since the slave who is in the station of I-ness and otherness is not permitted anything according to the way of the gnostics. If he comes out of this station, and becomes annihilated in the *hajj* and in the state of abiding therein, then everything becomes permissible for him; indeed, he is forbidden or permitted something in accordance with his own speech, since he is the caliph and has the authority to command and prohibit. The reader should take great care to understand this point: by it one may obtain gnosis of the station of prophethood and saintliness *(wilayah)* — since after the Truth, there is no other source of authority but them. He then takes on another *ihram* (the pilgrim's apparel) from the presence of the intellect which lies beneath the water-course of the heart. (The intellect is a water-course in relation to the heart since wisdom flows from the sea of the heart by way of the water-course of the intellect. Hence the words of the Prophet 'Whoever devotes forty mornings to Allah, springs of wisdom will appear from within his heart,' that is, on the tongue of the intellect which is the interpreter of the heart.)

He then makes his way to the 'Arafat of the mind and the mountain of gnosis, in order to gaze on the signs, gnoses and realities thereabout; this is so since the mind in relation to the body is sometimes like the mount of Abu Qabis or the Mount of Hira' and sometimes like the Throne of His Majesty or the

Throne of the Generous. It is in this station that gnoses descend between the spiritual Adam, which is the soul or spirit, and Eve, the Universal Soul. It is for just this reason that this station is called 'Arafat (from the Arabic root *'arafa* meaning knowledge); this is affirmed in the words of the Prophet, 'Whoever knows himself knows his Lord.'

The person then returns to the place of the rites and sacrifice, that is, he stands in the proximity of his own feelings and sensations both in the realm of form and inner meaning, in order to gaze upon the state of each one of them and to cause each to brought under the authority of its Creator and its Lord, in accordance with the words, 'I was his hearing and his sight and his tongue and his hand and his foot...'; this is because as long as the senses are under the authority of the slave then they are obedient to the soul which commands to evil and they follow the rebellious Satan of passion and desire. If they come under the authority of the Lord and are obedient to that which He has ordered, then they become obedient to the tranquil soul and follow the intellect: the intellect then becomes the emir and ruler in the city and region of the senses.

Then the person returns to Mina, to the realm of the breast and the heart, in order to throw the stones of his own blameworthy and base qualities of behaviour at the three *'jamrat'* (places of the devil), that is, the three realms of the mineral, vegetable and animal. This latter is the realm of the compound realities and all that is related to these realities; it is the state of sincerity and the station of great rank and risk, in accordance with the saying of the Prophet, 'All men are doomed to perish except those of action; those of action will perish except for the sincere and the sincere are in great risk.' Thus the person of this station, having discarded his bad qualities of behaviour during the taking on of the *ihram*, must take care not to return to them when he returns to the station of final perfection, attested to in the words of the people of this science, 'The final goal is a return to the beginning;' the reason for this is also evident in the words, 'The good actions of the righteous are the bad actions of those who have achieved the station of intimacy.' The person then goes on to cut the hair of his head, that is, to remove the 'I-ness' from the head of his self so that action, power and strength are perceived as coming from Allah (which is a higher station than the first cutting of the hair). He then continues towards the removal of the veils of the sacrifice of his self once more, such that no name or trace remains of his self.

Then he goes back to the Ka'bah to perform the second *tawaf*. What this means is that he inspects his heart once again in order to purify it from the impurity of seeing otherness in any way. This is the station contained in the saying of the Prophet, 'Surely trouble and vexation come over my heart and surely I seek forgiveness of Allah seventy times every day and night;' this is so since the Prophet is infallible and has none of the faults recognised as punishable by the *shari'ah* for which he must seek forgiveness of Allah. The only wrong action of the people of this grroup in their travelling along this spiritual path is the witnessing of otherness, even if it is only be for a moment and this occurs when the world of man and the corresponding force of the animal soul overcomes this spiritual station.

Then he goes on to pray two cycles in the station of Abraham, in gratitude for his arrival at the Beloved and at his goal. He then runs once more, that is between the Safa of the world of the soul and the Marwah of the world of corporeality, or we may say between the Safa of the heart and Marwah of the self, in order to witness therein the perfect signs of His manifestations and to witness the signs of His beauty and majesty. He performs the cutting of the hair in the Marwah of the self. By abandoning whatever remains therein of the witnessing of multiplicity in the world. of Oneness. He then returns to Mina to stone the devils during the three days following 'Arafat, that is, he returns from the Ka'bah of the heart once more to the Mina of the breast in the *ayyam al-tashriq*, which are the different days of divine unity (the *tawhid* of action, attribute and essence) in order to abandon everything which is other than these, such that nothing remains with him but the Real. In this station he rises up above perception of all creation, such that no trace at all of the existence of its creatures remains with him and existence remains with him; thus he witnesses the Real as the Real, sometimes in the world of His Oneness, stripped of all phenomenal manifestation, sometimes in the world of multiplicity in the guise of His Names, Attributes, beauty and majesty, and sometimes in the world which combines the two above-mentioned realms, that is, in the Muhammadi *tawhid* of gatheredness. It is this that is the goal of the *hajj* in the realm of meaning according to the masters of *tariqah*. If this is clear to the reader we shall now begin on a commentary of the *hajj* of the people of *haqiqah*.

iii) According to the people of *haqiqah*

The *hajj* of the people of this group refers to the spiritual journey in the esoteric realm towards the heart of the Great Man, which is the Greater House of Allah, also known as the *Bayt al-Ma'mur*, the Presence of Sanctity and the Universal Soul — just as the *hajj* of the people of *tariqah* refers to the journey towards the heart of the lesser man or microcosm. An explanation of this requires some introductory explanation, including the commentary of one of the gnostics with regard to the correspondence between the two worlds.

Know that just as the sultan of the individual soul, the soul of the lesser man, resides only in the brain, so too the sultan of the Universal Soul, the soul of the Great Man — also called the world — resides only in the Throne which is analogous to the brain in relation to us. Just as its first manifestation in the lesser man is the phenomenal heart, the source of life, so too its first manifestation in the Great Man is the fourth planetary sphere, the sphere of the sun and the source of life in this world. As for the heart in the realm of reality, it is the Universal Soul, also called the Preserved Tablet, the Clear Book and the Real Adam, referred to in the words of Allah, 'O people! Be careful of (your duty to) your Lord, Who created you from a simple being and created its mate in the same (kind) and spread of these two, many men and women.' The soul of the fourth planetary sphere is analogous to the animal or vital soul which resides in the heart whereby all the bodily limbs receive life; it is the *Bayt al-Ma'mur*, recognised in the *shari'ah* as being in the fourth heaven. It is by this that the revelation of Allah swears in the following *ayah*: 'I swear by the Mountain and the Book written in a fine outstretched parchment and the House (Ka'bah) that is visited and the elevated canopy and the swollen sea'. It is for this reason that the station of Jesus was made that of the Soul of Allah; indeed, among his miracles was the raising of the dead. The 'Mountain' referred to in the *ayah* is the Throne and the 'Book' is the Universal Soul, that is, the heart of the world. The words 'in fine outstretched parchment' refer to the eighth planetary sphere, being the manifestation thereof; 'the elevated canopy' may be either the Throne or the sky of this world; and 'the House (the Ka'bah) that is visited' may be either the fourth sphere or the Universal Soul — for the eighth planetary sphere is also the manifestation of the Universal Soul. 'The swollen sea' is the sea of the substance, flowing full of forms; it is possible that it is the world of the first interspace, composed of the worlds of the soul and the body, also called the Absolute Imagination and full of the forms of all existent beings. We shall now begin to explain this matter again in more detail.

The meaning of the *hadith* 'The Ka'bah was the first house...' has already been discussed in the section concerning the *hajj* of the people of the *tariqah*, namely that the Ka'bah is the Universal Soul, also known as the Greater House of Allah. The appearance on the surface of the water refers to worlds of the souls which issued from this Universal Soul before the worlds of corporeal realities: anything which is above anything else is of necessity on top of it and thus there is no doubt that the Universal Soul is above the individual souls and so it may also be said to be on top of them. The *ayah*, 'And He it is Who created the heavens and the earth in six periods — and His dominion (extends) on the water' also points to this same meaning.

It may be said that the water refers to the universal substance which is analogous to the water in relation to the Universal Soul. It is also possible that it refers to a time before the split took place when things were still in the closed-up state. This state of of being closed, in one entity, comprised the totality of all material things: the Intellect, the Soul, the Throne and the Footstool were one reality and a universal matter. This is referred to in Allah's words: 'Do not those who disbelieve see that the heavens and the earth were closed but We have opened them.' The gnostics have commented upon the meaning of being closed up, saying it comprises the totality of matter in the state of oneness, also known as the greater and absolute element which was closed-up before the creation of the heavens and the earth. It is also applied to the Presence of Oneness in relation to itself, before its subsequent manifestations, and to the esoteric realities hidden in the Essence of Oneness before separation; there are many examples of this, one among them being the likeness of the tree which is contained as a latent force within the seed.

Whoever disbelieves in this *hajj,* who does not perform it and does not aver its validity, then he is of the *mushrikun,* the people who associate others with Allah, the people who are veiled — surely Allah has no need of such people, be they man or jinn or from wherever they may be. This is because Allah is Self-Sufficient in relation to all the worlds and has no need of their obedience and worship, since He is He. Indeed, the benefit of obedience and worship is confined to the one whose duty it is to obey and to worship none other than Allah, Who is Self-Sufficient with respect to the worlds, their obedience and their worship. It is not permissible to say that this implies a completion of His perfection by what is other-than-Him because this benefit cannot return to Him. Moreover, no action on the part of the All-Wise, the Perfect, is done in jest and any action which issues from an actor without a purpose must be in jest — and jest is impossible of Allah, in accordance with His words, 'And We did not create the heavens and the earth and what is between them for sport' and His words, 'What! Did you then think that We had created you in vain and that you shall not be returned to Us?' Thus, of necessity, this creation has a specific purpose; since it is impossible that the benefit be for Him, it must be that it is for the sake of His slaves, and thus we may arrive at a satisfactory conclusion to this argument. It is for this reason that Allah says in various places in the Qur'an, 'Whoever does good, it is for his own soul and whoever does evil, it is against it' and His words, 'Indeed there have come to you clear proofs from your Lord; whoever will therefore see, it is for his own soul and whoever will be blind, it shall be against himself and I am not a keeper over you.' We shall conclude this particular topic at this point, although there are many other matters which may be taken into consideration. We shall now begin a detailed study of the nature of the pilgrimage, the manner of its performance and the arrival at the goal.

Know that whoever wants to go and visit this house, that is, to arrive therein, it is incumbent upon him in the first instance to take upon himself the *ihram,* namely the prohibition upon himself against witnessing the world of the sensory or the material forms and all the desires and sensual pleasures connected to them. The person must then go forward towards the world of the souls, that is, the realities which are analogous to the Haram, to Makkah, Bakkah and the other corresponding stations in the phenomenal world — until he actually arrives. On arrival, he must take on the qualities of these realities so that they become part of his own character. The person then goes towards the Ka'bah of the realm of reality, that is the Universal Soul, and circumambulates it twice. On completion of each *tawaf,* he attains to a gnosis of each of the seven spheres and the seven Qur'anic gnoses[1] indicated in the Prophet's words: 'Truly the Qur'an has an outward and an inward dimension and this latter has its own inward dimension — and so on up to seven inward dimensions.' The person then goes to the place of standing of Abraham, that is the station of oneness and the presence of oneness, also known as the First Intellect and the greater soul. The person prays therein two cycles of prayer out of gratitude for his arrival at that presence. These two cycles of prayer are an expression of his annihilation, in the first instance from the outer world and in the second from the inner world and all contained therein, including even himself.

---

[1] These seven knowledges are: knowledge of *tawhid,* divestment, annihilation, abiding; knowledge of the essence, the attributes and the divine actions; knowledge of prophethood, the message, *wilayah* and refined manners; knowledge of revelation, inspiration and unveiling; knowledge of the beginnings, the return, the gathering and the division of men accordingly; the knowledge of behaviour, politics, courtesy and instruction therein; knowledge of the cosmos, the individual souls and the correspondence between the two; these are the greatest and noblest of the sciences. It has been said that what is meant by the seven celestial spheres is other than we have maintained at the beginning; what we have said is nevertheless true and in accordance with the subject of our book.

He then goes to the place of running between Safa and Marwah, between the two worlds of the outer and inner, in order to perceive them once more by means of his running and striving; he eliminates any vision of multiplicity by perceiving every thing contained therein as the existence of the One. He then becomes established in the state of gatheredness, which is the true goal, in accordance with the words of the Prophet, 'This world is prohibited the people of the next world and the next world is forbidden the people of this world and they are both forbidden to the people of Allah;' the truth of this may be recognised in the division of the people into those of the left, those of the right and those of intimacy, as we have already mentioned above. The gnostic has also referred to this with his words: 'Awareness of these two things (this world and the next) is incumbent upon you; for surely the person who joins them both is the person who attains to true unity *(tawhid)* and is the one who gathers gatheredness; he reaches a sublime station and the ultimate goal.' The person does the cutting at Marwah, that is the elimination of the world of the outer and the end of multiplicity by removing from himself any trace of duality and the seeing of otherness. This then is the completion of the actions of the *'umrah* of *tamattu'* within this *hajj*.

He then makes for the Ka'bah once again in order to witness the Universal Soul and to apprise himself of its realities and to take the *ihram* of *hajj*, beneath the water-course of the intellect in the above-mentioned manner. He then moves to the station of the 'Arafat of the soul and the intellect, at the mountain of truth, which is the Throne of the phenomenal realm, and the manifestation of the First Intellect. In doing so, he unites with them both by the power of the gnosis obtained from his awareness that all is One. Beyond this presence there is no other, except for that of the Essence, forbidden of access to all; to arrive there and take on the Attributes of the Presence of Oneness with the Essence is impossible. Of this station therefore it has been said, 'There is no further village beyond Abadan (forever).' Here the Muhammadi *tawhid*, the unity of gatheredness, is obtained once again; the difference between the two is that in the first *tawhid*, creation as a whole is removed from his gaze, in accordance with

Allah's words, 'Everything is perishable but He', and in the second *tawhid,* all the attributes are removed, in accordance with the words of the divine gnostic: 'The first part of the way is gnosis of Him, and the perfection of gnosis of Him is affirmation of Him, and the perfection of affirmation of Him is recognition of His Oneness, and the perfection of this recognition is sincerity to Him, and the perfection of sincerity to Him is the negation of the attributes from Him, by bearing witness on the part of each attribute that it was something without attribute, and the bearing witness on the part of each thing possessing an attribute that it is without attribute. In this station man becomes a (true) man, the perfect man becomes (truly) perfected and the gnostic (truly) gnostic.' It is for this reason that a return to a completion of perfection and the world of multiplicity becomes necessary, in accordance with the words of Allah, 'and that they may warn their people when they come back to them that they may be cautious' and in accordance with the reply of the Shaykh Junayd when asked about the meaning of the end: 'It is a return to the beginning.' It is this that is the secret of the return of the one who is performing the *hajj* from 'Arafat to Mina; indeed there are still more secrets beyond those revealed here.

He then returns to Mina, the world of multiplicity, that is, the world of rites and sacrifice in the realm of the spheres, the planetary bodies, the elements and the three kingdoms; he perceives them with the perception of Oneness and he witnesses them as divine manifestations contemplating them as created from one aspect and as real from another aspect. He then becomes occupied with the execution of the rites and ceremonies of this station, by performing the stoning, the sacrifice and the cutting; he first of all stones the *Jamrat al-'Aqabah* (places of the devil), namely this world and its pleasures, comprising the seven levels of elemental and natural kingdoms. This stoning is the stoning in the visionary realm, not physical stoning. Thus when he returns to the above-mentioned worlds it is incumbent upon him to act with authority and certainty. He then sacrifices his self again, such that he is hardly alive any more with the superficial life of this world; rather he becomes alive with the life of the realm of reality, indicated in Allah's words, 'And reckon not those who are killed in Allah's way are dead; nay, they are alive and are provided sustenance from their Lord' and His words, 'Is he who was dead then We raised him to life and made for him a light by which he walked among the people like him whose likeness is that of one in utter darkness, whence he cannot come forth?'

He then shaves the head of his self from love of this world and its pleasures; he shaves it such that he hardly returns to the world at all. The goal is to remove any belief in the reality of this world, since an investigation of this world reveals that it is nothing but pure non-existence and a figment of the imagination; indeed it is maintained in existence by false conjecture which is mentioned in the saying of the Prophet, 'This world is maintained in existence by illusion' and in the words of the Imam, 'The destruction of what is imaginary comes with the sobriety of the Known'. Jesus has said: 'O seeker of this world, to behave correctly therein is to abandon it; this is more correct behaviour, this is more correct.'

He then returns from this station to the station of abiding in Allah after the annihilation. He also makes another *tawaf* of the Ka'bah, that is, he perceives it again from seven directions as demanded by the source of his own soul, that is the seven levels of his coming into being, in accordance with Allah's words, 'Indeed He has created you through various grades.' In this way he attains influence in the seven regions of the earth and the seven regions of the spheres, also known as the *malakut* and the *jabarut*. He then performs the two cycles of prayer for the two *'Id* festivals, namely the *'Id al-Adha* festivals, and that of *al-Fitr*, in the station of Abraham: one for his taking on of the attributes in the annihilation from all existence and one for his abiding in Allah after this annihilation. Moreover, the *'Id* prayer must be performed in a place specially reserved for this purpose, which is the station of Oneness in the realm of reality. The reader should mark this point well as it is subtle in character.

He then returns to Mina and the world of multiplicity within the three realms of the mineral, vegetable and animal; therein are three divine days for the perfection of higher aspirations: it is station of the final goal and ultimate aim of the spiritually noble. The following *ayah* refers in particular to this: 'This day I have perfected for you your religion and completed My favour on you and chosen for you Islam as a religion.' We ask Allah to grant us arrival to the like of this *hajj* by the truth of the Real. Herewith we conclude the commentary on the *hajj* of the people of *haqiqah*. We shall now begin with subject of *jihad;* and praise belongs to Allah alone and it is from Him that all help is sought and in Whom the people trust.

12

Jihad

i)   According to the people of *shari'ah*

According to the people of this group, the *jihad* (striving in the way of Allah or holy war) is one of the obligations of Islam, that is, it is an obligation of communal responsibility, so that if it is only performed by some, the obligation ceases to be binding on the rest. There are seven conditions to this obligation: being male, having reached the age of puberty, being of perfectly sound mind and health, being a free man, and not being an elderly person on whom sustenance of all the family depends, and that there be a just Imam or someone who represents him. If one of these conditions is not fulfilled, then there is no longer any obligation. The disbelievers against whom the *jihad* is obligatory are of two kinds. The first are those whom one must fight until they surrender or are killed or until they accept the *jizyah* tax.

As for the second kind, the *jizyah* is not accepted of them and they are fought until they surrender or are killed. If the *jizyah* is accepted then there is no fixed amount to be exacted according to the soundest opinion; rather the amount is to be determined by those of the Shiah *fuqaha'* (men of law) skilled in this science — and collected in accordance with the judgement of the Imam. The *jizyah* is either exacted per head or in accordance with the amount of land held by them; but it cannot be demanded of these two things together. Moreover it may be increased or reduced according to the judgement of the Imam. If the *jizyah* is exacted on land and they submit and become Muslims, then the obligation is no longer biding. *Jizyah* may not be taken from four groups of persons: children, mad persons, the foolish and women. Fighting should not be begun until they (the enemy) are invited to Islam, by way of the science of *tawhid*, justice and the establishment of the pillars. If they refuse to accept all or any of these things, then it is permitted to fight them. The person entrusted with inviting them to Islam should be the Imam or whoever is delegated by him; and Allah is more Knowing and more Wise.

ii)   According to the people of *tariqah*

The *jihad* of this group refers to the *jihad* or the struggle against the self in accordance with the saying of the Prophet, 'We have returned from the lesser *jihad* to the greater *jihad.'* What is meant by the lesser *jihad* is fighting of unbelievers and the greater *jihad* the struggle against the self *(nafs)*. When asked about this, he replied: 'It is the struggle against the soul (or self) which commands to evil.' It has also been related from the Prophet: 'Your greatest enemy is the self contained between the two sides of your body.' Any person of sound intellect would consider that the struggle against the greater of enemies is more important that the struggle against just the enemy, in particular when it exists between the sides of his own body. The *jihad* of the self is to oppose it in anything which contradicts the intellect and the *shari'ah,* in accordance with Allah's words, 'As for him who fears to stand in the presence of his Lord and forbids the soul from low desires, then surely the Garden is his abode.' This is because the self is always calling to evil in accordance with its inherent nature, described by Allah in His words: 'Most surely (man's) self is wont to command (him to do) evil.' Therefore opposing this kind of self is the source of goodness and perfect justice. This is reflected in the *hadith* of the Prophet with respect to women who are considered similar to the self: 'Take counsel of them and oppose them therein.' The people of Allah have established, in their study of correspondences, that the self of man is analogous to women in the cosmic realm: thus just as it is obligatory to oppose women in most states, it is also obligatory to oppose the self in most states. If it were not so, then opposing the self would not be the cause of immediate entry into the Garden. This same meaning is reflected in the *hadith,* 'The Fire is surrounded by desires and the Garden is surrounded by hated things' since the desires literally issue from the self and the Fire of necessity accompanies these desires; moreover, the hated things and opposition to them are dependent upon a sound intellect and the divine code of law and it must be that the fruit of this opposition is the Garden. Allah refers to this when He says, 'And (as for) those who strive hard for Us, We will most certainly guide them in Our ways; and Allah is most surely with the doers of good', and His saying that it is 'for Us' indicates that if the struggle against the self is not for Allah and in His way, then it is of no use and will not cause the person to enter the Garden and will not be a cause of guidance to Allah and to His straight path.

The Shaykhs are agreed that the spiritual wayfarer should be prevented from travelling the path on his own without a shaykh of perfection. These shaykhs, by their perception of the realities of gnosis, by their knowledge of the stations and the manner in which each may be crossed and how transfer may be effected from a lower to a higher one, are able to instruct the spiritual wayfarer and cause him to stand in the places of standing so that he may arrive at the desired goals without great hardship and difficulty. Undoubtedly a shaykh is well-equipped to do this because he himself has travelled along this path and therefore knows by experience which path is the easiest and quickest. The seeker cannot do this on his own: he needs help since there are numerous routes to travel and he must find out which of them will bring him to the goal. He may begin to travel one path when he encounters another, with the result that he leaves the former and is at pains to arrive at his destination; if he does arrive, then it is only after great trouble and after spending far more time in a particular station than the Imam or the Prophet had spent therein. The reason for this is that when the person begins the path on his own, he is not able to free himself of the tendency · to yield the demands of the self. Since travel on the path of Allah is based on constant opposition to the self, how then, one may ask, will this person travelling the path of Allah arrive at the goal by himself? Allah alludes to this in His words, 'And could you but see when the guilty shall hang down their heads before their Lord.' The movement of the one obedient to his self is always downwards; the person who hangs his head down and the person who stands in an upright position are as two distinct persons, the one moving upwards and the other downwards. Movement on the part of either of them only increases the distance between them. This downward movement is like the movement particular to the plants, as we have already mentioned;

this is self-evident and there is no need for any other rational proof. We therefore ask Allah by His grace for protection from this downward movement towards the lowest level of the natural world, that is the level of Gehenna, known as 'the lowest of the low' in the Qur'an. The following verse describes this kind of self:

> If the self is neglected, then it keeps company with mean-
> ness,
> And if it is urged on then, it longs for nobler qualities.

We have already discussed the manner in which the self ascends from its level of 'commanding to evil' to the 'reproachful' and from there to the 'inspired' and finally to the station where it is tranquil or 'at rest'; it then goes on from this station to the Divine Presence by the law of return in accordance with Allah's words, 'O soul that art at rest! Return to your Lord, well-pleased (with him), well-pleasing (Him) so enter among My servants and enter into My garden.' This entering means that they should accept the jurisdiction, authority, instruction and guidance of the Prophet, the Imam or the shaykh without any further argument. There are other secrets connected with the manner of arrival, although it would not be appropriate to include them here; we shall mention them, if Allah wills, at the end of the work in the final instructions.

The *jihad* of the people of *tariqah* is the struggle against the self and nothing else. Such people are always in a state of struggle · and they never forget their vigilance even for a moment. Just as *jihad* is a communal obligation for the people of the *shari'ah,* so for the people of this group it is an individual obligation, such that no one can perform it on one's behalf, and with them it is the first of obligations. This because it is impossible to set out on this path without it — and thus we arrive at the desired conclusion of our argument.

iii) According to the people of *haqiqah*

The *jihad* of the people of this group refers to their struggle against the theorising of the intellect: their struggle is overcoming its doubts and misgivings. This speculative intellect is always restricted to contingencies. What is desired, indeed the constant goal, is freedom from such restrictions: this is a state which is in accordance with the demands of passion and spiritual tasting. What a difference there is between the intellect and passion or yearning. It has been narrated from the Prophet that Allah has created the intellect to fulfil the claims of slavery, not for the perception of the reality or Lordship. Thus it is an obligation to use the intellect to carry out what is demanded by the state of slavery and not to speculate on the reality of Lordship. It is for this reason that the gnostic has said the following, which is not understood by the speculative intellect and its theorising because it is a science based on divine unveiling: 'It is a science whereby one may know the source of the world of forms which receives the souls.' Thus Fakr al-Din al-Razi has said:

> The ultimate perception of the intellect is limited
> And most men's striving is misguided.
> We will never benefit from our investigations throughout
> our life,
> Whether we fill it with argument or speculation.

On investigation we realise that intellect is to divine yearning as the faculty of conjecture is to the intellect: conjecture is never able to arrive at the level of perception of divine yearning and its gnoses; rather it usually seeks to deny it and obstruct its influence, just as the spirit of conjecture usually tries to deny the intellect and prevent it from functioning. It is for this reason that differences have arisen between the science of rhetoric and intellectual proof and the science of spiritual tasting. Indeed most of the laws of the *shari'ah* issue from the realm of spiritual tasting and yearning, that is, from a prophet or messenger, and they do not accord with the workings of the intellect and intellectual judgements. The doubts and misgivings of the philosophers and brahmins all arise from this source. Thus the philosphers deny the return and resurrection after death of the body in a physical way and they deny knowledge of the partial or individual entities existing in time; moreover, they ascribe certain attributes to Allah which have not been recorded in the law of the *shari'ah* and whose existence is not even possible in terms of the intellect, such as their assertion of divine simplicity and that God's existence is necessary by virtue of mere logical proof. They also believe that the world has existed since eternity and that the Real — may He be exalted — is the cause of this. All these matters are a result of the judgement of their shallow intellects which are incapable of grasping the secrets of the divine code of law and its subtleties. The same is true of the brahmins who deny the return and resurrection of man; they also oppose the prophets and their miracles and contradict the revealed texts and the divine codes of law, believing in the power of action and whatever issues from action. They persist in denying the prophets and following the dictates of their shallow intellects, claiming that if the prophets came with a message in harmony with the intellect, then there was no need for the prophets in the first place; if, however, they brought a message which was in opposition to the intellect, then they are not prepared to accept this message, arguing that their intellects are sufficient to find the best and most beneficial manner of living.

However, all these claims are incorrect. If the intellect were sufficient we would have no need of the revealed Books and the messengers; indeed the revelation of such Books and the sending of these messengers would be an act of jest and we have already shown that Allah is not capable of such a jest. Thus we realise that the intellect is in need of another kind of faculty of perception, known as logic by the philosophers and as divine light and justice by those who affirm and act according to the science of divine unity. Accordingly, just as *jihad* with the literal sword must be made against those who believe in a god other than Allah, so *jihad* with the symbolic sword must also be made against those who affirm an existence other than the existence of Allah. The former arises when a person follows the desires of his self and the latter when he follows the intellect, the resulting judgement being pure speculative thought. Indeed the first is an expression of manifest idolatry *(shirk)* and the second of hidden idolatry; the rejection of each is obligatory upon every man. Thus there is never a time or period when these two kinds of *jihad* are absent, whatever the circumstances, for just as the Muslims are always fighting the unbelievers in the different regions of the earth with the literal sword, so those who affirm the oneness of Allah are also constantly striving against the philosophers and brahmins in the different regions of the world with the symbolic sword.

The *jihad* of the people of the *haqiqah* is thus the struggle against the scholars of the intellect to destroy their dubious arguments and reject their misgivings; they strive to make them abandon intellectual speculation that they may follow the true way of tasting and divine passion, namely the way of revelation and inspiration. Similarly, the *jihad* of the people of *tariqah* is never anything other than the struggle against the self by removal of its doubts and misgivings and by overcoming its desires. The result of the first *jihad* is firm establishment on the path of the unity of gatheredness and arrival at the world of oneness after freeing oneself of the hidden idolatry; the result of the second is the journeying towards Allah by means of a sound intellect and the following of His command both outwardly and inwardly, after freeing oneself from manifet idolatry. It is exactly this which Allah intends by the term *jihad* since the goal of the literal *jihad* is also the figurative *jihad*.

Allah mentions those who struggle to establish the proof of Allah, saying they are above those of His slaves who are guilty of associating others with Him (*shirk*): 'Allah has made the strivers with their property and their persons to excell the holders back a (high) degree and to each (class) Allah has promised good; and Allah shall grant to the strivers above the holders back a mighty reward: high degrees from Him and protection and mercy, and Allah is Forgiving and Merciful.' What is meant by 'the holders back' are those who abandon these two kinds of *jihad*. What is meant by 'the strivers' are those who establish the *jihad* by way of those two things. Allah also refers to them in His words, 'And whoever does this seeking Allah's pleasure, We will give him a mighty reward.' We ask Allah to make us of those strivers by His grace and generosity.

As for our promise to describe the rest of the secrets of spiritual travel, secrets which are instrumental in bringing the traveller to the Real, His Sacred Presence and the worlds of light, then we would say the following: to accustom the self to beneficial things and to acquire the qualities of perfection such that they become inherent in your being is the first of your stations and your first contact with perfection. This then disappears with the rapidity of the station and what enters the self is the consciousness of thought; if this is from conjecture, then the thought occurring to the mind is Satanic or negative and its source are the passions and anger of the self which impede right action, whereas if this consciousness is consciousness of the Real then awareness of what has passed and regret for its passing leads one to turn to Him for forgiveness. The movement of the self when seeking is the will; the seeker of true purification is a *murid* or aspirant, a person who possesses will the excitment of the self with what it finds pleasant is hope; the pain it suffers for what is disliked is fear; its abstention from becoming engrossed in sensuality is doing without; its remaining unshaken by contingent events is patience; its perception of the blessings of Allah is gratitude; its perception of the judgement and the degree beyond the natural realm is trust; its acceptance of the judgement and decree is contentment; its vision of the realities in the mirror of this decree is gnosis; its pleasure in what it feels is love; its inhaling of the passing pleasure contained therein is a breath of freshness and the pleasure which lasts for some time is tranquillity; the presence of secrecy by way of His presence and seizing His word from the senses of the self is ecstasy; the secret manifestations which annul movement is intoxication; the perception of the origin and source is awe; the extinction of the word with respect to the beginnings is intimacy; its isolation from the physical world, such that the perception of the beginning of creation is contained in the vastness of His self-reliant existence, is divine unity; that which is dependent upon partial manifestations from the unseen is unveiling; and the bodily forms of the spheres, which cause a form to be given to the rational self and which manifests with its sudden appearance and vanishes with its disappearance, is time — it is for this reason that on many occasions a form gives rise to a state without great exertion or involvement; if it occurs frequently then it should be opposed. It is for this reason that the Prophet has said, 'Truly your Lord blows breaths of fragrance on certain days of your earthly time — during other than these days oppose such (manifestations).' The world is concealed in the perception of its essence by way of its Beloved and it is so utterly submerged in Him that all other sensations vanish. This station, that is, the station of annihilation, is the last of the levels and the highest of the stations of the path. In this concise description of the station of the spiritual wayfarers we have fulfilled the promise made earlier in the book. It should be remembered, however, that these paths to Allah, as the Messenger has said, are 'as many as the souls of creation' and they multiply or diminish in relation to one's intimacy or distance from the Beloved.

13

Final Word of Advice and Instruction

We have also promised to add a word of advice to the spiritual travellers on their way to the Lord of the Worlds. This concerns the qualities that they must adopt in order to reach their goal and arrive at their Beloved, to join and abide with Him after their annihilation. When your mind is fixed on the angelic realm *(malakut)*, busy in its duty of remembrance, a remembrance which issues from humility and submission, when this reflective awareness is subtle and lets the body consume less food and lets the passions and desires die, when it is prepared to remain awake at night in humility and submission before the majesty of the Lord, with sincere devotion and good intention, then it is not long before the flashes of light and delicious moments of recognition and understanding occur. Your soul attains perfection when it returns to its original sublime state, according to the individual capacity of each person. Thus the soul divests itself of all illusion and refines itself with the subtlety of its own secret by means of spiritual exercises aimed at a purification of the outer and inner from all obscurity and impurity. In this way your soul must seize authority over the body — and not vice-versa. The perfection of the soul lies in its relationship with the body and it is achieved by way of absolute justice, by a combination of wisdom, courage and chastity; and each one of these qualities must lie between the two bounds of excess and negligence. This middle path is itself a quality of excellence bounded as it must be on either side by two baser qualities: thus the first (wisdom) lies between foolishness and cunning, the second (courage) between cowardliness and impetuousness and the third (chastity) between covetousness and discouragement.

Up to this point we have been considering the principles or root qualities. As for the branches of wisdom, they are astuteness, eloquence, sound opinion, prudence and resolution, truthfulness, trustworthiness, mercy, modesty, earnestness, faithfulness and humility; the branches of chastity are contentment, generosity, patience, forbearance, open-heartedness, concealment of the secret and trust; the branches of courage are endeavour, power, firmness and constancy, determination, vitality, bravery and ambition. It is thus by adoption of these qualities that one attains to a completion of perfection.

Know too — and may Allah assist you and grant you success — that despite the differences in these terms, they are essentially similar in meaning. As for gnosis, it is preceded by love; wherever gnosis is perfected, then love of necessity is established, and whenever love is perfected, it calls up gnosis. If you possess astuteness and great foresight, then you are able to enquire after the truth of your state in your descent from the disclosure of painful states of separation; you are able too to reach your goal without great difficulty, unlike others who only reach this goal with intense hardship. But you must be ready to serve and eager to find out the truth.

Know that union with the world of sanctity and entry into the Presence of Allah refers to the removal of the veil, that is, union in the realm of the intellect. It must be realised that the sun does not become more in number by the multiplicity of its manifestations; likewise the One, the Real, does not become many by His being reflected in various mirrors. One town may have many roads leading to it, each different in length and difficulty and ease; most of the paths are full of danger, thus strive to prepare yourself by increasing your provision and means of transport. Above all, you must equip yourself with fear of Allah and sincerity in your intention, while respecting the laws of the *shari'ah* together with the divine commands and the prohibitions for these things are as a whip whereby Allah reprimands His servants. Restrain yourself from becoming occupied in anything superfluous to the detriment of what is more important and necessary. Seeking perfection in knowledge will bring you many qualities of excellence. Abstain from indulging in your sensual desires and pray in the darkness of the night. You should practise the daily *awrad* (the programme of *dhikr* or remembrance given by a shaykh) and the praising of Allah. You should cut out base and vile thoughts and increase your purification by way of the purification of the sacred soul. Illuminate your heart by attracting the presence of the illuminated and sacred souls; approach them with your self so that it may acquire similar qualities and so that some of their radiance may be reflected in it; and make your character their character. Cling steadfastly to the light of lights and stand at the gate of the *malakut* in humility and submission; oppose its perfumed exhalation and increase your supplications and your devotions towards the Presence of Existence, Generosity and Excellence. Ask of Him for He is the Bestower and the Giver of Gifts. Read His Wise and Precious Book with understanding and reflect in order that the self may gain assistance from the greatest of store-houses and the most generous of sources of benefit. In this way you will reach your goal.

Repeat the words of one of the masters of the spiritual path: 'O Maintainer (of the cosmos), darkness has surrounded me, serpent passions have bitten me, crocodile desires are preying on me and the scorpions of the world have stung me. You have become a stranger to me in the midst of my enemies, so free me O Lord. I call on You, O Lord, drowning as I am in the sea of natural sensations, perishing by the voracity of the passion. I have been turned away from the door of Your might. Would You regard with favour a poor man rejected from the gate of Your grace? I am your slave who seeks refuge in the domain of Your Power; release him by a momentary flash of Your radiance. May the Lord of power be exalted, the Sacred, the Holy, the Lord of the angels and the soul. My God, I am the slave who has run away from You, cure me of the sickness of disobedience; I have collapsed at your door weak with thirst. Why do You not pour a clear drink of Your forgiveness for one thirsty for Your Grace? You have cast Your light into the inner depths of My forerunners and You have manifested Your majesty to the souls of the spiritual wayfarers, annihilating those who gaze at the grandeur of the doorway. O make me of those who long passionately for You, of those who are aware of Your grace and kindness, O Lord of what is wondrous, Master of all that is vast and tremendous, the Originator of all substance and Creator of the smallest seeds of life, the Bestower of blessings and the One who manifests all that is good. Make me of those who are sincere in their devotion, who are grateful, who remember You, who are content with Your decree and who are patient in the face of Your trials. Truly You are the Sustainer of life, the Maintainer (of the cosmos), Possessor of great generosity and power; You are the

One Who forgives, the Merciful. O Lord of all lords, Who sustains the spiritual realm by the light of Your majesty; O You Who, if You manifest Your radiance to something, then that thing submits to You; O You Whose grace is concealed; O You Who have spread Your light over all dark things and have illuminated them thereby; O You Who have sent the torch of Your divine passion to the planetary spheres and have made them spin in their orbits. Your servants have felt humbled by Your greatness and their hard-heartedness has been softened in awe of You; the hearts have trembled in their pleasure at the remembrance of the Your spirit; the confused senses have been stilled by the radiance of Your glory, O You Whose most illustrious radiance fills the secret hearts of those who turn to Him and Who causes the deafening thunder claps of His awe to strike in the hearts of the fearful. O You Possessor of Sublime Speech and Lord of the greater tranquillity; grant us mercy from Yourself and pour the lights of your blessings on our selves and the radiance of Your goodness on our souls. Make us of the felicitous and of those who experience Your majesty and witness Your beauty and are fearful of You. Surely You are capable of all things.'

We shall conclude this exhortation and instruction by mentioning what has been reported of the spiritual experience by one of the gnostics and seekers of the truth, recorded on the tablet of remembrance in the intellects of the men of knowledge and in the persons of spiritual grandeur. The spiritual travellers move towards the light of the lights of Allah — may He be exalted — and they knock at the gates of light and request of Him with sincerity and patience the knowledge of reality and pleasing conduct and so He bestows upon them precious gifts from the angelic realm and radiant illumination. The water of the spring of majestic splendour and the sources of perfection and beauty are poured over them such that they are purified by the purification of light. Surely the Generous Benefactor loves purity in those who enter into His Presence — a purity obtained by means of knowledge from the realm of reality and pleasing behaviour.

The brothers of inward sight concur that Allah is independent of and above creation — both in the realm of inner meaning and speech. These brothers keep to the way of humility and silent supplication. They invoke the One Who orders the world of the elements, the world of the planetary spheres, the world of ideal form in the realm of dependence and the world of pure Lights. They avoid the realm of darkness and the sons of darkness. They plead with the keepers of the dungeons, seeking freedom for their prisoners bound in chains. They seize hold of brands of fire from His elements, taking as examples the pure of heart and the most intimate of the angels. They say, 'Glory be to the One Who has made the sun, His first light, a means of pouring out His generosity and glory be to Him Who has caused the sun and moons to continue such that the blessing of their radiant emanation may be enjoyed by His slaves.' They exclaim, 'O Lord remove the darkness of negligence and ignorance, for surely it is the cloak of the unjust. We have come to You in obedience. Our spirits extol You, seeking to ascend to the seat of Your majesty and the station of Your light. Therefore purify us by Your powerful hand and open our hands to Your provision of unveilings. Open our sight by Your light for surely we have found Your Majesty above the pillars of the realm of Absolute Dominion *(jabarut)*.'

The men of resolve and perfection are cleansed so that they may be worthy of a place next to Allah. They hate wrong actions and disobedience, and if it were not for them, then the heavens would have been thrown down upon the earth as a punishment for mankind and grievous destruction would be fall the unjust. When Allah sent His prophets to mankind in order that they might worship Him, one group of men established the rites and one group strayed from the right path. The former are raised to a witnessing of the Intellect; they enter into the ranks of the angels; they are purified by Allah and are granted constant blessings. As for the latter, they are removed from His side and they are covered in disgrace and ignominy; they have their heads lowered, existing in veils of darkness and the gloom of corporeal things. The purified souls emerge from the obscurity of physical forms and move towards the sublime stations of the lights. They are given wide expanses and space and return therein ennobled. Their recompense from Allah is to be taken to the proximity of the Real and the world of the intellect, at the very source of life in the sea of lights beside the well-springs of life itself. Thus those who are obedient to the Merciful are bathed in the flashing radiance of His light; His meeting with them causes them to be victorious; surely the mercy of Allah is granted to the doers of good actions. We ask Allah to make us and you of those who are prepared for this meeting. We ask Him to inspire within us and within you the best possible degree of certainty and to grant us and you victory with the victorious, with those of union, with the annihilated and with those who abide with Him, for surely He is the most Beneficent, the Merciful, and He does not withhold the outpourings of His blessings from those who are ready and have the capacity to receive.

In these words of remembrance there is instruction enough — sufficient to lead one to a station of proximity with the Truth, enough to free man from the ties and chains which might bind the seeker of salvation. It is for this reason that Allah has instructed His slaves to seek the capacity to persevere on the straight path — that is the path of those He has blessed with His special blessings, free from the confusion of anger and misguided love. The tongue of their station says: 'O our Lord, Your first divine all-encompassing beneficence was that You created us and this first favour conferred special status on each one of us.' The second kind of divine beneficence is that, by virtue of the all-encompassing nature of Your name, the One Who guides, You have encompassed the generality of the believers. You have expressed this in Your words: 'He has ordained mercy on Himself.' You have included us in this by the blessing of faith, obedience to Your command, submission to Your rule and affirmation of Your oneness. Therefore each one of us is ready to make remembrance of You, to praise You, to glorify You, to hand over affairs to You and to devote ourselves solely to Your worship after recognition of Your sovereignty. Each one of us must openly request help from You because of his incapacity and the deficiency inherent in created beings. Moreover, you have singled us out by Your second kind of mercy which holds sway by the special authority of Your name, the One Who guides. It is to this name that we directed our demands for the noblest kind of guidance and spiritual wayfaring. It is we who demand this from You since it brings with it victory and the ample blessings which are bestowed upon the perfected of Your beloved. It is these whom You cause to travel along the straightest and surest path until they throw down their staffs because they are ready for annihilation in You. Having attained the station of the truth, they obtain gnosis of You, a witnessing of You in Your profuse kindness and noblest of blessings. It is they who purify Your sacred presence from any notion of adulteration. 'Our Lord!' they pray, 'Grant us what You have promised us by Your apostles and disgrace us not on the day of resurrection; surely You would not fail to fulfil the promise.' So their Lord accepted their prayer. 'We ask you, O Allah, to make us of those who respond to You, who believe in Your promise and Your threat of punishment, and who fulfil their contract with You, and who establish Your caliphate which You have delegated to us, O Lord of the Worlds.'

Know that in the world of the intellect and the divine creation of Allah there are many wondrous things which may not be encompassed by the intellect of men engulfed in darkness; whatever wonders may be seen in the world of physical bodies, others still more wondrous and surprising may be seen in the other world. Thus our thoughts cannot contain Allah's exquisite organization of the beginning of existence nor His intricate management thereof: our darkness obscures and prevents us from witnessing these wonders. Whoever desires to perceive this world of the intellect when bound by the senses is as the diver submerged in the depths of the ocean: it is evident that he cannot see the sky in the same way as someone who is standing above in the open air. Therefore measure what you cannot see by what you can and the matter will become clear to you.

This is the last of the instructions which are addressed to you and which will permit you to arrive at your goal. As for the particular instructions of this book, you should take great care to observe them, for they are bestowed upon those who keep safely what is entrusted to them. Indeed you should always rely on these words and endeavour to extract the meanings therefrom with great precision; in this way they will remain present with you in the storehouse of your heart. Under no circumstances should you allow anyone to prevent you from seeking help in understanding the meanings of our words. Seek out the rare and subtle perceptions contained therein, for surely it is a book whose subject is of great import and which deals with sciences known only to a few. This book is like a tree containing much fruit and strong branches: in it I have placed wisdom and certainty from revealed sources and wondrously beneficial knowledge. Your path will be made easy if you commit it perfectly to memory and if you seek to understand the sources of its lights behind the veils — such that the suns of these lights shine as bright as day in your presence, as you stand in humility and submission illumined by the realities of truth from the realm of light, the sublime and subtle gnoses of the heart and the knowledge of Lordship from the realm of emanation. In this way the slave of Allah moves on upwards from the secrets of the *shari'ah* and meanings of the *tariqah:* these are the paths of our predecessors and our successors. Therefore rise up and strive in this way and preserve its secrets from betrayal on the part of those who censure; oppose such persons by your service of the King of creational phenomena. By serving Him, you will become one of the spiritual poles. I do not say this in excessive praise of myself, so that I be reckoned amongst the people of reknown and wonder: this would only result in my entering into darkness, veiled from the truth and without any desire for enlightenment. Besides, I am not saying that only I have attained to this degree of excellence; rather Allah's generosity extends to all and His bestowal of gifts is tremendous. Knowledge does not stagnate with a people such that it no longer flows to others; rather the One who pours His divine emanations into the source of certainty and into the drink of the pure springs of gnosis does not deny anyone knowledge of the unseen.

When I consider how the gentlemen of the age have made public the method of disputing employed by the Mu'tazilites and the Ash'arites, how they have thereby ascended the path of vainglory and repute, how discord and mutual rejection reign, how they have made their words a commerce for the sake of immediate worldly gain; when I consider that the only thing I found amongst them was excessive loquacity and questioning and answering without any achievement or result — for they are incapable of understanding what is hidden and subtle and it is as if their ideas rush headlong past without perceiving the reality of the subject — all this caused me to bring these secrets out into the open, extracting them from the rich lodes of gnosis beneath the surface of things; this I achieved by a process of rigorous reflection. In this way the spiritual wayfarer may journey to the path of the next world, leaving behind the above-mentioned commerce which leads only to ruin. I have travelled this path in the manner of all the spiritual wayfarers, in order that all ambiguity and obscurity may be removed from the true science of unity. I have published and described in clear terms what has been proven and confirmed. It is for this reason that I urge you to heed this book and shower it with praise. In it I have prepared for you a wealth of secrets; I have explained to you the way of the chosen few and the stations of the righteous; it is the way of the spiritual poles, the great saints, the prophets and those men who are a living example on earth of good conduct and spirituality and who determine and order the affairs of the world both now and in past ages.

Thus if you wish to gaze on these jewels and to dive for these pearls, then reflect well upon the contents of this book; consider the latter portion of the work and compare it with the beginning; gather together the different points and subjects which are dispersed throughout — for in each corner there is something hidden. Do not restrict your attention to the truths expounded in one specific place, but rather see them in the light of all the various subjects. If you treat the work as a whole and ponder on its contents you will find guidance. The aim of dispersing these hidden subtleties of knowledge is to arouse the reader's curiosity. Whoever imagines that this method is repetitious — and indeed this is the case — then it should be pointed out that these delicate matters of gnosis cannot be explained at once. Therefore a subject is repeatedly mentioned or is incorporated into another subject under a different title and in different terms. In this way the various facets of its amazing meanings are revealed in a satisfactory way; since it is only by means of the tongue of repetition that the blossoms of the tree of wonder may unfold. To this end I have followed the instructions of the Lord and the example of perfection set by the people of Allah and their elite. Thus gather this knowledge, commit it to memory and reflect upon its meanings: Allah will guide you to the right path; He is sufficient for us and the best of guardians.

I would also inform you, O you who pause to attend to its meanings, that I have chosen fine fruit for you, delicious and ready for eating; I have picked it from various gardens, watered by the water of divine blessings, 'well pleasing (Him) and well pleased (with Him)'. I hereby present you with the quintessence of what I myself have tasted from distant and diverse sources; I have lain patiently in wait for it for your benefit; I have contained it in a certain order and framework, and I have presented it to you. So take care to take good counsel from it and establish what it demands. Recognize too its true worth with profound discrimination — for it is a splendid example of a work on this science, a wonder of its kind and a rarity with regard to its subject. Allah has made this easy for me by His beneficence and generosity, something which others in a similar position have not found easy; this is by His bestowal of grace and favour on me; to Him is due much gratitude and to Him belongs overflowing praise. Therefore, O you who would gain spiritual victory, preserve this work from those who do not have the requisite understanding. Do not be miserly with it with respect to those who recognise its worth and are of the station of those of this science. Do not bestow wisdom on those who cannot appreciate it — and in so doing do it an injustice; nor should you prevent it from reaching those who do understand — and in doing so commit an injustice. Think well of all that is contained therein and do not rush to reject or negate: it may be that this knowledge is difficult for you to understand because of its outwardly concealed nature; indeed there are many expressions of great delicacy which, to be understood, require a corresponding subtlety of heart and refinement of temperament. Moreover, this work contains matters of such complexity that they may hardly be perceived without unveilings and spiritual assistance. This book and others of a similar nature are not open to discourse and are beyond the level

of the people of opinion and speculation. I am not saying this
to boast. The truth of our claim will be recognized by anyone
who investigates the work in its various dimensions and puts the
book to the test; its high standing will be evident to such a
person. Therefore do not allow doubt to enter your heart with
respect to any of the points which are obscure or contradict
appearances and what has become customary. If you abandon
the path of appearances and customs and concentrate your attention on what is beyond it, then you will understand the purpose
of the book and you will become aware of the knowledge of divine
truths and unveilings contained therein. Therefore scrutinise the
work, strive carefully to understand it and act accordingly; in this
way will reach your goal. Pause and reflect on what it contains
and seek to be sincere in your devotions — observing carefully
the conditions of worship described in the work. In this way you
will be victorious in attaining in full to the stations of the righteous; in this way you will travel far along the path of the prophets,
Imams and saints of Allah on the Day of Gathering. I give praise
to Allah and I give thanks to Him for that which He makes easy
for you at my hand. If you arrive and join with Him, then you
will have gained a great victory; you will have come to an abode
where you will be treated with honour by its inhabitants. I ask
of you that you do not forget to make good mention of me in
your prayers as a recompense for my attentiveness towards you
— by seeking forgiveness and salvation from the terror of the
Plain of Gathering after death and by asking for a place of refuge
in the abode of honour, far from the fearful events of the Day of
Resurrection. It may be that I shall benefit from your prayer
and that I shall share your reward, without any loss on your
part, for surely the Generous Bestower grants His gifts to me
and you alike. Although I praise the book, I do not laud myself
nor do I feel conceited — both my methods of thinking and
temperament are defective. How can this be otherwise when the
anguish and the impurity of the ages continue uninterrupted,
the lovers and companions are constantly being overwhelmed
by trial and tribulation, and the splintering of communities becomes more and more widespread. What we hope for from the
generosity of the reader is that he forgives our shortcomings from

the good nature of his heart, that he overlooks our deficiences and avoids divulging our secrets. We hope too that he will put right what he considers to be wrong and make good any lack or defect and with these words we conclude this work.

This arduous task was completed on a Saturday evening, 12th Ramadan 950 AH.[1] All praise belongs to Allah, the Possessor of Praise and we ask for blessings on Muhammad, the crown of splendour and glory, and on his family.[2]

---

[1] Another source relates that a copy written in the author's own hand was completed and corrected in th above-mentioned year.

[2] The editing and footnotes were completed on the evening in the month of Rajab 1400 AH by 'Abd al-Nasir Muhammad al-Khajavi, may Allah elevate his station throughout the days and the nights. All praise belongs to Allah, from the beginning to the end and may the blessings of Allah be upon our Master Muhammad and his purified family.

Index